Beiträge zum Kartellrecht

Edited by

Michael Kling und Stefan Thomas

32

Johannes Persch

Consumer Autonomy and Vertical Agreements

An Additional Pathway to Understanding EU Competition Law on Vertical Agreements, in Particular Online Sales Restrictions

Mohr Siebeck

Johannes Persch; studied law at the University of Mannheim, graduating in 2017 with the first state examination, 2018 LL.M. (University of Chicago), 2020 second state examination, Policy Officer at the European Commission's Directorate General for Competition in the Directorate for Policy and Strategy.
orcid.org/0009-0002-6927-5056

The Department of Law of the Faculty of Law and Economics at the University of Mannheim accepted this thesis as a dissertation in the fall/winter semester 2024/2025.

ISBN 978-3-16-164643-0 / eISBN 978-3-16-164644-7
DOI 10.1628/978-3-16-164644-7

ISSN 2626-773X / eISSN 2626-7748 (Beiträge zum Kartellrecht)

The Deutsche Nationalbibliothek lists this publication in the Deutsche Nationalbibliographie; detailed bibliographic data are available at *https://dnb.dnb.de.*

Printed on non-aging paper.

Mohr Siebeck GmbH & Co. KG, Wilhelmstraße 18, 72074 Tübingen, Germany
www.mohrsiebeck.com, info@mohrsiebeck.com

Preface

My heartfelt and sincere thanks go first to my academic mentor, Prof. Dr. Friedemann Kainer. Early in my studies, I had the opportunity to work at Professor Kainer's chair, where I was able to learn a great deal from him as well as from wonderful colleagues.

I would also like to thank Prof. Dr. Dr. Alexander Morell for taking on the role of second examiner and for his critical remarks, which have hopefully contributed to improving this work. Many thanks as well to Prof. Dr. Bülte for chairing the oral examination with his uniquely kind manner.

My gratitude also goes to Prof. Dr. Viktoria Robertson and Prof. Herbert Hovenkamp for making possible exciting research stays at WU Vienna and the University of Pennsylvania.

This work was supported by the *Studienstiftung des Deutschen Volkes*, the *Studienstiftung ius vivum*, and the *Deutsche Vereinigung für gewerblichen Rechtsschutz und Urheberrecht*.

Special thanks go to my friends Christian Weinmann, Simon Wizemann, Nico Halkenhäuser, Julius Netzer, Jascha Riedel, Tillmann Hauke Lüder Heise, Markus Lieberknecht, and Sarah Ponti, all of whom helped me in one way or another with this work – or with taking my mind off it. My heartfelt thanks also to my partner Eugénie, without whom life would be only half as beautiful.

Finally, I wish to thank my parents, who supported me in a very special way and whom I was able to get to know anew during the work on this dissertation. This work is dedicated to them.

Content Overview

Table of Contents

List of abbreviations

Art.	Article
BGH	Bundesgerichtshof
CMA	Competition and Markets Authority
DMA	Digital Markets Act
DoJ	Department of Justice
E.g.	For example
Ed(s).	Editor(s)
Et al.	And others
f.	Following
FTC	Federal Trade Commission
GDP	Gross Domestic Product
I.e.	That is
MAP	Minimum Advertised Prices
OECD	Organization for Economic Co-operation and Development
OEM(s)	Original Equipment Manufacturer(s)
P(p).	Page(s)
Para(s)	Paragraphs(s)
RPM	Resale Price Maintenance
TEU	Treaty on European Union
TFEU	Treaty on the Functioning of the European Union
VBER	Vertical Block Exemption Regulation
Vol.	Volume

Introduction

§ 1 Research questions

Online sales have become an increasingly important sales channel for a wide range of products.[1] The Covid-19 pandemic has further accelerated this trend.[2] Price is undoubtedly a factor that plays a role in consumers' decisions about which channel to choose, but other aspects are also important.[3] While offline purchases allow consumers to touch the product, online shopping comes with the opportunity to easily access detailed information and reviews about the product.[4] With the rise of online shopping, manufacturers have tried to restrict the availability of their products online. For example, the French garden, forestry, and agricultural equipment manufacturer STIHL allowed its authorized dealers to sell certain products only in the case of "personalized delivery" and thus de facto excluded internet sales.[5] Pierre Fabre, a manufacturer of cosmetic products, allowed its dealers to sell its products only in a physical room and in the presence of a qualified pharmacist.[6] In Germany, the sporting goods manufacturer ASICS prohibited its dealers from supporting the functionality of price comparison websites and from using ASICS trademarks on the websites of third parties, e.g., Amazon or eBay.[7] As these examples show, manufacturers often try to influence the distribution of their products. They want to have a say in how customers perceive the product and the context and environment in which it is sold.

Manufacturers, therefore, enter into agreements with their dealers on how they may distribute the product. Such agreements can range from stipulations on the product's price to its display (e.g., display in a shop window) or regulations on what other products it may be displayed with on the shelf. With the growing importance of online retail, specifications for sales via the internet have also become relevant. In some cases, manufacturers have attempted to prohibit the sale of their products over the internet altogether ('total bans'). In others, manu-

[1] *European Commission*, Study on Consumer Purchasing Behaviour in Europe, p. 18.

[2] *Eurostat*, 11/04/2022, Online Sales Efforts on the Rise due to the Pandemic, available at https://ec.europa.eu/eurostat/web/products-eurostat-news/-/ddn-20220411-1.

[3] *European Commission*, Study on Consumer Purchasing Behaviour in Europe, p. 39.

[4] *European Commission*, Study on Consumer Purchasing Behaviour in Europe, p. 36.

[5] Autorité de la Concurrence, 24/10/2018, Décision n° 18-D-23 STIHL.

[6] Autorité de la Concurrence, 29/10/2008, Décision n° 08-D-25 Pierre Fabre.

[7] Bundeskartellamt, 26/08/2015, B2–98/11 ASICS.wif

facturers restricted at least sales on platforms such as Amazon or eBay ('platform bans'). For consumers, such restrictions on distribution channels can be frustrating, as they make the products harder to find or more expensive. If you want to buy a product only sold at a specialist retailer, you may have to accept longer travel distances or shorter opening hours than, for example, with online shopping. Such restrictions can also mean a higher price for the product. However, the image created by these sales restrictions can also be the very reason why a customer considers buying certain goods at all. Particularly with products that are perceived as luxurious, the lifestyle associated with the product image plays an essential role in the purchase decision. The sales environment, reference prices, or consultation also suggests to the consumer a particular product value and benefit, whether true or false. There are many factors that influence the consumer's purchase decision. Many of them are predictable and can be strategically used by whoever is able to control the purchasing context and environment. For example, the music played in a retail store[8] or the design of the sales environment[9], although there is no direct link to product value, can impact consumers' purchase decisions. Controlling the purchasing context and environment is hence a valuable asset.

The division of control in this regard takes place between manufacturer and retailer through vertical agreements. These agreements stipulate, on the one hand, the retailer's obligations; for example, regarding the presentation, the advice to provide to customers, the location of their store, the quantity to be bought, or the retail price. On the other hand, they also govern the manufacturer's obligations, for example, a commitment by the manufacturer not to deliver to competing retailers in a territory reserved for the retailer. Obligations regarding the sale through the internet have recently become an important topic of vertical agreements. Manufacturers have imposed various obligations on retailers, ranging from total bans (prohibiting online sales altogether) to qualitative criteria on such sales or the prohibition of pure online retailers. The Court of Justice initially expressed a rather hostile view towards restrictions on online sales.[10] Later, it softened its earlier stance and acknowledged that online sales restrictions can be permissible in certain cases.[11] It maintained, however, that at least total online bans typically restrict competition and are prohibited under Art. 101 TFEU.[12] The topic has recently been included in the revision of the Vertical Block Exemp-

[8] *North et al.*, Nature 1997, 132.

[9] *Künzler*, Oxford Journal of Legal Studies 2017, 75 (90).

[10] Court of Justice, 13/10/2011, Case C-439/09 Pierre Fabre, ECLI:EU:C:2011:649.

[11] Court of Justice, 06/12/2017, Case C-230/16 Coty, ECLI:EU:C:2017:941.

[12] Court of Justice, 06/12/2017, Case C-230/16 Coty, ECLI:EU:C:2017:941, paras. 32–36.

tion Regulation ('VBER')[13] and the accompanying Vertical Guidelines[14]. The new VBER (in force since June 2022) now qualifies as a hardcore restriction, "the prevention of the effective use of the internet by the buyer or its customers to sell the contract goods or services".[15] Other restrictions of online sales can now, in principle, fall under the VBER where they do "not have the object of preventing the use of an entire online advertising channel."[16] Despite these developments, there are still voices that criticize the EU approach, specifically on internet sales restrictions, but also on vertical agreements in general.[17] They argue that vertical agreements, including online sales restrictions, are mostly benign and typically benefit consumers. Vergé, for example, criticizes the strict approach towards internet sales restrictions as follows:

> "The main question is not whether Internet sales can be prohibited or not, but simply whether we believe that the nature of the product justify that suppliers may be allowed to prevent some retailers – pure-internet players but also 'click-and-mortar' stores, and even discount brick and mortar store – from reselling the product."[18]

At the same time, for example, the German Federal Cartel Office ('Bundeskartellamt') appears more sceptical towards the benefits of online sales restrictions. In a 2018 note, it emphasized that a blanket marketplace ban is not necessary for the protection of branded products' images and that "the importance of different sales channels depends on the specific market conditions and consumer preferences in the respective Member States and can therefore lead to regionally different assessments".[19] The Bundeskartellamt's president, Andreas Mundt, also published a rather sceptical editorial on the updated VBER, stating that "it remains to be seen to what extent [the new rules on online sales restrictions] are practicable" and "will prove their worth".[20] The debate on vertical agreements and internet sales restrictions is not limited to their economic implications. Recently, another argument has gained prominence: the potential impact of online sales restrictions on consumer decision-making. The Bundeskartellamt, for example, in a background note, argues that online sales are important as they can

---

[13] Commission Regulation (EU) 2022/720 of 10 May 2022 on the application of Article 101(3) of the Treaty on the Functioning of the European Union to categories of vertical agreements and concerted practices, OJ L 134, 11.5.2022, pp. 4–13.

[14] Communication from the Commission, Guidelines on vertical restraints 2022, OJ C 248, 30.06.2022, p. 1, C/2022/4238 ('Vertical Guidelines'), para. 203.

[15] Art. 4 point (e) VBER.

[16] Art. 4 point (e)(ii) VBER.

[17] *Buccirossi*, Vertical Restraints for Online Sales, p. 32; *de la Mano et al.*, Competition Law & Policy Debate 2022, 12; *Vogel*, JECLAP 2013, 277 (281); *Waelbroeck/Davies*, JECLAP 2018, 431 (438).

[18] *Vergé*, in: Vertical Restraints, 31 (47).

[19] *Bundeskartellamt*, Wettbewerbsbeschränkungen im Internetvertrieb, p. 5.

[20] *Mundt*, ZVertriebsR 2022, 205 (207).

contribute to making consumer decisions more rational and less biased.[21] Even more explicitly, Künzler contends that

> "[i]ntratype competition may [...] be a precondition for consumers to search and may mitigate a product manufacturer's effort to manipulate consumer preferences based on subconscious appeal and affect-driven emotions."[22]

Schwaderer has also explored the idea that vertical agreements may negatively affect consumers' decision-making: she argues that manufacturers and retailers can use minimum resale price maintenance to influence consumers by creating an artificially high initial anchor through a uniform and elevated retail price.[23] However, it remains unclear whether these concerns fall within the normative scope of competition law and, if so, how restrictions on competition could be concretely identified on this basis.

Against this background, this thesis aims to address the following research question:

Can the treatment of vertical agreements under EU competition law, particularly concerning online sales restrictions, be justified based on a) economic considerations, and/or b) considerations of consumer autonomy?

This can be broken down into the following sub-questions:

(1) Are the current rules on vertical agreements concerning online sales restrictions aligned with economic theory?
(2) If not, can they be explained instead by a desire by courts and competition authorities to protect consumers' autonomous decision-making?
(3) Is consumer autonomy a valid normative concern that can be considered in the application of EU competition law?
(4) How can consumer autonomy, as a goal of competition law, be operationalized in the context of vertical agreements
(5) Can the rules on internet sales restrictions be justified when taking into account consumer autonomy in the analysis?

§ 2 Outline

Chapter 1 will first provide an overview of the current rules on vertical agreements. The focus will be on the treatment of online sales restrictions. The Chapter will explain the structure of the assessment, in particular the interplay between Art. 101 TFEU and the VBER. Second, it will evaluate the current framework from an economic perspective. Third, it will compare the European approach to the treatment of vertical agreements in the United States. Chapter 1 will show

[21] *Bundeskartellamt*, Wettbewerb und Verbraucherverhalten, pp. 11–14.
[22] *Künzler*, Restoring Consumer Sovereignty, p. 166.
[23] *Schwaderer*, Resale Price Maintenance, pp. 172–203.

that the EU's approach to vertical agreements remains, to some extent, categorical, focusing on the type of agreement rather than its effects on competition. This contrasts with economic theory, which advocates for a case-by-case assessment and considers EU law as overly strict. Online sales restrictions, in particular, are treated rather rigidly, with a quasi-blanket prohibition of total bans, regardless of their likely effects on the market. Compared to the United States, which applies a more economically driven, case-by-case approach, the EU's stance appears less aligned with economic theory.

Chapter 2 first examines how consumer autonomy considerations can help explain certain aspects of how vertical agreements are treated under EU law. Again, a particular focus will be on online sales restrictions. Second, it will show that protecting consumer autonomy may be a legitimate objective of EU competition law, alongside other goals such as consumer welfare.

Chapter 3 examines how the admittedly vague concept of consumer autonomy can be operationalized in the application of competition law. It explores the various ways in which vertical agreements influence consumer decision-making – sometimes enhancing it, sometimes distorting it. The chapter argues that competition law cannot protect individual consumer's autonomy for its own sake but may, in principle, safeguard consumers' role in the competitive process. In this context, it develops a potential theory of harm to identify anticompetitive vertical agreements that affect consumer decision-making. Finally, it demonstrates that while consumer autonomy may be a valid normative concern, it does not provide a justification for the current treatment of online sales restrictions under EU competition law.

§ 3 Terminology

I. Who is the relevant consumer?

There is ongoing debate about the definition of the relevant consumer in competition law, as the term is used with varying meanings across different legal texts.[24] For the purposes of this thesis, 'consumer' refers to the final consumer – i.e., the ultimate purchaser of a product or service for private use. This focus is justified because the final consumer differs from intermediate consumers – i.e., those who purchase a product or service for further processing or value creation – in two key ways.

First, the final consumer, as a general matter, is not able to exit the market. At least for essential goods and services, such as food or basic hygiene products, consumer demand cannot drop to zero.[25] In contrast, commercial consumers

[24] For a thorough analysis of the different usages of the term 'consumer' in competition law, see *Endler*, Verbraucher im Kartellrecht.

[25] *Endler*, Verbraucher im Kartellrecht, p. 155.

purchase products or services for resale or production. In response to unfavorable market conditions, they can not only switch to different intermediate products but also change their business entirely. For example, a clothing manufacturer could respond to a rise in cotton prices (e.g., due to a cartel) by using more synthetic materials like polyester. Alternatively, they could leave the clothing industry altogether and shift to furniture production. Consumers, however, do not have the same flexibility; they cannot simply stop being consumers. A consumer will not (entirely) stop buying clothes and buy only furniture instead. As a result, consumers are more vulnerable than other market participants.

Second, and more importantly, intermediate commercial consumers do not play the same role in the competitive process as final consumers. While their preferences may be relevant at the upstream market level, they are ultimately shaped by end consumers either directly or indirectly through downstream demand in a competitive market. This can be illustrated by revisiting the earlier example of a clothing manufacturer. They do not choose to buy and use cotton simply because they personally prefer it over other materials but because consumers are willing to purchase cotton-based clothing. Similarly, if consumer preferences shift, for instance, due to a study revealing that cotton causes cancer, the manufacturer would likely replace cotton with an alternative material. This substitution would not reflect a personal change in preference but rather a response to consumer demand. Ultimately, only the preferences of final consumers drive the market.

II. From consumer choice to consumer autonomy

The term *consumer choice* was introduced by Averitt and Lande[26] as part of a broader critique of the consumer welfare standard[27], which some commentators argue is overly focused on price while neglecting other factors important to consumers, such as quality, safety, variety, and innovation.[28] According to Averitt and Lande, consumer choice should be understood within the broader concept of consumer sovereignty, which highlights the consumer's active role in the competitive process. In this view, consumer sovereignty means that economic actors "act primarily in response to the aggregate signals of consumer demand, rather than in response to government directives or the preferences of individual business."[29] Consumers are 'sovereign' because they have "the power to define their own wants and the opportunity to satisfy those wants at prices not greatly in

[26] *Averitt/Lande*, Antitrust Law Journal 1997, 713; *Averitt/Lande*, Antitrust Law Journal 2007, 175.

[27] See for the consumer welfare standard below p. 162.

[28] *Foer/Durst*, Antitrust Bulletin 2018, 494; *Grimes*, GRUR International 2020, 3; *Steinbaum/Stucke*, University of Chicago Law Review 2020, 595; *Wu*, CPI 2018.

[29] *Averitt/Lande*, Antitrust Law Journal 1997, 713 (715).

excess of the costs borne by the providers of the relevant goods and services."[30] In a competitive marketplace, consumers have a meaningful range of options, whereas anticompetitive practices such as price fixing or (harmful) mergers can reduce this range of options. According to the consumer choice approach, competition law's task is to prevent such practices and thereby ensure the benefits that competition brings to consumers in terms of choice.[31] In the view of Averitt and Lande, competition law is accompanied by consumer protection laws that

> "ensure that consumers can choose effectively from among these options, with their critical faculties unimpaired by such violations as deception or withholding of material information."[32]

The core principle of a consumer sovereignty standard is that consumers, through their choices, provide the necessary signals to guide the economy. This can only work when two conditions are fulfilled: (1) sufficient options are available, and (2) consumers can freely choose among those options.[33] Averitt and Lande argue that competition and consumer protection laws must address market failures that may impair consumer sovereignty. They divide such failures into two categories, those taking place "outside the head" of the consumer and those "inside the consumer's head".[34] The first category includes what is generally perceived as antitrust problems, e.g., reduced choices due to cartels or monopolies.[35] The second category concerns the consumer's ability to properly "process information and distinguish the true from the false."[36] Consumer protection law generally deals with this kind of market failure. Discussing US law, Averitt and Lande refer to the laws against coercion, undue influence, deception, incomplete information, or confusing information.[37] The distinction also seems to generally apply to EU law that deals with the latter kind of problems through consumer protection law and the law on unfair commercial practices. These laws identify settings where the consumer's ability to make an informed decision is threatened due to information asymmetries or undue business behaviour rather than behaviour affecting the structure of markets. The identified market failures "in the consumer's head" are then remedied through measures like mandatory disclosure rules or prohibiting certain business practices. Although Averitt and Lande propose this dichotomy, they point out that effects may interact in complex ways and that market failures in one category can lead to market failures in

[30] *Averitt/Lande*, Antitrust Law Journal 1997, 713 (715–716).
[31] *Averitt/Lande*, Antitrust Law Journal 1997, 713 (713)
[32] *Averitt/Lande*, Antitrust Law Journal 1997, 713 (713–714)
[33] *Averitt/Lande*, Antitrust Law Journal 1997, 713 (716).
[34] *Averitt/Lande*, Antitrust Law Journal 1997, 713 (729).
[35] *Averitt/Lande*, Antitrust Law Journal 1997, 713 (729).
[36] *Averitt/Lande*, Antitrust Law Journal 1997, 713 (729).
[37] *Averitt/Lande*, Antitrust Law Journal 1997, 713 (733).

the other.[38] They give three examples where such overlap is possible. The first one is horizontal agreements that increase consumers' search costs.

Not only do these impair decision quality by limiting information about a product's relative price and value but they may also, in the long run, reduce the number of available options.[39] A second example is resale price maintenance which can be used as an incentive for dealers to push for the sale of a manufacturer's product irrespective of whether it best fits the needs and preferences of the consumer.[40] The last example they offer is tying of products, which reduces the consumers' options (only one combined product instead of two separate products) as well as their ability to evaluate the product's characteristics.[41] While Averitt and Lande primarily frame their discussion around consumer choice in terms of variety and market options, they also suggest that competition law may, in some cases, encompass broader consumer sovereignty concerns beyond the mere availability of options.

Consumer choice is also a topic of debate in the EU. There are meaningful contributions arguing for a consumer choice approach as an essential factor in the competitive analysis. In particular, Paul Nihoul, a judge at the EU General Court, has voiced strong support for this idea.[42] Even more explicitly than Averitt/Lande, Nihoul follows a broad definition of choice. He defines consumer choice as

> "the possibility, and the right, for customers to choose freely the products/services best corresponding to their needs, and the economic partners they want to deal with."[43]

This definition conveys an underlying concept that extends beyond merely the number and variety of options, emphasizing that choice must also be free. This broader perspective allows for the examination not only of the existence and outcomes of consumer choices but also of the very process of choosing. This is best expressed through adopting a broader view, which this thesis tries to offer with the concept of 'consumer autonomy'. Consumer autonomy[44] for the purpose of this thesis is understood as entailing:

(1) the (mental) capacities to form intentions and plan their execution, including some level of rationality; this includes factors such as sufficient information and time to make an informed choice; and
(2) independence of decision-making, in particular, freedom from coercion and manipulation.

---

[38] *Averitt/Lande*, Antitrust Law Journal 1997, 713 (734–735)

[39] *Averitt/Lande*, Antitrust Law Journal 1997, 713 (736–737)

[40] *Averitt/Lande*, Antitrust Law Journal 1997, 713 (737–738)

[41] *Averitt/Lande*, Antitrust Law Journal 1997, 713 (738–740)

[42] *Nihoul*, in: Consumer Choice, 9.

[43] *Nihoul*, in: Consumer Choice, 9.

[44] For an overview of different conceptions of autonomy, see *Hacker*, Verhaltensökonomik und Normativität, pp. 223–232; see also *Raz*, The Morality of Freedom, pp. 372–373.

While the range of options as emphasized by proponents of the consumer choice approach is also important, this thesis will focus on the process of choosing rather than on the range of options. As will become apparent, the question of what constitutes an 'adequate' range of options can only be answered through the operation of a functioning competitive market. This, however, presupposes that consumers can make autonomous decisions.[45]

III. Vertical agreements or vertical restraints?

This thesis will primarily use the term 'vertical agreement' rather than 'vertical restraint' because the second already implies that the agreement is restrictive of competition. Whether this is the case or not, however, is often still to be determined. One would also not speak of a 'horizontal restraint' to describe a horizontal agreement before one has determined whether it restricts competition. Nonetheless, courts and scholars sometimes use the terms 'vertical agreement' and 'vertical restraint' interchangeably without intending to imply that a certain agreement is restrictive of competition. Throughout the thesis, it may therefore occur in citations that the term 'vertical restraint' is also used. To avoid confusion, a vertical agreement that restricts competition in the sense of Art. 101(1) TFEU will typically be labelled a 'vertical restriction'.

§4 Basics of behavioural economics

This section will explain how behavioural economics has reshaped our understanding of human behaviour, particularly in a market context. It will first provide an overview of the traditional rational choice theory and the concept of homo oeconomicus (I.) to describe then how behavioural economics offers an alternative perspective on human decision-making (II.–III.). The section introduces behavioural economics briefly, as the thesis will build on some of its findings later. Readers already familiar with behavioural economics may wish to proceed directly to Chapter 1.

I. Traditional economic assumptions about market participants' behaviour: the homo oeconomicus

Economic sciences have traditionally characterized human behavior under the assumption of rationality. According to rational choice theory, individuals make rational choices to best satisfy their wants.[46] The factors influencing an individ-

[45] See, in particular, below from p. 208.
[46] *Kirchgässner*, Homo Oeconomicus, pp. 1–2.

ual's decision are their preferences and constraints.[47] Rational choice theory is rooted in the neoclassical model, which portrays the human as homo oeconomicus.[48] Its underlying assumptions are the following:[49]

- The individual's goal is to maximize their (subjective) utility.
- The individual's preferences are known, stable, and non-contradictory.
- The individual's decision is not influenced by how the alternatives are presented (invariance), nor do individuals consider features common to all options (independence).

Neumann and Morgenstern developed expected utility theory to describe decisions under conditions of uncertainty.[50] The core idea of this theory is that the decision-maker seeks to maximize their *expected* utility. A simplified example illustrates this[51]: A decision-maker has the choice between options A and B. Option A has a 10 % chance of resulting in a gain of $100, while Option B offers a 25 % chance of the same gain. The expected utility of Option A is $10 (100 × 0.1), while the expected utility of Option B is $25 (100 × 0.25). Therefore, Option B is the better choice.

II. Behavioural economics' critique of the conventional model

The rational choice and expected utility theory have long been criticized for relying on unrealistic assumptions.[52] Another point of critique is that the question "where [...] preferences come from, how they are formed and how they are (or can be) influenced" traditionally plays no role in these theories.[53] Rather than the process of choice, the results have been the centre of attention. The idea that 'real people' behave differently from homo oeconomicus has been further explored by the field of behavioral economics. Behavioural economics examines the extent to which people systematically differ from the homo oeconomicus.[54] Drawing from

---

[47] *Towfigh*, in: Ökonomische Methoden im Recht, 23 (28).

[48] *Albert*, in: Behavioral Economics und Wirtschaftspolitik, 3 (5); *Latzel*, Verhaltenssteuerung, Recht und Privatautonomie, p. 54; *Thaler*, American Economic Review 2016, 1577 (1578) who uses the term 'econ'; *Towfigh*, in: Ökonomische Methoden im Recht, 23 (32).

[49] *Varian*, Intermediate Microeconomics, pp. 223–226; *Towfigh*, in: Ökonomische Methoden im Recht, 23 (28–31); *Morell*, in: Ökonomische Methoden im Recht, 41 (42–56).

[50] *von Neumann/Morgenstern*, Theory of Games and Economic Behavior.

[51] After *Hanson/Kysar*, NYU Law Review 2000, 630 (641).

[52] *Hanson/Kysar*, NYU Law Review 2000, 630 (643).; *Kirchgässner*, Homo Oeconomicus, p. 25; *Latzel*, Verhaltenssteuerung, Recht und Privatautonomie, p. 57; *Thaler*, American Economic Review 2016, 1577 (1579).

[53] Compare *Kirchgässner*, Homo Oeconomicus, pp. 24, 35; *Künzler*, Restoring Consumer Sovereignty, p. 138.

[54] For a very detailed description of behavioural economics, including criticism, see *Hacker*, Verhaltensökonomik und Normativität, pp. 71–141; see also *Latzel*, Verhaltenssteuerung, Recht und Privatautonomie, p. 52.

psychology, it aims to provide a more accurate prediction of human decision-making.[55] Behavioural economics rejects the notion of stable preferences; instead, it assumes preferences to be intransitive and often only constructed in the process of decision-making. As such, preferences can be predictably influenced by the context and framing of the decision.[56] Behavioral economics, therefore, places greater emphasis on the process of decision-making.

1. The three bounds of decision-making

Jolls, Sunstein and Thaler identified three bounds that limit rational decision-making: bounded rationality, bounded willpower, and bounded self-interest.[57] They argue that because of these bounds, "most people depart from the standard economic model."[58]

a) Bounded rationality

It was Herbert A. Simon, who first developed the concept of bounded rationality as a more realistic model of decision-making. He highlighted the individual's limitations in "knowledge and computational capacity".[59] Under bounded rationality, the decision-maker is not always utility-optimizing but rather just satisficing: they set an aspiration level that suffices and that they can reasonably achieve and picks the first solution that meets this expectation.[60] Kahneman and Tversky showed that to cope with uncertainty, people use heuristics "which reduce the complex tasks of assessing probabilities and predicting values to simpler judgmental operations."[61] While these heuristics (or rules of thumb)[62] can often be helpful, in some cases they "lead to severe and systematic errors."[63] One of the most prominent examples in this context is the availability heuristic: the frequency or probability of an event (such as a car accident, a heart attack, a terrorist attack) is evaluated based on the availability of recalling similar instances.[64] Doing so might be a rational way of thinking: assessing frequency or probability based on availability makes sense because more frequent examples are often easier to recall.[65] If the costs of making a more accurate prediction are high, it can indeed be rational to fall back on the availability heuristic. However, the avai-

---

[55] *Thaler*, American Economic Review 2016, 1577 (1577).

[56] *Albert*, in: Behavioral Economics und Wirtschaftspolitik, 3 (6).

[57] *Jolls et al.*, Stanford Law Review 1998, 1471 (1476).

[58] *Jolls et al.*, Stanford Law Review 1998, 1471 (1476).

[59] *Simon*, in: Utility and Probability, 15 (15).

[60] *Simon*, Annual Review of Psychology 1990, 1 (9).

[61] *Tversky/Kahneman*, Science 1974, 1124 (1124).

[62] *Jolls et al.*, Stanford Law Review 1998, 1471 (1477).

[63] *Kahneman*, American Economic Review 2003, 1449 (1460); *Tversky/Kahneman*, Science 1974, 1124 (1124).

[64] *Tversky/Kahneman*, Science 1974, 1124 (1127).

[65] *Tversky/Kahneman*, Science 1974, 1124 (1127).

lability heuristic, like other heuristics, in some scenarios can lead to predictable errors: e.g., if one just witnessed the occurrence of an event (e.g., a car accident), the likelihood of the same event is overestimated.[66] Tversky and Kahneman refer to these predictable errors as 'biases'.[67]

b) Bounded willpower

Another deviation in human behaviour from the rational choice model is bounded willpower: individuals, in many cases, make decisions or take actions that conflict with their long-term preferences. Unlike rational choice theory suggests, preferences do not remain stable over time, but short-term and long-term preferences can be contradictory. Consequently, preferences can be time inconsistent. Englerth and Towfigh, in this regard, use the term 'present bias' for what they describe as an "extreme overvaluation of immediate consumption."[68] A prominent example is that of the smoker, whose long-term preference is to quit smoking, yet continues to purchase and consume cigarettes.[69]

c) Bounded self-interest

Finally, behavioural economics challenges the traditional assumption of self-maximizing behaviour. Unlike what rational choice theory suggests, people often care (or behave as if they care) about others, including strangers.[70] In particular, they care about the perceived 'fairness' of transactions.[71] Economists and psychologists have conducted a series of experiments to analyse how this can influence decisions. One of the most prominent examples is the ultimatum game:[72] Player 1 is asked to divide a certain amount of money (e.g. 20 $) between herself and player 2. Player 2 can accept or decline the offer. If they accept, the money is allocated as proposed by player 1. If they decline, none of the players gets anything. Under rational choice theory, one would expect player 1 to offer the smallest possible amount (e.g., 1 $) to keep the maximum amount for herself and that player 2 accepts any offer greater than zero. However, this result in experiments was rare. Most times, player 2 would decline offers below one-third of the total amount and player 1 would anticipate this behaviour in their offers.

---

[66] *Tversky/Kahneman*, Science 1974, 1124 (1127).

[67] *Tversky/Kahneman*, Science 1974, 1124 (1124).

[68] *Englerth/Towfigh*, in: Ökonomische Methoden im Recht, 216 (240).

[69] *Englerth/Towfigh*, in: Ökonomische Methoden im Recht, 216 (239); *Jolls et al.*, Stanford Law Review 1998, 1471 (1479).

[70] *Jolls et al.*, Stanford Law Review 1998, 1471 (1479).

[71] *Jolls et al.*, Stanford Law Review 1998, 1471 (1479).

[72] *Englerth/Towfigh*, in: Ökonomische Methoden im Recht, 216 (222); *Jolls et al.*, Stanford Law Review 1998, 1471 (1489–1497).

III. The consumer's decision-making process

This thesis will in Chapter 2 discuss whether and to what extent competition law may protect the consumer's decision-making process. To do so, it is first helpful to develop a general understanding of this decision-making process, drawing on insights from behavioural economic research. Not surprisingly, there is vast body of of literature analysing consumer behaviour from the discipline of business administration sciences, particularly marketing.[73] The following paragraphs will give an overview of consumers' decision-making and typical biases that can occur in a purchasing context.

1. Types of purchase decisions

How a consumer makes a purchase decision depends on the product in question, the consumer's knowledge of the product, and their preferences. Marketing literature often distinguishes between extensive, impulsive, limited, and habitual purchases.[74]

a) Extensive purchase

In an extensive purchase decision, the consumer is very attentive and/or actively seeks information about the product and is highly mentally involved.[75] This type of purchase decision typically concerns purchases of significant economic importance to the consumer, e.g., buying a car or even a house. The extensive purchase decision represents a situation where the real world aligns most closely with the economic model of homo oeconomicus. The consumer is relatively well-informed and tries to maximize their utility by choosing between different alternatives. They try to assert high cognitive effort to make a thorough and rational purchase decision.[76]

b) Impulsive purchase

In this type of purchase, the consumer is much less involved. The decision is more of a reactive behavior in response to external circumstances.[77] It results from an "unplanned, spontaneous impulse".[78] Examples of impulsive purchases include,

[73] In the same direction already *Leavitt*, Journal of Business 1954, 205; see *Tull et al.*, Journal of Business 1964, 186 (186) who already remarked that the consumer 'does not have all the information provided his theoretical brother, and search costs are frequently such as to make it uneconomic for him to obtain it.'; *Simonson*, California Management Review 1993, 68 (69) who states that '[...] customers' preferences should not be taken as given and fixed.'

[74] *Felser*, Werbe- und Konsumentenpsychologie, p. 156; *Kroeber-Riel/Gröppel-Klein*, Konsumentenverhalten, pp. 385–418.

[75] *Felser*, Werbe- und Konsumentenpsychologie, p. 156.

[76] *Kroeber-Riel/Gröppel-Klein*, Konsumentenverhalten, p. 396.

[77] *Felser*, Werbe- und Konsumentenpsychologie, pp. 157–158.

[78] *Baumeister*, Journal of Consumer Research 2002, 670 (670).

for instance, buying items at the grocery store because of a special offer. Impulsive purchases often conflict with the consumer's (long-term) goals.[79] For instance, buying a chocolate bar at the supermarket checkout may contradict the consumer's goal to eat healthier or to save money. Speaking in terms of behavioural economics, impulsive purchases are often linked to bounded willpower.[80]

c) Limited purchase

In a limited purchase situation, the consumer already has some experience regarding the purchase that they can rely on.[81] Unlike in an impulsive purchase, the consumer is relatively involved in the decision-making process and less influenced by external circumstances. However, the decision is not as cognitively elaborate as in an extensive purchase, either because the consumer lacks the time for a more detailed evaluation or because the economic significance of the item does not warrant the effort. In this context, the consumer relies heavily on heuristics.[82] This can be, for example, the price as an indicator of the quality of the good,[83] prior experience with goods of the same brand or the reputation of the country where the product was produced[84] (e.g., made in Germany as a proxy for good quality).[85]

d) Habitual purchase

Like impulsive purchases, habitual purchases involve minimal cognitive effort on the part of the consumer.[86] The consumer simply buys what they always buy. Typical items for habitual purchase include food and beverages; for example, consumers may consistently choose the same coffee or beer brand.[87] Unlike limited purchases, the consumer does not rely on heuristics in making these decisions. Instead, the habit forms either through the consumer's own experiences (learning) or by adapting to the observed behavior of others.[88] It is estimated that up to 50% of human behaviour is based on habitual decisions.[89] Habitual purchases are not always tied to the bounds of decision-making discussed earlier. It

---

[79] *Baumeister*, Journal of Consumer Research 2002, 670 (671).

[80] See above p. 12.

[81] Compare *Felser*, Werbe- und Konsumentenpsychologie, pp. 158–159; *Kroeber-Riel/Gröppel-Klein*, Konsumentenverhalten, p. 397.

[82] *Felser*, Werbe- und Konsumentenpsychologie, p. 158.

[83] *Kroeber-Riel/Gröppel-Klein*, Konsumentenverhalten, p. 399; *Leavitt*, Journal of Business 1954, 205 (209–210); *Tull et al.*, Journal of Business 1964, 186.

[84] *Simonson/Rosen*, Absolute Value, p. 32.

[85] For more examples of typical consumer heuristics, see *Solomon*, Consumer Behavior, p. 340.

[86] *Kroeber-Riel/Gröppel-Klein*, Konsumentenverhalten, p. 404.

[87] *Felser*, Werbe- und Konsumentenpsychologie, p. 159.

[88] *Kroeber-Riel/Gröppel-Klein*, Konsumentenverhalten, p. 406.

[89] *Kroeber-Riel/Gröppel-Klein*, Konsumentenverhalten, p. 405.

may be perfectly rational and in the consumer's best interest to consistently buy the same brand, but this is only true if the initial decision to do so was rational. For instance, if a consumer initially opts for a specific brand due to bounded rationality, they might later develop a habit of purchasing the same brand repeatedly. In other words, habitual purchases can reinforce the effects of boundedly rational decision-making.

e) Conclusion

Depending on the purchase, consumers may be more or less mentally involved in the decision-making. Often, they are unwilling or unable to invest significant cognitive effort and instead rely on heuristics or make impulsive choices.

2. The most common heuristics consumers rely on

The following paragraphs will provide more detailed examples of heuristics that consumers often rely on when making decisions, as well as discuss the impact of the purchasing environment on consumer choices.

a) Availability heuristic

In the context of consumer decisions, a consumer who can easily recall specific information related to their purchase decision will often assume that this information is particularly relevant. The implicit thinking rule behind it is that there must be a reason why one quickly remembers certain information.[90] This heuristic applies not only to events but also to product names or brands. A consumer who can easily remember a brand or product name often assumes it signifies popularity or widespread distribution.[91] A sales strategy that capitalizes on the availability heuristic, therefore, involves exposing the consumer to a brand or product as frequently as possible. The first product a consumer encounters in a store or the most visible product may serve as a reference point for their decision.[92]

b) Representativeness heuristic

When individuals are faced with assessing probabilities, they often rely on the representativeness heuristic.[93] According to this heuristic, the likelihood that an item belongs to a specific category is assessed based on its similarity to other items of the same type or, more generally, the correspondence "between an outcome

[90] *Felser*, Werbe- und Konsumentenpsychologie, p. 177.
[91] *Felser*, Werbe- und Konsumentenpsychologie, p. 177.
[92] *Zhou*, Journal of Economics & Management Strategy 2011, 1073 (1074).
[93] *Hanson/Kysar*, NYU Law Review 2000, 630 (664); *Tversky/Kahneman*, Science 1974, 1124 (1124).

and a model."[94] This can lead to biases when ignoring other important information due to sole reliance on representativeness. Understanding the representativeness heuristic can help explain why consumers might disregard negative information about a product. For example, a car with key features of a high-quality vehicle, such as a premium interior, high horsepower, and additional features, may be perceived as high-quality, even if it performs poorly in accident statistics. The heuristic can also explain the often-observed reliance on price as an indicator of quality.[95] The high price is a typical property of high-quality products, so consumers assume that an item with a high price is also of high quality, even if it is representative of high-quality products just regarding the price and not the quality (which is much harder to assess). Some scholars call this the "you pay for what you get"-heuristic.[96] Sales strategies leveraging this heuristic might involve setting relatively high prices and emphasizing certain 'representative' attributes of a product.

c) Anchor heuristic

The anchor heuristic describes a decision-making strategy where individuals use a specific numerical reference point to assess a numerical judgmen. As Kahneman and Tversky demonstrated, there is often insufficient adjustment from the initial anchor.[97] For example, list prices or recommended retail prices frequently serve as anchors, setting a high price in the consumer's mind. The same effect can occur when high-priced items are placed at eye level, making them the first ones the consumer sees. A salesperson can also use this strategy by first showing the consumer the highest-priced items. This can indeed be a promising sales strategy as the following example shows: in a pool table store, the manager for one week started the sale conversation with each customer by leading them to the cheapest available table; in the week after, he did so by showing them first the most expensive table. While the average sale in week 1 was $ 550, in week 2, it was over $ 1000.[98]

d) Mental accounting

Building on the work of Tversky and Kahneman[99], Thaler explored mental accounting as a way of decision-making.[100] He suggests that consumers engage in

---

[94] *Tversky/Kahneman*, in: Extensional Versus Intuitive Reasoning, 114 (116).

[95] *Lee*, International Journal of Marketing Studies 2012, 31.

[96] *Lichtenstein/Burton*, Journal of Marketing Research 1989, 429 (430); see also *Solomon*, Consumer Behavior, p. 342.

[97] *Tversky/Kahneman*, Science 1974, 1124; see also *Hanson/Kysar*, NYU Law Review 2000, 630 (667).

[98] *Ornstein*, Multimind, p. 86.

[99] In particular *Tversky/Kahneman*, Science 1981, 453.

[100] *Thaler*, Marketing Science 1985, 199.

'mental account management'.[101] In their head, the consumer allocates their expenses (e.g., time, money, efforts) to specific accounts. These can be, for example, accounts for professional expenses, accounts for entertainment, food etc. An account can eventually be exhausted, making it unlikely that the consumer continues to buy products that they allocate to this account. Tversky and Kahneman give the example of someone losing a cinema ticket worth 10 $ vs someone losing a 10 $ bill just before buying the ticket. The person losing the cinema ticket is much less likely to buy a (new) cinema ticket than the person who lost the bill because their 'cinema account' is depleted.[102] Felser describes the process of mental accounting as 'budget heuristic'.[103] Mental accounting can be used by framing a product for a purpose that is typically assigned to a specific mental account. Suppose a consumer in a store, for example, has already purchased an expensive suit for 'work purposes'. In that case, the salesperson could suggest buying another suit for 'leisure' as the leisure account is not yet depleted.[104]

e) Decoy effects

Often, the existence of irrelevant options influences the decision.[105] Consider the following example from Felser[106] (after Pratkanis and Aronson[107]): a consumer wants to go to a pizzeria and has two options, the Pizzeria Venezia and the Pizzeria Sole. The first is just a few steps away from their place, and the pizza is decent; the second is further away but has the best pizza. The consumer will decide according to a weighing of their preferences (better pizza vs less travel time). However, if they face a third choice – Pizzeria Palermo, which is as far as Sole, but the Pizza is better than at Venezia, they choose Sole more often than in the scenario with only two alternatives. This is striking as Palermo is an inferior choice to both other options (it is further away than Venezia, and the Pizza is less good than in Sole). However, bringing Palermo to the table gives greater importance to quality compared to distance.[108] The decoy effect can be used by adding irrelevant options that make the other options look more attractive. In a study by Solomon and Tversky[109] participants in one group were asked to choose between two cameras, one priced at $ 169.99, and the other at $ 239.99. Participants in a

---

[101] Compare *Felser*, Werbe- und Konsumentenpsychologie, p. 181.

[102] *Kahneman/Tversky*, American Psychologist 1984, 341 (347); see also *Felser*, Werbe- und Konsumentenpsychologie, p. 182.

[103] *Felser*, Werbe- und Konsumentenpsychologie, p. 181.

[104] Compare *Felser*, Werbe- und Konsumentenpsychologie, p. 182.

[105] *Hanson/Kysar*, NYU Law Review 2000, 630 (676); see also *Dahremöller/Fels*, Journal of Economic Behavior & Organization 2015, 437 modelling limited attention in the context of product design.

[106] *Felser*, Werbe- und Konsumentenpsychologie, pp. 187–188.

[107] *Pratkanis/Aronson*, Age of Propaganda, pp. 67–70.

[108] *Felser*, Werbe- und Konsumentenpsychologie, pp. 187–188.

[109] *Simonson/Tversky*, Journal of Marketing Research 1992, 281.

second group were asked to choose between the same two plus a third camera, which was priced at $ 469.99. In the second group, significantly more people chose the $ 239.99 camera than the cheapest one.[110] This example shows that people tend to go for the compromise item. A crafty salesperson can easily influence which item is perceived as the compromise item by adding or removing other options.[111] The mental processes leading to the decoy effect are considered to be largely intuitive.[112] When mental resources are depleted and, in consequence, the decision-maker takes a more intuitive and less elaborate decision, they are more likely to be subject to the decoy effect.[113]

f) Loss aversion and endowment effect

Loss aversion leads to an endowment effect in decision-making, where losses are valued more highly than equivalent gains.[114] There are numerous strategies that capitalize on the endowment effect and loss aversion. Framing outcomes as gains or losses can thus have a significant influence on the decision.[115] In many stores, it is possible to touch the items, which gives a feeling of possession over them.[116] Online shops can try to replicate this by encouraging customers to imagine the product in detail, e.g., by options to zoom in, turn the image, change colours or even individualize the product. Evoking the thought of touch is supposed to generate a sense of ownership.[117] Money-back guarantees, trial periods, free samples and similar strategies serve the same purpose: they make the consumer feel like they already own the product.[118]

g) Valuing irrelevant attributes

Carpenter et al. have demonstrated that a firm can achieve a competitive advantage not (only) through better catering to consumers' preferences but instead through product differentiation[119] using meaningless attributes.[120] They provide two examples of such differentiation: the first is the use of "flaked crystals" in

[110] *Simonson/Tversky*, Journal of Marketing Research 1992, 281 (290).

[111] Compare *Hanson/Kysar*, Harvard Law Review 1999, 1420 (1140).

[112] *Dhar/Gorlin*, Journal of Consumer Psychology 2013, 528 (536).

[113] *Dhar/Gorlin*, Journal of Consumer Psychology 2013, 528 (536).

[114] *Felser*, Werbe- und Konsumentenpsychologie, p. 189; *Thaler*, Journal of Economic Behavior & Organization 1980, 39 (43–47).

[115] *Jolls/Sunstein*, Journal of Legal Studies 2006, 199 (7).

[116] *Jansson-Boyd*, in: Handbook Consumer Psychology, 85 (87).

[117] Compare *Jansson-Boyd*, in: Handbook Consumer Psychology, 85 (87).

[118] *Hanson/Kysar*, NYU Law Review 2000, 630 (734).

[119] Product differentiation refers to strategies to make a product or service distinct from competing products or services, i.e. making them distinct in the eye of the consumer. This can be profitable for firms because it reduces competitive pressure from other products or services. See: *Lianos*, in: Brands, Competition Law and IP, 146.

[120] *Carpenter et al.*, Journal of Marketing Research 1994, 339.

Folger's instant coffee, which served to differentiate it from competing products, even though the attribute had no effect on the taste (unlike ground coffee, where the shape of coffee particles is relevant – greater surface area extracts more flavor).[121] The second example is the inclusion of silk in Alberto Culver Natural Shampoo, an ingredient that has no bearing on the quality of the product.[122] Consumers will often assign significant importance to such attributes, particularly when they are novel and, therefore, more salient in the consumption decision.[123] Such irrelevant attributes can make the differentiated brand more distinctive and, therefore, more salient in consumers' minds, making them more likely to purchase it.[124] The irrelevant attribute can offer a "simple, single-attribute decision rule".[125] This choice rule can even persist once the consumer learns about the attribute's irrelevance. Interestingly, the study's authors found that irrelevant attributes only influence consumers' valuations when the products are sold at relatively high prices. They conclude that this "suggests that differentiating from competitors by adding an irrelevant attribute and pricing *above* competitors can create a competitive advantage if consumer information is limited."[126] As the authors state, these "results are somewhat disquieting for the model of rational choice."[127] Irrelevant information and attributes become a relevant factor in consumers' decisions. This can lead to competition being not a race to "meet consumer needs at the lowest price" but instead one "over the structure of consumer preferences" with "little or no investment in product improvement."[128]

h) Salience and limited attention

The attributes upon which consumers base their choices depend largely on the salience of those attributes. Consequently, firms seek to highlight their products' outstanding features while downplaying areas where their products might not excel.[129] Consumers have only limited attention and are therefore unable to consider all product attributes or all available products.[130] As a result, they may fail to identify products that best align with their needs and preferences.[131]

---

[121] *Carpenter et al.*, Journal of Marketing Research 1994, 339.
[122] *Carpenter et al.*, Journal of Marketing Research 1994, 339.
[123] *Carpenter et al.*, Journal of Marketing Research 1994, 339 (341).
[124] *Carpenter et al.*, Journal of Marketing Research 1994, 339 (341).
[125] *Carpenter et al.*, Journal of Marketing Research 1994, 339 (341).
[126] *Carpenter et al.*, Journal of Marketing Research 1994, 339 (347) (emphasis in original).
[127] *Carpenter et al.*, Journal of Marketing Research 1994, 339 (348).
[128] *Carpenter et al.*, Journal of Marketing Research 1994, 339 (341).
[129] *Bordalo et al.*, Review of Economic Studies 2016, 481 (504).
[130] See *Hefti*, Journal of Economic Theory 2018, 318.
[131] See *Hefti*, Journal of Economic Theory 2018, 318 (319).

i) Conclusion: framing and context matter

These are just a few examples of how consumers make decisions in ways that deviate from traditional economic theory and how firms can leverage these insights. They illustrate that consumer decision-making can be influenced by various factors, including the sales context and the options presented. Tversky and Kahneman already pointed out in 1981 that framing and context matter.[132] The person who controls the anchor, presents the options in a specific order, or adds or removes decoys, for example, holds considerable influence over the decision-making process. To a certain extent, it allows them to programme the consumer's decision-making process. While this might not always lead to the decision that they envisage (e.g., the sale of a product), it can be a successful strategy in many cases. As Hanson and Douglas put it: "because individuals exhibit systematic and persistent cognitive processes that depart from axioms of rationality, they are susceptible to manipulation by those actors in a position to influence the decision-making context."[133]

---

[132] *Tversky/Kahneman*, Science 1981, 453.

[133] *Hanson/Kysar*, Harvard Law Review 1999, 1420 (1424–1425).

Chapter 1

Treatment of vertical agreements under EU competition law and economic evaluation

This Chapter will discuss the treatment of vertical agreements under EU competition law and provide an overview of their economic evaluation. It will also carry out a comparison with how vertical agreements are treated under US antitrust law. While the Chapter aims to provide a general overview of the treatment and evaluation of vertical agreements, its primary focus will be on agreements that restrict or prohibit online sales. The Chapter proceeds as follows: first, it will give an overview of the treatment of vertical agreements under EU competition law, showing that this treatment remains, to some extent, categorical and sometimes lacks proper identification of the restriction of competition (§ 1). This is followed by an assessment of whether the current approach rests on solid economic grounds (§ 2). In this regard, it will be demonstrated that the treatment of vertical agreements under EU competition law does not fully align with economy theory. Subsequently, the chapter will conduct a comparison with US antitrust law (§ 3), displaying that the more effects and less form-based approach in the United States follows from US antitrust law's clear and unambiguous goal of promoting economic efficiency. The chapter will then wrap up with a conclusion (§ 4).

§ 1 Current assessment of vertical agreements under EU competition law

I. Introduction

The Court of Justice in the 1966 Consten/Grundig case found that Art. 85 EEC Treaty [today: Art. 101 TFEU] applies not only to horizontal but also to vertical agreements.[1] Initially, the European Commission and the Court of Justice considered almost every vertical agreement a restriction of competition based on the understanding that it would restrict the retailer's economic freedom,[2] except were

[1] Court of Justice, 13/06/1966, Joined Cases 56 and 58–64 Consten/Grundig, ECLI:EU:C:1966:41, p. 342.

[2] *Colino*, Vertical Agreements, p. 61; *de la Mano/Jones*, in: Methods and Models, 167 (169).

the agreement was objectively justified.[3] Such justification was recognized for certain categories of agreements that proportionately pursue a legitimate (pro-competitive) objective. In Pronuptia, for example, the Court of Justice considered franchise agreements not to restrict competition under certain circumstances if they were "strictly necessary in order to ensure that the know-how and assistance provided by the franchisor do not benefit competitors" or "for maintaining the identity and reputation of the network identified by the common name or symbol."[4] Similarly, in the 1977 Metro I[5] case, the Court of Justice developed an exemption for selective distribution agreements.[6] Under certain conditions, those agreements do not fall within the ambit of Art. 101(1) TFEU (no restriction of competition).

Besides those inherent exceptions to Art. 101(1) TFEU, the application of Art. 101(3) TFEU also played a significant role as so many agreements were covered by the prohibition in the first place.[7] Since the adoption of Regulation 1/2003, Art. 101(3) TFEU is directly applicable without requiring an explicit exemption by the Commission or a national competition authority.[8] There are two ways in which Art. 101(3) TFEU can be applied to exclude an agreement from the prohibition under Art. 101(1) TFEU. First, by direct application of Art. 101(3) TFEU, so-called individual exemption; second, through the application of block exemption regulations. The latter allows the Commission, acting under delegated authority from the Council, to declare Art. 101(1) TFEU inapplicable to specific groups or categories of agreements based on a typifying competitive assessment.[9] For vertical agreements, the Commission has adopted the Vertical Block Exemption Regulation ('VBER'). If an agreement falls under the VBER, it is exempted from Art. 101(1) TFEU and no direct recourse to Art. 101(3) TFEU is needed. On the other hand, agreements that do not fulfil the requirements laid down in the VBER can nevertheless be exempted under Art. 101(3) TFEU.[10] Starting from the assumption that most vertical agreements restrict competition, the Commission's block exemption regulations played an important role in shaping vertical arrangements in the European Union.[11] Initially, the Commission adopted separate regulations for specific types of agreements,

[3] See *European Commission*, Green Paper on Vertical Restraints, para. 20.

[4] Court of Justice, 28/01/1986, Case 161/84 Pronuptia, ECLI:EU:C:1986:41, para. 27.

[5] Court of Justice, 25/10/1977, Case 26–76 Metro I, ECLI:EU:C:1977:167.

[6] See in more detail below p. 25.

[7] *de la Mano/Jones*, in: Methods and Models, 167 (169).

[8] Art. 1 (2) Regulation 1/2003; *Whish/Bailey*, Competition Law, p. 173.

[9] *Kumkar*, Online-Märkte und Wettbewerbsrecht, p. 180; *Whish/Bailey*, Competition Law, p. 176.

[10] *Whish/Bailey*, Competition Law, p. 707.

[11] *European Commission*, Green Paper on Vertical Restraints, para. 23.

such as exclusive distribution[12], exclusive purchasing[13] or franchising[14].[15] The block exemptions applied without regard to the involved companies' market shares.[16] This approach was criticized as form-based and suppressing innovation in the distribution chain by imposing a straitjacket on companies.[17] The Commission, reacting to this criticism, in the 1990s moved to a more effects-based approach, emphasizing that a reduction of competition between distributors ('intra-brand competition') is unlikely to have negative effects if competition between distributors of different suppliers ('inter-brand competition') is strong.[18] Since Regulation 2790/1990[19], in principle, all vertical agreements (below certain market share thresholds) are exempted, and only certain categories of agreements ('hardcore restrictions') are not covered by the Regulation.[20]

The current VBER, which is applicable since June 2022, in a continuation of this approach, relatively broadly exempts vertical agreements from Art. 101(1) TFEU. The VBER is complemented by the Commission's Vertical Guidelines[21], which albeit not legally binding, are of great importance for interpreting the VBER.[22] In principle, the VBER exempts vertical agreements concluded by undertakings with a market share not exceeding 30 % of the relevant market.[23] This threshold is applicable for supplier/manufacturer and buyer/retailer alike. The VBER presumes that under this condition, vertical agreements "generally lead to an improvement in production or distribution and allow consumers a fair share of the resulting benefits."[24] According to the Commission, the presumption

---

[12] Commission Regulation (EEC) No 1983/83 of 22 June 1983 on the application of Article 85 (3) of the Treaty to categories of exclusive distribution agreements, OJ L 173, 30.6.1983, pp. 1–4.

[13] Commission Regulation (EEC) No 1984/83 of 22 June 1983 on the application of Article 85 (3) of the Treaty to categories of exclusive purchasing agreements, OJ C 355, 30.12.1983, 7–15.

[14] Commission Regulation (EEC) No 4087/88 of 30 November 1988 on the application of Article 85 (3) of the Treaty to categories of franchise agreements, OJ L 359, 28.12.1988, pp. 46–52.

[15] *European Commission*, Green Paper on Vertical Restraints, para. 17.

[16] *European Commission*, Green Paper on Vertical Restraints, para. 102.

[17] *Hawk*, CMLR 1995, 973; *Vezzoso*, Vertikale Beschränkungen, p. 16; *European Commission*, Green Paper on Vertical Restraints, para. 251.

[18] *Colino*, Vertical Agreements, p. 70; *de la Mano/Jones*, in: Methods and Models, 167 (170); *Vezzoso*, Vertikale Beschränkungen, pp. 14–19; *European Commission*, Green Paper on Vertical Restraints.

[19] Commission Regulation (EC) No 2790/1999 of 22 December 1999 on the application of Article 81(3) of the Treaty to categories of vertical agreements and concerted practices, OJ L 336, 29.12.1999, pp. 21–25.

[20] *de la Mano/Jones*, in: Methods and Models, 167 (170).

[21] Communication from the Commission, Guidelines on vertical restraints 2022/C 248/01, OJ C 248, 30.6.2022, p. 1–85.

[22] *Christodoulou/Holzwarth*, NZKart 2022, 540 (541).

[23] Art. 2(1) and Art. 3 VBER.

[24] VBER, recital 8.

that vertical agreements are efficiency-enhancing does not hold for certain hardcore restrictions laid down in Art. 4 VBER.[25] Vertical agreements containing hardcore restrictions as a whole lose the exemption under the VBER.[26] The categorization as hardcore restriction has several important consequences beyond the loss of the safe harbour provided by the VBER.[27] First, the Commission generally considers hardcore restrictions to constitute restrictions by object so they can be "regarded as being harmful by their very nature to the proper functioning of normal competition" without assessing their effects.[28] While the Vertical Guidelines at the same time emphasize that "hardcore restrictions do not necessarily fall within the scope of Article 101(1) [TFEU]",[29] there is little guidance as to when they would not constitute a by object restriction. For restrictions of competition by object, no concrete effects must be established.[30] As Zelger puts it, "a rebuttable presumption of their illegality exists."[31] Vertical agreements that contain hardcore restrictions are seen as very likely to restrict competition and thus to fall within the scope of Art. 101(1) VBER. They are, moreover, unlikely to fulfil the conditions of Art. 101(3) TFEU.[32] Although they can, in principle, qualify for an individual exemption under Art. 101(3) TFEU if they pursue efficiency goals, they will normally not be indispensable to attaining these objectives. Second, qualifying an agreement as hardcore restriction has the further consequence that the De Minimis Notice[33], under which the Commission holds the view that certain agreements of minor importance do not appreciably restrict competition, does not apply.[34] The only (relative) safe harbour that still applies is the one provided by the Effect on Trade Guidelines[35].[36] Under this Guidelines, the Commission holds the view that agreements do usually not appreciably affect trade between Member States when the parties' aggregate market share does not

[25] VBER, recital 9.

[26] Vertical Guidelines, para. 177.

[27] *Jones*, European Competition Journal 2010, 649 (654).

[28] Vertical Guidelines, para. 179.

[29] Vertical Guidelines, para. 180.

[30] Court of Justice, 12/12/2012, Case C-226/11 Expedia, ECLI:EU:C:2012:795, para. 37; *Jones*, European Competition Journal 2010, 649 (654); *Mestmäcker/Schweitzer*, Europäisches Wettbewerbsrecht, § 11, para. 25 speaking in this context of strict liability ('Gefährdungshaftung'); *Zelger*, European Competition Journal 2017, 356 (360–361).

[31] *Zelger*, European Competition Journal 2017, 356 (364).

[32] Vertical Guidelines, para. 180; *de la Mano/Jones*, in: Methods and Models, 167, describing this as a 'double presumption of illegality'.

[33] Communication from the Commission, Notice on agreements of minor importance which do not appreciably restrict competition under Article 101(1) of the Treaty on the Functioning of the European Union, OJ C 291, 30.8.2014, p. 1–4 ('De Minimis Notice').

[34] De Minimis Notice, para. 13; see Court of Justice, 12/12/2012, Case C-226/11 Expedia, ECLI:EU:C:2012:795, para. 37.

[35] Commission Notice, Guidelines on the effect on trade concept contained in Articles 81 and 82 of the Treaty, OJ C 101, 27.4.2004, p. 81–96 ('Effect on Trade Guidelines').

[36] Vertical Guidelines, para. 25.

exceed 5 % and the aggregate annual EU turnover in the products covered by the agreement does not exceed 40 million EUR.[37] Third, by object restrictions are typically among competition authorities' enforcement priorities and attract high fines.[38] Including hardcore restrictions in vertical agreements, therefore, comes with a high risk for undertakings even when their market shares are low.[39]

II. How specific categories of vertical agreements are treated

The treatment of vertical agreements under both Art. 101(1) TFEU and the VBER/Art. 101(3) TFEU is still guided by the type of agreement in question. Therefore, the following sections will provide an overview of how different types of agreements are evaluated under EU law. Starting point of the assessment for each category is its treatment under the VBER. This approach corresponds to how the Commission conducts its assessment in practice. It assesses first whether the agreement is exempted under the VBER, and only where this is not the case assesses whether the agreement restricts competition in the first place.[40] Moreover, the treatment under the VBER already gives important indications for the treatment under Art. 101(1) TFEU as agreements that are blacklisted under the VBER (hardcore restrictions) are typically considered restrictions of competition by object.

1. Selective distribution agreements

Selective distribution agreements are particularly relevant for this thesis because online sales restrictions are often part of such agreements.[41] The VBER defines selective distribution as a

> "distribution system where the supplier undertakes to sell the contract goods or services [...] only to distributors selected on the basis of specified criteria and where these distributors undertake not to sell such goods or services to unauthorised distributors within the territory reserved by the supplier to operate that system."[42]

Selective distribution under the VBER is, in principle, permitted for all products regardless of their specific characteristics and the criteria applied for the selection of retailers.[43] Within a selective distribution system, restrictions of active or passive sales to end users by retailers, in principle, constitute hardcore restrictions.[44]

---

[37] Effect on Trade Guidelines, para. 52.

[38] *Goyder*, JECLAP 2011, 327 (327).

[39] *Jones*, European Competition Journal 2010, 649 (654, 670).

[40] Vertical Guidelines, para. 7.

[41] See *European Commission*, E-Commerce Sector Inquiry (Commission Staff Working Document), paras. 240–259.

[42] Art. 1(1) point (g) VBER.

[43] Vertical Guidelines (2010), para. 176.

[44] Art. 4 point (c) VBER.

There are, however, several exceptions to this. First, active sales outside the selective distribution system into a territory or to a customer group reserved to the supplier or allocated by the supplier exclusively to a maximum of five exclusive distributors can be restricted.[45] Second, the (active or passive)[46] sale by retailers, who are members of the selective distribution system and their customers to unauthorised distributors, can be restricted.[47] Third, restrictions regarding the place of establishment of the members of the selective distribution system are allowed.[48] This does not, however, allow to prohibit the opening of an online store.[49] Fourth, the wholesale and retail levels can be kept separate by restricting active and passive sales by an authorised wholesaler to end users.[50] Fifth, suppliers can restrict authorised distributors' "ability to actively or passively sell components for the purpose of incorporation, to customers who would use them to manufacture the same type of goods as those produced by the supplier".[51] On the other hand, restrictions on cross-supplies between retailers in a selective distribution system are hardcore restrictions.[52] It also constitutes a hardcore restriction to prevent active or passive sales to end users by members of a selective distribution system operating at the retail level.[53]

Where a selective distribution agreement does not fall under the scope of the VBER, it is necessary[54] to assess whether it constitutes a restriction of competition. Selective distribution agreements are *not* considered a restriction of competition where the Metro[55] criteria are fulfilled. Those have been further developed and clarified in the case Metro II[56] and can be summarized as follows:

(1) The characteristics of the product in question require selective distribution to preserve its quality or ensure its proper use,
(2) resellers are chosen based on objective and qualitative (vs quantitative[57]) criteria relating to the technical qualifications of the reseller and the suitability of their trading premises that are applied in a non-discriminatory manner,
(3) the selection criteria do not go beyond what is necessary, and

[45] Art. 4 point (c)(i)(1) VBER; Vertical Guidelines, para. 229.

[46] For the distinction between active and passive sales, see below from p. 31.

[47] Art. 4 point (c)(i)(2) VBER; Vertical Guidelines, para. 230.

[48] Art. 4 point (c)(i)(3) VBER.

[49] Vertical Guidelines, para. 231.

[50] Art. 4 point (c)(i)(4) VBER.

[51] Art. 4 point (c)(i)(5) VBER.

[52] Art. 4 point (c)(ii) VBER.

[53] Art. 4 point (c)(iii) VBER; Vertical Guidelines, para. 234.

[54] Often it is easier to establish whether the agreement is exempted under the VBER. Therefore, the question of whether there is a restriction of competition for practical reasons is conducted only as a second step.

[55] For more details on the Metro judgment, see below from p. 102.

[56] Court of Justice, 22/10/1986, Case 75/84 Metro II, ECLI:EU:C:1986:399.

[57] Vertical Guidelines, para. 147.

(4) the use of selective distribution systems in the market, in general, does not preclude other forms of distribution.[58]

The most important but controversial of the Metro criteria is the objective necessity of a selective distribution system to preserve the quality and the proper use of a product. The Court of Justice has held that selective distribution systems can be justified in particular for

"high-quality and technically advanced consumer durables, where a relatively small number of large and medium-scale producers offer a varied range of items which are readily interchangeable."[59]

It is recognized that the complexity of a product can require selective distribution in order to secure the provision of advice for proper product use. This has been understood relatively broadly, encompassing, inter alia, consumer electronics[60], watches[61], ceramic tableware and ornaments[62], newspapers and periodicals[63].[64] The Metro exception and the VBER overlap to a large extent, but there are some differences. First, qualitative and quantitative restrictions in selective distribution systems are traditionally treated differently under the Metro exception.[65] In principle, qualitative requirements fall under the Metro exception and thus escape the prohibition of Art. 101(1) TFEU irrespective of the participating companies' market position.[66] Quantitative requirements, on the other hand, are exempted only under the VBER and thus require that the companies' market shares do not exceed 30 %. It should be noted, however, that the Commission also tends to apply a relatively lenient approach to quantitative restrictions under Art. 101(3) TFEU. In the Vertical Guidelines, it states that

"[w]here selective distribution is applied by only one supplier on the market, quantitative selective distribution does not normally create net negative effects provided that the contract goods, having regard to their nature, require the use of a selective distribution system and on condition that the selection criteria applied are necessary to ensure efficient distribution of the goods in question."[67]

---

[58] *Colangelo/Torti*, European Competition Journal 2018, 81 (84); *Whish/Bailey*, Competition Law, p. 675; *Witt*, European Competition Journal 2016, 435 (440–441).

[59] Court of Justice, 22/10/1986, Case 75/84 Metro II, ECLI:EU:C:1986:399, para. 54.

[60] Court of Justice, 25/10/1983, Case 107/82 AEG/Commission, ECLI:EU:C:1983:293.

[61] Court of Justice, 13/01/1994, Case C-376/92 Metro/Cartier, ECLI:EU:C:1994:5.

[62] European Commission, 31/12/1985, IV.30.665 Villeroy&Boch.

[63] Court of Justice, 03/07/1985, Case 243/83 Binon/AMP, ECLI:EU:C:1985:284, para. 27, here the goal was to provide the consumer with a wider range of options, including foreign newspapers.

[64] *Kumkar*, Online-Märkte und Wettbewerbsrecht, p. 316; *Witt*, European Competition Journal 2016, 435 (443); *Whish/Bailey*, Competition Law, p. 675.

[65] *European Commission*, Green Paper on Vertical Restraints, para. 128.

[66] See Court of Justice, 03/07/1985, Case 243/83 Binon/AMP, ECLI:EU:C:1985:284, para. 34.

[67] Vertical Guidelines, para. 153.

While the difference in practice might not be great, legally, the distinction between quantitative and qualitative distribution remains in place.

Second, theoretically, the Metro exception could also apply to hardcore restrictions under the VBER. However, according to the Commission, such agreements do not meet the proportionality test required by the Metro exception.[68]

Most recently, in the context of online sales restrictions, the Court of Justice had to decide whether protecting a product's or brand's prestigious image justifies using a selective distribution system. Initially, in the 2011 Pierre Fabre case, it rejected maintaining a prestigious image as a legitimate goal of a selective distribution system.[69] The case concerned a total ban on online sales for high-priced cosmetic products of brands like Klorane and Avène.[70] In 2017, the Court of Justice, while maintaining a strict stand on total internet bans, in its Coty judgment,[71] accepted the product's luxury image as a legitimate concern of selective distribution agreements for luxury products under the Metro exception. The case concerned a selective distribution agreement which, while allowing online sales in principle, prohibited retailers' from selling on third-party platforms.

One thing that stands out from the case law is that there are few indicators of when and why selective distribution agreements restrict competition. The judgments go at great length to explain why a specific agreement does *not* restrict competition, e.g., because it fulfils the Metro requirements. This starts with the Metro I judgment, which explains why, as long as the Metro conditions are fulfilled, the agreement does not restrict competition but gives little guidance why it would in the absence of those criteria.[72] The view expressed in subsequent judgments is perhaps best illustrated by the Court of Justice's reasoning in Pierre Fabre:

> "As regards agreements constituting a selective distribution system, the Court has already stated that such agreements necessarily affect competition in the common market […]. Such agreements are to be considered, in the absence of objective justification, as 'restrictions by object'."[73]

This is also echoed in the more recent Coty judgment.[74] However, the Court has never explained why selective distribution agreements absent an objective justification would restrict competition. In Pierre Fabre, it only refers to AEG/Te-

---

[68] Vertical Guidelines, para. 150.

[69] Court of Justice, 13/10/2011, Case C-439/09 Pierre Fabre, ECLI:EU:C:2011:649, para. 46.

[70] Vertical Guidelines, para. 9.

[71] See in more detail below p. 35.

[72] Court of Justice, 25/10/1977, Case 26–76 Metro I, ECLI:EU:C:1977:167, paras. 19–22.

[73] Court of Justice, 13/10/2011, Case C-439/09 Pierre Fabre, ECLI:EU:C:2011:649, para. 39.

[74] Court of Justice, 06/12/2017, Case C-230/16 Coty, ECLI:EU:C:2017:941, para. 23; see also *Zelger*, European Competition Journal 2017, 356 (368); *Zelger*, European Competition Journal 2018, 445 (452–453).

lefunken, a 1983 case.[75] In the latter case, it states that "[i]t is common ground that agreements constituting a selective distribution system necessarily affect competition in the common market."[76] The Court in AEG/Telefunken does not explain where this "common ground" comes from. Just three years earlier, in the L'Oréal judgment, it had adopted a seemingly different approach, holding that while selective distribution agreements that do not fulfil the Metro requirements do, in principle, fall within the prohibition of Art. 85(1) (Art. 101(1) TFEU), the economic and legal context of the agreement has to be taken into account to evaluate their likely effects on competition.[77] Other judgments do not give more details or arguments either.[78] Ultimately, the Court of Justice, holds the view that every selective distribution agreement constitutes a restriction of competition if it is not objectively justified without ever having given any reasoning for this assumption.

A similar gap can also be observed in competition authorities' decisional practice. The Commission, for example, in Givenchy notes that obligations on retailers to only sell the products to final consumers or other members of the distribution network "constitute restrictions of competition" and then, in a second step, assesses whether they are justified under the Metro case law.[79] In Saba, it expressly states

> "where selective distribution agreements contain obligations upon the undertakings concerned which go beyond the limits indicated above [the Metro conditions] [...] fall under Article 85(1), but can in appropriate cases be exempted under Article 85(3)."[80]

Similarly, in Yamaha the Commission holds that "the restriction on cross supplies restricts competition because it seriously impedes the economic freedom of authorised dealers" without giving any further reasoning.[81] Echoing the AEG/Telefunken judgment, in Villeroy & Boch, the Commission states that "se-

[75] Court of Justice, 13/10/2011, Case C-439/09 Pierre Fabre, ECLI:EU:C:2011:649, para. 39.

[76] Court of Justice, 25/10/1983, Case 107/82 AEG, ECLI:EU:C:1983:293, para. 33.

[77] Court of Justice, 11/12/1980, Case 31/80 L'Oréal, ECLI:EU:C:1980:289, para. 19.

[78] Court of Justice, 16/06/1981, Case 126/80 Salonia, ECLI:EU:C:1981:136, para. 26 holding that it is for the national court to determine whether 'conditions exist which are capable of justifying' the selective distribution criteria; Court of Justice, 21/02/1984, Case 86/82 Hasselblad, ECLI:EU:C:1984:65, para. 46 stating that 'a prohibition of sales between authorized dealers constitutes a restriction of their economic freedom and, consequently, a restriction of competition'; Court of Justice, 03/07/1985, Case 243/83 Binon/AMP, ECLI:EU:C:1985:284, para. 35 holding that quantitative criteria in a selective distribution system restrict competition.

[79] European Commission, 10/12/1984, IV/30.299 Grohe, pp. 20–22; European Commission, 10/12/1984, IV/30.261 Ideal-Standard, pp. 40–41; similar European Commission, 10/07/1985, IV/29.420 Grundig, p. 3; European Commission, 24/07/1992, IV/33.542 Parfums Givenchy, pp. 16–18.

[80] European Commission, 21/12/1983, IV/29.598 SABA, para. 46.

[81] European Commission, 16/07/2003, AT.37975 PO Yamaha, para. 89.

lective distribution agreements necessarily affect competition in the common market".[82] In the Guess decision, concerning a selective distribution system that restricted online sales and advertisement, the Commission adopted a similar view and based its conclusion that the agreement restricted competition mainly on the lack of an objective justification rather than showing in the first place why absent of it, there would be a restriction.[83] Similarly, in its ASICS decision concerning online sales restrictions in a selective distribution system, the Bundeskartellamt also explains in much more detail why there is no exemption under Metro for the restriction of competition rather than the restriction, for which it attempts to find a justification, itself.[84]

2. Resale Price Maintenance ('RPM')

The VBER treats as hardcore restriction

> "the restriction of the buyer's ability to determine its sale price, without prejudice to the possibility of the supplier to impose a maximum sale price or recommend a sale price, provided that they do not amount to a fixed or minimum sale price as a result of pressure from, or incentives offered by, any of the parties."[85]

While efficiency defences under Art. 101(3) TFEU in individual cases remain possible, they are unlikely to be successful for minimum RPM.[86] It appears from the Vertical Guidelines that the Commission will consider a justification under Art. 101(3) TFEU only in exceptional cases, with a potentially more lenient approach when it comes to the introduction of new products.[87] The Commission also views indirect measures of imposing minimum prices, such as minimum advertised prices ('MAPs'), as falling under the hardcore restriction.[88] As with other hardcore restrictions, the Commission considers minimum and fixed RPM a restriction by object.[89] Hence, such agreements can, in principle, also not benefit from the De Minimis Notice.[90] Minimum RPM is thus treated close to per se illegal, even for undertakings with very low market shares.[91] The Court of Justice

[82] European Commission, 31/12/1985, IV.30.665 Villeroy&Boch, para. 22.

[83] European Commission, 17/12/2018, AT.40428 Guess, paras. 111–138, of the 44 pages long decision, only 5 are dedicated to explaining why the agreement restricts competition.

[84] Bundeskartellamt, 26/08/2015, B2–98/11 ASICS, pp. 253–256, only 3 paragraphs are dedicated to why there is a restriction and 11 to why the Metro criteria are not fulfilled.

[85] Art. 4 point (a) VBER.

[86] *Akhtar*, EuCML 2018, 5 (5); *Korn*, ZEuP 2020, 618 (633).

[87] Vertical Guidelines, para. 197.

[88] Vertical Guidelines, paras. 187, 189.

[89] *Korn*, ZEuP 2020, 618 (627).

[90] De Minimis Notice, para. 13; *Korn*, ZEuP 2020, 618 (628).

[91] *de la Mano et al.*, Competition Law & Policy Debate 2022, 12 (13); *Lugard*, in: Vertical Restraints, 193 (180); *Vergé*, in: Vertical Restraints, 31 (33); see, however, Vertical Guidelines, para. 195 stating that this does not amount to a 'per se' prohibition. From the examples provided in the Guidelines, it appears that short-term programs or RPM in the context of the introduction of new products might be permissible.

in Super Bock has recently held that in order to find a minimum RPM agreement to restrict competition

"regard must be had to the content of its provisions, its objectives and the economic and legal context of which it forms a part. When determining that context, it is also necessary to take into consideration the nature of the goods or services affected, as well as the actual conditions of the functioning and structure of the market or markets in question […]."[92]

This leaves it to some extent open what exactly competition authorities have to argue and what evidence they have to gather if they want to find a minimum RPM agreement to constitute a restriction by object. However, it does not as such put in question that minimum RPM typically constitutes a restriction of competition by object.

Like with selective distribution agreements, there is relatively little discussion in the case law and decisional practice as to why RPM restricts competition. The Court, in cases involving fixed or maximum RPM, does not provide any substantial reasoning why they restrict competition in the first place and refers mainly to its own case law and the wording of Art. 101(1) TFEU, which explicitly mentions "directly or indirectly fix purchase or selling prices" as an example of agreements which restrict competition.[93] Similarly, the Commission, when intervening against such agreements, typically restates the previous case law and assesses whether the agreement constitutes RPM without giving much further reasoning why it restricts competition.[94]

3. Territory or customer group restrictions in exclusive distribution systems

Territory or customer group restrictions in exclusive distribution systems, according to Art. 4 point (b) VBER, are also considered hardcore restrictions. In principle, the retailer shall be able to decide freely to whom and where they sell the products. Thus, whenever the supply of customers or customer groups is restricted or excluded, this constitutes a hardcore restriction. This also applies to restrictions of distribution channels. Art. 4 point (b) VBER contains five exceptions from the general rule that territory or customer restrictions are hardcore restrictions.

---

[92] Court of Justice, 29/06/2023, Case C-211/22 Super Bock Bebidas, ECLI:EU:C:2023:529, para. 35.

[93] See Court of Justice, 03/07/1985, Case 243/83 Binon/AMP, ECLI:EU:C:1985:284, para. 44; Court of Justice, 28/01/1986, Case 161/84 Pronuptia, ECLI:EU:C:1986:41, para. 25; Court of Justice, 01/10/1987, Case 311/85 ASBL, ECLI:EU:C:1987:418, para. 17; Court of Justice, 19/04/1988, Case 27/87 SPRL Louis Erauw, ECLI:EU:C:1988:183, para. 15.

[94] European Commission, 05/07/2000, AT.36516 Nathan-Bricolux, para. 88; European Commission, 16/07/2003, AT.37975 PO Yamaha, paras. 124–146; European Commission, 24/07/2018, AT.40465 ASUS, paras. 105–109, European Commission, 24/07/2018, AT.40181 Philips, paras. 59–64; European Commission, 24/07/2018, AT.40469 Denon&Marantz, paras. 90–95; European Commission, 24/07/2018, AT.40182 Pioneer, paras. 150–155; European Commission, 17/12/2018, AT.40428 Guess, paras. 136–137.

- Art. 4 point (b)(i) allows restrictions of active sales into the exclusive territory or exclusive customer group reserved or allocated by the supplier to a maximum of five other distributors (or the supplier itself). Active sales are defined as "actively targeting customers by visits, letters, emails, calls or other means of direct communication or through targeted advertising and promotion, offline or online".[95]
- Art. 4 point (b)(ii) VBER exempts the restriction of active or passive sales by the members of an exclusive distribution system to unauthorised distributors located in a territory where the supplier operates a selective distribution system from the hardcore restrictions.[96]
- Art. 4 point (b)(iii) VBER allows the restriction of an exclusive distributor's place of establishment. This does, however, not allow the prohibition of an online store.[97]
- According to Art. 4 point (b)(iv) VBER, restrictions of sales to end users by a buyer operating at the wholesale level of trade do not constitute hardcore restrictions. This includes prohibitions of active and passive sales alike. Thus, like under selective distribution, the supplier is permitted to keep the wholesale and retail levels of trade separate.[98]
- Art. 4 point (b)(v) VBER exempts the restriction of the buyer's ability to sell components supplied for incorporation to customers who would use them to manufacture the same type of goods as those produced by the supplier from the hardcore restriction.[99]

Where the exclusive distribution agreement does not remain within the limits that lead to an exemption under the VBER, it is considered to restrict competition by object. This is particularly true for agreements limiting parallel trade (e.g., export bans).[100] The reasoning for finding a restriction of competition in such cases again is rather short. It lies in their alleged frustration of the Treaties' "objective of achieving the integration of national markets through the establishment of a single market."[101] The Court of Justice, in line with the applicable standard for by object restrictions, does not assess whether such frustration actually takes place (i.e., whether the agreement is likely to have a market-partitioning effect).[102]

[95] Art. 1(1) point (l) VBER.

[96] Vertical Guidelines, para. 223.

[97] Vertical Guidelines, para. 224.

[98] Vertical Guidelines, para. 225.

[99] Vertical Guidelines, para. 226.

[100] Court of Justice, 01/02/1978, Case 19/77 Miller, ECLI:EU:C:1978:19, paras. 7, 18; Court of Justice, 06/10/2009, Joined Cases C-501/06 P, C-513/06 P, C-515/06 P C-519/06 P GlaxoSmithKline, ECLI:EU:C:2009:610, para. 59.

[101] Court of Justice, 06/10/2009, Joined Cases C-501/06 P, C-513/06 P, C-515/06 P C-519/06 P GlaxoSmithKline, ECLI:EU:C:2009:610, para. 61.

[102] See also below p. 96, regarding the internal market goal.

4. Restrictions outside of exclusive or selective distribution

Outside of selective and exclusive distribution ('free distribution'[103]), restrictions of active or passive sales in a territory or to a customer group are, in principle, considered hardcore restrictions.[104] As with other hardcore restrictions, there are exceptions to this rule. This concerns first the protection of exclusively allocated territories from active sales.[105] Second, where the supplier operates a selective distribution system in another territory, they can restrict active and passive sales in that territory alike.[106] Third, similar to other hardcore restrictions, the supplier may also impose a location clause on the buyer[107], which does not apply to online stores.[108] Fourth, manufacturers can also keep the wholesale and retail level of trade separate.[109] Finally, the supplier can restrict a buyer of components from reselling them to the supplier's competitors if they are supplied to the buyer for incorporation.[110]

5. Restrictions regarding the supply of spare parts

Art. 4 point (f) VBER sets out a hardcore restriction for agreements that restrict access to spare parts from the manufacturer of those parts. In principle, the manufacturer of the end product can thus not prevent the manufacturers of its spare parts from selling those spare parts to end users, independent repairers or service providers.[111]

6. Excluded restrictions under Art. 5 VBER

Art. 5 VBER excludes certain obligations contained in vertical agreements that, as such, benefit from the VBER.[112] Unlike agreements which contain a hardcore restriction, restrictions excluded under Art. 5 VBER do not render the entire vertical agreement to fall out of the VBER. This applies notably to the obligation on members of selective distribution systems not to sell the brands of particular competing suppliers.[113] This rule shall discourage horizontal collusion on the manufacturer level to exclude particular brands.[114] Art. 5 VBER further excludes non-compete obligations that exceed a duration of five years[115] and post-term

[103] Vertical Guidelines, para. 116.
[104] Vertical Guidelines, para. 238; Art. 4 point (d) VBER.
[105] Vertical Guidelines, para. 240; Art. 4 point (d)(i) VBER.
[106] Art. 4 point (d)(ii) VBER.
[107] Art. 4 point (d)(iii) VBER.
[108] Vertical Guidelines, para. 242.
[109] Vertical Guidelines, para. 243; Art. 4 point (d)(iv) VBER.
[110] Vertical Guidelines, para. 244; Art. 4 point (d)(v) VBER.
[111] Vertical Guidelines, para. 245.
[112] Vertical Guidelines, para. 246.
[113] Art. 5(1)(c) VBER.
[114] Vertical Guidelines, paras. 159, 252.
[115] Vertical Guidelines, paras. 247–249; Art. 5(1) point (a) VBER.

non-compete obligations[116]. Finally, across-platform (wide) parity obligations imposed by suppliers of online intermediation services are excluded.[117] Unlike hardcore restrictions, the provisions mentioned in Art. 5 VBER are not treated as restrictions of competition by object.[118]

7. Online sales restrictions

The updated VBER and Vertical Guidelines contain explicit rules regarding online sales restrictions.[119] These are primarily based on the Court of Justice's Coty case law.[120] Initially, in Pierre Fabre[121], the Court of Justice expressed quite a sceptical view towards online sales restrictions. In Coty, however, the Court of Justice confined the Pierre Fabre judgment to its facts, holding that only an absolute and general online ban cannot satisfy the Metro conditions nor be exempted under the VBER.[122] The vertical agreement that led to the Coty case allowed retailers to sell online but prevented them from selling Coty products on third-party platforms such as Amazon.[123] Regarding the specific selective distribution system applied by Coty, the Court of Justice found that, in principle, it can fulfil the Metro criteria.[124] In particular, the prohibition of sales through online platforms was appropriate to preserve the quality and luxury image of the goods in question.[125] The Court of Justice also considered vertical agreements which limited the use of third-party platforms for online sales as not constituting a hardcore restriction under Art. 4 point (b) of the previous VBER because third-party platform customers are no distinct group within the group of online purchasers.[126] From the Court of Justice's case law, it can thus be extracted that total bans are generally not permissible, whereas other restrictions, in principle, can be permissible under the Metro exception and the VBER. The following paragraphs will explain the current framework in more detail.

---

[116] Vertical Guidelines, paras. 250–251; Art. 5(1) point (b) VBER.

[117] Vertical Guidelines, para. 253; 5(1) point (d) VBER.

[118] Vertical Guidelines, para. 246.

[119] See for the legal situation before *Botteman/Barrio*, JECLAP 2019, 519; *Emde*, ZVertriebsR 2019, 69; *Dreyer/Ahlenstiel*, NZKart 2019, 130; *Szot/Amza*, YARS 2018, 241; *Zelger*, European Competition Journal 2018, 445.

[120] *Christodoulou/Holzwarth*, NZKart 2022, 540 (545–547).

[121] See above p. 28.

[122] *Colangelo/Torti*, European Competition Journal 2018, 81 (102).

[123] Court of Justice, 06/12/2017, Case C-230/16 Coty, ECLI:EU:C:2017:941, paras. 8–9.

[124] Court of Justice, 06/12/2017, Case C-230/16 Coty, ECLI:EU:C:2017:941, paras. 37–58.

[125] Court of Justice, 06/12/2017, Case C-230/16 Coty, ECLI:EU:C:2017:941, para. 46.

[126] Court of Justice, 06/12/2017, Case C-230/16 Coty, ECLI:EU:C:2017:941, paras. 66–67.

a) Total online bans

Under Art. 4 point (e) VBER, "the prevention of the effective use of the internet by the buyer or its customers" is now explicitly considered a hardcore restriction irrespective of the type of distribution system. It remains, however, possible to impose on the buyer "other restrictions of online sales" (i) or "restrictions of online advertising that do not have the object of preventing the use of an entire online advertising channel" (ii). The assessment of what constitutes a total online ban does not depend on the "market-specific circumstances or the individual characteristics of the parties."[127] The Vertical Guidelines give several examples of agreements that indirectly have the object of preventing the effective use of the internet.[128] Those include, inter alia, forcing the buyer to geoblock consumers, requiring them to terminate consumers' online transactions where their credit card data reveal an address not within the buyer's territory, requiring to sell only in a physical space or in physical presence of personnel, requiring authorization before online transactions, prohibiting the buyer from using the supplier's trademarks or brand names on websites or online stores or prohibiting the buyer from using an entire online advertising channel.[129] Total online bans are thus not exempted under the VBER (hardcore restriction), and they are typically considered a restriction of competition by object.[130] Where they are part of selective distribution systems, they will typically not fulfil the Metro criteria because they are not proportionate.[131] Where internet bans, as usually, are part of selective distribution agreements, competition authorities and courts rely on the established per object restriction for selective distribution and do not engage in a substantial assessment why they restrict competition in the first place.[132] Even outside of selective distribution agreements, however, there is no clear reasoning why they restrict competition in the first place. In CIBA vision, the Bundeskartellamt, for example, stated (in one single paragraph) that requiring written consent for selling contact lenses on the internet restricts competition by object and effect without any assessment why this is the case.[133] It then goes on to explain that the restriction is not objectively justified by health-related reasons or to prevent free-riding.[134] In essence, competition authorities hence mainly assess whether and to what extent retailers remain able to sell products online rather than evaluating why a prohibition to sell online would restrict competition.

---

[127] VBER, recital 15; see also *Christodoulou/Holzwarth*, NZKart 2022, 540 (546).

[128] Vertical Guidelines, para. 206.

[129] Vertical Guidelines, para. 206.

[130] *de la Mano/Jones*, in: Methods and Models, 167 (173) (for the VBER 2010) argue that they are treated as per se illegal.

[131] Vertical Guidelines, para. 150.

[132] See above from p. 30.

[133] Bundeskartellamt, 25/09/2009, B 3 – 123/08 CIBA Vision, para. 18.

[134] Bundeskartellamt, 25/09/2009, B 3 – 123/08 CIBA Vision, paras. 20–32.

b) Qualitative criteria on online sales in general

Under the previous Vertical Guidelines[135], qualitative criteria for online sales were only considered permissible if they were "equivalent to the criteria imposed for the sales from the brick and mortar shop".[136] They needed to pursue the same objectives and achieve comparable results.[137] However, the application of the equivalence test to third party platform bans was questionable for these platforms are innovative distribution channels that can hardly be compared with brick and mortar shops.[138] Under the new Vertical Guidelines, the Commission follows a different approach. It considers that qualitative criteria for online sales can be exempted irrespective of whether or not they are equivalent to those on brick and mortar stores.[139] The Vertical Guidelines mention as examples for qualitative criteria, inter alia, the requirement of an online help desk or specifications for delivery (e.g., using bicycles).[140] Such qualitative criteria are, in principle, exempted under the VBER, where the market share threshold is met. Where this is not the case, the Commission will carry out a "full competition analysis", taking into account, inter alia, the nature of the agreement and the market circumstances to establish whether the agreement restricts competition.[141]

c) Marketplace bans

Restrictions on the use of online marketplaces are, in principle, exempted under the VBER as long as they do not prevent the effective use of the internet.[142] Agreements that go beyond, constitute hardcore restrictions and by object restrictions. If the VBER is not applicable, on the other hand, because the market share threshold is exceeded, it is unclear whether an agreement restricts competition in the first place. Where such a ban is part of a selective distribution agreement, it can be covered by the Metro exception, provided that the restriction pursues a legitimate goal and does not go beyond what is necessary.[143] Where the Metro criteria are not fulfilled, according to the Court of Justice's case law, the selective distribution agreement will be considered a restriction of competition by object.[144] The Vertical Guidelines, however, argue that adverse effects for con-

[135] Guidelines on Vertical Restraints, OJ C 130, 19.5.2010, p. 1–46 ('Vertical Guidelines 2010').

[136] Vertical Guidelines (2010), para. 56.

[137] Vertical Guidelines (2010), para. 56.

[138] *Lohse*, WuW 2014, 120 (128); *European Commission*, Impact Assessment Report on the VBER and Vertical Guidelines (Commission Staff Working Document), p. 18.

[139] Vertical Guidelines, paras. 235, 332–342; *Christodoulou/Holzwarth*, NZKart 2022, 540 (545).

[140] Vertical Guidelines, para. 235.

[141] Vertical Guidelines, para. 278.

[142] Vertical Guidelines, paras. 335–336.

[143] Vertical Guidelines, para. 338.

[144] See above p. 28.

sumers are unlikely even in such cases if there is sufficient inter-brand competition.[145]

Previous to the Coty judgment, the permissibility of marketplace bans was disputed.[146] For example, the District Court of Amsterdam found platform bans as, in principle, suitable under the Metro exception.[147] The clause at issue was a limited platform ban allowing retail through certain authorized marketplaces but excluding other platforms (e.g., Amazon). In the Caudalie case, the Paris Court of Appeals initially found a platform ban to constitute a hardcore restriction.[148] The case concerned luxury cosmetic products that Caudalie wanted to prevent from being sold on the online pharmacy 1001pharmacies.com. After the Coty ruling, the French Court of Cassation invalidated the decision and referred the case back.[149] The Court of Appeals then followed in line and held that the agreement fulfilled the Metro conditions and was thus exempted from Art. 101(1) TFEU.[150] The Bundeskartellamt in ASICS considered a marketplace ban likely to constitute a restriction of competition by object.[151] German courts were divided on the issue. The Higher Regional Court Munich found a sporting goods manufacturer's third-party marketplace ban (outside of a selective distribution system) to constitute a restriction of competition by object, which was, however, exempted under the (previous) VBER.[152] The Higher Regional Courts Karlsruhe[153] and Berlin[154] held that a platform ban (concerning auction platforms such as eBay) within a selective distribution system could fulfil the Metro conditions and hence may not restrict competition. The Higher Regional Court Frankfurt a.M. found that platform bans (targeting, in this case, Amazon) but not price comparison bans may be permissible within a selective distribution system that satisfies the Metro requirements.[155] The Higher Regional Court Schleswig found a platform ban outside selective distribution to constitute a restriction of competition by object and hardcore restriction.[156]

---

[145] Vertical Guidelines, para. 341.

[146] *Ezrachi*, World Competition 2017, 47; *Lohse*, WuW 2014, 120; *Lubberger*, WRP 2015, 14; *Mäger/Schreitter*, NZKart 2015, 62; *Robertson*, ECLR 2012, 179; *Wartinger/Solek*, World Competition 2016, 291; *Witt*, European Competition Journal 2016, 435.

[147] Rechtbank Amsterdam, 04/10/2017, C/13/615474/HA ZA 16–959 NIKE.

[148] Paris Court of Appeals, 02/02/2016, 15/01542 Caudalie.

[149] Cour de Cassation, 13/12/2017, 16–15.067 Caudalie, ECLI:FR:CCASS:2017:CO01070.

[150] Paris Court of Appeals, 13/07/2018, 17/20787 Caudalie.

[151] Bundeskartellamt, 26/08/2015, B2–98/11 ASICS (Fallbericht), pp. 10–11.

[152] OLG München, Urt. 02/07/2009, U (K) 4842/08 Plattformverbot, MMR 2010, 35.

[153] OLG Karlsruhe, Urt. 25/11/2009, 6 U 47/08 Kart. Schulranzen, GRUR-RR 2010, 109.

[154] KG Berlin, 19/09/2013, 2 U 8/09 Schulranzen, ZVertriebsR 2014, 104.

[155] OLG Frankfurt, Urt. 22/12/2015, 11 U 84/14 (Kart) Funktionsrucksäcke, NZKart 2016, 84.

[156] OLG Schleswig, Urt. 05/06/2014, 16 U (Kart) 154/13 Digitalkameras, NJW 2014, 3104.

Even after the Coty judgment, the debate has not entirely cooled down. While, for example, the Higher Regional Court Hamburg found that a third-party platform ban for food supplements can fulfil the Metro requirements,[157] the Higher Regional Court Frankfurt a.M., which had submitted the preliminary question in the Coty case, in its subsequent judgement left open whether in the case at hand the Metro requirements were fulfilled (but held the agreement to be exempted under the VBER).[158] The court left open whether the general prohibition of the sale through externally recognizable third-party platforms, regardless of its specific form, was proportionate to the object pursued (protection of the luxury image).[159] It expressed some doubt in this regard and considered that there could be contractual arrangements less harmful to competition.[160] The court also noticed that platform sales are far more important in Germany than in other Member States and the EU average.[161] This was also emphasized by the Bundeskartellamt, which indicated that the assessment in Germany might be stricter than the one suggested by the Court of Justice in Coty.[162]

d) Dual pricing

Dual pricing, i.e., agreements that the distributor shall pay a higher price for products intended to be sold online than for those intended to be sold offline, were considered hardcore restrictions under the previous Vertical Guidelines.[163] Such agreements have been subject to investigations by the Bundeskartellamt which in three cases came to the preliminary conclusion that dual pricing constitutes a hardcore restriction.[164] However, under the updated Vertical Guidelines, the Commission considers that dual pricing agreements can benefit from the VBER as long as they do not have "the object of preventing the effective use of the internet by the buyer to sell the contract goods or services to particular territories or customers."[165]

e) Online advertising restrictions

Restrictions on the use of online advertising channels are also discussed in the Vertical Guidelines.[166] The most important online advertising channels are search

---

[157] OLG Hamburg, Urt. 22/03/2018, 3 U 250/16 Aloe2Go, GRUR 2018, 750.

[158] OLG Frankfurt, 12/07/2018, 11 U 96/14 (KART) Coty, GRUR 2018, 1171.

[159] OLG Frankfurt, 12/07/2018, 11 U 96/14 (KART) Coty, GRUR 2018, 1171, para. 74.

[160] OLG Frankfurt, 12/07/2018, 11 U 96/14 (KART) Coty, GRUR 2018, 1171, para. 70.

[161] OLG Frankfurt, 12/07/2018, 11 U 96/14 (KART) Coty, GRUR 2018, 1171, para. 71.

[162] *Bundeskartellamt*, Wettbewerbsbeschränkungen im Internetvertrieb, p. 5.

[163] Vertical Guidelines (2010), para. 52(d).

[164] Bundeskartellamt, 13/12/2011, B5–100/10 Dornbracht; Bundeskartellamt, 05/12/2013, B5–144/13 Gardena; Bundeskartellamt, 23/12/2013, B7–11/13 Bosch.

[165] Vertical Guidelines, para. 209; *Christodoulou/Holzwarth*, NZKart 2022, 540 (545).

[166] Vertical Guidelines, paras. 206(g) and 210.

engines and price comparison websites.[167] In principle, restrictions on online advertising in the form of qualitative requirements are permissible under the VBER. However, according to the Vertical Guidelines, excluding entire online advertising channels (e.g. price comparison websites or search engines) amounts to a hardcore restriction under Art. 4 point (e) VBER.[168] Quality standards on price comparison websites, on the other hand, can be exempted.[169] Similarly, restrictions on the use of online search engines can be exempted under the VBER as long as they do not "prohibit the use of an entire online advertising channel, such as an obligation not to use the supplier's trademarks or brand names for bidding to be referenced in search engines [...]."[170] The exclusion of a particular search engine shall also, in principle, be allowed.[171] Where the "use of the most widely used advertising services in the particular online advertising channel" is prohibited, however, this may amount to a hardcore restriction as it comes close to the exclusion of search engines as an entire online advertising channel.[172] This can be interpreted as meaning that a manufacturer cannot prevent their retailers from advertising on Google since, otherwise, they would have little chance of being found through online advertising at all.

This is in line with the Commission's Guess decision (adopted before the new VBER), where the Commission condemned a clause that prohibited retailers from using or bidding on Guess' brand names and trademarks in Google AdWords as anti-competitive because

> "the online search advertising restrictions cannot be said to serve the legitimate objective of Guess' selective distribution system claimed by Guess, namely to protect the brand image."[173]

Where restrictions go beyond what is permissible under Art. 4 point (e) VBER, they constitute hardcore restrictions and thus, in principle, also by object restrictions. For agreements for which the VBER does not apply in the first place because one of the parties' market share exceeds the 30% threshold under the VBER, the Commission will carry out an analysis of the agreement's effects.[174] The Vertical Guidelines express some scepticism towards price comparison restrictions. They emphasize several potential adverse effects of restrictions on price comparison websites, including softening price competition or partitioning markets and "restricting the possibility for the buyer to inform potential customers about lower prices."[175] Where price comparison bans are included in selective

[167] Vertical Guidelines, paras. 206(g).
[168] Vertical Guidelines, paras. 206(g).
[169] Vertical Guidelines, para. 349.
[170] Vertical Guidelines, para. 206.
[171] Vertical Guidelines, para. 206.
[172] Vertical Guidelines, para. 206.
[173] European Commission, 17/12/2018, AT.40428 Guess, para. 119.
[174] Vertical Guidelines, paras. 352–355.
[175] Vertical Guidelines, para. 352.

distribution agreements, according to the Vertical Guidelines, they are unlikely to be proportionate and fulfil the Metro criteria.[176]

f) Summary: treatment of online sales restrictions

The VBER and the Vertical Guidelines contain rules and explanations on the use of the internet as a sales channel and the restrictions that distributors can impose thereon. They can be summarized as follows:

[1] Complete bans of online sales (total bans) can never be exempted under the VBER and will be considered a restriction of competition by object, irrespective of the distribution system.
[2] Dual pricing is not considered a hardcore restriction (anymore).
[3] Platform restrictions under the Vertical Guidelines and the Court of Justice's Coty judgement are considered qualitative criteria and, thus, in principle, exempted under the VBER.
[4] The Vertical Guidelines state that price comparison website bans constitute hardcore restrictions as they ban an entire online advertising channel. Qualitative criteria on such price comparison websites, however, remain permissible.
[5] The same applies to other online search restrictions, such as bans on search engine advertising. Where they amount to the exclusion of an entire online advertising channel, it constitutes a hardcore restriction and thus also a restriction of competition by object.

The treatment of online sales restriction is based on the Pierre Fabre and Coty case law concerning selective distribution agreements. The rules focus on evaluating the agreement's effect on the retailer's ability to sell the manufacturer's products online rather than on the effect on competition.[177] The Court of Justice developed its case law on internet sales restrictions by asking whether or not the agreement is objectively justified rather than asking why, absent of a justification, it would restrict competition. In Coty, for example, the Court of Justice emphasized that the manufacturer may have a legitimate interest in prohibiting the sale on third-party platforms because it cannot otherwise preserve their products' luxury image.[178] Conversely, total bans go beyond what is necessary to safeguard the manufacturers' interests.

[176] Vertical Guidelines, para. 351.

[177] See Vertical Guidelines, para. 203: 'The assessment of whether a restriction is hardcore within the meaning of Article 4, point (e) of Regulation (EU) 2022/720 may take into account the content and context of the restriction, but it cannot depend on market-specific circumstances or the individual characteristics of the parties to the vertical agreement.'

[178] Court of Justice, 06/12/2017, Case C-230/16 Coty, ECLI:EU:C:2017:941, paras. 51–57.

III. Conclusion: it remains in some cases unclear what the restriction of competition is

When assessing the rules on vertical agreements in EU competition law, it becomes apparent that the system remains relatively complex. Some agreements are considered not restrictive of competition in the first place, whereas others are only exempted under the VBER. The demarcation between the two is to some extent arbitrary. From the current rules, it is relatively straightforward to identify agreements that either clearly do not restrict competition (e.g., selective distribution agreements where the Metro criteria are fulfilled) or are exempted under the VBER. There is, however, little guidance on when and why other agreements restrict competition.[179] The case law and decisional practice largely revolve around the interpretation of the VBER and the inherent exceptions developed by the Court of Justice (such as Metro), thus shedding more light on when a vertical agreement does not restrict competition or is at least justified than on when it restricts competition in the first place.[180]

This is in particular the case for those categories of vertical agreements that are deemed restrictions of competition by object (for example, hardcore restrictions or selective distribution systems failing to meet the Metro criteria). Moreover, such restrictions are typically regarded as illegal despite the theoretical possibility of justifying them under Art. 101(3) TFEU, and companies have little guidance or legal certainty on when they can include such clauses in their vertical agreements.[181] Indeed, the treatment of vertical agreements, despite the shift to a more general block exemption regulation in the 1990s, remains based on certain categories of agreements rather than on an agreement's effect on the market. Moreover, the analysis still contains traces of the previous approach to categorize vertical agreements as restrictive of competition if they are not objectively justified.[182] This framework makes it particularly difficult for companies to assess new distribution models and practices that are not yet reflected in the VBER and Guidelines.[183] The now-cooled debate around restrictions on online sales is a prime example. Initially, it was quite unclear to what extent such restrictions were (1) restrictive of competition and (2) justifiable under the VBER and Art. 101(3) TFEU.[184] The updated Vertical Guidelines and VBER have since provided more clarity regarding which types of online restraints are permissible (those that do not constitute a hardcore restriction and that are applied by companies with

[179] See, for some general guidance, Vertical Guidelines, paras. 278–290; compare *Jones*, European Competition Journal 2010, 649 (669).

[180] Even the Vertical Guidelines only devote 13 paragraphs (out of 397) exclusively to this question, see Vertical Guidelines, paras. 278–290.

[181] *de la Mano/Jones*, in: Methods and Models, 167 (175).

[182] *de la Mano/Jones*, in: Methods and Models, 167 (177).

[183] *de la Mano/Jones*, in: Methods and Models, 167 (192).

[184] See above p. 34.

market shares not exceeding 30 %). The current framework is built primarily on the case law and decisional practice of the Court of Justice and the European Commission. Its reference point remains largely the existence (or lack thereof) of an objective justification for the agreement rather than an evaluation of whether (and to what extent) the agreement restricts competition in the first place.

Relatedly, a shortcoming of the treatment of vertical agreements is that there is not always a clear distinction between the reasoning relating to whether a vertical agreement restricts competition versus whether the agreement brings efficiencies. While this might, at first sight, appear irrelevant – after all, the result (legal/illegal) does not depend on it – it can blur the debate and may influence the burden of proof.[185] Moreover, it can make it difficult to evaluate and discuss the VBER substantially. The purpose of the Regulation is, after all, to exempt those agreements which satisfy the conditions of Art. 101(3) TFEU, i.e., for which the efficiency-enhancing effects outweigh the restriction of competition.[186] Art. 101(3) TFEU requires that the restriction must not be indispensable to the attainment of the objectives pursued. This condition is an expression of the principle of proportionality.[187] It remains unclear how a meaningful proportionality assessment can be conducted when the restriction is not adequately identified. To give an example therefor: the VBER exempts restrictions on active sales by the exclusive distributor into a territory or to a customer group reserved to the supplier or allocated by the supplier exclusively to a *maximum of five* other exclusive distributors.[188] The Commission explains that "[a]bove that number, there is an increased risk that the exclusive distributors may free-ride on each other's investments, thereby eliminating the efficiency that exclusive distribution is intended to achieve."[189] Why now is there a higher risk of free-riding when there are more than five distributors for a given territory or customer group? The answer is simple and yet confusing: because there is more competition among retailers. While efficiencies might be lower if there are more distributors, the restriction of competition (if there is one) must hence also be less severe. If the number of exclusive distributors, however, exceeds five, which means more competition, under the current framework, this amounts to a hardcore restriction and thus a restriction of competition by object.[190] As this example illustrates, it is difficult to

[185] While the Commission has to prove that there is a restriction of competition, the undertakings bear the burden of proof regarding the conditions of Art. 101(3) TFEU, see Vertical Guidelines, para. 276.

[186] VBER, recital 5.

[187] *Mestmäcker/Schweitzer*, Europäisches Wettbewerbsrecht, § 14, para. 68; see also *Whish/Bailey*, Competition Law, p. 168 speaking of 'a balancing of pro- and anticompetitive effects'.

[188] Art. 4 point (b)(i) VBER.

[189] Vertical Guidelines, para. 121.

[190] It thus also has the rather absurd result that companies enjoy a safe harbour for an agreement that restricts competition more (five distributors) compared to one that restricts competition less (more than five distributors).

draw conclusions from the categorization of agreements as hardcore restrictions (which are based mainly on efficiency considerations and do not always consider how much competition is actually restricted) regarding whether or not an agreement restricts competition in the first place. This casts some doubt on the treatment of hardcore restriction as restrictions of competition by object. The lack of a differentiated identification of what constitutes restrictions of competition in the case of hardcore restrictions can also make it challenging to assess an individual exemption under Art. 101(3) TFEU, which also requires that the agreement's benefits "outweigh its anti-competitive effects".[191]

The treatment of vertical agreements under EU law remains to some extent form-based, relying primarily on the type of agreement instead of the concrete market circumstances. Detailed hardcore restrictions render the inclusion of such clauses in vertical agreements, while not per se illegal, rather risky for companies.[192] Against this background, it is not surprising that some commentators argue that vertical agreements tend to be considered anti-competitive irrespective of their "likely impact on competition."[193]

§ 2 Economic evaluation of the EU's current rules on vertical agreements, particularly on online distribution

The extent to which vertical agreements are efficient and benefit or harm consumers has been subject to an ongoing discussion in economic literature. In this context, 'efficiency' refers to 'welfare-maximization', which can encompass either total welfare or consumer welfare.[194] Hence, when economists contemplate that vertical agreements are 'efficient', they mean that they increase welfare. Typically, at least in the context of EU competition law, the focus is only on consumer welfare, leaving producer welfare out of the equation.[195] While the term consumer welfare in its wording appears relatively broad (and indeed, at least by the European Commission, is also interpreted in this way[196]), economists typically define consumer welfare as 'aggregated consumer surplus'. Consumer surplus is the difference between the benefits consumers derive from a good, as they themselves perceive it, expressed through their willingness (and ability) to pay and the

[191] Vertical Guidelines, para. 6.

[192] See above p. 24.

[193] *de la Mano/Jones*, in: Methods and Models, 167 (177); compare also *Monti*, World Competition 2013, 489.

[194] *Verouden*, Antitrust Law Journal 2003, 525 (526) footnote 4.

[195] See *Cseres*, Competition Law and Consumer Protection, p. 312 for a discussion why a total welfare standard is no attractive policy option; it should further be noted that it is often understood that a European consumer welfare standard would include all 'users', including intermediate consumers, see *Albors-Llorens*, Yearbook of European Law 2014, 163 (169).

[196] See below p. 161.

price.[197] Consumer welfare thus increases with lower prices, better quality (without corresponding price increase), or more and new products (assuming that they are sold at prices below consumers' willingness to pay).

It is undisputed that some degree of vertical cooperation is required to allocate labour efficiently between manufacturers and distributors.[198] Without such cooperation, a manufacturer would have to circulate all their products directly to the consumers. Unlike agreements between competitors, vertical agreements take place between producers of complementary products (production and distribution) and, as such, are prima facie considered efficient by economists.[199] Economists argue that it is mainly inter-brand competition that creates consumer welfare as consumers derive most value from the product itself rather than the retailers' service.[200] Moreover, manufacturers facing strong inter-brand competition have little interest in high retail prices, as this reduces the number of their products being sold.[201] Consequently, vertical agreements are considered to typically increase the profits of manufacturers and distributors and often simultaneously increase consumer welfare.[202] Although anti-competitive effects are possible, they very much depend on the circumstances and context of the agreement.[203]

This section will first examine, in general, the possible pro-competitive (I.) and potential anti-competitive effects of vertical agreements (II.), as well as their effects from a behavioural economic perspective (III.), and provide a brief overview of the existing empirical evidence (IV.), followed by a conclusion (V.). Against this background, it will demonstrate that EU law and economic theory on vertical agreements do not fully align (VI.).

I. Possible positive effects

In particular the Chicago School has long argued that vertical agreements are generally pro-competitive.[204] They enable to adapt the terms of distribution to

[197] The term goes back to *Marshall*, Principles of Economics, p. 103; see also *Dworkin*, Journal of Legal Studies 1980, 191 (191–192) calling it 'individual wealth maximization'; *Foer/Durst*, Antitrust Bulletin 2018, 494 (497); *Hertfelder*, Consumer Welfare, p. 20; *Motta*, Competition Policy, p. 17.

[198] *Colino*, Vertical Agreements, pp. 19–20.

[199] *Verouden*, in: Issues in Competition Law and Policy, 1813 (1814–1815); *Winter/Iacobucci*, in: Handbook International Antitrust Economics, 351 (355).

[200] *Buccirossi*, Journal of Competition Law & Economics 2015, 747 (749).

[201] *Buccirossi*, Journal of Competition Law & Economics 2015, 747 (749); *Thomas*, ZHR 2020, 223 (226).

[202] *Hovenkamp*, Federal Antitrust Policy, p. 657; *Monti*, World Competition 2013, 489 (490); *Verouden*, in: Issues in Competition Law and Policy, 1813 (1814).

[203] *Verouden*, in: Issues in Competition Law and Policy, 1813 (1816).

[204] This goes back in particular to the work of *Bork*, Antitrust Paradox, pp. 289–290; see *Verouden*, in: Issues in Competition Law and Policy, 1813 (1814–1815).

consumer preferences, thereby offering an improved overall package, consisting of product and distribution to the consumer. Manufacturers generally value competition on the retail level as it can lead to higher wholesale prices and more sales, benefitting the manufacturer. Therefore, economists argue that manufacturers typically do not have the incentive to restrict intra-brand competition[205] but that they will make use of vertical agreements mainly where this is efficient.[206] The following paragraphs discuss some of the most important possible pro-competitive effects in more detail.

1. Solving the free-riding problem

One of the main arguments in favour of allowing vertical agreements is that they are needed to prevent free-riding:[207] if a retailer provides particularly attractive (and thus expensive) services to the consumer to promote the product, e.g., customer advice, attractive shopping environment, after-sales services etc., this will promote the attractiveness of the manufacturer's products overall. Other retailers not offering similar services can also profit from this attractiveness (spill-over benefits).[208] Because they do not provide similar services, they have lower costs and can sell the product at a lower price.[209] This reduces any retailer's incentive to offer high-quality services because they have to share the fruits of their investments with the other retailers.[210] The common terminology describes the retailer who does not invest but benefits from other retailers' sales efforts as 'free-rider'.[211] Although it is not the consumer who is free-riding, their behaviour is insofar relevant as it determines the success of a retailer's free-riding activities. Free-riding can be successful only when consumers purchase from the free-riding retailer while being informed or motivated to buy by the investing retailer.[212] Vertical agreements can help to solve this problem. Exclusive territorial distribution, for instance, allows each retailer to profit exclusively from their service and advertising investments, as consumers cannot simply buy the product at a different retailer. RPM can also help solve the problem by preventing price-cutting from competing retailers.[213] Similarly, selective distribution can prevent

[205] *Caffarra*, in: Vertical Restraints, 55 (73); *de la Mano/Jones*, in: Methods and Models, 167 (180).

[206] *Caffarra*, in: Vertical Restraints, 55 (73); *Colino*, Vertical Agreements, p. 22; *de la Mano/Jones*, in: Methods and Models, 167 (180).

[207] This argument is attributed to *Telser*, Journal of Law & Economics 1960, 86.

[208] *Cheng*, Virginia Law & Business Review 2017, 1 (8).

[209] *Verouden*, in: Issues in Competition Law and Policy, 1813 (1821).

[210] *Motta*, Competition Policy, p. 314.

[211] *Telser*, Journal of Law & Economics 1960, 86 (91).

[212] *Turner et al.*, Competition Law & Policy Debate 2022, 30 (31).

[213] *Motta*, Competition Policy, p. 314; *Verouden*, in: Issues in Competition Law and Policy, 1813 (1821).

free-riding as the manufacturer then can simply require all retailers to offer a similar level of services.[214]

It should be noted that the extent to which free-riding causes concerns is disputed.[215] Many services a retailer can offer (e.g., after-sales services, pleasant shopping environment, credit to consumers) may be directly attributed to them and not only to the brand as such.[216] Free-riding may also not explain vertical agreements when consumers do not actually value the services, as can be the case for simple goods with low search costs for consumers.[217] Telser, who first developed the idea of the free-riding defence in the context of RPM, recognised his argument's limits, suggesting its application only in some instances, e.g., "branded products […] unfamiliar to the mass of consumer".[218] He argued that once a product "has gained wide consumer acceptance, its producer no longer needs to maintain a minimum retail price."[219] Since, in Telser's view, RPM "substitutes to some extent for […] advertising",[220] with easier means of advertising (e.g., online advertising), the free-riding rationale, according to Künzler, may be weaker today than when it was developed in the 1960s.[221]

Today one of the main concerns of manufacturers is free-riding from online shops: a consumer could visit a brick and mortar store, profit from the advice offered there, select a certain product but then buy it online (profiting from a lower price).[222] Free-riding-consistent behaviour can, however, also happen in the other direction (e.g., to get the product without waiting for delivery). A recent study showed that "free-riding between online and offline channels is only relevant for about 2–15 % of all consumers/purchases, depending on the product."[223] This suggests a careful approach to free-riding as an explanation for vertical agreements on online sales. In the context of online shopping, the traditional account of the free-riding hypothesis also seems to shift its focus. While initially, it would mean that one retailer would offer less pre- or aftersales service and

---

[214] *Verouden*, in: Issues in Competition Law and Policy, 1813 (1821).

[215] Arguing for a narrow scope of the free-riding hypothesis *Grimes*, Southwestern University Law Review 1992, 1285 (1295); *Künzler*, Oxford Journal of Legal Studies 2017, 75 (81); see also *Scherer*, Antitrust Law Journal 1983, 687; and *European Commission*, Green Paper on Vertical Restraints, para. 563.

[216] *Motta*, Competition Policy, p. 314; *Scherer*, Industrial Market Structure, p. 551; *Tirole*, Theory of Industrial Organization, p. 183.

[217] *van den Bergh/Camesasca*, Comparative Competition Law and Economics, pp. 251–252; *Hovenkamp*, Federal Antitrust Policy, p. 616.

[218] *Telser*, Journal of Law & Economics 1960, 86 (95).

[219] *Telser*, Journal of Law & Economics 1960, 86 (95).

[220] *Telser*, Journal of Law & Economics 1960, 86 (95).

[221] *Künzler*, Restoring Consumer Sovereignty, p. 28; *Schwaderer*, Resale Price Maintenance, pp. 85–88.

[222] *European Commission*, Support Studies for the Evaluation of the VBER: Final Report, pp. 66–67.

[223] *European Commission*, Evaluation of the Vertical Block Exemption Regulation, p. 42.

therefore save money, this cannot be directly transferred to the online context. Online retailers often do provide valuable services to consumers (fast delivery, extended guarantees etc.) that are just different from the ones brick and mortar retailers can offer (e.g., personal advice by a sales agent).[224]

2. *Quality certification and image creation*

Another economic argument for vertical agreements is that they help ensure that manufacturers profit from the quality certification of being stocked in (and thus associated with) a high-quality store.[225] This is arguably be the most common motivation behind selective distribution in Europe.[226] The underlying idea is analogous to the free-riding problem: if a good is listed in a high-quality store (be it due to its features, such as location, interior design, sales personnel or due to a particularly thorough selection of the products sold), consumers perceive the products as more attractive.[227] Other (less high-quality) retailers can try to profit from this by offering the products in question at a lower price (assuming that they face lower costs because of less thorough product selection, lower quality services etc.)[228], thus cutting sales from the high-quality retailer. This can deteriorate the consumers' perception (i.e., the 'image') of the product/brand, making it overall less attractive.[229] In the case of luxury products, this deterioration could be so severe that the product loses its luxury appeal and vanishes from the market.[230]

Vertical agreements are viewed as a solution to solve this problem.[231] For instance, a selective distribution system can prevent sales by unauthorized, and presumptively lower-quality, retailers. The threat of an 'image deterioration' is particularly brought forward to explain exclusions of online sales as 'low-price' channels.[232] RPM can have similar effects as selective distribution because consumers generally prefer to shop in a high-quality store if they cannot get a better price in a low-quality store.[233] It can even be a high price itself that the manufacturer considers as a way to "lure consumers and increase sales volume."[234] Such a

---

[224] *European Commission*, E-Commerce Sector Inquiry (Commission Staff Working Document), para. 164.

[225] *Hovenkamp*, Federal Antitrust Policy, pp. 617–618; *Motta*, Competition Policy, p. 334.

[226] *European Commission*, Support Studies for the Evaluation of the VBER: Final Report, p. 65.

[227] *Tirole*, Theory of Industrial Organization, p. 183; compare *Buettner et al.*, European Competition Journal 2009, 201 (206–207) who discuss this problem directly under the free-riding hypothesis; *Marvell/McCafferty*, RAND Journal of Economics 1984, 346 (349).

[228] *Marvell/McCafferty*, RAND Journal of Economics 1984, 346 (350).

[229] *Motta*, Competition Policy, pp. 334–335.

[230] *Motta*, Competition Policy, p. 334.

[231] Critical to this view *Grimes*, Southwestern University Law Review 1992, 1285 (1310).

[232] *Buettner et al.*, European Competition Journal 2009, 201 (49).

[233] *Motta*, Competition Policy, p. 335.

[234] *Orbach*, Antitrust Bulletin 2010, 277 (278).

strategy can work where consumers are willing to pay for the exclusive status linked to the high prices.[235]

3. Addressing consumer heterogeneity

Manufacturers seek to influence their retailers' behaviour on two dimensions: (1) they want retailers to compete with one another to attract consumers, i.e., to draw customers into their stores, (2) they want retailers to steer consumers toward purchasing the manufacturer's own products.[236] The second dimension is crucial because a manufacturer gains little if a consumer simply shops at a retailer that carries their brand but ultimately purchases a competing brand.[237]

These two dimensions, however, may conflict due to consumer heterogeneity. Consumers who respond to efforts aimed at attracting them to a store (i.e., those who search and switch between retailers) typically face low search costs and are better informed; for these consumers, price is the most important criterion, making it the key factor in retailer competition. In contrast, consumers who are more impulsive and less likely to switch retailers are more responsive to initiatives that persuade them to buy a specific product at a given retailer. These consumers tend to be less price-sensitive and more attracted by the shopping environment, sales services, and the specific brand image conveyed. Since such shoppers are less likely to switch retailers, the retailer has little incentive to compete on these dimensions, leading to retailers competing excessively on prices rather than services.[238] Selective distribution can address this problem by establishing consistent service levels and a uniform shopping environment among retailers. This can be in the manufacturer's interest if they believe that their products will attract more customers in such an environment compared to other products. RPM or exclusive distribution can also address the problem by guaranteeing the retailer a higher margin on the sale of the covered products, giving them the incentive to sell these rather than competing products.[239]

4. Solving hold-up problems

Another possible economic justification for vertical agreements is that they can resolve hold-up problems.[240] Such problems can arise when entering a retail market for a specific product requires high initial relationship-specific investments.[241]

---

[235] *Orbach*, Antitrust Bulletin 2010, 277 (279).

[236] *Buettner et al.*, European Competition Journal 2009, 201 (208); *Klein*, in: Handbooks Economics of Law, 174 (178–182); *Klein/Murphy*, Journal of Law & Economics 1988, 265.

[237] *Buettner et al.*, European Competition Journal 2009, 201 (208).

[238] *Buettner et al.*, European Competition Journal 2009, 201 (208).

[239] *Klein*, in: Handbooks Economics of Law, 174 (178–184).

[240] *Buccirossi*, Journal of Competition Law & Economics 2015, 747 (750); *Rey/Caballero-Sanz*, Economic Analysis of Vertical Restraints, p. 16; *Verouden*, in: Issues in Competition Law and Policy, 1813 (1822–1823).

[241] *Buccirossi*, Journal of Competition Law & Economics 2015, 747 (750).

Once these investments are made, the retailer finds itself in a relatively bad negotiation position towards the manufacturer, who can even threaten to enter the retail market herself. This situation could enable the manufacturer to significantly worsen the retailer's selling conditions once these investments have been made. Consequently, the retailer might refrain from making such investments in the first place due to the risk of not recouping them. Vertical agreements such as exclusive distribution agreements can mitigate the retailer's risk and thus solve such hold-up problems.

5. Preventing double-marginalization

Scherer provides one of the most illustrative example of double marginalisation[242]: in the 18th century, on the river rhine in Germany, several local monarchs (the prototype of 'robber barons') each held a monopoly over the part of the river running through their territories. As a result, each monarch charged passing ships a toll, without considering that additional tolls would be imposed further downstream by other monopolists. This double marginalization significantly suppressed river traffic.[243]

A similar problem can occur when the retailer and the manufacturer both possess market power. Absent vertical agreements, the manufacturer in this scenario will charge a supracompetitive wholesale price and the retailer will add a margin, setting a supracompetitive retail price.[244] The consumer, thus, must pay a double-marginalized price. This price will typically be higher than the price a vertically integrated firm (with equal market power) would ask as the retailer does not take into account the effects that their price has on the manufacturer's profits and vice versa.[245]

One straightforward solution is a two-part tariff: the manufacturer sets a wholesale price equal to marginal cost and charges an additional fixed fee.[246] This arrangement allows the retailer to act as a single monopolist and set the retail price to maximize the joint profit of the vertical structure, while the manufacturer recovers part of that profit through the fixed fee. A similar outcome can be achieved through maximum RPM or quantity forcing, more directly influencing the price the retailer charges to consumers.[247] Vertical agreements in such a sce-

[242] *Scherer*, Antitrust Bulletin 2004, 841 (852).

[243] Scherer argues that free passage along the Rhine, which was introduced in 1831, was an important contributor to Germany's industrialisation afterwards.

[244] *van den Bergh/Camesasca*, Comparative Competition Law and Economics, p. 249; *Buccirossi*, Journal of Competition Law & Economics 2015, 747 (750–751); *Rey/Vergé*, in: Handbook Antitrust Economics, 354 (360–361); *Tirole*, Theory of Industrial Organization, p. 174; *Verouden*, in: Issues in Competition Law and Policy, 1813 (1818).

[245] *van den Bergh/Camesasca*, Comparative Competition Law and Economics, p. 249.

[246] *Tirole*, Theory of Industrial Organization, p. 176; this, however, shifts all the risk to the retailer and might therefore not be feasible where the retailer is risk averse, see *Rey/Caballero-Sanz*, Economic Analysis of Vertical Restraints, p. 15.

[247] *Buccirossi*, Journal of Competition Law & Economics 2015, 747 (750–751); *van den*

nario can thus result in a lower price for consumers that increases output as well as manufacturers' and retailers' profits and are hence considered welfare-enhancing.[248]

Similar coordination problems can affect retailers' decisions to invest in attractive sales services. Where demand depends on prices and retailer services alike, a retailer with some degree of market power will set prices (too high) and services (too low) at a level that differs from the optimum for the combined vertical structure.[249] When it comes to services, RPM will not be sufficient where the retailer has market power (even at high prices, they do not have the incentive to invest in more services).[250] Selective distribution or other agreements that directly require the provision of services are better suited in this regard. A two-part tariff can also give the retailer the right incentives.[251]

The double-marginalisation problem arises only in scenarios of market power, so the more limited competition there is upstream and downstream, the more beneficial a vertical agreement addressing double marginalisation will be.[252] Introducing strong intra-brand competition is, therefore, an alternative way of solving problems of double marginalization.[253]

II. Possible negative effects

While economists typically view vertical agreements as beneficial, they recognize that vertical agreements can also have anticompetitive effects, albeit usually only where either manufacturer or retailer have market power. The most well-established risks commonly accrued to vertical agreements are horizontal in nature.[254] These risks include collusion on the upstream or downstream market, dampening competition or foreclosing markets.[255] The following paragraphs provide an overview of the most important negative effects discussed in economic literature.

Bergh/Camesasca, Comparative Competition Law and Economics, pp. 249–250; *Tirole*, Theory of Industrial Organization, p. 177; *Verouden*, in: Issues in Competition Law and Policy, 1813 (1818).

[248] *Rey/Vergé*, in: Handbook Antitrust Economics, 354 (362); *Tirole*, Theory of Industrial Organization, p. 177.

[249] *Buccirossi*, Journal of Competition Law & Economics 2015, 747 (751); *Verouden*, in: Issues in Competition Law and Policy, 1813 (1818–1819); *Tirole*, Theory of Industrial Organization, pp. 177–178.

[250] *Tirole*, Theory of Industrial Organization, p. 178.

[251] *Verouden*, in: Issues in Competition Law and Policy, 1813 (1819–1820).

[252] *Rey/Caballero-Sanz*, Economic Analysis of Vertical Restraints, p. 12; *Tirole*, Theory of Industrial Organization, p. 181.

[253] *Rey/Caballero-Sanz*, Economic Analysis of Vertical Restraints, p. 12.

[254] *Winter/Iacobucci*, in: Handbook International Antitrust Economics, 351 (356).

[255] *Bishop*, Economics of EC Competition Law paras. 5.043–5.046; *Hovenkamp*, Federal Antitrust Policy, p. 659; *Monti*, World Competition 2013, 489 (494); *Rey/Vergé*, in: Handbook Antitrust Economics, 354 (369–384).

1. Facilitating collusion

One possible anticompetitive effect of vertical agreements is that they can facilitate collusion either between retailers (downstream) or manufacturers (upstream).

a) Downstream collusion

Retailers can use vertical agreements, in particular RPM, to better organise collusion on the downstream market: the supplier is often in a better position to monitor the retailers' pricing (or other) policies since these are generally not in direct contact with each other.[256] Retailer collusion, however, appears to be a serious risk only in scenarios where either the manufacturer possesses market power or the restriction is widely used, covering products from most manufacturers.[257] This is because, otherwise, prices would only go up for the products of one manufacturer, and consumers could easily switch to other manufacturers' products.[258] While in markets where manufacturers have market power, vertical agreements could facilitate collusion on the retail level, the manufacturer, in general, is not interested in this happening: retailer collusion will reduce output, resulting in lower profits for the manufacturer.[259] They might nevertheless not always be able to resist such cartels when they need the retailers to distribute their products.[260] This is particularly the case where vertical integration is difficult, and the manufacturer cannot easily enter the retail market herself.[261] Most products are sold by multi-brand and multi-product retailers that are difficult to replicate by a manufacturer, making such scenarios relatively probable to occur.[262] For example, a shampoo manufacturer would struggle to enter the retail market directly because consumers generally purchase shampoo alongside other products, and they often prefer having a choice among different brands.

b) Upstream collusion

Vertical agreements can also facilitate collusion between manufacturers.[263] Cartels are inherently difficult to monitor and enforce, and every member has the

---

[256] *Hovenkamp*, Federal Antitrust Policy, p. 604; *Tirole*, Theory of Industrial Organization, pp. 184–185; *Winter/Iacobucci*, in: Handbook International Antitrust Economics, 351 (368).

[257] *Hovenkamp*, Federal Antitrust Policy, p. 604.

[258] *Hovenkamp*, Federal Antitrust Policy, p. 604.

[259] *Hovenkamp*, Federal Antitrust Policy, p. 605.

[260] *Carstensen*, Antitrust Law Journal 2001, 569 (581).

[261] *Hovenkamp*, Federal Antitrust Policy, pp. 606–607.

[262] *Hovenkamp*, Federal Antitrust Policy, p. 608.

[263] *Jullien/Rey*, RAND Journal of Economics 2007, 983; *Rey/Vergé*, in: Handbook Antitrust Economics, 354 (373); *Winter/Iacobucci*, in: Handbook International Antitrust Economics, 351 (368).

incentive to cheat. For example, in a price-fixing agreement, a cartel member can boost its profits by lowering its prices below the agreed-upon level. Detecting violations of horizontal anti-competitive agreements can be difficult. This is particularly so for price fixing agreements on the manufacturer level because prices at this level are difficult to observe.[264] They are typically embedded in larger contracts between manufacturers and retailers and are not publicly available. Through RPM, at least at the retail level, prices become easier to observe.[265] RPM makes prices across retailers uniform, which can allow drawing conclusions from the retail to the wholesale price.[266] The retail prices can serve as indirect evidence for deviations from price-fixing agreements on the manufacturer level.[267] Similarly, territorial restraints can make the number of sales on the retail level more easily observable,[268] potentially serving to detect deviations from output restriction cartels. As with retailer collusion, however, effective collusion among manufacturers usually requires that the participating manufacturers hold a sufficiently high combined market share.[269] Upstream collusion is mainly considered a problem for RPM, not for other vertical agreements such as selective distribution.[270] Non-price restraints, from this perspective, are considered less harmful.[271]

2. Dampening competition

Dampening upstream competition can occur where vertical agreements signal to competing manufacturers that no aggressive price competition is intended.[272] In doing so, vertical agreements can demonstrate a commitment to passivity, thereby reducing competition at the manufacturer level.[273] This effect has been primarily discussed in the context of exclusive territorial distribution, where the vertical agreement effectively delegates some power from the manufacturer to the retailers.[274] A retailer facing limited intra-brand competition due to, for example,

[264] *Buettner et al.*, European Competition Journal 2009, 201 (213); *Hovenkamp*, Federal Antitrust Policy, p. 609.

[265] *Geradin et al.*, EU Competition Law and Economics, para. 8.19; *Hovenkamp*, Federal Antitrust Policy, p. 609.

[266] *Jullien/Rey*, RAND Journal of Economics 2007, 983 (985).

[267] *Jullien/Rey*, RAND Journal of Economics 2007, 983 (996).

[268] *Hovenkamp*, Federal Antitrust Policy, p. 609.

[269] *Hovenkamp*, Federal Antitrust Policy pp. 609–610; *Scherer*, Industrial Market Structure, p. 550 suggesting that there are only few documented cases where vertical restraints were used for upstream collusion.

[270] *Buettner et al.*, European Competition Journal 2009, 201 (213–214).

[271] *Jullien/Rey*, RAND Journal of Economics 2007, 983 (997).

[272] *Bonanno/Vickers*, Journal of Industrial Economics 1988, 257; *Bowman*, University of Chicago Law Review 1954, 825 (838); *Rey/Vergé*, in: Handbook Antitrust Economics, 354 (369–370).

[273] *Buettner et al.*, European Competition Journal 2009, 201 (212); *Rey/Caballero-Sanz*, Economic Analysis of Vertical Restraints, pp. 17–18.

[274] *Rey/Stiglitz*, European Economic Review 1988, 561; *Rey/Vergé*, in: Handbook Antitrust Economics, 354 (370–371).

exclusive distribution, in the case of a reduction of the wholesale price, will pass on only part of the lower price to consumers (as due to limited intra-brand competition, they do not have to operate at marginal costs).[275] This makes it more attractive for manufacturers to operate at a high price level. Other distributors in such a scenario can trust prices to stay high, giving them an incentive also to raise their prices.[276] Vertical agreements that limit retailers' power, as is typically the case for selective distribution or RPM, are not generally considered to be able to dampen competition between manufacturers.[277]

3. Foreclosure

Vertical agreements can also result in market foreclosure for rivals.[278] For example, in single branding arrangements, if one manufacturer binds a sufficiently large number of retailers to exclusive purchasing agreements, those retailers will not stock or sell rival products.[279] Rivals then would have to build up their own distribution system to enter the market.[280] Vertical agreements can thus follow a strategy of raising rivals' costs. Such strategies can be directed not only against existing rivals but also potential new entrants.[281] While retailers provide some checks on such strategies (they will prefer to carry more than one manufacturer's products if this is profitable)[282], they can be compensated by a share of the extra profits the manufacturer achieves through foreclosing rivals.[283]

Vertical agreements can also lead to foreclosure on the retail level.[284] When a manufacturer is particularly influential, or when a large number of manufacturers adopt similar selective or exclusive distribution systems, new market entrants

[275] *Verouden*, in: Issues in Competition Law and Policy, 1813 (1834).

[276] *Vezzoso*, Vertikale Beschränkungen, p. 109.

[277] *Rey/Caballero-Sanz*, Economic Analysis of Vertical Restraints, p. 118; *Rey/Vergé*, in: Handbook Antitrust Economics, 354 (372).

[278] *Comanor/Rey*, Review of Industrial Organization 2000, 135; *Rey/Caballero-Sanz*, Economic Analysis of Vertical Restraints, p. 19; *Rey/Vergé*, in: Handbook Antitrust Economics, 354 (377–384); *Tirole*, Theory of Industrial Organization, p. 186; *Verouden*, in: Issues in Competition Law and Policy, 1813 (1827–1828); *Winter/Iacobucci*, in: Handbook International Antitrust Economics, 351 (368).

[279] Vertical Guidelines, para. 298 defines single branding as 'agreements which have as their main element the fact that the buyer is obliged or induced to concentrate its orders for a particular type of product with one supplier'.

[280] *Rey/Caballero-Sanz*, Economic Analysis of Vertical Restraints, p. 19; *Rey/Vergé*, in: Handbook Antitrust Economics, 354 (378).

[281] *Rey/Vergé*, in: Handbook Antitrust Economics, 354 (378).

[282] *Verouden*, in: Issues in Competition Law and Policy, 1813 (1827–1828).

[283] *Rey/Caballero-Sanz*, Economic Analysis of Vertical Restraints, p. 19; *Rey/Vergé*, in: Handbook Antitrust Economics, 354 (378).

[284] *Verouden*, in: Issues in Competition Law and Policy, 1813 (1831–1832).

in the retail sector may be unable to obtain the necessary products to stock their (online or offline) shelves.[285]

4. Increasing search costs

Another, albeit less discussed, effect of vertical agreements is that they can increase search costs. This has first been considered for exclusive dealing.[286] The underlying idea is that exclusive dealing makes in-store inter-brand comparison more difficult. When a consumer can buy a product of a certain brand only in a store that sells that brand exclusively, it will be more costly (in terms of time and effort) to compare the product's attributes and price with a competing product by another manufacturer.

Other types of vertical agreements can also raise search costs, affecting both inter-brand and intra-brand comparisons. For example, selective distribution may hinder in-store inter-brand comparisons by reducing the range of products offered by retailers (e.g., limiting the selection to only high-quality and high-priced products). Exclusive territories can complicate intra-brand comparisons across retailers, as fewer retail outlets are available, potentially increasing transportation and other search costs associated with comparison shopping.

Minimum Advertised Prices ('MAPs') can also impact search costs, as explored by Asker and Bar-Isaac.[287] Unlike RPM, MAPs do not require the retailer to *sell* at a specific price but impose a price floor on the price at which they can *advertise*.[288] This can increase consumers' search costs, making it "more difficult [...] to find the retailer charging the lowest prices and lead to retail price dispersion".[289] MAPs can also facilitate price discrimination: consumers with high search costs will not shop around to make a better deal but buy from the retailer with the lowest advertised price (rather than the one with the lowest actual price).[290] Consumers who face lower search costs will still look for better deals and are likely to find the retailer with the lowest actual price. In such a scenario, each retailer has the incentive to charge a different price than their competitors by either catering mainly to those consumers with high search costs by charging a high price or by catering to those with low search costs by setting a low price. As always with price discrimination, the welfare effects are unclear and depend on the circumstances.[291] Additionally, Asker and Bar-Isaac offer a service-based explanation for MAPs: by softening competition between retailers, MAPs allow

---

[285] *Geradin et al.*, EU Competition Law and Economics, p. 8.22; *Verouden*, in: Issues in Competition Law and Policy, 1813 (1830).

[286] *Verouden*, in: Issues in Competition Law and Policy, 1813 (1834).

[287] *Asker/Bar-Isaac*, Journal of Law & Economics 2020, 111.

[288] *Asker/Bar-Isaac*, Journal of Law & Economics 2020, 111 (114).

[289] *Asker/Bar-Isaac*, Journal of Law & Economics 2020, 111 (118).

[290] *Asker/Bar-Isaac*, Journal of Law & Economics 2020, 111 (119–125).

[291] *Asker/Bar-Isaac*, Journal of Law & Economics 2020, 111 (125).

retailers to earn higher margins, which can encourage further investment in service.[292]

While vertical agreements can potentially increase search costs, economists do not conclude that they should be prohibited solely on that basis. There are two reasons for this. First, high search costs are not necessarily detrimental to consumer welfare. Second, vertical agreements typically affect the search costs for a single manufacturer's products (intra-brand), which can even be efficiency-enhancing.

Turning to the first argument[293]: Raising search costs does not automatically lead to higher prices or lower consumer welfare. Although search costs are ubiquitous and contribute to imperfect competition,[294] a further increase in search costs does not necessarily cause additional harm, nor is a reduction always beneficial. The relationship between search costs, prices and welfare is complex.[295] While reducing search costs may reduce prices,[296] this is not always true. For instance, Mitsukuni and Remer model a situation where reduced search costs diminish consumer heterogeneity; in such a case, firms have less incentive to target consumers with low search costs, which may lead to less price dispersion or higher prices.[297] They suggest that this mechanism could explain observed price increases for gasoline after the introduction of price transparency regulations.

Similarly, Nermuth et al. propose that increased search costs for consumers who already compare prices primarily redistribute welfare to well-informed consumers, with overall prices potentially rising.[298] Piccolo et al. argue that even deceptive practices can be welfare-enhancing.[299] In their model, there are two sellers, one of which sells a high-quality good and one of which sells a low-quality good. If now both goods are advertised as high quality, thus one is deceptively advertised, from the buyer's perspective, both products appear as substitutes. This puts downward pressure on prices. The lower price, in their model, can outweigh the potential loss from acquiring the low-quality product.[300] Fabra and

[292] *Asker/Bar-Isaac*, Journal of Law & Economics 2020, 111 (130).

[293] For a literature review on search costs, see *Anderson/Renault*, in: Handbook of Game Theory and Industrial Organization, 177.

[294] *Anderson/Renault*, in: Handbook of Game Theory and Industrial Organization, 177; *Diamond*, Journal of Economic Theory 1971, 156; *Stiglitz*, in: Handbook Industrial Organization, 769 (818); *Wolinsky*, Quarterly Journal of Economics 1986, 493; for a useful overview of the different models to explain price dispersion, see *Baye et al.*, in: Economics and Information Systems, 323.

[295] *Mitsukuni/Remer*, Economics Letters 2018, 1; *Pereira*, Information Economics and Policy 2005, 61.

[296] See, for example *Lynch/Ariely*, Marketing Science 2000, 83.

[297] See *Mitsukuni/Remer*, Economics Letters 2018, 1.

[298] *Nermuth et al.*, Games and Economic Behavior 2013, 21.

[299] *Piccolo et al.*, RAND Journal of Economics 2015, 611.

[300] *Piccolo et al.*, RAND Journal of Economics 2015, 611 (612); see also *Rhodes/Wilson*, RAND Journal of Economics 2018, 348.

Montero analyse a model of firms' product choice in competitive markets with search costs and show that in such markets, buyer search costs can induce firms to carry overlapping product lines and thus create head-to-head competition.[301] Rhodes and Zhou further contend that reducing search frictions may increase prices and harm consumers by altering retail market structures: high search frictions encourage multiproduct firms to offer a one-stop convenience, whereas lower search frictions allow for more diverse retail formats and finer market segmentation.[302] Yang highlights another important aspect of search costs: their effects on product variety.[303] Where search costs are low, firms will target niche consumers more, resulting in greater product variety. While this appears positive at first sight, it also can have negative implications: it makes the mainstream product markets less competitive (fewer firms). Therefore, Yang describes the effects of a decrease in search costs on consumer utilities as ambiguous.[304] Finally, González et al. analyze how reduced search costs affect which consumers choose to search.[305] If consumers who already search do so even more, firms are pressured to lower prices; conversely, if previously high search cost consumers begin to search, firms might raise prices. Thus, the net effect of changes in search costs depends on which effect dominates.

Turning to the second argument: Increasing search costs for a single manufacturer's products can yield positive effects. Search costs can be achieved without vertical agreements – for example, by requiring consumer registration, using doormen at storefronts, omitting price tags, or imposing a 'fitting fee' (as experimented by luxury wedding designer Vera Wang in China).[306] Taylor shows that these measures enable firms to avoid 'wasting' resources on unlikely buyers and instead invest in serving likely buyers, thereby enhancing welfare.[307] A similar logic applies to vertical agreements. Low search costs can facilitate free-riding, as consumers can easily compare retailers after receiving services.[308] When it is harder for consumers to find another retailer selling the same product, free-riding is less likely. Vertical agreements can thus reduce free-riding by increasing search costs. When it comes to online sales restrictions, for example, reduced search costs online are one of the arguments put forward by manufacturers for why they need to restrict internet sales (to increase search costs again).[309] Where search

[301] *Fabral/Montero*, C.E.P.R. Discussion Paper 2017.

[302] *Rhodes/Zhou*, Management Science 2019, 2607.

[303] *Yang*, RAND Journal of Economics 2013, 733.

[304] *Yang*, RAND Journal of Economics 2013, 733 (750),

[305] *Moraga-González et al.*, RAND Journal of Economics 2017, 125.

[306] *Junqian*, China Daily, 28/03/2013, Vera Wang cancels fitting fees following criticism, available at http://www.chinadaily.com.cn/china/2013-03/28/content_16353645.htm. (accessed: 11 March 2025); *Taylor*, RAND Journal of Economics 2017, 387 (388).

[307] *Taylor*, RAND Journal of Economics 2017, 387.

[308] *European Commission*, Final Report on the E-commerce Sector Inquiry, para. 11.

[309] *European Commission*, Support Studies for the Evaluation of the VBER: Final Report, p. 66.

costs have effects mainly on intra-brand competition (for example, by making prices of the same brand across retailers less observable for consumers), they raise little concern from an economic perspective since intra-brand competition as such is considered less important than inter-brand competition. Additionally, reduced search costs often come with increased price transparency, which can facilitate collusion.[310]

5. Price discrimination

Vertical agreements also enable manufacturers with market power to engage in price discrimination among different customer groups.[311] Territorial restraints, for example, can be used to price-discriminate between consumers in different areas (third-degree price discrimination[312]). Similarly, customer restrictions can separate the retail between different groups of customers, e.g., private and commercial customers, allowing manufacturers to charge different prices accordingly. Although it is widely accepted that vertical agreements can lead to price discrimination, the overall welfare effects remain ambiguous.[313] Consequently, some commentators advocate for a relatively lenient treatment of price discrimination under competition law.[314] In the Vertical Guidelines, the Commission discusses price discrimination as a potential harm of exclusive distribution and tying.[315] In contrast, RPM tends to result in more uniform prices at the retail level and can thus prevent price discrimination by retailers. Geradin et al. even name this as a potential anti-competitive effect, nothing RPM can prevent "efficient price discrimination by retailers".[316] Similarly, selective distribution generally leads to more uniform rather than dispersed prices. The effects of internet sales restrictions on price discrimination are more complex. A total ban on online distribution can increase price discrimination by making it harder for consumers

---

[310] See above p. 51.

[311] *Bowman*, University of Chicago Law Review 1954, 825 (840); *Carstensen*, Antitrust Law Journal 2001, 569 (585); *Hovenkamp*, Federal Antitrust Policy, pp. 610–611.

[312] *Varian*, Intermediate Microeconomics, p. 487; *Varian*, in: Handbook Industrial Organization, 598 (600).

[313] *Carstensen*, Antitrust Law Journal 2001, 569 (587) concluding that price discrimination should not justify vertical restraints; *Gehrig/Stenbacka*, Swedish Competition Authority Pros and Cons Series 2005; *Hovenkamp*, Federal Antitrust Policy, p. 611; *Katz*, American Economic Review 1987, 154; *Stole*, in: Handbook Industrial Organization, 2221; *Sullivan/Grimes*, Law of Antitrust, p. 354 emphasizing that price discrimination tends to target the less powerful or less knowledgeable buyers; *Varian*, in: Handbook Industrial Organization, 598 (619–623); *Wright/Ginsburg*, Fordham Law Review 2013, 2405 (2412) arguing even that 'price discrimination is generally efficient and welfare increasing'.

[314] *Geradin/Petit*, Journal of Competition Law & Economics 2006, 479; *Winter/Iacobucci*, in: Handbook International Antitrust Economics, 351 (357).

[315] Vertical Guidelines, paras. 119, 392.

[316] *Geradin et al.*, EU Competition Law and Economics, para. 8.19.

to compare prices across retailers, while also standardizing retailers' cost structures.

6. Reducing dynamic efficiency

Limiting intra-brand competition can also reduce dynamic efficiency. Absent vertical agreements, each retailer has the incentive to organize their business efficiently and ask for a low price to increase their sales.[317] This will also encourage retailers to invest in innovative retail strategies and thus lead to dynamic efficiency.[318] Such innovations in the past included, inter alia, mail-order catalogues, specialized boutiques, drive-in stores and, most recently, online shopping.[319] In contrast, vertical agreements can reduce retailers' abilities and incentives to innovate.[320] Price restrictions, for example, prevent retailers from profiting from efficiency and innovation by competing with other retailers on prices. Exclusive distribution can have similar effects.[321] Selective distribution systems often directly impose on the retailer how the product is to be sold and, by nature, tend to prevent retailers from innovating as innovations often don't fit the 'straitjacket' of qualitative criteria for choosing the retailers.[322] Vezzoso and Vezzoso/Kerber[323] also emphasise the importance of unrestricted vertical exchange for innovation on the manufacturer level. Exclusivity arrangements, for example, can make market access of newcomers with innovative products more difficult.[324] Moreover, retailers in many markets serve as selectors and, to some extent, as gatekeepers: to properly reach consumers, it is often necessary to find a retailer that sells a manufacturer's products.[325] The more heterogenous retailers exist in a market, the easier it is especially for manufacturers of new products, to find a retailer willing to stock their product.[326] Vertical agreements, such as selective distribution agreements, which reduce variety on the retailer level, can thus negatively affect innovation on the inter-brand level.[327] However, vertical agreements can also be beneficial from an evolutionary economics perspective.[328] For example, a manufacturer who wants their retailers to engage in new and innovative distribution methods may do so with the help of vertical agreements.[329]

---

[317] *Sullivan/Grimes*, Law of Antitrust, pp. 334–335.

[318] *Sullivan/Grimes*, Law of Antitrust, p. 335.

[319] *Sullivan/Grimes*, Law of Antitrust, p. 335; *Comanor*, Antitrust Bulletin 2013, 107 (110).

[320] *Sullivan/Grimes*, Law of Antitrust, pp. 341–342.

[321] *Tirole*, Theory of Industrial Organization, p. 188 emphasizes that exclusive distribution can use decentralized knowledge regarding demand.

[322] *Vezzoso*, Vertikale Beschränkungen, pp. 212–214.

[323] *Kerber/Vezzoso*, World Competition 2005, 507.

[324] *Vezzoso*, Vertikale Beschränkungen, p. 158.

[325] *Vezzoso*, Vertikale Beschränkungen, p. 159.

[326] *Vezzoso*, Vertikale Beschränkungen, p. 159.

[327] *Vezzoso*, Vertikale Beschränkungen, p. 159.

[328] *Vezzoso*, Vertikale Beschränkungen, pp. 181–202, 205–207.

[329] *Vezzoso*, Vertikale Beschränkungen, pp. 205–206.

7. Harming the inframarginal consumer

Some commentators argue that the welfare effects of vertical agreements, particularly regarding the efficient level of services provided by retailers, are ambiuozs.[330] Comanor has shown that manufacturers' and consumers' interests do not always align. Notably, he points out that Telser's famous article "why manufacturers want fair trade"[331] explains exactly what is indicated in the title[332]: manufacturers want vertical agreements to ensure that retailers provide certain services. However, the article does not address whether these services benefit consumers, that is, whether the additional services justify the higher prices.[333]

The traditional view is that a manufacturer can only increase sales through vertical agreements if consumers value the additional services more than the associated price increase; otherwise, consumers would switch to a competitor offering the product at a lower price without the extra services. According to Comanor, this is only true for the 'marginal consumer', i.e., the consumer whose current willingness to pay is approximately equal to the product's price.[334] These consumers are sensitive to any change in the product's price/service composition. If the product (under vertical agreements) is now sold only with additional services but at a higher price, they will buy more or less of the product, depending on how much they value the services. In contrast, the 'infra-marginal consumer', whose willingness to pay substantially exceeds the price (without vertical agreements) is less price sensitive and will often continue to buy the product, albeit receiving a lower surplus from this transaction. This dynamic can lead to an oversupply of services that ultimately harms overall consumer welfare.[335] Ultimately, the positive effects on the marginal consumers must be balanced with the negative effects on the inframarginal consumers. The more inframarginal consumers exist in a market and the less price sensitive they are, the more likely it is that the benefits do not outweigh the overall costs. This suggests that vertical agreements can be harmful for well-established and differentiated products.[336]

The issue of inframarginal consumers is implicitly acknowledged in the Vertical Guidelines, which state in the context of free-riding on promotional efforts:

"Whether consumers actually benefit overall from extra promotional efforts depends on whether the extra promotion informs and convinces and thus benefits many new customers

[330] *van den Bergh/Camesasca*, Comparative Competition Law and Economics, p. 253.

[331] *Telser*, Journal of Law & Economics 1960, 86.

[332] The term fair trade comes from the so-called State 'fair trading laws' that allowed RPM under Miller-Tydings Act of 1937, see below from p. 85.

[333] *Comanor*, Harvard Law Review 1985, 983 (988); *Comanor*, Review of Industrial Organization 1990, 99 (106–107).

[334] *Comanor*, Harvard Law Review 1985, 983 (991); *Comanor*, Review of Industrial Organization 1990, 99 (107).

[335] *Comanor*, Harvard Law Review 1985, 983 (992).

[336] *Comanor*, Harvard Law Review 1985, 983 (999).

or mainly reaches customers who already know what they want to buy and for whom the extra promotion only or mainly implies a price increase."[337]

Although this discussion refers primarily to promotion and service, it may also have implications for certification and luxury products. Just as additional services that inform consumers do not necessarily enhance a product's value for everyone, an improved product image may not benefit all consumers equally. For example, if a widely used shampoo is repositioned as a premium product through a strict selective distribution system – sold exclusively through pharmacies – some consumers may be willing to pay more for the enhanced image, while others may find it unaffordable or unchanged in their evaluation.

The effects on the inframarginal consumers do not play a prominent role in the economic discussion around vertical agreements, partly because they are difficult to measure.[338] Moreover, some argue that negative impacts on inframarginal consumers are common across the economy and not necessarily harmful – after all, product innovations may primarily benefit marginal consumers even though all consumers are ultimately asked to pay for them.[339]

III. Behavioural economic discussion of vertical agreements

Vertical agreements have received relatively little attention in the literature on behavioural economics.[340] However, there are a few notable exceptions.

First, Tor and Rinner discuss RPM and behavioural economics, focusing on boundedly rational manufacturers.[341] They argue that behavioural economics suggests that manufacturers may overestimate the expected harm from price-cutting by retailers and overestimate the benefits by retailers due to several biases, e.g., anchoring, representativeness, loss aversion and thus overuse RPM.[342] This can induce manufacturers to use RPM in cases where they are neither beneficial for manufacturers nor for society.[343] They argue that, nevertheless, a rule of reason is the appropriate standard for RPM.[344] While their analysis focuses on manufacturer behaviour rather than consumer behavior, it reinforces the view

---

[337] Vertical Guidelines, para. 16b footnote 22.

[338] *Hovenkamp*, Federal Antitrust Policy, p. 622.

[339] *Hovenkamp*, Federal Antitrust Policy, p. 622.

[340] *Ahlert et al.*, Vielfalt durch Gestaltungsfreiheit, pp. 185–193 making the very general argument that behavioural economics provide more support for the efficiency of vertical restraints; *Heinemann*, in: European Perspectives on Behavioural Law and Economics, 211 (221); for a review of the related but broader literature on experimental economics, see *Landeo*, in: Handbook Behavioral Law and Economics, 75.

[341] *Rinner/Tor*, University of Illinois Law Review 2011, 805; for a critical perspective, see *Wright/Stone*, Cordoza Law Review 2012, 1517 (1543–1544).

[342] *Rinner/Tor*, University of Illinois Law Review 2011, 805 (821–822).

[343] *Rinner/Tor*, University of Illinois Law Review 2011, 805 (854–855).

[344] *Rinner/Tor*, University of Illinois Law Review 2011, 805 (854–855).

that vertical agreements are not always efficiency-driven. Their findings underscore the limitations of broad generalizations about the effects of such agreements.

Second, Helfrich and Herweg analyse the effects of internet bans under the assumption of context-dependent preferences[345]: consumers tend to focus on and hence overvalue either price or quality; if the price level is higher, consumers tend to focus more on quality, leading to a higher willingness to pay.[346] In their model, the attribute quality is salient[347] "if and only if the quality ratio is larger than the ratio of average prices across channels."[348] Therefore, an overall higher price level is beneficial to higher-price (and quality) goods. A lower price level, on the other hand, makes the price more salient, shifting consumer attention away from quality. Online sales can induce lower prices because of high competition in online retail markets (as well as lower distribution costs). A multibrand brick and mortar retailer can induce a quality-salient environment only by raising prices for fringe (non-branded/low-price) goods or for branded and fringe products alike. If they raise prices only for the branded goods, the price will be salient because of the fringe products' better price/quality ratio. If they raises prices for the fringe products, however, they will forego sales of these products: some consumers will buy the more expensive product instead, and other consumers that still prefer lower-priced goods will buy them elsewhere, e.g., online (harming the retailer). If the manufacturer wants their retailers to induce a quality-salient environment, they need to secure them a higher margin on the sale of branded products that compensates for the foregone sales in low-price products that come with the quality-salient environment. This can be done by prohibiting online sales of the branded product (reducing price competition between retailers). The multibrand retailer can then "charge a higher markup on the branded product than on competing products."[349] According to Helfrich and Herweg, prohibiting internet sales can align manufacturers' and retailers' interests.[350] However, they argue that this can harm consumer and total welfare.[351] Under the assumption that consumers slightly prefer to shop in brick and mortar stores, consumers that prefer low-quality/price products are harmed because they will buy the fringe product online rather than in a brick and mortar store (where it is too expensive due to the induced higher price). Restrictions on online sales for branded products can

---

345 *Helfrich/Herweg*, Journal of Behavioral and Experimental Economics 2020, 101556.

346 *Helfrich/Herweg*, Journal of Behavioral and Experimental Economics 2020, 10155 (2).

347 See for salience already above p. 19.

348 *Helfrich/Herweg*, Journal of Behavioral and Experimental Economics 2020, 101556 (4).

349 *Helfrich/Herweg*, Journal of Behavioral and Experimental Economics 2020, 101556 (11).

350 *Helfrich/Herweg*, Journal of Behavioral and Experimental Economics 2020, 101556 (11).

351 *Helfrich/Herweg*, Journal of Behavioral and Experimental Economics 2020, 101556 (8–9).

therefore actually lead to inefficient overuse of the internet as a sales channel for non-branded products. Consumers that prefer higher-quality products, on the other hand, are harmed because they must pay higher prices for the branded product. Helfrich and Herweg offer an interesting model of the reasons for restrictions on online sales, considering behavioural economics. Yet, their conclusions on the welfare implications seem questionable. In particular, they do not consider any utility that consumers can derive from the scarcity and prestige of the product that is not available online. Nevertheless, their analysis is valuable, highlighting the need for a more cautious approach to vertical agreements on online sales.

Third, Dertwinkel-Kalt and Köster discuss salience effects linked to price dispersion through online channels.[352] Their underlying assumption about salience differs from the one adopted by Helfrich and Herweg. A price-salient environment under their model occurs "if and only if the available offers 'vary more' along the price than along the quality dimension."[353] Salience here comes from a contrast effect drawing most attention to the attribute that differs most between options.[354] They assume in their model that there are two types of consumers: those who prefer offline shopping (offline consumers) and those that are indifferent between online or offline (online consumers). Moreover, they assume that retail costs are lower online and that all consumers are aware of online and offline prices. Vertical agreements, according to Dertwinkel-Kalt and Köster, can potentially address inefficiencies that result from salience.[355] Absent restraints, if there is only a small share of online consumers, manufacturers can overproduce quality to prevent a price-salient environment or underproduce quality where prices are salient. If the share of online consumers is large, price salience can lead to an equilibrium in which brick and mortar stores are no longer profitable and in which, therefore, only online consumers can be served. If the share of online consumers is low, manufacturers produce too high quality (with the goal of preventing a price-salient environment). For intermediate shares of online consumers, the manufacturer invests insufficiently in quality as they cannot prevent a price-salient equilibrium from occurring if they want all consumers to be served. A (total) ban on internet sales, they argue, will prevent price salience (less contrasting prices) and all consumers will be served in brick and mortar stores at an efficient quality level. At the same time, however, such bans lead to inefficiently high retail costs by forcing (all) consumers to buy at brick and mortar stores instead of at cheaper online retailers.[356] The welfare implications, according to

[352] *Dertwinkel-Kalt/Köster*, Journal of Economics & Management Strategy 2022, 64.

[353] *Dertwinkel-Kalt/Köster*, Journal of Economics & Management Strategy 2022, 64 (66–67).

[354] *Dertwinkel-Kalt/Köster*, Journal of Economics & Management Strategy 2022, 64 (66–67).

[355] *Dertwinkel-Kalt/Köster*, Journal of Economics & Management Strategy 2022, 64 (72–74)

[356] *Dertwinkel-Kalt/Köster*, Journal of Economics & Management Strategy 2022, 64 (73).

Dertwinkel-Kalt and Köster, therefore, depend on which effect is greater, which in turn depends on how large the share of online consumers is.[357] Similar to an online ban, RPM can prevent price salience (as it ensures uniform prices across channels). Unlike a ban, however, it does not prevent efficient online sales, but it does prevent low prices and can hence reduce consumer welfare, again depending on the share of online consumers.[358] Dual pricing has similar effects in their model.[359] So under Dertwinkel-Kalt's and Köster's model, the consumer welfare implications of vertical agreements in the context of online sales depend primarily on the relative number of online users.

Dertwinkel-Kalt's and Köster's analysis assumes that salience depends on variation. Helfrich and Helweg base their model on the assumption that salience depends on the quality vs the price ratio. These different assumptions already show how difficult it is to draw clear conclusions. Vertical agreements have not yet been sufficiently researched from a behavioural economic lens to allow clear conclusions about their welfare effects. They could be welfare-enhancing or welfare-reducing. Nevertheless, one important element crystallizes from the literature: vertical agreements can influence the consumer's decision-making and lead them to make different decisions than absent such agreements. Usually, however, these effects are generally perceived as positive: typically, the consumer buys more, leading to higher output and, thus, higher consumer welfare. Behavioural economics is somewhat more cautious in this regard.

IV. Empirical evidence

Empirical evidence on the effects of vertical agreements remains scarce and inconclusive, with most studies focusing primarily on RPM. Two main methods are commonly used to assess whether vertical agreements are more likely to be beneficial or detrimental to consumer welfare.

The first approach is to look at incidences of vertical agreements and explain the likely motivation behind them (incidence/motivation studies). There are two prominent literature reviews, one by Ippolito and one by Overstreet. Both have gained prominence by being cited in the 2007 US Supreme Court opinion Legin[360]. Ippolito, in her 1991 paper, studies reported litigated RPM cases in the US between 1976 and 1982 (when RPM was still per se illegal in the US)[361].[362] She tested whether, in these cases, RPM was likely to be motivated either by collusion or by procompetitive motives. She used RPM cases that also included a horizontal price-fixing allegation as an indicator of how often collusion played a role,

[357] *Dertwinkel-Kalt/Köster*, Journal of Economics & Management Strategy 2022, 64 (73).
[358] *Dertwinkel-Kalt/Köster*, Journal of Economics & Management Strategy 2022, 64 (73).
[359] *Dertwinkel-Kalt/Köster*, Journal of Economics & Management Strategy 2022, 64 (74).
[360] US Supreme Court, 28/06/2007, No. 06–480 Leegin, 551 U.S. 877, p. 10.
[361] See for the legal treatment of vertical agreements in the US below from p. 84.
[362] *Ippolito*, Journal of Law & Economics 1991, 263.

finding that this was the case in only 13.1 % of the sampled cases.[363] This approach, however, has been criticized: the mere fact that the plaintiff did not make the allegation of collusion does not rule out that it existed.[364] Given RPM's per se illegality at the time, plaintiffs may have chosen to focus solely on RPM violations rather than introducing collusion claims, which would have required additional evidence. In her study, Ippolito did not test other potential harms (e.g., foreclosing, dampening competition). As an indicator of pro-competitive motives, Ippolito used the nature of the covered products. Complex products were assumed to indicate the procompetitive rationale of preventing free-riding[365] on retailer services. Infrequently purchased goods, fashion goods and new entrants' cases were used to indicate the quality certification rationale[366]. Ippolito concluded that more than 60 % of the sample included such goods.[367] Simple goods were used as an indicator for the pro-competitive rationale to enhance dealer sales efforts (consumer heterogeneity[368]).[369] Ultimately, Ippolito's assessment provides little conclusive evidence of procompetitive results: three different categories of products were used, and a pro-competitive rationale was assumed for each product category. However, her conclusions remain inconclusive: she assumes, rather than proves, that these rationales were the true motivations behind RPM in the cases analyzed.[370] Moreover, it is disputed whether the used sample of cases is representative. Tor and Rinner argue that, under the per se rule, strong cases were often settled, leaving the litigated cases skewed toward weaker evidence.[371]

Overstreet, in his study, examines RPM cases brought by the US Federal Trade Commission between 1965 and 1982.[372] He uses the market circumstances (the size of the firms using RPM, the structure of the retailer and manufacturer market) to estimate the likelihood of horizontal collusion through RPM, concluding that RPM is unlikely motivated by collusion in most cases.[373] Overstreet's approach also faces some difficulties. First, it only tests one rationale (collusion) and leaves out others. Second, Overstreet empirically tests the prediction that RPM is not frequently used to facilitate collusion. His results, however, rest on the assumption that certain market circumstances (e.g., a high con-

---

[363] *Ippolito*, Journal of Law & Economics 1991, 263 (281–282).

[364] *Schwaderer*, Resale Price Maintenance, p. 48.

[365] See in this regard above p. 45.

[366] See in this regard above p. 47.

[367] *Ippolito*, Journal of Law & Economics 1991, 263 (283–284).

[368] See in this regard above p. 48.

[369] *Ippolito*, Journal of Law & Economics 1991, 263 (289–290).

[370] *Brunell*, Antitrust Bulletin 2007, 475 (510); *Ippolito*, Journal of Law & Economics 1991, 263 (293) recognizing that her 'study is based on admittedly limited plausability tests of the various theories of RPM.'

[371] *Rinner/Tor*, University of Illinois Law Review 2011, 805 (816–817) footnote 77; this is also recognized by *Ippolito*, Journal of Law & Economics 1991, 263 (274).

[372] *Overstreet*, RPM: Economic Theories and Empirical Evidence, pp. 63–100.

[373] *Overstreet*, RPM: Economic Theories and Empirical Evidence, pp. 80–82.

centration ratio) indicate collusion. His study does not test whether or not this assumption is correct. Third, the study faces the same critique regarding the sample selection as Ippolito's.[374] Overstreet himself recognizes that

"the information generated and retained for this sample of RPM cases is, in most instances, inadequate to determine rigorously whether the associated economic conditions correspond best with procompetitive or anticompetitive hypotheses".[375]

Both studies focus only on a limited set of rationales – such as whether preventing free-riding was the likely motivation behind a restraint – rather than providing a comprehensive assessment. Their findings must further be considered with scepticism as they do not stricto sensu provide evidence of the agreements' welfare implications. Even if a manufacturer *wants* to achieve a pro-competitive result (e.g., solving free-riding problems), the actual effects of the restraint might be anti-competitive. For instance, such a restriction could inadvertently facilitate collusion at the retailer level. This is not the least because the manufacturer may act boundedly rationally.[376] The undertakings' subjective procompetitive motivation behind an agreement does not rule out a violation of Art. 101 TFEU.[377] Moreover, both studies ignore the effects on the inframarginal consumer.[378] Besides these methodological problems, the studies use data from before 1982, so their results cannot necessarily be transferred to today's context.[379]

The second approach to empirically analysing the effects of vertical agreements is to look not at the likely motivation but at their effects on an observable market variable, e.g., price, output or stock market returns (effects studies).[380] These studies typically compare variables across regions, assess differences between firms that do or do not employ vertical agreements, or examine market conditions before and after a regulatory change (e.g., the introduction of a new *per se* rule for or against vertical agreements). Since the Supreme Court in Leegin (2007) has overruled the long-standing per se rule against RPM in the United States, RPM is governed by a rule of reason.[381] In practice, this means that almost no cases are brought against RPM, and those brought are very difficult to win. RPM is now relatively common in the US and covers a wide range of products, including electronics, pet foods, rental cars, and home accessories.[382] Prominent

---

[374] *Schwaderer*, Resale Price Maintenance, p. 47.

[375] *Overstreet*, RPM: Economic Theories and Empirical Evidence, p. 66.

[376] See above p. 60.

[377] This is only relevant in so far as fines can only be imposed on firms who intentionally or negligently violent competition law, see Art. 23(2) Regulation 1/2003. In the context of vertical agreements, often times disputes arise between distributor and manufacturer as the validity of the contract and in this respect, negligence or intent does not matter.

[378] *Schwaderer*, Resale Price Maintenance, p. 50.

[379] *Schwaderer*, Resale Price Maintenance, pp. 50–52.

[380] *Schwaderer*, Resale Price Maintenance, p. 53.

[381] See for a more detailed account of US law below from p. 84.

[382] *Pereira*, Wall Street Journal, 28/08/2016, Price-Fixing Makes Comeback After Su-

examples include Sony and Samsung, which introduced RPM in 2012.[383] However, some states have introduced legislation that made RPM per se illegal in their territory. This provides a natural experiment that MacKay and Aron Smith have used to empirically test the effects of RPM in an effects study by comparing the price and quantity developments of consumer goods post-Leegin in those states that adhered strictly to the federal precedent (rule of reason states) compared to those that remained hostile towards RPM (control group states).[384] They find that in the period following Leegin, in the rule of reason states, prices increased relative to the control group. Their study finds an increase in prices of 0.33 per cent (average) and an overall decrease in quantities of 3.8 %.[385] They do not find significant effects on increased distribution or broader inventories in the rule of reason states.[386]

More broadly looking at vertical agreements, Lafontaine and Slade, in a review of the empirical literature based on effect studies, concluded that most privately initiated restraints (e.g. based on agreements between manufacturers and retailers) – vs government-mandated restraints (e.g. laws that require that wholesalers are given exclusive territories) – had positive effects on consumer welfare.[387] Of the 14 articles they reviewed, eight showed positive effects, and only three showed negative effects of vertical agreements on consumer welfare. As with other effects studies, Lafontaine's and Slade's approach faces the challenge that the market variables they use are, at most, imperfect indicators for consumer welfare. Lafontaine and Slade consider positive any restraint that leads to increased consumption, even at increased prices.[388] This appears to disregard any trade-off between the surplus of marginal and inframarginal consumers. Cooper et al., in another literature review, also conclude that empirical evidence favours a pro-competitive rationale for vertical agreements in most cases.[389] However, they survey not only literature that measures market variables but also include incidence/motivation studies such as the one by Ippolito mentioned above. Their review in this regard must face the same objections. The Cooper et al. survey has

preme Court Ruling, available at https://www.wsj.com/articles/SB121901920116148325 (accessed: 11 March 2025); *MacKay/Smith*, SSRN 2014, p. 5.

[383] *Zimmerman*, Wallstreet Journal, 23/05/2012, Sony, Samsung rein in Retailers' Discounts on TVs, available at http://online.wsj.com/article/SB10001424052702304791704577420383631021786.html.

[384] *MacKay/Smith*, SSRN 2014; similar studies have been conducted regarding a change in the legality of RPM in 1975 through the abolishment of the Miller-Tydings Act. In states that previously allowed RPM, this led to a reinstatement of the per se rule against maximum resale price maintenance; see for an account of these studies *Rinner/Tor*, University of Illinois Law Review 2011, 805 (816–817); and *Shepard*, Journal of Consumer Affairs 1978, 220.

[385] *MacKay/Smith*, SSRN 2014, p. 17.

[386] *MacKay/Smith*, SSRN 2014, pp. 19–20.

[387] *Lafontaine/Slade*, in: Handbook Antitrust Economics, 391 (409).

[388] *Lafontaine/Slade*, in: Handbook Antitrust Economics, 391 (407).

[389] *Cooper et al.*, International Journal of Industrial Organization 2005, 639 (658).

been heavily criticized. Scherer et al. point out the non-representative selection of papers reviewed that ignored studies pointing in other directions.[390] Moreover, in both the Lofaintane and Slade and the Cooper et al. survey, some products (such as gasoline and cable TV) appear overrepresented. As an additional point of critique, the market conditions, e.g., whether the analysed markets are competitive or not, are not always distinguished. Additionally, the usefulness of empirical results on the effects of vertical agreements that aggregate data in general is disputed.[391] It is difficult to draw conclusions from one case to another as vertical agreements' effects are very heterogenous, depending on the market circumstances and the restraint at issue.[392]

To conclude, empirical studies have not definitively confirmed the theoretical prediction that vertical agreements are predominantly used for pro-competitive reasons and typically enhance consumer welfare. However, they also fail to provide conclusive evidence for the opposite claim. Given these mixed findings, the empirical record supports a case-by-case approach rather than the imposition of strict, categorical rules.

V. Conclusion

In economic literature, the view prevails that vertical agreements often benefit consumers.[393] Potential for harm is mainly seen concerning inter-brand competition. The effects on intra-brand competition are generally considered less significant, except when they involve collusive behavior among retailers or where market power is at play.[394] Vertical agreements are seen as fostering an efficient and appropriate level of services due to inter-brand competition. If consumers do not sufficiently value the services imposed by vertical agreements, they will simply switch to products from other manufacturers.[395] Emphasizing the manufacturer's interest in vivid competition between retailers, Caffarra even characterizes

> "the idea that competition authorities should be concerned about promoting intra-brand competition when inter-brand competition is low" as "the 'intra-brand competition' fallacy".[396]

---

[390] *Scherer et al.*, SSRN 2005.

[391] *Verouden*, in: Issues in Competition Law and Policy, 1813 (1838–1839); *Winter*, CPI 2006, 75.

[392] *Verouden*, in: Issues in Competition Law and Policy, 1813 (1838).

[393] For a more nuanced approach, however, see *Rey/Vergé*, in: Handbook Antitrust Economics, 354.

[394] *Thomas*, ZHR 2020, 223 (224–226); note, however, that even this is not unambiguous as vertical restraints to solve double marginalization are efficient only if there is market power, see *Rey/Vergé*, in: Handbook Antitrust Economics, 354 (361–362).

[395] *Monti*, World Competition 2013, 489 (496).

[396] *Caffarra*, in: Vertical Restraints, 55 (73).

Furthermore, different types of vertical agreements are largely viewed as interchangeable, and pro- or anticompetitive effects do not depend so much on the kind of agreement but rather on the market circumstances, particularly the existence of market power upstream or downstream.[397] While in some scenarios, for example, RPM can be beneficial if it avoids double marginalization, in others, it can facilitate collusion and thus reduce welfare.[398] Therefore, the main argument to be distilled from economic literature is that vertical agreements should be evaluated based on their effects on the market, requiring a case-by-case approach. Only when it comes to the distinction between price and non-price restraints it seems accepted that a stricter stance towards the former compared to the latter is appropriate.[399]

Empirical evidence has not definitively proven that vertical agreements are pro-competitive in most cases, nor has it demonstrated the opposite. Therefore, it supports a case-by-case approach to evaluating these agreements. The same conclusion can be drawn from the emerging literature in behavioral economics. While this literature suggests that vertical agreements may be used more frequently than is socially optimal, it does not provide conclusive evidence regarding whether specific types of vertical agreements are generally pro- or anti-competitive.

VI. Assessing the EU's stance on vertical agreements: are the rules economically justified?

After examining both the legal and economic evaluations of vertical agreements, it becomes clear that both areas share a considerable degree of complexity. However, this shared complexity does not necessarily mean that the legal treatment aligns with economic theory. This section will show that the treatment of vertical agreements under EU law cannot fully be justified on economic grounds. The section will focus on agreements that can lead to restrictions on online sales. However, RPM will also be discussed as it is the prototype of vertical agreements and the starting point of many economic discussions and hence central to understanding the economic evaluation of vertical agreements.

---

[397] *Rey/Caballero-Sanz*, Economic Analysis of Vertical Restraints, pp. 21, 41; *Rey/Vergé*, in: Handbook Antitrust Economics, 354 (384); *Secrieru*, Journal of Economic Surveys 2006, 797; *Tirole*, Theory of Industrial Organization, p. 186; *Verouden*, in: Issues in Competition Law and Policy, 1813 (1838); this is, in principle, even recognized by the Commission, see *European Commission*, Green Paper on Vertical Restraints, para. 87.

[398] *Rey/Caballero-Sanz*, Economic Analysis of Vertical Restraints, p. 21.

[399] *Rey/Vergé*, in: Handbook Antitrust Economics, 354 (386); *Verouden*, in: Issues in Competition Law and Policy, 1813 (1838–1839).

1. The Metro exception for selective distribution from an economic viewpoint

First, the Metro exception for selective distribution agreements will be discussed from an economic viewpoint. Here, it needs to be distinguished between the relatively more lenient approach that it brings as such (a) and the criteria to determine the scope of the exception (b).

a) Allowing selective distribution agreements as such

The Metro exception for selective distribution, exempting such agreement from the ambit of Art. 101(1) TFEU, in most cases,[400] is generally welcomed from an economic perspective as selective distribution is considered to be typically welfare-enhancing. It can reduce transaction costs, allow for an efficient distribution of the products, and solve the free-riding problem[401] regarding advice and pre-sales services.[402] Similarly, selective distribution systems can be used to protect a certain image of the product.[403] Besides the free-riding rationale, selective distribution can also help to address consumer heterogeneity[404].[405] The welfare effects can nevertheless be somewhat ambiguous due to a possible oversupply of services. This is because the manufacturer will consider only the marginal consumers, but the welfare effects also concern the average (or inframarginal) consumers[406].[407] Nevertheless, from an economic perspective, the treatment of selective distribution agreements as generally permissible is justified: while they might not always be in the consumers' interest, there is also no basis for presuming the opposite, so a laissez-faire approach is preferred.[408] Moreover, selective distribution is less likely than other vertical agreements to dampen competition or facilitate collusion between manufacturers.[409] In particular, selective distribution still allows (some) price competition, making prices not entirely uniform across retailers, so conformity with price agreements between manufacturers remains hard to observe. Further, selective distribution, particularly when it purports to protect a brand's image and uniqueness, tends to increase brand differentiation, making collusive behaviour less likely due to more heterogenous goods in the market.[410] While selective distribution agreements are typically considered harm-

---

[400] See above p. 26.

[401] See above from p. 45.

[402] *Monti*, World Competition 2013, 489 (502); *Witt*, European Competition Journal 2016, 435 (441); this is also recognized by the Commission, see *European Commission*, Evaluation of the Vertical Block Exemption Regulation, p. 37.

[403] See above p. 47.

[404] See above p. 48.

[405] *Buettner et al.*, European Competition Journal 2009, 201 (207).

[406] See above from p. 59.

[407] *Buettner et al.*, European Competition Journal 2009, 201 (210).

[408] *Buettner et al.*, European Competition Journal 2009, 201 (210–211, 214)

[409] *Buettner et al.*, European Competition Journal 2009, 201 (213–214)

[410] Compare *Sullivan/Grimes*, Law of Antitrust, p. 322.

less from an economic perspective, this does not mean they never restrict competition (e.g., through foreclosure). Such risks are, however, limited to scenarios where one of the companies involved has market power.[411] Against this background, economic theory favours a lenient approach towards selective distribution agreements.

b) The applicable criteria

Nevertheless, the Metro exception is not fully supported by economic theory as it is a rather formalistic framework, ignoring the concrete circumstances of the market. The Metro exception applies irrespective of the companies' market position and, thus also, where they have market power.[412] Economic literature, on the other hand, identifies market power as the most important element to evaluate the pro- and anticompetitive effects of selective distribution. The distinction between qualitative and quantitative criteria under the Metro exception also raises questions from an economic point of view. The Vertical Guidelines, in this regard, emphasize that quantitative criteria restrict more directly the potential number of dealers than qualitative criteria, which do so only indirectly.[413] One potential reason for the different treatments could therefore be the different market foreclosure effects of quantitative and qualitative selective distribution systems. However, quantitative criteria appear to bear a relatively low risk of market foreclosure on the inter-brand level. The category of quantitative restrictions covers a wide range of restraints, including, for instance, minimum or maximum sales requirements or fixing the number of dealers.[414] However, fixing the number of dealers seems unlikely to have foreclosure effects on the inter-brand level: the fewer retailers sell a specific manufacturer's products, the more other retailers have shelf space available for other manufacturers' products. Finding a retailer willing to carry a market entrant's products will thus potentially be easier. Minimum or maximum sales requirements are more ambiguous. On the one hand, a minimum sales requirement can reduce the number of retailers that sell a specific manufacturer's products if not all retailers can or want to match the minimum sales requirement. Minimum sales requirements can have similar effects as fixing the number of retailers and thus make more retail shelve space available to other manufacturers, including new market entrants. On the other hand, among those retailers who are part of the selective distribution system, minimum sales requirements will reduce their ability and willingness to stock competing manufacturers' products, making it more difficult for market entrants to find a distributor. The effects can therefore be ambiguous. Maximum sales requirements appear to have again different effects. They actually increase the

---

[411] *Monti*, World Competition 2013, 489 (493).
[412] See above p. 27.
[413] Vertical Guidelines, para. 144.
[414] Vertical Guidelines, para. 144; Vertical Guidelines (2010), para. 175.

number of retailers who are able to carry one manufacturer's products since each retailer can only sell a limited amount. As each retailer will still be able to carry other manufacturers' products, it is also unlikely that such a requirement will lead to market foreclosure for other manufacturers who can still sell through the same retailer. The same is true regarding market foreclosure on the retail level – new retailers will not typically face problems in meeting the requirement of maximum sales. The distinction between quantitative and qualitative criteria also appears questionable when looking at the potential effects on innovation.[415] Qualitative criteria, when used widely, can make market entry for new entrants particularly difficult.[416] Suppose the manufacturer imposes such qualitative criteria and thereby determines the price-service mix for the retail of their products. In that case, retailers may not themselves experiment and discover alternative price-service bundles and new forms of retail.[417] Quantitative criteria do not similarly affect the distributor's price service mix. In this sense, qualitative criteria could be even more harmful than quantitative criteria, casting doubt on the usefulness of the current distinction.

The fourth Metro condition (stemming from the Metro II judgment) requires that on the affected market, there must not be a wide-spread use of similar selective distribution systems that forecloses new forms of distribution.[418] This has some economic merit, especially from an evolutionary economics perspective[419]: the widespread use of a certain distribution system can make it more difficult for market entrants on the manufacturing level to find distributors for their new products.[420] The more distributors exist, and the more heterogeneous they are, the easier it gets for new entrants to find a distribution partner.[421] Selective distribution, if too common in a particular market, can thus harm dynamic efficiency.[422] Moreover, this is also in line with the theory of harm that vertical agreements can lead to collusion among retailers. Such collusion will only work if the manufacturer whose products are affected has market power or if retailers manage to conclude similar distribution agreements with a number of manufacturers; otherwise, consumers could just switch to products not covered by the agreement.[423] A larger number of similar vertical agreements can thus facilitate collusion. However, it should be noted that collusion is not the main concern of selective distribution but rather of price-related restraints.[424] Besides this, the

[415] See above from p. 58.

[416] *Vezzoso*, Vertikale Beschränkungen, p. 212.

[417] *Kerber/Vezzoso*, World Competition 2005, 507 (520).

[418] See above p. 27.

[419] See above from p. 58.

[420] *Vezzoso*, Vertikale Beschränkungen, p. 212.

[421] *Kerber/Vezzoso*, World Competition 2005, 507 (522); *Vezzoso*, Vertikale Beschränkungen, p. 212.

[422] Compare *Kerber/Vezzoso*, World Competition 2005, 507 (522).

[423] *Hovenkamp*, Federal Antitrust Policy, p. 604.

[424] See above p. 51.

criterion also faces the problem that the widespread use of a particular distribution system could simply indicate that this is the most efficient one. In the luxury sector, for example, selective distribution is very common. There are good reasons to believe this is not based on collusion among manufacturers or retailers but on consumers' preferences to purchase luxury items in luxury stores.[425]

c) Conclusion

To conclude, the Metro exception for selective distribution is generally welcomed by economists because it permits a more lenient approach to vertical agreements. However, its specific requirements – such as the distinction between quantitative and qualitative criteria, and the fact that it applies regardless of market conditions, even for companies with market power – are not fully supported by economic theory.

2. Coty: protecting the product's image

The Coty judgment[426], which extended the Metro exception to selective distribution agreements that safeguard or improve a product's image seems largely in line with economic theory.[427] Economists generally endorse vertical agreements with image goals, even if this is not related to any physical property of the good. Image, in this view, is a source of value in and of itself.[428] If a selective distribution system helps to create such an image, it creates value. The very fact that consumers buy the product, thereby expressing their preference for the image, which is (at least partly) created through vertical agreements, is considered evidence enough.[429] The image can create value through two distinct mechanisms, conspicuous and inconspicuous consumption.[430] In the case of conspicuous consumption, the consumer's product valuation depends on their ability to use it as a status symbol.[431] Conspicuous consumption requires exclusivity and rareness of the product.[432] Examples include fashion items from brands like Burberry, Car-

---

[425] See *Buettner et al.*, European Competition Journal 2009, 201 (221).

[426] See in more detail on Coty and related cases below from p. 108.

[427] *Buettner et al.*, European Competition Journal 2009, 201 (219–223); *Buettner et al.*, European Competition Journal 2009, 613 (614); *Franck*, WuW 2010, 772 (778–779); *Buccirossi*, Vertical Restraints for Online Sales, p. 19.

[428] *Buettner et al.*, European Competition Journal 2009, 201 (220); *Buettner et al.*, European Competition Journal 2009, 613 (614); *Caffarra*, in: Vertical Restraints, 55 (58); *Iacobucci/Winter*, Antitrust Law Journal 2016, 47 (58); *Orbach*, Antitrust Bulletin 2010, 277 discussing RPM.

[429] *Buettner et al.*, European Competition Journal 2009, 201 (221); *Witt*, European Competition Journal 2016, 435 (455).

[430] See *Schwaderer*, Resale Price Maintenance, pp. 151–153.

[431] This idea was initially developed by *Veblen*, The Theory of the Leisure Class, pp. 83–121; see *Leibenstein*, Quarterly Journal of Economics 1950, 183 (202–205); *Orbach*, Antitrust Bulletin 2010, 277 (290–293).

[432] See *Ackert*, Texas Law Review 1994, 1185 (1199–1205).

tier and Versace.[433] In the case of inconspicuous consumption, the consumer's evaluation of the image does not depend on others observing their consumption, but the consumer nevertheless derives pleasure from the luxury image.[434] Inconspicuous consumption would include, for example, luxury cosmetic products, as their consumption is not typically observable by others.[435] Irrespective of the underlying reasons, consumers' preferences in classical economic theory must not be questioned as this would amount to paternalism.[436] Iacobucci and Winter bring the economic reasoning to the point:

> "Product image is as valid an investment as the extra horsepower in a Lamborghini or Ferrari. The investment should not be second-guessed by regulators."[437]

Safeguarding a product's or brand's image is therefore recognized as a legitimate goal[438] and selective distribution as suitable to achieve it: the manufacturer can exclude those retailers who do not fulfil the requirements to maintain and contribute to the product's or brand's image.[439] It is generally accepted that the sales experience, location of shops, and other elements often prescribed in selective distribution systems contribute to the product image.[440] However, this is not unequivocally endorsed. While not directly discussing selective distribution, Sullivan and Grimes argue that vertical agreements can lead to greater brand differentiation and, thus, lower demand elasticity.[441] They argue that intra-brand competition as a countervailing force and a disciplining mechanism is particularly important in such a situation.[442] However, the argument that intra-brand competition is more important in markets with high brand differentiation is not generally accepted in economic literature. Product differentiation from an economic perspective is often seen as positive as it responds to varying consumer needs.[443]

The only element of Coty that raises doubts in the literature is the requirement that luxury products must be concerned for a manufacturer to protect their image. Critics argue that, in principle, a manufacturer should be able to protect any type of brand image.[444] In terms of legitimacy, this is certainly true: a brand is not less worthy of protection if it is not conveying an aura of luxury but instead

---

[433] *Orbach*, Antitrust Bulletin 2010, 277 (287).

[434] *Dilbary*, George Mason Law Review 2006, 605 (622).

[435] *Dilbary*, George Mason Law Review 2006, 605 (622).

[436] See *Iacobucci/Winter*, Antitrust Law Journal 2016, 47 (58); *Orbach*, Antitrust Bulletin 2010, 277 (307).

[437] *Iacobucci/Winter*, Antitrust Law Journal 2016, 47 (63).

[438] See already above from p. 47.

[439] Critical to this view: *Grimes*, Southwestern University Law Review 1992, 1285 (1310).

[440] *Waelbroeck/Davies*, JECLAP 2018, 431 (434).

[441] *Sullivan/Grimes*, Law of Antitrust, p. 331.

[442] *Sullivan/Grimes*, Law of Antitrust, p. 331.

[443] See in more detail below from p. 195.

[444] *Witt*, European Competition Journal 2016, 435 (457).

focuses on other criteria. For example, one can imagine sustainability or fair working criteria (e.g., fair prices for farmers who produce milk) as equally legitimate goals of vertical agreements.

3. The distinction between active and passive sales

The VBER distinguishes between active and passive sales regarding exclusive distribution.[445] The manufacturer can designate a certain territory exclusively to a retailer (or herself) and prohibit other retailers from actively selling to customers in this territory. They cannot, however, prevent retailers from responding to unsolicited requests by customers (passive selling).[446] From an economic viewpoint, de la Mano et al. describe this distinction as "artificial and unnecessary".[447] First, they emphasize that there is no clear distinction between active and passive sales, particularly online.[448] Second, they argue that the pro- and anticompetitive effects do not differ along the lines of active and passive selling.[449] This distinction thus seems to be not entirely explainable by economic reasoning.[450] This critique once more sheds light on the fact that there is limited guidance on why certain agreements restrict competition in the first place. It is, for example, typically considered a form of active selling to offer a language option (except English) in an online store which is different from the main language spoken in the territory where the seller is established.[451] Therefore, a retailer in an exclusive distribution system whose exclusively assigned territory lies only in Germany could be prevented from offering a French language option on their website but not from selling and delivering the goods to customers in France. It is questionable if also preventing the latter would add much to the impact of the exclusive distribution system on the market. This is somewhat mitigated by the very broad interpretation of what constitutes passive sales, in particular, that setting up an online store and offering English-language options is included.[452] Nevertheless, the distinctions remain somewhat arbitrary. An exclusive retailer for Belgium (main languages: Dutch and French), for example, could offer a website in Dutch, French (and English), whereas an exclusive retailer in Germany could be prevented from offering other language options than German and English, although both can sell and deliver to customers throughout the EU. More importantly, exclusive retailers from smaller Member States whose inhabitants speak the same language as those of some bigger Member States (again, think of Belgium but

[445] See above from p. 31.

[446] Vertical Guidelines, paras. 211–215.

[447] *de la Mano et al.*, Competition Law & Policy Debate 2022, 12 (15); *de la Mano/Jones*, in: Methods and Models, 167 (186).

[448] *de la Mano et al.*, Competition Law & Policy Debate 2022, 12 (15).

[449] *de la Mano et al.*, Competition Law & Policy Debate 2022, 12 (15–16).

[450] *Rey/Caballero-Sanz*, Economic Analysis of Vertical Restraints, p. 27.

[451] Vertical Guidelines, para. 213.

[452] Vertical Guidelines, paras. 212–214.

also Austria) must always face competition from online shops in the same language established in other Member States. While preventing restrictions on passive sales, therefore, can mitigate the impact on competition, it can also undermine the efficiencies of exclusive distribution.

4. The treatment of online sales restrictions

Total online bans are considered restrictions of competition by object and cannot be exempted under the VBER or the Metro exception (within selective distribution systems).[453] On the other hand, platform bans can be permissible under the VBER and the Metro exception.[454] In general, qualitative criteria can be imposed on internet sales, whereas excluding the internet or an entire online advertising channel (e.g., search engines or price comparison websites) is not permissible. The following paragraphs will demonstrate that economic literature generally supports a more lenient approach towards vertical agreements that restrict online sales than the one applied under EU law.

a) Total bans

What are the potential economic effects of prohibiting internet sales altogether? A possible negative effect of internet sales restrictions is that they might be used to segment markets and price discriminate between different groups of consumers.[455] However, internet bans do not necessarily lead to market segmentation as long as no exclusive dealership exists.[456] Moreover, economists tend to evaluate any negative effects of online bans as unlikely: first, unlike RPM, such restrictions do not seem likely to facilitate collusion.[457] Whereas RPM makes prices easier observable for cartel members[458], prohibiting internet sales is likely to have the opposite effect: prices on online sales are, as a general matter, easier to observe than offline prices. So, prohibiting them will make prices more and not less difficult to observe.[459] Second, it seems unlikely that total internet bans negatively affect competition between manufacturers (inter-brand competition).[460] Suppose one manufacturer restricts the availability of their products online. In that case, consumers are likely to buy from other manufacturers who continue to offer their products online, so internet bans are unlikely to have exclusionary effects.[461] Third, it can be possible that an internet ban affects intra-brand com-

---

453 See above from p. 35.
454 See above p. 36.
455 *Kinsella Obe et al.*, European Competition Journal 2009, 227 (238–139).
456 *Buettner et al.*, European Competition Journal 2009, 613 (619).
457 *Buettner et al.*, European Competition Journal 2009, 613 (616–617).
458 See above from p. 51.
459 *Iacobucci/Winter*, Antitrust Law Journal 2016, 47 (50–51).
460 Inter-brand competition, however, is given more importance than intra-brand competition, see above pp. 44 and 67.
461 *Iacobucci/Winter*, Antitrust Law Journal 2016, 47 (51).

petition by cementing the market position of a certain (often traditional) type of retailer at the expense of modern forms of distribution. This, however, would only apply where the restraint is adopted upon pressure from retailers because the manufacturer generally does not have an interest in limiting the supply of their products.[462] Buettner et al. argue that manufacturers will only restrict internet sales if and so far as the negative effects (free-riding) outweigh the positive effects of online distribution.[463] The image free-riding defence applies, in principle, also to restraints on internet sales and seems to indeed be what motivates many manufacturers. Restrictions on internet sales are generally held to be motivated by the desire to increase competition in dimensions other than price, in particular the product's image, consumer information and advice.[464] The rationale here is that there is a risk that some consumers are attracted by the product's image, which is created, inter alia, through the retail environment, but buy the product cheaper online.[465] Retailers will thus be unable to harvest all the fruits of their investment in the retail store, making them invest less.[466] The manufacturer's intentions, it is argued, are thus generally not anti-competitive.

Nevertheless, this does not mean that restrictions on the use of the internet as a sales channel are necessarily welfare-enhancing: consumers' and manufacturers' interests are not always aligned, and some consumers are better off with and other consumers without the distribution restrictions.[467] However, economists tend to still argue for a relatively 'laissez-faire' approach as it is unclear in which cases antitrust intervention against restrictions on internet sales would raise welfare.[468] It is generally perceived that it is not competition law's task to intervene merely because a certain distribution system is not the one that most increases welfare.[469] Moreover, it is argued that the internet is not sufficiently distinct from other sales channels to justify the special treatment it receives under EU law.[470] Vergé best expresses this critique:

"The main question is not whether Internet sales can be prohibited or not, but simply whether we believe that the nature of the product justify that suppliers may be allowed to

[462] *Iacobucci/Winter*, Antitrust Law Journal 2016, 47 (51).

[463] *Buettner et al.*, European Competition Journal 2009, 613 (615).

[464] *Iacobucci/Winter*, Antitrust Law Journal 2016, 47 (54).

[465] *Buettner et al.*, European Competition Journal 2009, 613 (615).

[466] *Buettner et al.*, European Competition Journal 2009, 613 (615).

[467] *Buettner et al.*, European Competition Journal 2009, 613 (615); *Monti*, World Competition 2013, 489 (506); *Verouden*, in: Issues in Competition Law and Policy, 1813 (1819–1820).

[468] *Buettner et al.*, European Competition Journal 2009, 613 (617); *Iacobucci/Winter*, Antitrust Law Journal 2016, 47 (54–55).

[469] *Buettner et al.*, European Competition Journal 2009, 613 (616); *Monti*, World Competition 2013, 489 (506–507); see also *Vogel*, JECLAP 2013, 277 (283) speaking of a 'bias in favour of internet sales'.

[470] *Caffarra*, in: Vertical Restraints, 55 (57); *Vergé*, in: Vertical Restraints, 31 (47).

prevent some retailers – pure-internet players but also 'click-and-mortar' stores, and even discount brick and mortar stores – from reselling the product."[471]

If it is accepted that certain products require selective distribution and qualitative criteria, e.g., excluding discount stores, there is no reason why no product could ever justify the exclusion of internet sales altogether. EU law is thus perceived to favour a particular distribution channel without any economic justification.[472]

Hence, the strict approach under EU law towards total online bans from an economic perspective is generally perceived as too severe.[473]

b) Platform bans

Whereas total internet bans are treated as hardcore restrictions, EU law takes a more lenient approach towards platform bans.[474] They can be exempted under the VBER (no hardcore restriction) and, as established in Coty, fall under the Metro exception (relevant for undertakings with market shares exceeding 30 %).

Some voices argue that online bans should not be treated too leniently. First, it is emphasized that the risk of image deterioration through sales on online platforms is only small.[475] Manufacturers could use minimum qualitative standards rather than blanket bans, and some platforms offer significant quality in presentation and service.[476] Second, platforms are considered a valuable tool of market entry for small and medium-sized enterprises: selling on third-party platforms requires only little upfront investments, and consumers can easily find offers on platforms through search engines.[477] Limiting distribution through online platforms thus risks favouring larger and established retailers and reducing price competition.[478] Platforms are also an important way for smaller and less established retailers to reach consumers since consumers often already have an account with those platforms and trust them.[479] On the other hand, proponents of allowing platform bans argue that even if platforms can facilitate entry and platform bans thus foreclose markets; this would only affect less efficient firms.[480]

---

[471] *Vergé*, in: Vertical Restraints, 31 (47).

[472] *Caffarra*, in: Vertical Restraints, 55 (77); *Vergé*, in: Vertical Restraints, 31 (47–49); *Vogel*, JECLAP 2013, 277 (281).

[473] *Buccirossi*, Vertical Restraints for Online Sales, p. 32; *Vogel*, JECLAP 2013, 277 (281); *Waelbroeck/Davies*, JECLAP 2018, 431 (438).

[474] See above from p. 36.

[475] Bundeskartellamt, 26/08/2015, B2–98/11 ASICS (Fallbericht), p. 11.

[476] *Brömmelmeyer*, NZKart 2018, 62 (66–67); *Janal*, EuZW 2017, 844 (848); *Schweda/Rudowicz*, WRP 2013, 590 (593–594); *Bundeskartellamt*, Wettbewerbsbeschränkungen im Internetvertrieb, p. 5.

[477] *Ezrachi*, World Competition 2017, 47 (49–50); *Janal*, EuZW 2017, 844 (845); *Schweda/Rudowicz*, WRP 2013, 590 (592).

[478] *Ezrachi*, World Competition 2017, 47 (61); Bundeskartellamt, 27/06/2014, B3–137/12 Adidas (Fallbericht), p. 4.

[479] Bundeskartellamt, 27/06/2014, B3–137/12 Adidas (Fallbericht), pp. 4–5.

[480] *Waelbroeck/Davies*, JECLAP 2018, 431 (440).

Because the manufacturer is typically not in a direct contractual relationship with the platform through which their retailer sells the products, they cannot ensure that the platform complies with qualitative criteria.[481] Platforms, it is argued, host a wide range of retailers selling various kinds of products, including lower-quality and even counterfeit goods.[482] This can put the manufacturer's (and their products') image at risk.[483] As regards quality standards for platforms, it is argued that retailers, because of their dependence on large platforms, would not be able to negotiate that the latter comply with the requirements.[484]

As often, the debate circles around the possible efficiencies rather than how to establish a restriction of competition. If one focuses too much on the potential efficiencies, one can easily conclude that platform bans are less efficient than total online bans. After all, free-riding of online shops can still occur, and image problems do not generally appear as an issue for all platforms. However, fewer efficiencies do not necessarily imply a restriction of competition in the first place or a more severe restriction.

Overall, the prevailing economic view on platform bans is that they should, in principle, be permissible. Considering that the same is true for the even more restrictive total online bans described above, this does not come as a surprise. If already complete internet bans can be efficient, this applies a fortiori to platform bans since they are less restrictive. Like total internet bans, they can protect the products' image from free-riding retailers and ensure that consumers are adequately advised.

c) Other internet sales restrictions

In principle, the above-made argumentum a fortiori also applies to other restrictions on online sales. If total bans can be efficient, this must also be true for less severe restraints, such as restrictions on price comparison websites, search engines or advertising. While potential efficiencies of such restraints appear less likely, the same is true for anti-competitive effects. Moreover, distinctions between the effects of different types of online bans seem artificial.[485] For example, price comparison websites (bans are typically not permissible)[486] and online marketplaces (bans are typically permissible)[487] differ from the outset but share many characteristics at closer sight. Some price comparison websites allow for direct

---

[481] *Waelbroeck/Davies*, JECLAP 2018, 431 (440).

[482] *Waelbroeck/Davies*, JECLAP 2018, 431 (441).

[483] *Waelbroeck/Davies*, JECLAP 2018, 431 (441).

[484] *Waelbroeck/Davies*, JECLAP 2018, 431 (441). It should be noted that this argument is rather circular: if a certain platform does not fulfill the qualitative standards, the manufacturer would then indeed be able to exclude it (or terminate its relationship with the retailer selling on the platform).

[485] *Mullan/Timan*, Competition Law & Policy Debate 2017, 11 (22–23).

[486] See above p. 38.

[487] See above p. 36.

intermediation of transactions (rather than just serving as a link to the retailer's website).[488] At the same time, consumers can use marketplaces to inform themselves about product prices and attributes.

As with most other internet restrictions, from a purely economic perspective, there is little reason to prevent restrictions on the use of price comparison websites. Again, the argumentum a fortiori applies: if total online bans from an economic perspective should already be, in principle, permissible (at least for companies with small market shares), restrictions with similar goals but which fall short of total bans should similarly not constitute hardcore restrictions. The standard argument applies: a manufacturer will only impose (or agree to) restrictions of intra-brand competition if they benefit from it, allowing the conclusion that such restrictions are normally efficient or at least neutral.[489] As with other restraints, bans on price comparison tools can protect a specific image and induce retailer services. However, price comparison restrictions seem somewhat less important in that regard: a manufacturer's image is not likely to be significantly impaired when a product is visible on a price comparison website if, after visiting the comparison website, the consumer still has to go through the retailer's website (where the manufacturer can easily impose qualitative requirements).[490] While free-riding concerns also appear less important than for some other restrictions, price comparison websites can intensify price competition among retailers and thus reduce their ability to invest in better services.[491] When it comes to anti-competitive effects, there appears to be no particular reason to consider price comparison bans as more dangerous than platform bans (which are exempted under the VBER).[492] Once more, EU law and economics are not completely aligned.

d) Conclusion

Economic literature argues for a relative laissez-faire approach towards vertical agreements that limit the sale either through online channels in general (total ban) or other online sales restrictions, e.g., third party-platforms bans.[493] Under EU law, only the latter is, in principle, considered permissible (under the VBER

---

[488] However, the Vertical Guidelines in para. 344 emphasize that '[u]nlike online marketplaces, price comparison services typically do not offer sale and purchase functionality, but rather re-direct customers to the online store of the retailer, enabling the initiation of a direct transaction between the customer and the retailer outside the price comparison service.'

[489] *Mullan/Timan*, Competition Law & Policy Debate 2017, 11 (14–15).

[490] *Mullan/Timan*, Competition Law & Policy Debate 2017, 11 (15).

[491] See *European Commission*, E-Commerce Sector Inquiry (Commission Staff Working Document), para. 537.

[492] *Mullan/Timan*, Competition Law & Policy Debate 2017, 11.

[493] *Winter/Iacobucci*, in: Handbook International Antitrust Economics, 351 (367) arguing that '[R]estrictions to limit sales through the Internet are not part of a scheme to limit competition among manufacturers and should not be regulated.'

and the Metro case law). Total internet bans, on the other hand, are presumed to be illegal. Law and economic theory, therefore, do not fully align.

5. Allowing the exclusion of pure online retailers

As with most aspects of the EU law on vertical agreements that show a somewhat more lenient approach, economists generally applaud that excluding pure online retailers from a selective distribution system is permissible.[494] From an economic viewpoint, this is a legitimate business practice and can solve free-riding problems that are considered particularly prevalent between pure online retailers and their brick and mortar counterparts.[495] However, many economists argue for a more lenient approach that would also permit the exclusion of hybrid retailers. They see no economic justification for allowing pure online retailers to be excluded while permitting hybrid retailers, who operate both physical stores and online platforms, to sell online. These hybrid retailers could minimise their offline activities, leading to similar free-riding issues.[496] Therefore, while economists approve of excluding pure online retailers, they challenge the distinction between pure and hybrid retailers and advocate for allowing all internet sales restrictions.

6. Dual pricing

Dual pricing under the previous Vertical Guidelines was considered a hardcore restriction and thus not exempted.[497] The rationale was that dual pricing could effectively disincentivize retailers from using the internet as a sales channel.[498] It gives the manufacturer control over their retailers' online vs offline sales distribution. Theoretically, the manufacturer could set the price for online sales so high that retailers do not sell online at all. However, as with internet bans as such, economic theory suggests that allowing the manufacturer to control the proportion of internet sales is welcomed: they will choose the offline/online mix that is the most efficient.[499] Lower wholesale prices for goods sold offline vs those sold offline are a way for the manufacturer to reward the retailer for specific (offline) sales efforts.[500] The updated Vertical Guidelines now treat dual pricing more leniently, as long as it does not significantly hinder online sales.[501] Economists generally support this revised approach, as it acknowledges the manufacturer's legitimate interest in managing the proportion of online and offline sales.[502]

---

494 *Buettner et al.*, European Competition Journal 2009, 201 (224).
495 *Buettner et al.*, European Competition Journal 2009, 201 (224).
496 *Buettner et al.*, European Competition Journal 2009, 613 (224).
497 See above p. 38.
498 *Bundeskartellamt*, Vertical Restraints in the Internet Economy, pp. 20–21.
499 *Caffarra*, in: Vertical Restraints, 55 (69).
500 *Caffarra*, in: Vertical Restraints, 55 (68).
501 Vertical Guidelines, para. 209.
502 *de la Mano et al.*, Competition Law & Policy Debate 2022, 12 (17).

7. Resale price maintenance

RPM can facilitate upstream collusion among manufacturers or downstream collusion among retailers.[503] Moreover, RPM is more likely than some other vertical agreements to soften competition between retailers and/or manufacturers.[504] Nevertheless, even maximum RPM is not necessarily considered significantly more harmful than other vertical agreements. When it comes to dampening competition, for example, risks appear higher for restraints that delegate pricing power to distributors (such as exclusive distribution) compared to RPM.[505] It is also undisputed that RPM can have positive effects; notably, the free-riding argument[506] was initially developed for this type of restraint.[507] Besides addressing free-riding, RPM can also serve as quality certification where consumers associate high quality with a high price, and it can give high-quality retailers an incentive to carry the product.[508] Further, from an economic perspective, the price is an important attribute of a product that the manufacturer should, at least to some extent, be able to control.[509] The price conveys important information.[510] For example, it can signal a product's quality or image.[511] Therefore, allowing even minimum RPM in certain cases can have beneficial economic effects.[512] Nevertheless, the generally tougher stand of EU law on price restraints compared to non-price restraints as such seems to be justified.[513] This is because the manufacturer's goals can often be achieved with other restraints that do not always carry the same risks for competition. For example, considering the goal of signalling quality through a high price, the manufacturer, through a qualitative selective distribution system, can ensure that only high-price retailers sell the product. They can also set a high wholesale price herself, making (very) low prices improbable. Also, from an evolutionary economics perspective, a rather strict approach towards RPM appears reasonable. Price restraints reduce incentives for retailers to innovate as they will not be able to fully benefit from improved services and techniques through lowering prices and increasing their share of sales.[514]

[503] See above from p. 51.

[504] *Buccirossi*, Vertical Restraints for Online Sales, p. 7.

[505] *Rey/Caballero-Sanz*, Economic Analysis of Vertical Restraints, p. 30.

[506] See above p. 45.

[507] *Akhtar*, EuCML 2018, 5 (7); *Geradin et al.*, EU Competition Law and Economics, para. 8.19; *Rey/Caballero-Sanz*, Economic Analysis of Vertical Restraints, p. 28.

[508] *Geradin et al.*, EU Competition Law and Economics, para. 8.19; *Korn*, ZEuP 2020, 618 (622).

[509] *Inderst/Maier-Rigaud*, CPI 2015.

[510] *Völckner*, Journal of the Academy of Marketing Science 2008, 359.

[511] *Völckner/Hofmann*, Marketing Letters 2007, 181.

[512] *Inderst/Maier-Rigaud*, CPI 2015; *Orbach*, Antitrust Bulletin 2010, 277.

[513] *Vergé*, in: Vertical Restraints, 31 (38).

[514] *Vezzoso*, Vertikale Beschränkungen, p. 218.

Nevertheless, the relatively rigid approach under EU law towards minimum and fixed RPM may, to some extent, still conflict with economic theory.[515] While generally, a stricter approach towards price versus non-price restraints seems economically justified; many economists advocate for a more flexible approach than the one currently pursued under EU law.[516] Suggestions for reform include incorporating RPM in the De Minimis Notice, thus effectively allowing it for companies with a market share of each below 15 %, or requiring the competition authority to present a plausible theory of harm in each individual case.[517] Going even further, de la Mano et al. suggest entirely removing RPM from the list of hardcore restrictions.[518]

8. Conclusion: the EU's approach to vertical agreements cannot entirely be explained by economic considerations

A purely economic perspective cannot fully explain the treatment of vertical agreements under EU competition law. This is particularly evident with regard to the following:

[1] The rather strict prohibition of RPM, even for undertakings with very small market shares;
[2] the distinction between active and passive sales;
[3] the strict approach towards restrictions on online sales that prohibits total online bans and bans on an entire online advertising channels (such as price comparison websites);
[4] the formal distinction between qualitative and quantitative criteria in selective distribution systems under the Metro case law.

Economic theory cannot entirely explain the EU rules on vertical agreements. Indeed, some economists argue that the EU is over-enforcing antitrust law in the context of vertical agreements and that the concept of hardcore restrictions should be abandoned altogether.[519] Economic theory argues for a more case-by-case approach rather than rigidly focusing on the type or category of agreement in question.[520]

---

[515] *Lugard*, in: Vertical Restraints, 193; *Vergé*, in: Vertical Restraints, 31 (40).

[516] *Klein*, in: Handbook International Antitrust Economics, 277; *de la Mano et al.*, Competition Law & Policy Debate 2022, 12 (13); *de la Mano/Jones*, in: Methods and Models, 167 (188).

[517] *Korn*, ZEuP 2020, 618 (638–641).

[518] *de la Mano et al.*, Competition Law & Policy Debate 2022, 12 (14).

[519] *de la Mano et al.*, Competition Law & Policy Debate 2022, 12 (13, 20).

[520] *de la Mano/Jones*, in: Methods and Models, 167 (191).

VII. The problem of a case-by-case analysis

While the integration of economic tools into competition law can enhance decision-making, it also faces a fundamental problem: it risks becoming excessively occupied with developing sophisticated models to predict outcomes for very specific cases. This can lead to lengthy and costly proceedings, which, even in an ideal world, may result in correct individual decisions at the expense of effective and timely enforcement of the law.[521] While it may be possible to arrive at the perfect economic result in each case in a world of unlimited time and resources, in reality, requiring a lengthy individual assessment in each case is not only impractical but also violates the spirit of competition law. Restoring competition under such an approach risks coming too late. Moreover, courts could be overwhelmed,[522] and firms face legal uncertainty in deciding which strategies they can adopt without violating competition law.[523] Where every case has to be assessed individually and new models developed for it, this could indicate that the existing models suffer from 'regression overfitting'. This term describes a model that is too precise (too many parameters relative to the amount of data) and thus cannot be generalized and used to predict values that have not yet been observed.[524] As long as there are no more general models available towards vertical agreements which can apply across different scenarios, there are important limits to the integration of economic theory into the application of the law. The answer that economists give to vertical agreements, i.e., that they need to be assessed on a case-by-case basis, is, therefore, unsatisfactory at best.[525]

However, even recognizing that a pure case-by-case approach is little feasible, the question remains on which criteria a categorization shall be based. In the European Union, this categorization is two-layered: first, the most relevant criterion is the companies' market shares. This corresponds well with economic theory, which identifies market power as the most important element in the competition analysis (at least for most cases).[526] Second, EU law distinguishes

---

[521] *Christiansen/Kerber*, Journal of Competition Law & Economics 2006, 215; *Overstreet*, RPM: Economic Theories and Empirical Evidence, pp. 171–175; *Podszun*, EuCML 2018, 57 (64–65); *Rey/Caballero-Sanz*, Economic Analysis of Vertical Restraints, p. 41; *Stucke*, U.C. Davis Law Review 2008, 1375 (1460–1466).

[522] It needs to be kept in mind that ordinary courts in all EU Member States are competent for questions of EU competition law, in the case of private enforcement even without the involvement of a competition authority.

[523] *Podszun*, EuCML 2018, 57 (65); for a detailed analysis of the problems that the 'more economic approach' poses to the rule of law and legal certainty, see *Dreher/Adam*, ZWeR 2006, 259; *Wardhaugh*, Competition Law Review 2016, 215 (221–224); *Wardhaugh*, Competition, Effects and Predictability.

[524] *Backhaus*, Multivariate Analysemethoden, pp. 92–93.

[525] See *Hovenkamp*, Federal Antitrust Policy, p. 658 arguing that despite high costs of a rule of reason standard, 'the present state of knowledge seems to permit no alternative.'

[526] However, the relevance of market share as an indicator of market power, is disputed. See in this regard below p. 250.

between the types of agreements (e.g., RPM, selective distribution, internet bans etc.). Depending on the type of agreement, more or less strict standards apply. This treatment is difficult to reconcile with economics. Different types of agreements are seen as largely interchangeable from an economic perspective.[527] While recognizing that some level of formalization is necessary, the rigid classification of certain types of agreements remains difficult to justify from an economic standpoint.[528]

§ 3 A comparative perspective: vertical agreements under US law

This section examines the differences in how vertical agreements are assessed under US and EU competition law. This comparative part aims to help draw conclusions from the results of the previous section. The following three theses will be tested: (1) US antitrust law on vertical agreements differs significantly from the European approach. (2) The US approach can be explained by the sole economic goal of consumer welfare. (3) If this is the case, this indicates that US and EU law may not fully pursue identical goals, leading to the question of which other goals may potentially support the EU's treatment of vertical agreements.

I. Introduction

Like in the European Union, antitrust law in the US is based on a few general clauses, the most important being Section 1 Sherman Act, stating that "every contract, combination in the form of trust or otherwise, or conspiracy, in restraint of trade or commerce [...] is declared to be illegal." This provision has been held to apply not only to horizontal but also to vertical restrictions early on. The Supreme Court first judged a classical vertical restraint in the 1911 Dr. Miles case concerning minimum retail price fixing.[529] The Supreme Court recognized the protection of intra-brand competition through US antitrust law by finding the price-fixing agreement illegal because through it, "all room for competition between retailers, who supply the public, is made impossible."[530] Under US law, it must be distinguished between situations that are per se violations of antitrust

---

[527] *Overstreet*, RPM: Economic Theories and Empirical Evidence, pp. 168–170; *Rey/Caballero-Sanz*, Economic Analysis of Vertical Restraints, pp. 21, 41; *Rey/Vergé*, in: Handbook Antitrust Economics, 354 (384); *Secrieru*, Journal of Economic Surveys 2006, 797; *Tirole*, Theory of Industrial Organization, p. 186; *Verouden*, in: Issues in Competition Law and Policy, 1813 (1838); this is also recognized by the Commission, see *European Commission*, Green Paper on Vertical Restraints, para. 87.

[528] See *Rey/Caballero-Sanz*, Economic Analysis of Vertical Restraints, p. 42 who suggest distinguishing between different market scenarios.

[529] US Supreme Court, 03/04/1911, No. 72 Dr. Miles, 220 U.S. 373.

[530] US Supreme Court, 03/04/1911, No. 72 Dr. Miles, 220 U.S. 373, p. 400.

law and those that are subject to a rule of reason analysis.[531] The per se rule prohibits those

> "agreements or practices which, because of their pernicious effect on competition and lack of any redeeming virtue, are conclusively presumed to be unreasonable, and therefore illegal without elaborate inquiry as to the precise harm they have caused or the business excuse for their use."[532]

No further inquiry or evidence beyond the existence of the (per se illegal) practice or agreement is required under the per se rule.[533] In contrast, where the rule of reason applies, the effects of a practice/agreement must be established, and positive and negative effects on competition must be balanced against each other.[534] Over time, the US Supreme Court has moved away from applying per se rules to vertical agreements, increasingly favoring a rule of reason analysis instead.[535]

II. Price restraints

The US Supreme Court's Dr. Miles decision established a strict per se prohibition against minimum RPM, barring any case-by-case assessment or defenses based on specific circumstances.[536] However, this rigid stance was softened by the 1919 Colgate decision, in which the Court ruled that Section 1 of the Sherman Act does not prevent "a private business from announcing in advance the prices at which his good may be resold and refusing to deal with wholesaler and retailers who do not conform to such price."[537] According to the Court, the Sherman Act's requirement of finding a contract, combination or conspiracy is not fulfilled in such cases.[538] Further limitations to the Dr. Miles doctrine emerged in the 1926 U.S. v. General Electric decision, where the Court permitted manufacturers to set resale prices when goods remained their property and were sold on commission by retailers.[539] Moreover, another even more important exception to the Dr. Miles rule was created by Congress with the Miller-Tydings Act[540] in 1937, which allowed state laws to authorize vertical price restraints (so called 'fair trading laws'). The act was repealed only in 1975, putting the per se rule against minimum vertical price fixing back in place.[541] Even vertical maximum fixed prices were

[531] See *Colino*, Vertical Agreements, p. 51.
[532] US Supreme Court, 10/03/1958, No. 59 Northern Pacific, 356 U.S. 1, p. 5.
[533] *Gerber*, Competition Law and Antitrust, p. 99.
[534] *Gerber*, Competition Law and Antitrust, p. 98.
[535] For a brief overview of the history, see *Rooney et al.*, Columbia Business Law Review 2019, 1; *Rey/Vergé*, in: Handbook Antitrust Economics, 354 (355–357).
[536] US Supreme Court, 03/04/1911, No. 72 Dr. Miles, 220 U.S. 373.
[537] US Supreme Court, 02/06/1919, No. 828 Colgate, 250 U.S. 300, p. 301.
[538] US Supreme Court, 02/06/1919, No. 828 Colgate, 250 U.S. 300, p. 307.
[539] US Supreme Court, 23/11/1926, No. 113 General Electric, 272 U.S. 476.
[540] US Ch. 690, tit. VIII, 50 Stat. 693.
[541] *Sullivan/Grimes*, Law of Antitrust, pp. 320–321.

prohibited under a per se rule according to the Albrecht v. Herold ruling.[542] Historically, this strict approach was criticized not on the grounds of efficiency but rather with the opposite claim: vertical agreements would hinder entry by large and more efficient retailers and thus protect small businesses (the typical 'mom and pop store').[543] One of the starkest proponents of RPM was Louis Brandeis[544], who now lends his name to the new progressive antitrust movement in the US.[545] Legislative efforts to allow RPM were thus generally not passed to promote efficiency but to protect small businesses.[546] The breakthrough for vertical agreements, however, a couple of decades later, came with a shift to efficiency with the rise of the Chicago School. While before that, some had argued that vertical agreements should be allowed because they are socially desirable as they allow for some inefficiencies, the argument was now that vertical agreements should be allowed because they enhance efficiency.[547]

With the judgment GTE Sylvania, which will be dealt with in more detail in the context of non-price restraints[548], came a generally more open approach towards restraints of intra-brand competition. The Supreme Court first issued two rulings in the 1980s (Monsanto[549] and Sharp[550]) trying to limit the Dr. Miles approach to a narrower set of circumstances by interpreting restrictively what constitutes a price restraint.[551] Later on, it held in the case State Oil v. Khan from 1997 that for maximum price restraints, the rule of reason applies, overruling the Albrecht v. Herold decision.[552] Maximum price restraints subsequently have been treated as nearly always legal or not been subject to enforcement in the first place.[553] The US Supreme Court's shift toward a more lenient approach to vertical agreements culminated in the 2007 Leegin decision, which overturned Dr. Miles and subjected even RPM to the rule of reason.[554] This ruling was primarily driven by economic considerations, emphasizing the potential positive effects of vertical agreements, e.g., preventing free-riding, providing incentives for investments in brand quality and carrying a larger inventory.[555] As a result, under US

---

[542] US Supreme Court, 04/03/1968, No. 43 Albrecht v. Herald Co., 390 U.S. 145.

[543] *Carstensen*, Antitrust Law Journal 2001, 569 (572).

[544] *Carstensen*, Antitrust Law Journal 2001, 569 (572).

[545] See for the New Brandeis Movement *Khan*, JECLAP 2018, 131; and *Crane*, Antitrust Bulletin 2019, 531.

[546] *Carstensen*, Antitrust Law Journal 2001, 569 (572).

[547] *Carstensen*, Antitrust Law Journal 2001, 569 (572).

[548] See below from p. 87.

[549] US Supreme Court, 20/03/1984, No. 82–914 Monsanto, 465 U.S. 752.

[550] US Supreme Court, 02/05/1988, No. 85–1910 Business Electronics v. Sharp, 485 U.S. 717.

[551] *Sullivan/Grimes*, Law of Antitrust, pp. 321–322.

[552] US Supreme Court, 04/11/1997, No. 96–871 State Oil v. Khan, 522 U.S. 3.

[553] *Sokol*, Antitrust Law Journal 2014, 1003 (1010).

[554] US Supreme Court, 28/06/2007, No. 06–480 Leegin, 551 U.S. 877.

[555] US Supreme Court, 28/06/2007, No. 06–480 Leegin, 551 U.S. 877, pp. 890–892; see *Sullivan/Grimes*, Law of Antitrust, p. 331.

federal antitrust law, the rule of reason applies also to minimum RPM. However, it should be noted, however, that several State antitrust laws continue to treat this restraint as per se unlawful in the US.[556]

III. Non-price restraints

In the 1950s and the beginning of the 1960s, the US DoJ adopted a strict stance on territorial and customer restrictions, treating them as per se illegal and aggressively prosecuted such practices.[557] While the Supreme Court initially appeared more cautious in its White Motor decision[558] (where it considered that it did not know enough about the effects of territorial restrictions to apply a per se rule), in the 1967 Schwinn case[559], it held that all non-price vertical agreements are illegal per se.[560] There was, however, an emphasis on who is the owner of the product, as the judgment states: "If the manufacturer parts with dominion over his product or transfers risk of loss to another, he may not reserve control over its destiny or the conditions of its resale."[561] So where the manufacturer transferred their property rights to the retailer, it could not impose any vertical agreements.[562] In the US v. General Motors case, for example, the US Supreme Court held a clause prohibiting retailers from opening new selling locations to be per se illegal.[563] The case concerned a distribution system which, by today's standards, would be classified as selective distribution: General Motors allowed the sale only through authorized sales outlets, thus prohibiting discount retailers. The Supreme Court did not consider the potentially positive effects on inter-brand competition.[564] Only where the manufacturer retained property, i.e., allowing the retailers only to sell on commission, vertical agreements were subject to a rule of reason analysis.[565] Similar to vertical price restraints, non-price restraints thus faced very strict limits under US antitrust law until the 1970s.

However, shortly after that, the rise of the Chicago School of antitrust began, leading to a sea change in the treatment of vertical agreements. The Supreme Court's GTE Sylvania case[566] was the first landmark judgment that endorsed the potential positive effects of vertical agreements and clearly prioritized inter-

---

[556] For an overview of the different States' approach, see *Lindsay*, The Antitrust Source, 04/2017, Overview of State RPM, available at https://www.dorsey.com/-/media/files/newsresources/publications/2017/apr17_lindsay_chart.pdf?la=en (accessed: 11 March 2025).

[557] *Sullivan/Grimes*, Law of Antitrust, p. 325.

[558] US Supreme Court, 03/03/1963, No. 54 White Motor, 372 U.S. 253.

[559] US Supreme Court, 12/06/1967, No. 25 Schwinn, 388 U.S. 365.

[560] *Sullivan/Grimes*, Law of Antitrust, p. 325.

[561] US Supreme Court, 12/06/1967, No. 25 Schwinn, 388 U.S. 365, p. 379.

[562] *Sullivan/Grimes*, Law of Antitrust, p. 325.

[563] US Supreme Court, 28/04/1966, No. 46 General Motors, 384 U.S. 127.

[564] For a critical analysis of the case, see *Colino*, Vertical Agreements, pp. 77–78.

[565] *Sullivan/Grimes*, Law of Antitrust, p. 325.

[566] US Supreme Court, 23/06/1977, No. 76–15 Sylvania, 433 U.S. 36.

brand over intra-brand competition.[567] The Supreme Court argued that inter-brand competition

"provides a significant check on the exploitation of intra-brand market power because of the ability of consumers to substitute a different brand of the same product."[568]

Since Sylvania, all non-price vertical agreements are subject to a rule of reason analysis.[569] This treatment has been confirmed, among others, in the case Sharp Electronics in 1988.[570] The burden of proof that a vertical restraint is unreasonable is on the person alleging the antitrust violation. As inter-brand competition is the primary concern of US antitrust law after the Sylvania ruling, the mere showing of an adverse effect on intra-brand competition is not enough to shift the burden of proof to the alleged infringer.[571] Under US law, at least non-price vertical agreements are now generally considered lawful except in cases of market power of the participating firms.[572] Sagers even argues that vertical agreements in the US "have become more or less per se legal as a practical matter."[573] In the Amex case, the lenient approach towards vertical agreements under US law has most recently been reconfirmed and refined by the US Supreme Court.[574] The case concerned non-steering provisions by the credit card company American Express ('Amex') (Visa and Mastercard used similar provisions, but these companies had settled the case[575]). Amex prohibited merchants from steering consumers to use a non-Amex credit card, inter alia, by telling them the merchant fees related to the transaction or offering discounts or incentives for a particular type of payment.[576] The Supreme Court applied the rule of reason and confirmed the lower courts' burden-shifting framework: first, the plaintiff must prove that "the challenged restraint has a substantial anticompetitive effect that harms consumers […]."[577] If he carries that burden, the burden then shifts to the defendant "to

---

[567] See US Supreme Court, 23/06/1977, No. 76–15 Sylvania, 433 U.S. 36, pp. 54–55; *Rooney et al.*, Columbia Business Law Review 2019, 1 (10–11); *Sullivan/Grimes*, Law of Antitrust, p. 326.

[568] US Supreme Court, 23/06/1977, No. 76–15 Sylvania, 433 U.S. 36 footnote 19.

[569] *Sullivan/Grimes*, Law of Antitrust, p. 327.

[570] US Supreme Court, 02/05/1988, No. 85–1910 Business Electronics v. Sharp, 485 U.S. 717.

[571] US 9th Circuit Court, 29/09/1982, No. 79–4131 Continental v. GTE Sylvania, 694 F.2d 1132; *Sullivan/Grimes*, Law of Antitrust, p. 346.

[572] *Colino*, Vertical Agreements, p. 81.

[573] *Sagers*, Antitrust 2019, 103 (104).

[574] US Supreme Court, 25/06/2018, No. 16–1454 Amex, 585 U.S. __ (2018); for a critical discussion of the judgment, see *Hovenkamp*, Columbia Business Law Review 2019, 35.

[575] *US DoJ*, 04/10/2010, Press Release of 04/10/2010, Justice Department Sues American Express, Mastercard and Visa to Eliminate Rules Restricting Price Competition, available at https://www.justice.gov/opa/pr/justice-department-sues-american-express-mastercard-and-visa-eliminate-rules-restricting (accessed: 11 March 2025).

[576] US Supreme Court, 25/06/2018, No. 16–1454 Amex.

[577] US Supreme Court, 25/06/2018, No. 16–1454 Amex, p. 9.

show a procompetitive rationale for the restraint". If he succeeds in showing this, the burden "shifts back to the plaintiff to demonstrate that the procompetitive efficiencies could be reasonably achieved through less anticompetitive means."[578] In Amex, in the Supreme Court's view, the plaintiff did not meet the initial burden of proof. It neither showed direct (e.g., reduced output or higher prices) nor indirect evidence (proof of market power "plus some evidence that the challenged restraint harms competition") of anticompetitive effect.[579] Reiterating that the promotion of inter-brand competition is the primary purpose of antitrust law, the Court did not find anticompetitive effects but, even though the practices had increased merchant fees, held that "Amex's business model has spurred robust inter-brand competition and has increased the quality and quantity of credit-card transactions."[580] It argued that the effects could not be evaluated based only on the side of the merchants but needed to take into account also the effects on consumers using Amex credit cards.[581] In a footnote, the Court expressed the opinion that vertical agreements are generally benign and that a condemnation always requires finding market power:

> "Vertical restraints often pose no risk to competition unless the entity imposing them has market power, which cannot be evaluated unless the Court first defines the relevant market."[582]

This leads to a very high initial burden of proof for the plaintiff.[583]

The Supreme Court did not consider the impact of Amex's practices on consumer decision-making. While Amex charges higher merchant fees than competitors, it also provides cardholders with benefits like rewards. Many merchants accept Amex despite the fees because Amex cardholders tend to be wealthier and higher-spending.[584] Without Amex's anti-steering provisions, merchants could have offered discounts or other incentives to encourage consumers to use alternative payment methods.[585] Thus, consumers would have been able to make an informed choice between the benefits of using the Amex card (e.g., rewards) and whatever benefits the merchants would have offered them for using another card. Despite higher prices, the Supreme Court accepted the practice, mainly because output (in terms of transactions) increased at the same time. However, critics

578 US Supreme Court, 25/06/2018, No. 16–1454 Amex, pp. 9–10.

579 US Supreme Court, 25/06/2018, No. 16–1454 Amex, p. 10.

580 US Supreme Court, 25/06/2018, No. 16–1454 Amex, p. 20.

581 US Supreme Court, 25/06/2018, No. 16–1454 Amex, pp. 19–20.

582 US Supreme Court, 25/06/2018, No. 16–1454 Amex, p. 11, footnote 7.

583 See Justice Breyer's dissent, arguing that 'because the relevant question is a comparison between reality and a hypothetical state of affairs, to require actual proof of reduced output is often to require the impossible-tantamount to saying that the Sherman Act does not apply at all.' US Supreme Court, 25/06/2018, No. 16–1454 Amex, p. 20.

584 See the explanation in Justice Breyer's dissent, US Supreme Court, 25/06/2018, No. 16–1454 Amex, p. 23.

585 See Breyer's dissent, US Supreme Court, 25/06/2018, No. 16–1454 Amex, p. 23.

argue that the decision overemphasized output growth and ignored the role of informed consumer choice. If consumers had known the true costs of using an Amex card, they might have opted for other payment methods, making output an unreliable measure of welfare in this case.[586] Therefore, the fact that they chose Amex without knowing the actual costs is a poor indicator of welfare.

Given the high threshold for intervention, it is unsurprising that vertical agreements are rarely enforced in the US.[587] Unlike EU law, US antitrust law does not differentiate between specific categories of non-price restraints. Instead, all vertical agreements are assessed under a rule of reason analysis on a case-by-case basis. As a result, distinctions such as active versus passive sales do not exist[588], and selective distribution is not treated as a separate category under US competition law[589].

IV. Online distribution restraints

Unlike in the EU, there is little debate around vertical[590] online distribution restraints as a distinct antitrust issue. In its contribution to the OECD Competition Committee's 'Round Table on Vertical Restraints for Online Sales', the US delegation stressed that "the extent of online sales in a market does not, by itself, add probative value" to the competitive analysis.[591] It devotes an entire section to explaining that there is no "basis for treating vertical restraints differently depending on the presence or extent of online sales in the market."[592] In particular, it argues that free-riding can occur in both directions (offline-online and online-offline)[593] and that the competitive analysis will be similar[594]. As a result, the competitive analysis for online sales restrictions is generally treated the same as for brick and mortar sales. Both are assessed under the rule of reason, and such restrictions are typically deemed permissible in most cases.

---

586 *Newman*, Iowa Law Review 2022, 563 (608–612).

587 *Sagers*, Antitrust 2019, 103 (104).

588 *OECD*, Roundtable on Vertical Restraints for Online Sales – Note by the United States, para. 36.

589 *Witt*, European Competition Journal 2016, 435 (442).

590 The FTC has, however, condemned horizontal online advertising restrictions, see Federal Trade Commission, 07/11/2018, No. 9372 1–800 Contacts.

591 *OECD*, Roundtable on Vertical Restraints for Online Sales – Note by the United States, para. 3.

592 *OECD*, Roundtable on Vertical Restraints for Online Sales – Note by the United States, para. 28.

593 *OECD*, Roundtable on Vertical Restraints for Online Sales – Note by the United States, para. 29.

594 *OECD*, Roundtable on Vertical Restraints for Online Sales – Note by the United States, para. 31.

V. Main differences between the regimes

Vertical agreements are treated very differently in the US and the EU. This concerns first the technical structure of the law and its application. In the US, all vertical agreements are assessed under a similar rule of reason on a case-by-case basis, with the primary focus being market power. Formally, there is not even a distinction between price and non-price restraints, although the former are generally still considered more likely to be harmful. Additionally, there is no specific distinction made between types of vertical agreements, such as selective distribution or online sales limitations.

In contrast, the EU adopts a more categorical approach. The VBER outlines several hardcore restrictions to which the exemption of the Regulation does not apply. Such hardcore restrictions, while not automatically illegal, are difficult to justify in practice.[595] Regarding the substance of the law, EU competition law is much stricter on vertical agreements than its US counterpart.[596] This is particularly apparent for restrictions on online sales. Total online sales bans, for example, are typically prohibited in the EU, while such restrictions are generally permissible under US antitrust law. This difference is also evident in the treatment of price restraints, which are treated strictly in the EU but are usually allowed in the US under the rule of reason.

VI. Different rules due to different goals?

US law on vertical agreements, in its current form, is grounded solely on the goal of promoting economic efficiency.[597] This economic focus has been unequivocally endorsed by the US Supreme Court in the Sylvania ruling, in which the Court argued that any deviation from the rule of reason would require "demonstrable economic effects".[598] This becomes even more vivid when looking at the historical development of the law: the per se illegality of price restraints in Dr. Miles was not based on economic criteria but on property rights arguments and the retailers' freedom.[599] The later case law that has subjected vertical agreements to a rule of reason analysis (and endorsed their efficiency-enhancing effects) often makes explicit references to scholars of the Chicago school, such as Bork and Posner,

---

[595] See above from p. 21, in particular p. 30.

[596] *de la Mano/Jones*, in: Methods and Models, 167 (195–196); *Sagers*, Antitrust 2019, 103 (104).

[597] *Colino*, Vertical Agreements, p. 49; *de la Mano/Jones*, in: Methods and Models, 167 (195) arguing that the Sherman Act is a 'consumer welfare prescription'.

[598] US Supreme Court, 23/06/1977, No. 76-15 Sylvania, 433 U.S. 36, p. 59; *Colino*, Vertical Agreements, p. 49.

[599] US Supreme Court, 03/04/1911, No. 72 Dr. Miles, 220 U.S. 373, p. 404; *Colino*, Vertical Agreements, p. 52.

who argue that economic efficiency or 'consumer welfare' is the exclusive goal of antitrust law[600].[601]

Although there is some critique that antitrust law in the United States is underenforced, particularly concerning mergers and abuse of dominance[602], this critique is rarely directed at the treatment of vertical agreements[603]. It appears that in this area, the law as it is applied aligns with its goal of promoting economic efficiency. Posner, in a 1981 article, even argued for an even more lenient approach to vertical agreements, suggesting per se legality.[604] However, it is now generally accepted that vertical agreements can have welfare-detrimental effects, at least when market power is involved. The US approach, which is relatively lenient but still allows for condemnation of vertical agreements in extreme cases, appears to align well with economic theory.

The EU approach to vertical agreements is undeniably stricter than the US approach, especially concerning RPM, selective distribution, and restrictions on internet sales. However, unlike the United States, EU law has never embraced economic efficiency as its sole objective.[605] This raises the question: what other goal of European competition law may drive the differences between the EU's treatment of vertical agreements and the American approach, as well as economic theory?[606] This question will be explored in the next Chapter.

§ 4 Conclusion

[1] The treatment of vertical agreements under EU competition law remains relatively categorical, despite significant changes, particularly in the 1990s. The focus of the assessment is, to some extent, still the type of agreement rather than the effects on competition.

[2] This approach does not fully align with economic theory which considers that different vertical agreement types are often interchangeable. Economic theory lends support for a more lenient and more case-by-case approach towards

---

[600] See *Bork*, Antitrust Paradox; *Posner*, Antitrust Law.

[601] The Supreme Court in Sylvania, for example, extensively cites Posner and Bork, see US Supreme Court, 23/06/1977, No. 76–15 Sylvania, 433 U.S. 36.

[602] *Baker et al.*, Yale Law Journal 2018, 1916; *Lancieri et al.*, SSRN 2022, pp. 5–7.

[603] Note, however, that the Utah Statement (a document laying out some of the reform proposals made by the so-called neo brandeisians) does emphasize that 'Vertical coercion, vertical restraints, and vertical mergers should enjoy no presumption of benefit to the public' *Wu*, OneZero, 19/11/2019, The Utah Statement: Reviving Antimonopoly Traditions for the Era of Big Tech, available at https://onezero.medium.com/the-utah-statement-reviving-antimonopoly-traditions-for-the-era-of-big-tech-e6be198012d7.

[604] *Posner*, University of Chicago Law Review 1981, 6.

[605] See *Stylianou/Iacovides*, Legal Studies 2022, 620.

[606] This question is also raised by *Sagers*, Antitrust 2019, 103 (104).

vertical agreements as, in many cases, they are considered efficiency-enhancing or at least neutral.

[3] From an economic perspective, EU law seems overly strict. In particular, the treatment of hardcore restrictions as (typically) restrictions by object is criticised. This is, on the one hand, because it does not fully take into account the market situations and even the market shares of the companies and, on the other hand, because it typically considers that agreements that bring less or no efficiencies, therefore, must restrict competition.

[4] EU law's treatment of vertical agreements still partly resembles an approach that holds all vertical agreements restrictive of competition except where they are objectively justified.

[5] There is no fully coherent framework to assess when a vertical agreement restricts competition in the first place. The analysis, to some extent, conflates restriction and efficiency and finds agreements restrictive of competition for the mere fact that they bring fewer efficiencies than other agreements, even where there are, at the same time, lower risks of restrictions.

[6] There are no economic reasons to treat online sales differently from other sales channels. In the context of online sales restrictions, the EU approach is particularly categorical: a total ban on online sales is prohibited, irrespective of the companies' market shares, the nature of the product and other market conditions. This cannot entirely be justified based on economic reasoning.

[7] This becomes even more apparent when comparing the rules with their US counterpart. In the US, based on a pursuit of solely economic goals, all vertical agreements are assessed case-by-case. Regarding online sales restrictions, they are not treated as a distinct category under US antitrust law and are typically considered benign.

Chapter 2

A different explanation for the EU's stance on vertical agreements: consumer autonomy?

The previous Chapter has shown that the treatment of vertical agreements under EU competition does not fully align with economic theory.

This Chapter explores whether consumer autonomy, as a normative objective, may offer an alternative pathway for understanding and potentially justifying the treatment of vertical agreements under EU competition aw. For this purpose, the Chapter will first show that consumer autonomy, besides other arguments, may be seen as an argumentative force in the case law and decisional practice (§ 1). It will then argue that consumer autonomy may, in principle, be considered a component of the broader normative goals of EU competition law (§ 2). The chapter concludes with a summary of its findings (§ 3). Importantly, this chapter is limited to examining whether consumer autonomy can plausibly play a role within competition law more generally. It does not seek to determine whether this justifies the current approach to online sales restrictions – a question that will be addressed in Chapter 3.

§ 1 Consumer autonomy as an argumentative force behind the EU's approach to vertical agreements

While economic theory generally supports a more permissive stance on vertical agreements, EU law follows a stricter approach. The fact that a manufacturer may have a legitimate interest in vertical agreements does not automatically mean that their interests prevail over other interests.[1] In its 1997 Green Paper on Vertical Restraints, the Commission emphasized: "It is clear that economic theory cannot be the only factor in the design of policy."[2] This section will explore which other rationales and goals can plausibly explain and/or justify the EU's relatively strict approach to vertical agreements. It will first analyse the role that internal market and industrial policy arguments play (I.), then explore the role of arguments based on property rights (II.) and retailers' freedom of action (III.)

---

[1] *Franck*, WuW 2010, 772 (777).

[2] *European Commission*, Green Paper on Vertical Restraints, para. 13.

and finally discuss consumer autonomy as an argumentative force that shaped the European rules on vertical agreements (IV.).

I. Internal market and industrial policy: promoting growth in e-commerce

In the EU, competition law does not operate in isolation but must be understood within the broader framework of EU law and the overarching objectives of the European Union. One distinctive feature compared to other jurisdictions is its close connection to the EU's goal of establishing and maintaining an internal market: market partitioning through private restraints to re-establish barriers to the internal market must be avoided.[3] The objective of market integration particularly guided the Commission before its shift to a more economic approach in the 1990s. In the 1997 Green Paper on Vertical Restraints, the Commission, for example, referred to this goal to explain the strict approach towards absolute territorial protection.[4] The current Vertical Guidelines still mention the goal of market integration.[5] However, this line of argument lies somewhat outside the scope of conventional economic reasoning.[6] Monti, for example, contends that at least vertical agreements between undertakings with small market shares cannot re-establish barriers between Member States.[7] Moreover, the impact of vertical agreements on market integration can be ambiguous. When taking an ex-ante perspective, vertical agreements can be necessary to allow the development of a distribution system in other Member States for the first time.[8] Without distribution restraints, the risk of free-riding could prevent manufacturers from entering markets in other Member States. Their effect can hence even be beneficial to market integration. The goal of market integration is thus not generally accepted as a valid justification for the EU's strict treatment of certain types of vertical agreements.[9] Nonetheless, it has featured prominently in the reasoning of the Commission and the European Courts, particularly in earlier case law.[10]

---

[3] *Colino*, Vertical Agreements, p. 23; *Gerber*, Law and Competition, pp. 354–356 using the internal market goal to explain the relative focus on vertical agreements in the past; *van den Bergh*, Antitrust Bulletin 2016, 167 (177).

[4] *Cseres*, Competition Law and Consumer Protection, pp. 246–247; *European Commission*, Green Paper on Vertical Restraints, para. 118.

[5] Vertical Guidelines, para. 5.

[6] *Cseres*, Competition Law and Consumer Protection, p. 247.

[7] *Monti*, World Competition 2013, 489 (495).

[8] *Cseres*, Competition Law and Consumer Protection, p. 274; *van den Bergh*, Antitrust Bulletin 2016, 167 (178–179).

[9] *Franck*, Europäisches Absatzrecht, pp. 337–341; *Gyselen*, CMLR 1984, 647 (666–667); *Hawk*, CMLR 1995, 973 (981); *van den Bergh*, Antitrust Bulletin 2016, 167 (178–179).

[10] See Court of Justice, 13/06/1966, Joined Cases 56 and 58–64 Consten/Grundig, ECLI:EU:C:1966:41, p. 389; Vertical Guidelines, para. 5: 'Undertakings may not use vertical agreements to re-establish private barriers between Member States where State barriers have been successfully abolished.'

Another possible and related rationale for the EU's strong stance, although limited to the strict treatment of internet sales restrictions may lie in industrial policy motivations: it has been the EU's declared goal to foster growth in e-commerce. E-commerce is seen as a way to "transcend national borders and enable businesses and consumers to get the most of the European Single Market".[11] The underlying logic is simple and compelling: e-commerce has the potential to allow for more cross-border transactions. The Court of Justice's and Commission's approach not to allowing complete internet bans could be seen as a way of instrumentalizing competition law to facilitate this goal.[12] In the ASICS case, the Bundeskartellamt has also emphasized the importance of the internet as a retail channel that vertical agreements should not overly restrict.[13] It is, however, not clear that such a policy can possibly have any positive impact on e-commerce. Just because manufacturers cannot prevent their retailers from selling online, this does not set the incentives, nor does it provide the infrastructure for retailers to increase their online activities. Moreover, the EU does not fare better when it comes to e-commerce compared to the United States, where limitations on the use of the internet as a sales channel generally do not face antitrust scrutiny.[14] Furthermore, online shopping has seen significant growth in the European Union over the last few years. For example, in 2021, 74 % of internet users in the EU shopped online[15], compared to 57 % in 2010[16]. In 2021, 66 % of individuals aged 16 to 74 in the EU bought goods or services online (compared to 51 % in 2016).[17] This trend, however, is unlikely explainable by the strict policy on vertical agreements but may rather reflect a general trend that has been further accelerated through the Covid-19 pandemic. Similar developments can also be observed in the United States with its very different policy on vertical agreements where 74.3 % of the population purchased goods online in 2021, compared to 63.1 % in 2017.[18] Hence, on the one hand, it is unlikely that the EU's vertical agreements policy has contributed much to the growth in e-commerce. On the other hand, this growth is a reality today, and there appears to be little need to enhance it even

---

[11] *European Commission*, Online Services, including E-commerce, in the Single Market (Commission Staff Working Document), p. 3.

[12] *Monti*, World Competition 2013, 489 (509).

[13] Bundeskartellamt, 26/08/2015, B2–98/11 ASICS, para. 22.

[14] See *Monti*, World Competition 2013, 489 (509).

[15] *Eurostat*, 01/2022, E-Commerce Statistics for Individuals, available at https://ec.europa.eu/eurostat/statistics-explained/index.php?title=E-commerce_statistics_for_individuals.

[16] *European Commission*, Online Services, including E-commerce, in the Single Market (Commission Staff Working Document), p. 6.

[17] *Eurostat*, 12/2021, Digital Economy and Society Statistics – Households and Individuals, available at https://ec.europa.eu/eurostat/statistics-explained/index.php?title=Digital_economy_and_society_statistics_-_households_and_individuals.

[18] *Statista*, Statista, 14/11/2022, U.S.: Digital Buyer Penetration 2017–2025, available at https://www.statista.com/statistics/273958/digital-buyer-penetration-in-the-united-states/ (accessed: 11 March 2025).

further. The Commission recognizes the latter in its Explanatory Note to the new VBER, arguing that "online sales have developed into a well-functioning sales channel that no longer requires special protection relative to offline sale."[19] Nevertheless, the special treatment continues as at least some forms of online sales restrictions (in particular total bans) are still treated very strictly.[20]

While the promotion of e-commerce and the goal of internal market integration help to explain the evolution of EU law on vertical agreements to some extent, they no longer offer a sufficient justification for the current treatment of internet sales restrictions.

II. Arguments based on property rights

One way to approach disputes over vertical agreements is through the lens of property rights, whether in favor of the manufacturer or the retailer.[21] One could argue that the manufacturer has a property right not to sell their goods to a retailer in the first place, and a fortiori must also have the right to subject the sale to conditions as they wish. On the other hand, however, the property rights argument can be turned around: a retailer shall be free to do whatever they want with the duly purchased products. Ultimately, the property rights argument is therefore not helpful in determining the scope of competition law in the realm of vertical agreements.[22] Under EU law, the notion of property rights does not appear to play a role in the Court of Justice's or Commission's reasoning in antitrust cases.

III. Arguments based on retailers' freedom of action

Similarly, one could argue that vertical agreements restrict competition because they limit the retailer's freedom of action. For instance, a retailer bound by a selective distribution agreement is not free to distribute the product at will. This kind of argumentation has indeed played a role in the development of the rules on vertical agreements in the EU.[23] However, the freedom argument as such cannot

[19] *European Commission*, Explanatory Note on the new VBER and Vertical Guidelines, p. 4; see also *European Commission*, Impact Assessment Report on the VBER and Vertical Guidelines (Commission Staff Working Document), pp. 11–12.

[20] See above from p. 34.

[21] *Sullivan/Grimes*, Law of Antitrust, p. 313.

[22] *Sullivan/Grimes*, Law of Antitrust, p. 313.

[23] See Court of Justice, 25/10/1977, Case 26–76 Metro I, ECLI:EU:C:1977:167, para. 41; Court of Justice, 21/02/1984, Case 86/82 Hasselblad, ECLI:EU:C:1984:65, para. 46; Court of Justice, 28/01/1986, Case 161/84 Pronuptia, ECLI:EU:C:1986:41, para. 25; European Commission, 19/12/1974, IV/23.013 Goodyear Italiana-Euram, para. 7; European Commission, 16/07/2003, AT.37975 PO Yamaha, para. 89; *Colino*, Vertical Agreements, p. 61; *Hawk*, CMLR 1995, 973 (979).

help in finding a restriction of competition.[24] Every contract limits both parties' freedom of action for the future. Yet, the ability to enter into the contract extends the freedom of action. Prohibiting an agreement simply because it binds the parties for the future would thus not protect but restrict their freedom of action. Moreover, if one were to protect the retailer's freedom of action to organise their business how they like, one would have to do the same for the manufacturer's freedom of action to structure their distribution system. Thus, as with the property rights arguments, vertical relationships are ultimately a zero-sum game.[25] Under the current framework, retailers' freedom of action seems to be largely disregarded as a stand-alone argument. For example, the VBER and the Vertical Guidelines do not reference this objective. The Vertical Guidelines further explicitly recognize the supplier's freedom "to organise the distribution of its goods or services as it sees fit."[26]

The retailer's freedom is hence not relevant for its own sake or for the retailer's protection. This, however, is not to exclude that in some instances, the retailer's freedom of action (or rather: the determination of a relevant parameter such as price or the availability of a product online by the retailer rather than the manufacturer)[27] is relevant because it is considered to have positive effects on competition. This type of reasoning was already present in the Metro judgment, where the Court of Justice stated that

> "since the function of a wholesaler is not to promote the products of a particular manufacturer but rather to provide for the retail trade supplies obtained on the basis of competition between manufacturers, so that obligations entered into by a wholesaler which limit his freedom in this respect constitute restrictions on competition."[28]

What matters is not the limitation of the wholesaler's freedom as such but the limitation of their ability to provide neutral advice and, thus, the effect on other market actors who are not parties to the agreement.

IV. Arguments based on consumer autonomy

Economic theory typically embraces the effects of vertical agreements on the consumer's decision-making. This is closely linked to the revealed-preference approach: if a consumer is convinced to buy something, they reveal a preference for the item they buy.[29] This increases welfare, as measured in consumer surplus.

[24] *Areeda/Hovenkamp*, Antitrust Law, Vol. 8, para. 1600c3; *Colino*, Vertical Agreements, p. 61; *Hawk*, CMLR 1995, 973 (979).

[25] *Wagner-von Papp*, in: Münchener Kommentar Wettbewerbsrecht, § 1GWB, para. 395.

[26] Vertical Guidelines, para. 115.

[27] See Vertical Guidelines, para. 150: 'where the authorised distributor remains free to operate its own online store', and para. 185: 'restricting the buyer's ability to determine its sale price'.

[28] Court of Justice, 25/10/1977, Case 26–76 Metro I, ECLI:EU:C:1977:167, para. 40.

[29] See below p. 166.

Economic theory generally does not question the consumer's motivation behind or the usefulness of their purchase. However, some voices argue that vertical agreements can also negatively affect consumer decision-making.[30] This section will explore to what extent arguments based on consumer autonomy play a role in the context of vertical agreements in the EU. It will first look at the Court of Justice's case law on vertical agreements, particularly selective distribution (1.). In this regard, it will give a brief overview of the Court of Justice's most fundamental case law on vertical agreements with a specific focus on arguments employed that are related to consumer autonomy. Then it will show that the European Commission and other competition authorities have regularly employed arguments based on consumer autonomy (2.). This will be followed by a conclusion (3.).

1. The Court of Justice's case law

a) Consten/Grundig

Already in Consten/Grundig[31], the effects of vertical agreements on consumers' decision-making played a certain role. The German company Grundig had entered into a contract with the French company Consten, appointing the latter as Grundig's 'sole representative' in France. Grundig would thus not make deliveries to other persons or companies in the areas covered by the agreement. Consten, in turn, promised to provide appropriate publicity, set up a repairs workshop, and carry out guarantee and after-sales services and not to sell competing goods. The Commission found this contract to violate Art. 85 EEC Treaty [today: Art. 101 TFEU].[32] The companies challenged the decision before the Court of Justice, arguing that the prohibition of anti-competitive agreements exclusively applies to horizontal and not to vertical agreements.[33]

The Court of Justice rejected this argument.[34] According to the Court, agreements between undertakings at different levels of the distribution chain carry the risk that they bring an unjustified advantage at the expense of the consumer or user of the product.[35] Therefore, under Art. 101(1) TFEU, there is no room to balance restrictions of intra-brand competition with their possible benefits for

[30] *Grimes*, California Law Review 1992, 815; *Grimes*, Antitrust Law Journal 1995, 83; *Künzler*, Restoring Consumer Sovereignty; *Künzler*, Oxford Journal of Legal Studies 2017, 75; see also *Elhauge/Geradin*, Global Competition Law and Economics, p. 697.

[31] Court of Justice, 13/06/1966, Joined Cases 56 and 58–64 Consten/Grundig, ECLI:EU:C:1966:41.

[32] European Commission, 23/09/1964, IV/A-00004–03344 Consten/Grundig.

[33] Court of Justice, 13/06/1966, Joined Cases 56 and 58–64 Consten/Grundig, ECLI:EU:C:1966:41, pp. 307, 339.

[34] Court of Justice, 13/06/1966, Joined Cases 56 and 58–64 Consten/Grundig, ECLI:EU:C:1966:41, p. 342.

[35] Court of Justice, 13/06/1966, Joined Cases 56 and 58–64 Consten/Grundig, ECLI:EU:C:1966:41, p. 339.

inter-brand competition. The Court explicitly rejected conducting a 'rule of reason' type analysis because the "principle of freedom of competition concerns the various states and manifestations of competition."[36] The Court also recognized the possible effects of product differentiation[37] on the consumer by holding that:

> "the more producers succeed in their efforts to render their own makes of product individually distinct in the eyes of the consumer, the more the effectiveness of competition between producers tends to diminish."[38]

The Consten/Grundig judgment was thus concerned with vertical agreements' effects on consumers, including their decision-making. This is also apparent in the Court of Justice's argumentation concerning a justification of the agreement under Art. 85(3) EEC Treaty [today: Art. 101(1) TFEU]. The undertakings had argued that the territorial protection awarded to Consten was necessary as Consten would otherwise have to refuse those services for Grundig machines imported by other distributors who do not provide similar services. This would be contrary to the interests of consumers and Grundig's reputation.[39] While not generally rejecting that such considerations could justify the agreement, the Court did not find Grundig's reputation at risk. In fact, a competitor who had already started selling Grundig products in France and who offered after-sales services only against remuneration (but also offered a free guarantee), according to the Court, had not harmed Grundig's reputation.[40] Moreover, the Court emphasized that through advertising efforts, the consumer could be informed about the advantages of buying the product from the official distribution network. The Court hereby rejected the free-riding argument that Consten's advertising efforts would benefit competitors to the same extent.[41]

Overall, the judgment appears to place some emphasis on how the agreement in question affected consumers and their decision-making. Notably, the Court of Justice suggests that product differentiation achieved through vertical agreements may reduce competition between producers. For companies with strong brands, there is concern that such agreements could serve as a shield from com-

[36] Court of Justice, 13/06/1966, Joined Cases 56 and 58–64 Consten/Grundig, ECLI:EU:C:1966:41, p. 342.

[37] Product differentiation refers to strategies to make a product or service distinct from competing products or services, i.e. making them distinct in the eye of the consumer. This can be profitable for firms because it reduces competitive pressure from other products or services. See above, p. 18.

[38] Court of Justice, 13/06/1966, Joined Cases 56 and 58–64 Consten/Grundig, ECLI:EU:C:1966:41, p. 343.

[39] Court of Justice, 13/06/1966, Joined Cases 56 and 58–64 Consten/Grundig, ECLI:EU:C:1966:41, p. 349.

[40] Court of Justice, 13/06/1966, Joined Cases 56 and 58–64 Consten/Grundig, ECLI:EU:C:1966:41, p. 343.

[41] Court of Justice, 13/06/1966, Joined Cases 56 and 58–64 Consten/Grundig, ECLI:EU:C:1966:41, p. 343.

petition by further enhancing product differentiation, thereby reducing the importance of inter-brand competition relative to intra-brand competition.[42] The judgment, however, leaves open the question of when inter-brand variety is sufficient so that intra-brand variety becomes less important. More generally, it offers no clear indicators to distinguish anticompetitive from permissible agreements. Under the broad protection of intra-brand competition expressed in the Consten/Grundig case, one might infer that many vertical agreements could restrict competition, although the precise implications remain uncertain.[43]

b) Metro

While the Consten/Grundig case implemented a relatively strict protection of intra-brand competition and allowed to consider possible positive effects of an agreement on inter-brand competition only under Art. 101(3) TFEU, the Court of Justice followed a different approach in the context of selective distribution systems. The Court of Justice considers them to fall outside the scope of Art. 101(1) TFEU under certain conditions.[44] The landmark case for selective distribution systems is the 1977 case Metro I[45]: SABA, a German electronic equipment manufacturer, had established a selective distribution system. Wholesalers and retailers were appointed by SABA and could not sell to non-authorized wholesalers or retailers. Authorised retailers had to fulfil several qualitative criteria. They had to achieve an adequate turnover in SABA products, keep a corresponding stock of SABA products in a representative manner, maintain retail premises suitable for advertising and displaying SABA products and maintain appropriate servicing facilities.[46] Only specialized retailers with more than 50% of their turnover relating to the sale of electronic products for leisure purposes or with a special department for such products could become authorised SABA retailers.[47] Further, retailers had to conclude long-term contracts covering the entire range of SABA products.[48] Setting prices and selling equipment from competing manufacturers remained at the retailer's discretion.[49]

Metro, a self-service wholesale retailer not authorized to sell SABA products, lodged a complaint against SABA's selective distribution system with the European Commission. The Commission adopted a decision, declaring that there

---

[42] This conflicts with economic theory, which mostly sees product differentiation positively, see below from p. 195.

[43] The Consten/Grundig judgment set the basis for the approach that basically every vertical agreement was held to restrict competition absent an objective justification, see above from p. 21.

[44] See above p. 26.

[45] Court of Justice, 25/10/1977, Case 26–76 Metro I, ECLI:EU:C:1977:167.

[46] Court of Justice, 25/10/1977, Case 26–76 Metro I, ECLI:EU:C:1977:167, p. 1880.

[47] Court of Justice, 25/10/1977, Case 26–76 Metro I, ECLI:EU:C:1977:167, p. 1881.

[48] Court of Justice, 25/10/1977, Case 26–76 Metro I, ECLI:EU:C:1977:167, p. 1881.

[49] Court of Justice, 25/10/1977, Case 26–76 Metro I, ECLI:EU:C:1977:167, p. 1881..

were no grounds for action under Art. 85(1) EEC [today: Art. 101(1) TFEU] concerning the qualitative criteria imposed on wholesalers and retailers and granting an exemption under Art. 85(3) concerning the quantitative criteria.[50] According to the Commission, the qualitative criteria in the selective distribution system were necessary to market the products adequately.[51] The Commission emphasized that to adequately sell consumer electronic equipment, "trained personnel must be available to sell the goods from premises suitable for their display, stocking and demonstration" and that the selective distribution system in question would only exclude "those dealers not capable of selling electronic equipment for domestic leisure purposes in a manner satisfactory to the consumer".[52] Quantitative criteria, on the other hand, would restrict the freedom of choice of non-authorized retailers and consumers.[53] Metro challenged this decision before the Court of Justice, arguing that the Commission had failed to recognize that Art. 85 does protect freedom of competition and "not the coincident interests of a manufacturer and a given group of traders who wish to secure selling prices which are considered to be satisfactory by the latter."[54]

The Court dismissed the application and, agreeing with the Commission's assessment, held that selective distribution systems can constitute

> "an aspect of competition which accords with Article 85(1) [Art. 101(1) TFEU], provided that resellers are chosen on the basis of objective criteria of a qualitative nature relating to the technical qualifications of the reseller and his staff and the suitability of his trading premises and that such conditions are laid down uniformly for all potential resellers and are not applied in a discriminatory fashion."[55]

The Court's reasoning in Metro I was largely based on the need for selective distribution to preserve the existence of specialist wholesalers and retailers and to allow non-price competition between those in the interest of consumers.[56] The Court explicitly adressed the agreement's impact on consumers' decision-making. The applicant had argued that

> "the obligation on wholesalers and retailers (systematically) to promote SABA products and their related obligation to attain sales quotas encourages distributors to influence their customers in favour of SABA products rather than giving them an objective choice".[57]

[50] European Commission, 15/12/1975, IV/847 SABA.

[51] European Commission, 15/12/1975, IV/847 SABA, para. 28.

[52] European Commission, 15/12/1975, IV/847 SABA, para. 28.

[53] European Commission, 15/12/1975, IV/847 SABA, para. 31.

[54] Court of Justice, 25/10/1977, Case 26–76 Metro I, ECLI:EU:C:1977:167, para. 19.

[55] Court of Justice, 25/10/1977, Case 26–76 Metro I, ECLI:EU:C:1977:167, para. 20.

[56] Compare Court of Justice, 25/10/1977, Case 26–76 Metro I, ECLI:EU:C:1977:167, para. 21; Court of Justice, 25/10/1983, Case 107/82 AEG/Commission, ECLI:EU:C:1983:293, para. 33.

[57] Court of Justice, 25/10/1977, Case 26–76 Metro I, ECLI:EU:C:1977:167, p. 1884.

The Court picked up this argument in the context of the quantitative criteria and the requirement that wholesalers had to participate in "the creation of a distribution network". Unlike qualitative criteria, these parts of the agreement[58] fell under Art. 85(1) in the first place because they could negatively affect the customers' decision-making.[59] Here, the Court did not share the Commission's view that the obligation to participate in the creation of a distribution network is exempted from the ambit of Art. 85(1). In particular, the Court of Justice, echoing the applicant, emphasized that

> "the function of a wholesaler is not to promote the products of a particular manufacturer but rather to provide for the retail trade supplies obtained on the basis of competition between manufacturers, so that obligations entered into by a wholesaler which limit his freedom in this respect constitute restrictions on competition."[60]

Thus, the restriction of competition identified by the Court was linked to the risk of wholesale customers being deprived of an objective choice. In the case at hand, the restriction was ultimately exempted under Art. 85(3) because the Court found it to improve stability in distribution.[61] Qualitative criteria which, according to the Court of Justice, did not restrict competition, on the other hand, were found to have rather positive effects on the consumer's decision-making: the Court of Justice emphasized that selective distribution systems for complex products can be necessary to ensure that retailers provide necessary sales and after-sales services. One of the contested requirements of the selective distribution systemin question was that retailers needed to have qualified staff and to give proper advice and supply technical service to customers.[62] In light of the products in question – consumer electronics such as television, tape-recording or radio equipment (relatively complex products at the time) – the Court considered these requirements necessary for properly distributing the products. At the heart of the argumentation was the importance of 'consumer information'.[63] Preserving specialist retailers was therefore seen as being in the "interest of the consumer."[64] The Court found it legitimate, at least for complex products, to safeguard the specialized retailer as a distribution channel because of its possible positive effects on consumers' decision-making by providing more and better information. Endorsing a free-riding rationale for selective distribution of technically complex products that require consumer advice, the Court of Justice argued that, without such restraints, retailers who do not invest in advisory services would free-ride on

---

[58] These were, inter alia, that wholesalers had to conclude supply contracts with SABA at least six months in advance, maintain an appropriate stock of SABA products and to display the products to their best advantage and receive an adequate turnover in SABA products.

[59] Court of Justice, 25/10/1977, Case 26–76 Metro I, ECLI:EU:C:1977:167, paras. 39–40.

[60] Court of Justice, 25/10/1977, Case 26–76 Metro I, ECLI:EU:C:1977:167, para. 40.

[61] Court of Justice, 25/10/1977, Case 26–76 Metro I, ECLI:EU:C:1977:167, paras. 43–50.

[62] Court of Justice, 25/10/1977, Case 26–76 Metro I, ECLI:EU:C:1977:167, para. 20.

[63] Court of Justice, 25/10/1977, Case 26–76 Metro I, ECLI:EU:C:1977:167, p. 1886.

[64] Court of Justice, 25/10/1977, Case 26–76 Metro I, ECLI:EU:C:1977:167, para. 21.

those who do – ultimately reducing the overall incentive to provide adequate advice. This could leave consumers insufficiently informed and unable to select the product that best fits their needs. In this respect, the Metro I judgment aligns with Telser's free-riding theory concerning advisory services.

However, the judgment remains somewhat unclear regarding why selective distribution agreements that fail to meet the Metro requirements should be considered restrictive of competition. While the Court emphasizes that wholesalers should offer neutral advice, it does not articulate a clear theory of harm.

c) Metro II

Metro II presented facts very similar to those in the original Metro case, involving the same companies: SABA and Metro, disputing SABA's selective distribution system, which had remained in place and had been cleared again by the Commission after some minor changes. Metro argued that the market structure since the first Metro judgment had evolved, notably due to a significant increase in selective distribution systems operated by major consumer electronics manufacturers.[65] It argued that the Commission should have considered these changes and, therefore, not have granted an exemption to SABA's distribution system (again).[66] The Court of Justice rejected this argument based on the facts of the case. While there were other selective distribution systems in the same sector, these were not similar to those of SABA,[67] and Metro had access to the products of other leading manufacturers.[68] Moreover, the Court found that sufficient price competition persisted both among SABA retailers and between manufacturers, preventing the emergence of a rigid price structure.[69] The Court of Justice also considered whether television sets as one of the product categories covered by the selective distribution system could still be considered complex enough to require sales and after-sales services "specially adapted to characteristics and linked to their distribution."[70] The Court of Justice found that the products were complex enough to justify "a distribution network involving specialized wholesalers and retailers" because they can be used in different ways and combined with other complementary or accessory equipment.[71] Again, no restriction of competition was found as regards the qualitative criteria since they could improve consumer decisions and because variety was ensured by the market situation in the intra- and inter-brand dimensions. The judgment looked in more detail at the concrete market circumstances. It stated, for example, that the degree of concentration

[65] Court of Justice, 22/10/1986, Case 75/84 Metro II, ECLI:EU:C:1986:399, para. 35.

[66] Court of Justice, 22/10/1986, Case 75/84 Metro II, ECLI:EU:C:1986:399, para. 36.

[67] Court of Justice, 22/10/1986, Case 75/84 Metro II, ECLI:EU:C:1986:399, paras. 38–46.

[68] Court of Justice, 22/10/1986, Case 75/84 Metro II, ECLI:EU:C:1986:399, para. 63.

[69] Court of Justice, 22/10/1986, Case 75/84 Metro II, ECLI:EU:C:1986:399, para. 44.

[70] Court of Justice, 22/10/1986, Case 75/84 Metro II, ECLI:EU:C:1986:399, para. 54.

[71] Court of Justice, 22/10/1986, Case 75/84 Metro II, ECLI:EU:C:1986:399, para. 55.

must be taken into account in the assessment under Art. 85(3) because in markets with high concentration, vertical agreements could "eliminate price competition or [...] oust other channels of distribution."[72] Further, the Court emphasized that parallel use of similar distribution systems could be harmful because this can have "an impact on the structure of competition on the market."[73] While the judgment remained relatively vague, it already identified the market structure as an important element of the competitive analysis.

d) Vichy

Vichy[74] was one of the first cases in which the Court of First Instance addressed issues concerning luxury products and selective distribution. Vichy – a luxury cosmetics manufacturer – had established a (highly) selective distribution system that permitted its products to e sold *only* in pharmacies. The Commission had characterised this criterion as quantitative, which rendered the Metro exception inapplicable, and led to the denial of an exception under Art. 85(3). Notably, the Commission based this assessment on the fact that there was a numerus clausus for pharmacists in some Member States.[75] The Court concurred, holding that the requirement constituted a quantitative restriction on the number of distribution outlets[76] and was "not necessary for the proper distribution" of the products.[77] Unlike medicinal products, (luxury) cosmetics did not require sale through pharmacies.[78] Thus, Vichy's sales strategy was not concerned with protecting the consumer from danger to their health or with properly advising them but was solely "a marketing strategy intended to create and maintain a brand image benefitting from the reputation of the pharmaceutical profession."[79] The argument could be made that Vichy was free-riding on the limited competition (due to regulation) between pharmacies.

The Commission and the Court clearly distinguished between a requirement that products be sold exclusively in pharmacies and one that mandates sale in the presence of a trained pharmacist – since any concerns regarding proper advice could be addressed by the latter.[80] Moreover, because Vichy products were also available under different brand names in other retail channels, any health-related justification appeared to be merely a pretext. The Commission raised concerns regarding the consumer's freedom of choice in that regard. If the same product is sold under different brands through different distribution channels, the consum-

[72] Court of Justice, 22/10/1986, Case 75/84 Metro II, ECLI:EU:C:1986:399, para. 88.
[73] Court of Justice, 22/10/1986, Case 75/84 Metro II, ECLI:EU:C:1986:399, para. 89.
[74] Court of First Instance, 27/02/1992, Case T-19/91 Vichy, ECLI:EU:T:1992:28.
[75] Court of First Instance, 27/02/1992, Case T-19/91 Vichy, ECLI:EU:T:1992:28, para. 54.
[76] Court of First Instance, 27/02/1992, Case T-19/91 Vichy, ECLI:EU:T:1992:28, para. 67.
[77] Court of First Instance, 27/02/1992, Case T-19/91 Vichy, ECLI:EU:T:1992:28, para. 69.
[78] Court of First Instance, 27/02/1992, Case T-19/91 Vichy, ECLI:EU:T:1992:28, para. 70.
[79] Court of First Instance, 27/02/1992, Case T-19/91 Vichy, ECLI:EU:T:1992:28, para. 71.
[80] Court of First Instance, 27/02/1992, Case T-19/91 Vichy, ECLI:EU:T:1992:28, para. 96.

er cannot exercise their freedom of choice in full knowledge of the fact.[81] This was one of the main reasons for declining to grant an exception under Art. 85(3). The Court shared this view, arguing that Vichy was "depriving the consumer of the possibility of making an informed choice" and, therefore, not offering them a fair share of the benefits of the practice.[82]

In effect, the judgment focused on the distribution system's impact on consumers' decision-making, implicitly rejecting the argument that increased sales at higher prices automatically benefit consumers. From a behavioral economics perspective, Vichy's strategy might be seen as exploiting consumers' reliance on a 'health is priceless' heuristic[83] or mental accounting – where expenses incurred in a pharmacy are accounted as health expenditures rather than beauty expenditures. Ultimately, the desire to induce consumers to pay more was not accepted as a sufficient justification for the restraint. However, the restraint itself was not clearly identified and the Court did not consider any effects on the market structure.

e) Interim conclusion

The Court of Justice's reasoning in its early case law on vertical agreements can partly be explained by a desire to protect autonomous consumer decisions. Initially, the Court was rather cautious regarding the impact of vertical agreements on consumers' decision-making. In Consten/Grundig, for example, it expressed skepticism toward horizontal product differentiation via vertical agreements because such differentiation might reduce inter-brand competition. Similarly, in *Vichy*, the Court of First Instance implicitly rejected the notion that higher consumer willingness to pay for products sold under vertical agreements necessarily indicates efficiency.

In contrast, in the Metro case law concerning selective distribution agreements, the Court of Justice considered both the negative and the positive effects of vertical agreements on consumers' decision-making. Qualitative selective distribution criteria in Metro were viewed as non-restrictive of competition because they could enhance consumer decision-making through improved retail advice services. Quantitative criteria, on the other hand, bear the risk that the retailer or wholesaler tries to steer their consumers'/customers' choices in a particular direction, thus limiting their autonomy (as they typically expect the retailer/wholesaler to be a neutral agent). Consequently, quantitative selective distribution agreements are generally considered to restrict competition and are only justifiable under the conditions of Art. 101(3) TFEU.

---

[81] Court of First Instance, 27/02/1992, Case T-19/91 Vichy, ECLI:EU:T:1992:28, para. 89.
[82] Court of First Instance, 27/02/1992, Case T-19/91 Vichy, ECLI:EU:T:1992:28, para. 98.
[83] See *Felser*, Werbe- und Konsumentenpsychologie, p. 182; *Hanson/Kysar*, NYU Law Review 2000, 630 (763); *Kahneman/Tversky*, American Psychologist 1984, 341 (347); *Thaler*, Marketing Science 1985, 199.

Nevertheless, the Court does not develop a fully coherent theory of harm. While it sometimes emphasizes the importance of market structure effects, it stops short of assessing the likelihood of such effects, particularly in relation to quantitative criteria in selective distribution agreements.

f) LeClerc, Copad, Pierre Fabre and Coty: selective distribution to protect the product or brand image – endorsing the image free-riding rationale

While in Consten/Grundig, the Court of Justice was initially skeptical of horizontal product differentiation through vertical agreements, its approach became more lenient over time. In the 1985 Commission case Villeroy & Boch[84], which concerned luxury goods (ceramic tableware), the brand's 'prestige' was already mentioned as a goal of selective distribution. However, in that case the emphasis was more on preventing consumer confusion and preserving the consumer's ability to choose than on the selective distribution system actively creating a prestige image.[85] It was only later that the concept of using vertical agreements to protect and cultivate a product's luxury image gained prominence – a development that began with the LeClerc decision and culminated in the Coty case. This evolution will be explored in the following paragraphs.

aa) LeClerc

In 1996, the Court of First Instance, in the cases LeClerc/Yves Saint Laurent[86] and LeClerc/Givenchy,[87] took the view that preserving the "aura of exclusivity and prestige" is in the interest of consumers and can require a selective distribution system under the Metro case law.[88] This led to an extension of the Metro exception, endorsing an image free-riding defence. Both cases concerned a selective distribution system for luxury cosmetic products with detailed selection criteria.[89] The Court of Justice argued that absent selective distribution, a product's luxury image and, thus, "the very character" of the product could be damaged.[90] According to the Court of First Instance, a product's luxury character is derived not only from its intrinsic quality, high price, and advertising but also from its

[84] European Commission, 31/12/1985, IV.30.665 Villeroy&Boch.

[85] European Commission, 31/12/1985, IV.30.665 Villeroy&Boch, para. 27.

[86] Court of First Instance, 12/12/1996, Case T-19/92 LeClerc/Yves Saint Laurent, ECLI:EU:T:1996:190.

[87] Court of First Instance, 12/12/1996, Case T-88/92 LeClerc/Givenchy, ECLI:EU:T:1996:192.

[88] Court of First Instance, 12/12/1996, Case T-19/92 LeClerc/Yves Saint Laurent, ECLI:EU:T:1996:190, paras. 119–123.

[89] Court of First Instance, 12/12/1996, Case T-19/92 LeClerc/Yves Saint Laurent, ECLI:EU:T:1996:190, paras. 10–18; Court of First Instance, 12/12/1996, Case T-88/92 LeClerc/Givenchy, ECLI:EU:T:1996:192, paras. 9–15.

[90] Court of First Instance, 12/12/1996, Case T-19/92 LeClerc/Yves Saint Laurent, ECLI:EU:T:1996:190, para. 120.

selective distribution.[91] In this view, selective distribution plays a role in fostering inter-brand competition by contributing to the very creation of a luxury product, thereby enhancing variety in the inter-brand market. Doctrinally, this is somehow at odds with the Consten/Grundig case law, according to which a balance between intra- and inter-brand competition is reserved for the analysis under Art. 101(3) TFEU. In the case at hand, the rationale for the selective distribution system was not to provide consumers with specialized advice for purchasing complex goods but to preserve the prestigious image of Yves Saint Laurent's luxury cosmetic products.[92] Although the argument remainsrooted in principles established in Metro, the justification is very different. Unlike in Metro, the argument is not that consumers need special advice or services (to make better choices) but rather that selective distribution can help the manufacturer preserve a prestigious image. The Commission's submission in the case best encapsulates the underlying argument:

> "Although consumers are initially willing to buy luxury products from retail outlets which do not reflect their luxury nature, over a period of time the availability of these products in such outlets gives them a down-market image and they then cease to be luxury products, with the result that consumers ultimately stop buying them."[93]

In essence, selective distribution serves as a marketing tool that prevents a product from being downgraded, particularly in the context of luxury goods.[94] The Court of First Instance acknowledges the psychological effects that selective distribution can have on consumers.[95] This marketing activity – creating or preserving an aura of luxury and rarity – creates value as it 'improves' the product or at least how it is perceived in consumers' minds and ultimately raises their willingness to pay. According to the Court, it is thus "in the interests of consumers seeking to purchase luxury cosmetics that such products are appropriately presented in retail outlets."[96] Besides a product's price, its high intrinsic quality and the manufacturer's advertising campaigns, selective distribution can contribute to a product's luxury image.[97] Therefore, according to the Court of First In-

[91] Court of First Instance, 12/12/1996, Case T-19/92 LeClerc/Yves Saint Laurent, ECLI: EU:T:1996:190, para. 120.

[92] Court of First Instance, 12/12/1996, Case T-19/92 LeClerc/Yves Saint Laurent, ECLI: EU:T:1996:190, para. 116.

[93] Court of First Instance, 12/12/1996, Case T-19/92 LeClerc/Yves Saint Laurent, ECLI: EU:T:1996:190, para. 77.

[94] Court of First Instance, 12/12/1996, Case T-19/92 LeClerc/Yves Saint Laurent, ECLI: EU:T:1996:190, para. 120.

[95] Court of First Instance, 12/12/1996, Case T-19/92 LeClerc/Yves Saint Laurent, ECLI: EU:T:1996:190, para. 114.

[96] Court of First Instance, 12/12/1996, Case T-19/92 LeClerc/Yves Saint Laurent, ECLI: EU:T:1996:190, para. 119.

[97] Court of First Instance, 12/12/1996, Case T-19/92 LeClerc/Yves Saint Laurent, ECLI: EU:T:1996:190, para. 120.

stance, luxury products are, in principle, suitable for the Metro exception, if the other Metro requirements are fulfilled. The judgment, however, adds little to finding whether and why selective distribution agreements restrict competition in the first place. The Court of First Instance relied on the Metro case law, assuming that every selective distribution agreement not justified under the Metro criteria inherently restricts competition.[98] Nonetheless, it considers the market structure to some extent, noting that there was workable competition in the market for luxury cosmetics.[99]

bb) Copad

The Court of Justice in Copad[100], albeit in a case concerning trademark law, seemingly confirmed the Court of First Instance's view. The company SIL manufactured luxury corsetry goods under the trademark Christian Dior, licensed by Dior, the trademark owner. As part of the licence agreement, SIL was not to sell to "wholesalers, buyers' collectives, discount stores, mail order companies, door-to-door sales companies or companies selling within private houses" without Dior's prior consent to "maintain the repute and prestige of the trade mark".[101] SIL, facing economic difficulties, asked Dior for permission to market the branded goods outside its selective distribution system, which Dior refused. Despite the refusal, SIL sold the branded goods to Copad, a company operating discount stores.[102] Dior, therefore, brought an action against SIL for infringement of its trademark before a Regional Court in France. The case eventually made its way to the Court of Cassation, which asked the Court of Justice for a preliminary ruling on the interpretation of the Trademarks Directive[103].

The questions, in essence, concerned the scope of protection of trademarks. In principle, under the Trademarks Directive, the proprietor of a trademark could not prohibit the use of the trademark in relation to goods that have lawfully been put on the market (Art. 7(1)). They could only oppose further commercialisation of those goods where there existed legitimate reasons, especially "where the condition of the goods is changed or impaired after they have been put on the market" (Art. 7(2)). However, under Art. 8(2), the proprietor could invoke their trade mark rights against a licensee "who contravenes any provision in his licensing contract with regard to its duration, the form covered by the registration in which the trade mark may be used, the scope of the goods or services for which the

[98] Court of First Instance, 12/12/1996, Case T-88/92 LeClerc/Givenchy, ECLI:EU:T:1996:192, para. 118.

[99] Court of First Instance, 12/12/1996, Case T-88/92 LeClerc/Givenchy, ECLI:EU:T:1996:192, paras. 190–192.

[100] Court of Justice, 23/04/2009, Case C-59/08 Copad, ECLI:EU:C:2009:260.

[101] Court of Justice, 23/04/2009, Case C-59/08 Copad, ECLI:EU:C:2009:260, para. 8.

[102] Court of Justice, 23/04/2009, Case C-59/08 Copad, ECLI:EU:C:2009:260, para. 10.

[103] Council Directive 89/104/EEC of 21 December 1988 to approximate the laws of the Member States relating to trademarks, OJ L 40, 11.2.1989, pp. 1–7.

licence is granted, the territory in which the trade mark may be used, the scope of the goods or services for which the licence is granted, the territory in which the trade mark may be affixed, or the quality of the goods manufacturer of the services provided by the licensee."

The Court of Justice held that for luxury goods, the aura of luxury is essential for it enables consumers to distinguish them from similar goods and that, therefore, an impairment of this aura can damage the very quality of the goods.[104] Selective distribution systems could contribute to the reputation of goods and their aura of luxury.[105] Therefore, Art. 8(2) of the Trademarks Directive was, in principle, applicable to sales capable of damaging the allure and prestigious image of the brand. The judgment is particularly relevant to the questions addressed here since the Trademark Directive's goal is to prevent consumer confusion: the trade mark shall enable the consumer to distinguish branded products and attribute them to a single company responsible for their quality.[106] In terms of confusion, however, SIL's non-authorized sales seem to have posed little problems: the goods were the same as those sold in the authorized stores, and they were equally branded, making the product attributable to Dior. There was no risk of consumer confusion. However, the protection of the selective distribution system through trademark law was justified by its positive effects on the brand's image. In the Court of Justice's view, the image is part of a product's qualities and must hence be protected.[107] The trademark owner could thus prevent sales that damage the reputation of their trademark. However, the Court of Justice remained relatively strict: not every sale outside an approved selective distribution system necessarily impairs the mark's luxury image. Instead, it needs to be established on a case-by-case basis whether the allure and prestigious image is actually damaged.[108]

cc) Pierre Fabre

In the 2011 Pierre Fabre case[109], the Court of Justice had the chance to decide on the validity of the protection of a luxury image to justify selective distribution under Art. 101(1) TFEU. The case concerned a selective distribution system by the French cosmetic manufacturer Pierre Fabre, the proprietor of brands like Klorane and Avène.[110] The products sold under these brands are cosmetic and

---

[104] Court of Justice, 23/04/2009, Case C-59/08 Copad, ECLI:EU:C:2009:260, paras. 27–28.

[105] Court of Justice, 23/04/2009, Case C-59/08 Copad, ECLI:EU:C:2009:260, para. 29.

[106] Court of Justice, 23/04/2009, Case C-59/08 Copad, ECLI:EU:C:2009:260, para. 22.

[107] Court of Justice, 23/04/2009, Case C-59/08 Copad, ECLI:EU:C:2009:260, paras. 28–30.

[108] Court of Justice, 23/04/2009, Case C-59/08 Copad, ECLI:EU:C:2009:260, para. 37.

[109] Court of Justice, 13/10/2011, Case C-439/09 Pierre Fabre, ECLI:EU:C:2011:649.

[110] Court of Justice, 13/10/2011, Case C-439/09 Pierre Fabre, ECLI:EU:C:2011:649, para. 9.

personal care products not subject to specific public health regulations.[111] Under the distribution contracts, Pierre Fabre's retailers could only sell "in a physical space, in which a qualified pharmacist must be present."[112] This requirement effectively excluded all forms of online selling.[113] This requirement was intended both to provide individualized consumer advice and to maintain the products' prestigious image.[114]

The Court reaffirmed that such a selective distribution system is liable to restrict competition by object because it reduces the ability of an authorised distributor to sell the contractual products to customers outside its contractual territory or area of activity.[115] It then explains that, nevertheless, such agreements can be exempted when the Metro conditions are fulfilled.[116] In particular, it emphasizes that in the context of freedom of movement, it had already held that the goal of providing individual advice to consumers and preventing incorrect use of products in the context of non-prescription medicines and contact lenses does not justify a ban on internet sales.[117] Therefore, the objective of providing individual advice can not justify a requirement in a selective distribution system that excludes online sales. Moreover, the Court of Justice rejected Pierre Fabre's argument that the requirement was necessary to maintain the prestigious image of the products at issue, holding:

> "The aim of maintaining a prestigious image is not a legitimate aim for restricting competition and cannot therefore justify a finding that a contractual clause pursuing such an aim does not fall within Article 101(1) TFEU."[118]

Hence, the Metro conditions were not fulfilled.[119] Moreover, the Court found that the conditions for a block exemption under the VBER[120] were not fulfilled

[111] Court of Justice, 13/10/2011, Case C-439/09 Pierre Fabre, ECLI:EU:C:2011:649, para. 10.

[112] Court of Justice, 13/10/2011, Case C-439/09 Pierre Fabre, ECLI:EU:C:2011:649, para. 12.

[113] Court of Justice, 13/10/2011, Case C-439/09 Pierre Fabre, ECLI:EU:C:2011:649, paras. 14, 37.

[114] Court of Justice, 13/10/2011, Case C-439/09 Pierre Fabre, ECLI:EU:C:2011:649, paras. 17, 45.

[115] Court of Justice, 13/10/2011, Case C-439/09 Pierre Fabre, ECLI:EU:C:2011:649, paras. 38–39.

[116] Court of Justice, 13/10/2011, Case C-439/09 Pierre Fabre, ECLI:EU:C:2011:649, paras. 40–47.

[117] Court of Justice, 13/10/2011, Case C-439/09 Pierre Fabre, ECLI:EU:C:2011:649, para. 44; referring to Court of Justice, 11/12/2003, Case C-322/01 DocMorris, ECLI:EU:C:2003:664, paras. 106, 107, 112; and Court of Justice, 02/12/2010, Case C-108/09 Ker-Optika, ECLI:EU:C:2010:725, para. 76.

[118] Court of Justice, 13/10/2011, Case C-439/09 Pierre Fabre, ECLI:EU:C:2011:649, para. 46.

[119] Court of Justice, 13/10/2011, Case C-439/09 Pierre Fabre, ECLI:EU:C:2011:649, para. 47.

[120] Here, this refers to the VBER 1999 (Commission Regulation (EC) No 2790/1999 of 22

either.[121] While Pierre Fabre had a market share below 30 %, making the company in principle eligible to benefit from the VBER, the de facto exclusion of internet sales had as its object the restriction of passive sales to end users.[122] Thus, according to Art. 4 point (c) VBER, it could not benefit from the block exemption. Pierre Fabre, therefore, seems to contradict the cases Copad and LeClerc.[123] The Court of Justice, however, did not address this conflict in its judgment.[124]

The ruling has sparked debate on the Court's motives as well as the judgment's implications. First, the judgment questioned the extent to which manufacturers could justify selective distribution systems for the sake of better advice to consumers. Previously, this had been interpreted relatively broadly and was accepted for a wide range of products (e.g., television sets, watches, ceramics).[125] It is hard to see how such products are more complex and require more advice than cosmetic products – and for the latter, the Court in Pierre Fabre seems to have rejected the necessity of advice.[126] One possible explanation is that in 2011 when the Pierre Fabre case was decided, the average consumer was less in need of advice than in 1977 when Metro was decided. In particular, the rise of the internet made it easier for consumers to inform themselves about products and their attributes; information became much more easily accessible.[127] Therefore, the argument as such seems to have lost some of its appeal over the decades.[128] In the judgments to which the Court of Justice refers (Doc Morris[129] and Ker-Optica[130]), it does express at least some sympathy for the internet as a sales channel that allows for informed consumer decisions. The Court of Justice, in Doc Morris and Ker-Optica, emphasized that it is not impossible to provide the consumer with adequate advice and information when they are shopping online, and that online shopping comes with certain advantages for the consumer, including the ability to shop from home but also "to have time to think about the questions to ask the pharmacists".[131] According to the Court of Justice, the risk of incorrect use can

---

December 1999 on the application of Article 81(3) of the Treaty to categories of vertical agreements and concerted practices, OJ L 336, 29.12.1999, pp. 21–25), which was in place until 31.05.2010.

[121] Court of Justice, 13/10/2011, Case C-439/09 Pierre Fabre, ECLI:EU:C:2011:649, paras. 48–58.

[122] Court of Justice, 13/10/2011, Case C-439/09 Pierre Fabre, ECLI:EU:C:2011:649, paras. 53–54.

[123] *Enchelmaier*, in: Competition on the Internet, 5 (21) emphasizing that the policy considerations of the two cases can be 'assessed side by side'.

[124] *Witt*, European Competition Journal 2016, 435 (436).

[125] See above p. 27.

[126] *Witt*, European Competition Journal 2016, 435 (447).

[127] *Enchelmaier*, in: Competition on the Internet, 5 (6).

[128] *Künzler*, Restoring Consumer Sovereignty, p. 28.

[129] Court of Justice, 11/12/2003, Case C-322/01 DocMorris, ECLI:EU:C:2003:664.

[130] Court of Justice, 02/12/2010, Case C-108/09 Ker-Optika, ECLI:EU:C:2010:725.

[131] Court of Justice, 11/12/2003, Case C-322/01 DocMorris, ECLI:EU:C:2003:664, para. 113; Court of Justice, 02/12/2010, Case C-108/09 Ker-Optika, ECLI:EU:C:2010:725, para. 73.

further be reduced through "on-line interactive features".[132] This suggests that the Court of Justice may see less need for advice through specialist brick and mortar retailers today, making online sales restrictions harder to justify.

Second, the Court of Justice questioned the validity of protecting a product's image or aura of luxury as a legitimate objective of selective distribution systems.[133] Iacobucci and Winter have criticized the Pierre Fabre judgment in this regard, accusing it of paternalism.[134] They argue that the image of a product is worthy of protection just as much as its quality and that other measures taken by manufacturers to improve their products' images are (rightly) not regulated.[135] More importantly, they emphasize that, from a purely economic perspective,[136] the Court of Justice's approach (and even EU law's approach in general) is not explainable as economic theory supports "a relatively laissez-faire policy towards selective distribution restraints established by manufacturers."[137] Ackermann suggests that the Court of Justice was motivated by a concern that image-creating vertical agreements could exploit consumers' bounded rationality and result in unwanted purchases: consumers could buy as a result of herd behaviour without properly assessing whether the product and its attributes actually justify the price.[138] He emphasizes, however, that this position would require a proper behavioural economic foundation.[139] This interpretation of the judgment would indeed mean that the Court of Justice once more took into account the consumers' decision-making and tried to protect consumers' autonomy. The case also shows some similarity to the Vichy case[140]: here, too, the manufacturer attempted to free-ride on pharmacists' reputation and frame their products as 'health products'.

The Pierre Fabre judgment does not identify any concrete market effect or evaluate the likelihood thereof. Instead, the Court simply states that agreements constituting a selective distribution system "necessarily affect competition in the common market"[141] and concluded that since they were not, the agreement must restrict competition. This approach, while consistent with earlier case law, falls short of clearly identifying the restriction of competition.

---

[132] Court of Justice, 11/12/2003, Case C-322/01 DocMorris, ECLI:EU:C:2003:664, para. 114.

[133] GA Mazák had argued that this is a legitimate objective but the total ban of internet sales is disproportionate, see General Advocate Mazák, 03/03/2011, Case C-439/09 Pierre Fabre, ECLI:EU:C:2011:113, para. 57.

[134] *Iacobucci/Winter*, Antitrust Law Journal 2016, 47 (63).

[135] *Iacobucci/Winter*, Antitrust Law Journal 2016, 47 (58).

[136] See above from p. 69.

[137] *Iacobucci/Winter*, Antitrust Law Journal 2016, 47 (55).

[138] *Ackermann*, in: Herausforderungen für die Wettbewerbsordnung, 73 (83).

[139] *Ackermann*, in: Herausforderungen für die Wettbewerbsordnung, 73 (83).

[140] See above p. 106.

[141] Court of Justice, 13/10/2011, Case C-439/09 Pierre Fabre, ECLI:EU:C:2011:649, para. 39.

dd) Coty

As the Court of Justice did not explicitly overrule the LeClerc judgement, its decision in Pierre Fabre created a lot of uncertainty and was harshly criticized.[142] It was not until 2017 that the Court of Justice had the chance to clarify the issue in its Coty judgment.[143] The Higher Regional Court Frankfurt am Main had asked the Court in a preliminary reference question whether a third-party platform ban in a selective distribution agreement for luxury cosmetics can be compatible with Art. 101(1) TFEU. This question arose between Coty Prestige, a manufacturer of luxury cosmetics and Parfümerie Akzente, an authorized Coty retailer that operated brick and mortar stores but also wanted to sell Coty products on Amazon.[144] The latter was not permissible under the selective distribution agreement. Like Pierre Fabre, Coty argued that the restriction was necessary to preserve the luxury image of its goods.

The Court of Justice reaffirmed that selective distribution systems "necessarily affect competition in the internal market."[145] Only when the Metro criteria are met, such agreements do not fall under Art. 101(1) TFEU. The Court of Justice then refers to the Copad case and emphasizes that the quality of luxury goods "is not just the result of their material characteristics, but also of the allure and prestigious image which bestow on them an aura of luxury".[146] Consequently, luxury products can require selective distribution systems to preserve the quality of those goods and ensure their proper use; thus, the Metro test is applicable.[147] The Court of Justice, as a result, effectively confined the Pierre Fabre judgement to its facts, i.e., an absolute and general online ban.[148] While the Court of Justice tried to distinguish the facts of the cases by arguing that Pierre Fabre was concerned not with luxury goods but with cosmetics,[149] it effectively changed its jurisprudence. Regarding the specific selective distribution system applied by Coty, the Court of Justice found that, in principle, it can fulfil the Metro criteria.[150] In particular, the prohibition of sales through online platforms was deemed appropriate for preserving the quality and luxury image of the goods in question.[151] The Court of Justice saw "a risk of deterioration of the online presentation of those goods which is liable to harm their luxury image and thus their very character" in the sale through online platforms.[152]

---

[142] *Colangelo/Torti*, European Competition Journal 2018, 81 (93); *Monti*, World Competition 2013, 489 (501–502); *Witt*, European Competition Journal 2016, 435 (448).
[143] Court of Justice, 06/12/2017, Case C-230/16 Coty, ECLI:EU:C:2017:941.
[144] Court of Justice, 06/12/2017, Case C-230/16 Coty, ECLI:EU:C:2017:941, paras. 8–9.
[145] Court of Justice, 06/12/2017, Case C-230/16 Coty, ECLI:EU:C:2017:941, para. 23.
[146] Court of Justice, 06/12/2017, Case C-230/16 Coty, ECLI:EU:C:2017:941, para. 25.
[147] Court of Justice, 06/12/2017, Case C-230/16 Coty, ECLI:EU:C:2017:941, paras. 28–29.
[148] *Colangelo/Torti*, European Competition Journal 2018, 81 (102).
[149] Court of Justice, 06/12/2017, Case C-230/16 Coty, ECLI:EU:C:2017:941, para. 32.
[150] Court of Justice, 06/12/2017, Case C-230/16 Coty, ECLI:EU:C:2017:941, paras. 37–58.
[151] Court of Justice, 06/12/2017, Case C-230/16 Coty, ECLI:EU:C:2017:941, para. 46.
[152] Court of Justice, 06/12/2017, Case C-230/16 Coty, ECLI:EU:C:2017:941, para. 49.

Thus, the Court endorsed the image free-riding rationale[153] for selective distribution systems under the Metro conditions. In doing so, it adopted a more economic perspective on consumer decision-making – arguing that if a manufacturer enhances its image to boost consumers' willingness to pay, consumers *must* derive greater benefits from the product, in line with the revealed preferences approach.[154] Under the Coty judgment, it is legitimate that manufacturers use vertical agreements to influence consumers' preference formation.

However, this was not the Court of Justice's only argument. Referring to Copad, the Court of Justice also emphasized that the "aura of luxury" is "essential in that it enables consumers to distinguish [the goods in question] from similar goods".[155] In this way, the Court maintained its concern for consumer decision-making as a normative objective, presuming that selective distribution systems which protect a product's image ultimately enhance consumers' ability to make informed choices.

g) Conclusion

The EU Courts have considered the effects of vertical agreements on consumers' decision-making. Such effects have helped to determine whether an agreement restricts competition (where it deprives consumers of neutral advice) or does not restrict competition (where it leads to better retail advisory services).

The Court of Justice in Coty accepted that agreements designed to protect or enhance a product's or brand's image can fall outside the scope of Art. 101(1) TFEU. Although earlier cases like Consten/Grundig viewed product differentiation by vertical agreements as detrimental, later judgments have endorsed product differentiation as a means to create distinct products – albeit primarily for luxury goods.

The Court of Justice typically presupposes a prima facie restriction of competition and evaluates whether this restriction is objectively justified.[156] This approach is unsatisfactory because it does not clearly explain why a restriction is identified in the first place. Although consumer autonomy appears to play a certain role, there is no coherent framework or theory of harm for incorporating it in the competition law analysis. Moreover, the line between which factors are relevant to find or exclude a restriction of competition and what can serve as a justification under Art. 101(3) TFEU remains unclear.

[153] See above from p. 47.

[154] See for this approach below p. 166.

[155] Court of Justice, 06/12/2017, Case C-230/16 Coty, ECLI:EU:C:2017:941, para. 25.

[156] See in this regard already above from p. 41.

2. Competition authorities and consumer autonomy

"Due to such [online] bans, retailers reach fewer consumers. Consumers, in turn, are robbed from having the greater choice and lower prices that competition on the Internet would give them."[157]

As illustrated by this excerpt from a speech by former Commissioner for Competition Italianer, the EU's approach to online sales restrictions may be partly explained by a consumer-focused perspective that takes into account consumers' decision-making. A key concern emphasized by competition authorities is that online sales restrictions may increase search costs and thereby harm consumers. In the Vertical Guidelines, for example, the Commission bases the prohibition of (total) price comparison bans on an increase in consumer search costs:

"Restrictions on the use of price comparison services may increase consumer search costs and thereby soften retail price competition. They may also restrict the buyer's ability to reach potential customers, inform them about its offering and direct them to its online store."[158]

Likewise, in its E-Commerce Sector Inquiry, the Commission states:

"The results of the sector inquiry show that the increased price transparency online is the feature that most affects the behaviour of customers and retailers. It lowers search costs for customers who are able to instantaneously obtain and compare product and price information online and switch swiftly from one channel to another (online/offline)."[159]

This rationale helps explain why the EU adopts a stricter stance on bans targeting price comparison websites compared to those on online marketplaces. Price comparison websites are seen as particularly valuable for lowering search costs, since they allow consumers to search and compare products from a wide range of providers.[160]

Furthermore, the Commission has adopted several decisions that correspond to the focus on the internet's positive effects on consumer decisions. In the context of an authorisation of a selective distribution system operated by Yves Saint Laurent, the Commission emphasised that internet selling was possible in this system.[161] In B&W loudspeakers, it cleared a selective distribution system after the company had agreed to remove certain hardcore restrictions, including a ban

---

[157] *Italianer*, 07/03/2014, Speech at the Competition Policy in the Digital Age 47th Innsbruck Symposium – 'Real sector economy and the internet – digital interconnection as an issue for competition policy', available at http://ec. europa.eu/competition/speeches/text/sp2014_01_en.pdf.

[158] Vertical Guidelines, para. 347.

[159] *European Commission*, E-Commerce Sector Inquiry (Commission Staff Working Document), para. 147.

[160] *Mullan/Timan*, Competition Law & Policy Debate 2017, 11 (17–18) who note, however, that there is no empirical evidence that consumers actually make use of price comparison websites and online marketplaces in different ways.

[161] European Commission, 15/07/2001, AT.36533 Yves Saint Laurent.

on sales through the internet.[162] In the Guess decision, the Commission considered that the requirement in the selective distribution system that retailers may not use or bid on the Guess brand name and trademarks for online advertising constitutes a restriction of competition by object.[163] According to the Commission, this clause did not pursue a legitimate objective because it reduced the "findability" of Guess retailers[164] and because there was "no risk of confusion as to the origin of the products."[165]

Some national competition authorities have made similar arguments. The French Competition Authority, in a contribution to the OECD competition roundtable, states

"that e-commerce appears to be a factor that encourages competition, especially in terms of price and diversity of choice for consumers. [...] The advent of e-commerce especially requires traders to be more adaptable. They can themselves invest in this new distribution channel and/or innovate so as to differentiate themselves and create added value for consumers."[166]

In its Pierre Fabre decision (which eventually led to the Court of Justice's Pierre Fabre judgment), the Authority found a total internet ban to restrict competition by object.[167] Regarding a possible justification under Art. 101(3) TFEU, the authority emphasized that "[t]he use of the internet [...] facilitates access to product information and allows consumers to make price comparisons."[168] In STIHL, the Authority also emphasized the advantages of "being able to compare prices and products available online"[169] in finding that a total online ban restricts competition by object.[170]

Likewise, the UK Competition and Markets Authority ('CMA') in Ping, concerning an online sales (but not advertising) ban, stressed the importance of the internet as a tool for consumers to facilitate comparison across products and retailers, in particular through price comparison websites.[171] This was one of the arguments put forward to find a restriction of competition by object.

The strongest proponent of the internet as a sales channel, however, appears to be the Bundeskartellamt which regularly expresses very positive views on the

[162] European Commission, 24/06/2002, AT.37709 B&W Loudspeakers.

[163] European Commission, 17/12/2018, AT.40428 Guess, paras. 114–126.

[164] European Commission, 17/12/2018, AT.40428 Guess, para. 120.

[165] European Commission, 17/12/2018, AT.40428 Guess, para. 117.

[166] *OECD*, Roundtable on Vertical Restraints for Online Sales – Note by France, p. 100.

[167] Autorité de la Concurrence, 29/10/2008, Décision n° 08-D-25 Pierre Fabre, paras. 56–59.

[168] Autorité de la Concurrence, 29/10/2008, Décision n° 08-D-25 Pierre Fabre, para. 82 (translation by the author).

[169] Autorité de la Concurrence, 24/10/2018, Décision n° 18-D-23 STIHL, para. 232.

[170] Autorité de la Concurrence, 24/10/2018, Décision n° 18-D-23 STIHL, paras. 240–244.

[171] Competition and Markets Authority, 24/08/2017, Case 50230 Ping paras. 4.54 and 4.76.

internet.[172] In its contribution to the OECD roundtable on vertical restraints, for example, it emphasizes:

“Beyond lower prices, reduced transaction costs as well as new or additional services (like convenient ‘business hours’ or home delivery) consumers can benefit from – and increasingly make use of the enhanced availability of information on different prices and quality (like test reports, the experiences of other consumers or the exchange of information on social networks). The increased availability of information (e.g., collection and evaluation of customer data in online shops) also allows businesses to better adapt product features, services and marketing efforts to customers’ preferences and competitors’ strategies.”[173]

Similarly, in a background note on vertical agreements in the internet economy, it emphasizes that online sales increase market transparency and reduce consumers’ search costs, thereby intensifying competition.[174] According to the Bundeskartellamt, this enhanced transparency can contribute to making consumer decisions more rational and less biased.[175] The authority further argues that search costs could be increased through platform bans.[176] In the ASICS decision, the Bundeskartellamt also referred to reduced search costs through online sales and a reduction of the information asymmetry between consumers and retailers.[177] In the related case report, it praised online retail by stating:

“The end consumer is put in a position to compare offers in a more time-saving and cost-effective manner in terms of quality and price than is possible in stationary retail, and can also include considerably more offers in his comparison.”[178]

The case concerned various restrictions on online sales for ASICS retailers (e.g., on advertising and price comparison website compatibility) within a selective distribution system. The Bundeskartellamt relied on the case law that selective distribution agreements, in principle, restrict competition where they are not objectively justified (Metro).[179] It, therefore, limited itself to a very short explanation regarding the restriction of competition.[180] One key element thereof was that “the intensification of competition, particularly in terms of price, which is generally possible through the use of the internet as a distribution channel, is thus restricted.”[181]

[172] Outside of the European Union, the competition authority of Chinese Taipei also seems quite fond of internet sales, see *OECD*, Roundtable on Vertical Restraints for Online Sales – Note by Chinese Taipei, p. 138.

[173] *OECD*, Roundtable on Vertical Restraints for Online Sales – Note by Germany, p. 111.

[174] *Bundeskartellamt*, Vertical Restraints in the Internet Economy, p. 15; *Bundeskartellamt*, Wettbewerbsbeschränkungen im Internetvertrieb, p. 3.

[175] *Bundeskartellamt*, Wettbewerb und Verbraucherverhalten, pp. 11–14.

[176] *Bundeskartellamt*, Vertical Restraints in the Internet Economy, pp. 23–24.

[177] Bundeskartellamt, 26/08/2015, B2–98/11 ASICS, paras. 78–80; see also Bundesgerichtshof, 12/12/2017, KVZ 41/17 ASICS, NZKART 2018, 96, para. 25.

[178] Bundeskartellamt, 26/08/2015, B2–98/11 ASICS (Fallbericht), p. 2.

[179] Bundeskartellamt, 26/08/2015, B2–98/11 ASICS, paras. 246–251.

[180] Bundeskartellamt, 26/08/2015, B2–98/11 ASICS, paras. 253–255.

[181] Bundeskartellamt, 26/08/2015, B2–98/11 ASICS, para. 255.

Albeit not the sole motivation for the above-mentioned cases, a certain pattern of argumentation may be distilled: (1) the internet reduces search costs for consumers and increases competition, and in turn, (2) any restriction on internet sales must restrict competition.

3. Conclusion: consumer autonomy plays a role in the realm of vertical agreements

The EU Courts have considered the effects of vertical agreements on consumers' decision-making in their case law. This concern first emerged in in Consten/Grundig where the Court warned that excessive product differentiation (products that are "individually distinct in the eyes of the consumer") through vertical agreements could undermine effective competition.[182] The effects of vertical agreements on consumers' decision-making were also relevant in the Metro case law. This concerns, on the one hand, the reasoning as to why certain selective distribution systems do *not* restrict competition and, on the other hand, the limits to this exception. It is a legitimate objective of selective distribution systems to ensure that consumers receive appropriate advice. The Court of Justice's line of argumentation rested on the assumption that selective distribution systems can *positively* influence the consumer's decision-making abilities, i.e., help the consumer to choose the product that best fits their needs. That explains the restrictive criteria under Metro, in particular, that the characteristics of the product in question need to require selective distribution to preserve its quality or ensure its proper use. This can be traced back to Telser's free-riding hypothesis.[183] Selective distribution was hence seen as "an aspect of competition which accords with Article 85(1) [Art. 101(1) TFEU]" because it can increase consumers' abilities to choose between different offers and make proper use of a product.[184] The Metro exception's limitation to qualitative rather than quantitative criteria can also be explained by concerns for the consumer's decision-making. This limitation is motivated by the idea that retailers should be neutral marketers and not steer the consumer to purchase a particular product for reasons other than that it best fits consumers' needs. In this way, the Court has drawn a distinction based on consumer autonomy: agreements that enhance the consumer's decision-making process are generally considered pro-competitive, while those that impair it and disrupt the link between market success and consumer choice are viewed as anti-competitive.

Most recently, consumer autonomy has played an important role in the debate on online sales restrictions. Competition authorities – including the Bundeskartellamt, the European Commission, the French Competition Authority, and the Competition and Markets Authority – have emphasized that the internet reduces

[182] Court of Justice, 13/06/1966, Joined Cases 56 and 58–64 Consten/Grundig, ECLI: EU:C:1966:41, p. 343.

[183] See above p. 45.

[184] *Künzler*, Journal of Antitrust Enforcement 2019, 249 (257).

search costs by facilitating easier price and product comparisons, and have argued that, in turn, bans on online sales restrict competition.

Although consumer autonomy has played a certain role in assessing whether selective distribution agreements and online sales restrictions are objectively justified, case law has yet developed a theory of harm that can precisely identify a competition restriction based on concerns for consumer autonomy. This thesis will address this gap in Chapter 3.

§ 2 Consumer autonomy as a goal of EU competition law

This section will analyse how consumer autonomy can plausibly form part of the normative goals of EU competition law. It will first discuss how consumer autonomy can fit into the values of EU law in general (I.) and show a growing focus on the consumer as an active market participant and agent for the internal market (II.) and how consumer autonomy can be a concern for competition law and consumer protection law alike (III.). Subsequently, it will analyse how consumer autonomy can fit into the broader structure of EU competition law (IV.) and its ordoliberal tradition (V.). This is followed by a discussion on the relationship between consumer welfare and consumer autonomy as different aspects and goals of competition law (VI.). Further, the section explores how a series of important antitrust decisions, mainly outside of the realm of vertical agreements, have already taken up the notion of consumer autonomy in their analyses and results (VII.). The section closes with a conclusion (VIII.).

I. Protecting autonomy as a fundamental value of the EU

This section will reflect on how consumer autonomy can fit in the constitutional structure of EU fundamental rights. Podszun raised this question, claiming that Art. 16 of the Charter of Fundamental Rights (freedom to conduct a business) provides an additional argument to protect the autonomy of economic actors, including consumers.[185] Addressing the question of whether consumer autonomy as a matter of EU fundamental rights and values shall play a role in antitrust law requires, as a first step, establishing whether EU competition law can *at all* be influenced by those factors (1.). As a second step, it will be discussed whether consumer autonomy can be recognized as a fundamental value of the EU (2.).

1. Are fundamental rights or values relevant for the interpretation of competition law?

It is sometimes argued that competition law ought to remain apolitical, grounded solely in considerations of economic efficiency, with all other values excluded

[185] *Podszun*, SSRN 2019, pp. 25–26.

from the analysis.[186] Indeed, considering that competition law on the EU level is largely laid down in the Treaties themselves and thus forms part of primary law, it must be addressed whether antitrust law is an insular field that should be shielded from other influences which threaten to water it down. However, a closer examination reveals that this is not the case.[187]

It is a long-standing principle of EU law

> "that every provision of community law must be placed in its context and interpreted in the light of the provisions of community law as a whole, regard being had to the objectives thereof and to its state of evolution at the date on which the provision in question is to be applied."[188]

This is supported by Art. 7 TEU, which explicitly states that the Union "shall ensure consistency between its policies and its activities." There is no stand-alone provision and no insular area of EU law – everything needs to be seen in the broader context, and interdependencies cannot be ignored. This can be illustrated by the Court of Justice's case law on the relationship between internal market freedoms and fundamental rights. Both sets of rules, like the competition law provisions, are primary law and thus equally ranked in the EU legal order.[189] The Court of Justice has consistently taken into account the interdependencies between these fields. As neither generally prevails over the other, the Court of Justice has developed a breach/justification model: fundamental freedoms can justify the restriction of fundamental rights and vice versa.[190] In Schmidberger, for example, fundamental rights served to justify a Member State's restriction on the free movement of goods.[191] This relationship also works in reverse. The Court of Justice has accepted the internal market freedoms as a reason to justify restrictions of fundamental rights.[192] Further, fundamental rights constitute a limitation on restrictions of internal market freedoms: while such restrictions can be justified for reasons of "overriding requirements in the public interest", this term,

---

[186] *Bork*, Antitrust Paradox; *Posner*, Antitrust Law; *Posner*, University of Chicago Law Review 1977, 1 (13); *Wright*, Yale Law Journal 2012, 2216; *Wright/Ginsburg*, Fordham Law Review 2013, 2405.

[187] This section is partly based on an article published in the European Competition Journal in 2021, see *Persch*, European Competition Journal 2021, 542.

[188] Court of Justice, 10/06/1982, Case 283/81 C.I.L.F.I.T., ECLI:EU:C:1982:335, para. 20; see also the very early judgement Court of Justice, 07/12/1962, Case 9/61 Netherlands/High Authority, ECLI:EU:C:1962:27, p. 235; regarding the Court of Justice's interpretative methods see *Lenaerts/Gutierrez-Fons*, Columbia Journal of European Law 2013, 3.

[189] *Trstenjak/Beysen*, ELR 2013, 293 (315).

[190] *Jarass*, EuR 2013, 29 (31); *Trstenjak/Beysen*, ELR 2013, 293 (314).

[191] Court of Justice, 06/12/2003, Case C-112/00 Schmidberger, ECLI:EU:C:2003:333, paras. 65–95; see also Court of Justice, 14/10/2004, Case C-36/02 Omega, ECLI:EU:C:2004:541, para. 35; Court of Justice, 14/02/2008, Case C-244/06 Dynamic Medien, ECLI:EU:C:2008:85, paras. 41–42.

[192] Court of Justice, 15/07/2010, Case C-271/08 Commission/Germany, ECLI:EU:C:2010:426, paras. 43–49.

according to the Court of Justice, has to be interpreted "in light of the general principles of EU law, in particular, the fundamental rights henceforth guaranteed by the Charter".[193] Thus, if a national rule that restricts an internal market freedom is not compatible with fundamental rights, it cannot be justified.[194] On the other hand, there can also be overlaps in the scope of protection between fundamental rights and fundamental freedoms, e.g., the freedom to conduct a business (Art. 16 of the Charter) and the freedom of establishment (Art. 49 TFEU).[195] In such cases, the Court of Justice conducts a single proportionality assessment.[196] Ultimately, the case law demonstrates that a fair balance must be struck between fundamental rights and fundamental freedoms. This supports the conclusion that no formal hierarchical relationship is required in order to reconcile the normative weight of different sets of rules.

In many respects, competition law is analogous to the fundamental freedoms: it is enshrined in primary law and shares the overarching objective of market integration While the fundamental freedoms primarily target barriers imposed by Member State measures, competition law serves a complementary function by preventing such barriers from being re-established through the conduct of private undertakings. If fundamental rights and EU values can inform the interpretation and application of the fundamental freedoms, the same must logically apply to competition law. The Court of Justice has also taken into account other legitimate objectives in the application of EU competition law in its Meca-Medina[197] and Wouters[198] case law.

This argument also extends more broadly to the Union's foundational values as laid down in Article 2 TEU. According to this provision, the Union is founded on the values of respect for human dignity, freedom, democracy, equality, the rule of law and respect for human rights. The provision is not purely symbolic; it follows already from its systematic position as one of the first Treaty provisions in Title I TEU ('common provisions') that the 'Union values' are relevant for the interpretation of the Treaties as a whole.[199] This is also in line with the Court of Justice's case law that has taken into account the 'objectives of the Treaty' (Art. 3 TEU) – similarly laid down in the 'common provisions' – when interpreting EU

[193] Court of Justice, 04/03/2014, Case C-390/12 Pfleger, ECLI:EU:C:2014:281, para. 35.

[194] Court of Justice, 18/06/1991, Case C-260/89 ERT, ECLI:EU:C.1991:254, paras. 43–45; Court of Justice, 26/06/1997, Case C-368/95 Familiapress, ECLI:EU:C:1997:325, paras. 24–29; Court of Justice, 04/03/2014, Case C-390/12 Pfleger, ECLI:EU:C:2014:281, para. 35.

[195] Court of Justice, 20/12/2017, Case C-322/16 Global Starnet, ECLI:EU:C:2017:985, para. 50.

[196] Court of Justice, 20/12/2017, Case C-322/16 Global Starnet, ECLI:EU:C:2017:985, para. 50..

[197] Court of Justice, 18/06/2006, Case C-519/04 P Meca Medina, ECLI:EU:C:2006:492

[198] Court of Justice, 19/02/2002, Case C-309/99 Wouters, ECLI:EU:C:2002:98.

[199] *Potacs*, EuR 2016, 164 (167); *von Bogdandy*, in: Europäisches Verfassungsrecht, 13 (33–36); compare also *Lenaerts*, EuGRZ 2017, 639.

primary law in general[200] and its antitrust rules in particular[201].[202] Promoting the Union's values is further explicitly mentioned as one of the EU's objectives in Art. 3 TEU, leading to the logical conclusion that when the Union's goals are used for the Treaties' interpretation, the same must be true for its values.

The situation in Europe differs markedly from that in the United States, where the prevailing view seems to be that non-economic considerations are generally excluded from the scope of antitrust law[203]. In contrast, EU law permits a more integrated approach: the interpretation and application of competition rules can be informed by broader considerations, including fundamental rights and the core values of the Union. This does not imply that reference needs to be made to fundamental rights and values in each antitrust case. However, it requires at least a minimum level of consistency between the different areas of law. If consumer autonomy is a fundamental value of the EU – as discussed in the next section – this would indicate that it can, in principle, also be considered in the context of competition law.

2. Consumer autonomy as a value of the EU

According to Art. 38 of the Charter, consumer protection is a fundamental principle of the EU and may therefore be relevant for the interpretation of competition law.[204] Even more explicitly, according to Art. 12 TEU, consumer protection requirements shall be taken into account in defining and implementing other Union policies and activities – a principle that also applies to competition law.[205] Moreover, according to Art. 169 TFEU the Union shall promote the interests of consumers and ensure a high level of consumer protection and shall therefore "contribute to protecting the health, safety and economic interests of consumers, as well as to promoting their right to information, education and to organise themselves in order to safeguard their interests."

Without delving into the details of the consumer image that underlies the relevant provisions and the corresponding substantive requirements that must guide consumer protection law,[206] it can be concluded from the Treaty and the

---

[200] Court of Justice, 23/03/1982, Case 53/81 Levin, ECLI:EU:C:1982:105, para. 15; Court of Justice, 25/02/1988, Case 15/81 Gaston Schul, ECLI:EU:C:1982:135, para. 33; Court of Justice, 25/02/1988, Case 299/86 Drexl, ECLI:EU:C:1988:103, para. 24.

[201] Court of Justice, 21/02/1973, Case 6–72 Continental Can, ECLI:EU:C:1973:22, para. 25.

[202] *Müller/Christensen*, Juristische Methodik, pp. 84–85; *Pechstein/Drechsler*, in: Europäische Methodenlehre, 181 (194–197).

[203] *Colino*, Journal of Business Law 2019, 329 (341); *Day*, Fordham Law Review 2020, 1315 (1321); *Shapiro*, International Journal of Industrial Organization 2018, 714 (716).

[204] Court of Justice, 20/12/2011, T-224/10 Test Achat, ECLI:EU:T:2011:588, para. 43; *Endler*, Verbraucher im Kartellrecht, p. 18; *Stuyck*, Journal of Consumer Policy 2005, 1.

[205] Court of Justice, 20/12/2011, T-224/10 Test Achat, ECLI:EU:T:2011:588, para. 43; *Endler*, Verbraucher im Kartellrecht, pp. 15–16.

[206] See in this regard *Schmitt*, Verbraucherleitbild.

Charter that consumer autonomy is an important value of the Union. In particular, the wording of Art. 169 TFEU shows that consumer protection is not limited to safeguarding consumers' economic and physical interests but instead aims at empowering them to take active decisions in the market. They shall be able to raise their voices through informed and educated consumption decisions on the one hand, as well as through collective efforts (through consumer associations) on the other hand. One important area in this context is the protection of consumers' preferences.[207] This refers to a strengthening of consumers' freedom to choose and make independent decisions.[208] Consumers must not only be protected in the exercise of their preferences, i.e., through consumption decisions but also regarding the very formation of those preferences. This is reflected by Art. 169 TFEU emphasizing the education of consumers. It fits neatly in the definition of autonomy underlying this thesis[209]: consumers must have sufficient cognitive and mental capacities as well as education to take autonomous decisions. EU law and policy, according to Art. 12, 169 TFEU and Art. 38 of the Charter, must take this into account as an important goal and value.

Furthermore, consumer protection under Article 38 of the Charter must be viewed in the wider context of the Charter as a whole. It complements Article 16, which protects the freedom to conduct a business, and highlights that the European economic model is not exclusively producer-oriented.[210] The freedom to conduct a business, however, necessarily relies on the autonomy of economic actors.[211] The same autonomy must also be guaranteed for consumers on the demand side of the market. Art. 38, as part of Title IV of the Charter (Solidarity), also fits into the general concept of this Title that is aimed at securing the autonomy and well-being of European citizens as employees and consumers.[212] While Art. 38 of the Charter does not contain a subjective right, it nonetheless constitutes a general principle.[213] As such, it is relevant for the interpretation and application of other areas of EU law, including antitrust law.

II. Focusing on the consumer as an agent for competition and the internal market

The previous section demonstrated that consumer autonomy is a recognised value within the EU legal order. Building on this normative foundation, the present section examines how the role of the consumer as an active and empowe-

[207] *Schmidt-Kessel*, in: Frankfurter Kommentar EUV/GRC/AEUV, Art. 12 AEUV, paras. 47–49.

[208] *Krebber*, in: Calliess/Ruffert, Art. 169 AEUV, para. 9.

[209] See above from p. 6.

[210] Compare *Giesecke*, in: Meyer/Hölscheidt, EU-Grundrechtecharta, Art. 38, para. 7.

[211] *Podszun*, SSRN 2019, p. 25.

[212] *Benöhr*, European Union Law and Consumer Rights, p. 57.

[213] *Giesecke*, in: Meyer/Hölscheidt, EU-Grundrechtecharta, Art. 38, paras. 11–12.

red participant in competition and in the internal market[214] is further reflected in EU secondary law. This analysis provides additional support for an argument that there is a broader trend in EU law to empower the consumer and their active role.

1. The consumer as an agent for market integration: the Consumer Rights Directive

Such a trend is most prominently observable in the field of consumer protection law. Going back to the European Commission's Green Paper on Consumer Protection from 2001[215], the empowerment of the consumer and their role as an active market participant in the internal market is at the forefront of the EU's consumer protection policy. In the Green Paper, the Commission identified fragmented regulation in the field of consumer protection as a barrier to the internal market.[216] According to the Commission,

> "it is the cross-border movement of goods and services that allows consumers to search out bargains and innovative products and services and thus ensures that they *optimise their consumption decision*."[217] This approach goes beyond the traditional account of consumer protection law to protect the consumer as the weak party in a situational imbalance[218].

Instead, the goal is to empower consumers to act as agents of market integration by fostering trust and confidence in the internal market. This is to be achieved by establishing a uniform and high level of consumer protection across the Union.[219] Consumer protection and internal market law onceptually and functionally intertwined at the EU level. This approach has a long-standing history in EU law.[220] The focus here shifted more and more from protecting the consumer as the weak party to a conception of consumer law as 'market conduct law' that aims at remodelling the consumer's role in order to enable them to perform their function as an agent for the creation of the internal market.[221]

The emphasis on the consumer as an active market participant has been accompanied by some legislative developments. The Consumer Rights Directive, for example, in its Art. 22, requires the trader to seek the consumer's express

---

[214] See also *Stuyck*, Journal of Consumer Policy 2005, 1.

[215] *European Commission*, Green Paper on European Consumer Protection, COM (2001) 531 final ('Green Paper on Consumer Protection').

[216] *European Commission*, Green Paper on Consumer Protection, p. 3.

[217] *European Commission*, Green Paper on Consumer Protection, p. 3. (emphasis added).

[218] *Endler*, Verbraucher im Kartellrecht, pp. 36–37.

[219] Directive 2011/83/EU of the European Parliament and of the Council of 25 October 2011 on consumer rights, amending Council Directive 93/13/EEC and Directive 1999/44/EC of the European Parliament and of the Council and repealing Council Directive 85/577/EEC and Directive 97/7/EC of the European Parliament and of the Council, OJ L 304, 22.11.2011, pp. 64–88 ('Consumer Rights Directive'), recitals 6–7.

[220] *Stuyck*, CMLR 2000, 367 (379).

[221] *Reich*, Sidney Law Review 1992, 23 (26).

consent – contrary to using default options – to any extra payment. This prevents traders from using 'opt-out' mechanisms, that is pre-selected additional services coming with additional costs which are automatically added to the consumer's order if they do not explicitly reject them (often by un-checking a pre-ticked box). Such practices had been deployed, for example, by hotels regarding extra options such as breakfast and by airlines and travel agencies regarding extra luggage, seat options, priority check-in or travel insurance.[222] A similar rule is also included in Art. 23 of the Air Services Regulation[223], which explicitly requires that optional price supplements to airfares and air rates are communicated in a clear, transparent and unambiguous way at the start of the booking process and accepted by the customer on an opt-in basis. These provisions reflect the idea that the consumer shall make active choices in the market and that those decisions must not be superseded by traders.

2. *Allowing cross-border comparison: the Geoblocking Regulation*

Another insightful piece of legislation regarding consumer autonomy is the Geoblocking Regulation[224] which aims at "widening customer choice and access to goods and services".[225] It prevents traders from blocking or limiting customers'[226] access to online interfaces based on their nationality, place of residence or establishment (Art. 3(1)). A customer must hence be able to access each country-specific online store and view its offers.[227] A French shopper, for example, must be able to access a German online shop and must not be automatically redirected to its French equivalent (which may have different options and prices).[228] The idea is to increase transparency within the internal market; consumers shall be able to access product information and compare prices and offers across countries.[229] This, too reflects an understanding of the consumer as an active market participant who is seeking the best possible offer in the internal market and who does not have to settle for the offer presented to them in their home state. The underlying idea is clear: even if the Directive does not force traders to conclude

[222] For examples, see *Schirmbacher/Schmidt*, Computer und Recht 2014, 107 (118).

[223] Regulation EC 1008/2008 of 24 September 2008 on common rules for the operation of air services in the Community, OJ L 293, 31.10.2008, pp. 3–20 ('Air Services Regulation').

[224] Regulation (EU) 2018/302 of the European Parliament and of the Council of 28 February 2018 on addressing unjustified geo-blocking and other forms of discrimination based on customers' nationality, place of residence or place of establishment within the internal market and amending Regulations (EC) No 2006/2004 and (EU) 2017/2394 and Directive 2009/22/EC, OJ L 60I, 2.3.2018, pp. 1–15.

[225] Geoblocking Regulation recital 5; for the relationship between geoblocking regulation and VBER, see *Christodoulou/Holzwarth*, NZKart 2022, 540 (543).

[226] According to Art. 2(13), the Directive uses the term 'costumer' to refer to consumers but also to undertakings when they are end users of the purchased product or service.

[227] *Bernhard*, NJW 2019, 472 (474).

[228] *Kohler*, ZEuP 2020, 253 (255).

[229] Geoblocking Regulation, recital 18; *Kohler*, ZEuP 2020, 253 (255).

cross-border trades,[230] the opportunity to compare prices and offers across countries alone will empower consumers to pressure traders in the home country to match offers elsewhere.[231] In this regard, the Regulation also has a competition dimension.[232] Traders under this concept shall not prevent the consumer from learning about products and prices in different Member States. This enhances consumers' abilities to make an informed consumption decision and can thus be said to enhance autonomy: the consumer is less dependent on the information provided to them by the traders in their own Member States.

3. Revealing nudges: the Unfair Commercial Practices Directive

In line with the overarching goals of EU consumer protection law, the Unfair Commercial Practices Directive seeks to foster cross-border activities and increase consumer confidence in the internal market.[233] As such, consumer choice shall be increased.[234] According to Art. 5 of the Directive, unfair commercial practices shall be prohibited, and a practice shall be unfair if it is contrary to the requirements of professional diligence and materially distorts or is likely to materially distort the economic behaviour with regard to the product of the relevant (average) consumer. Similarly, omitting material information can be misleading, according to Art. 7 of the Directive. Of particular interest here are some of the most recent amendments to the Directive regarding online shopping through the Directive on Modernisation of Consumer Protection Rules[235] as part of the 'New Deal for Consumers'[236]. The amended Directive introduces several new rules on traders engaged in online shopping in general and online marketplaces specifically.

First, the amended Directive in its Art. 7 point (4a) sets forth rules concerning the ranking of offers. These are based on the assessment that "higher ranking or any prominent placement of commercial offers within online search results" has an important impact on consumers.[237] When consumers are provided with the possibility to search for products, the main parameters determining the ranking

---

[230] Geoblocking Regulation, recital 18; *Bernhard*, NJW 2019, 472 (475).

[231] Compare *Kohler*, ZEuP 2020, 253 (258).

[232] *Picht*, JECLAP 2020, 244 (244–245).

[233] Unfair Commercial Practices Directive, recitals 2–5.

[234] Compare *Klagge*, Normative Kohärenz des deutschen Lauterkeitsrechts, p. 39.

[235] Directive (EU) 2019/2161 of the European Parliament and of the Council of 27 November 2019 amending Council Directive 93/13/EEC and Directives 98/6/EC, 2005/29/EC and 2011/83/EU of the European Parliament and of the Council as regards the better enforcement and modernisation of Union consumer protection rules, OJ L 328, 18.12.2019, pp. 7–28 ('Directive on Modernisation of Consumer Protection Rules').

[236] *European Commission*, Communication from the Commission to the European Parliament, the Council and the European Economic and Social Committee – A New Deal for Consumers.

[237] Directive on Modernisation of Consumer Protection Rules, recital 18.

of products presented to the consumer and the relative importance of those parameters is considered material information and, thus, in principle, must be disclosed. The information obligation is not limited to online marketplaces but can apply to other intermediaries (e.g., comparison websites) as well as online shops offering only the operator's own products.[238] The ranking parameters need to be made available in a specific section of the online interface "directly and easily accessible from the page where the query results are presented". As the information obligation is limited to the ranking's main parameters, firms do not have to disclose their ranking and search algorithm.[239] Further, the obligation does not apply to general search engines (e.g., Google).[240] This new obligation aims at empowering consumers to make informed and active choices in the market. While traders are not obliged to present and rank options in a neutral manner, they must make sure that consumers are empowered to understand why they see what they see. It tries to reduce the power that a particular trader can have over the choice context by forcing them to reveal their motivation and strategy.

Second, according to the newly introduced Art. 7(6),

> "[w]here a trader provides access to consumer reviews of products, information about whether and how the trader ensures that the published reviews originate from consumers who have actually used or purchased the product shall be regarded as material."

Omitting such information is thus an unfair commercial practice and illegal. This rule is also not limited to online marketplaces but applies to every trader who provides access to consumer reviews. This addresses the risk of manipulated ratings.[241] Notably, traders are *not* required to conduct any steps to control the reliability of the reviews to which they provide access. They just have to disclose whether or not they have a process in place to do so and, if yes, the basic features of this process.[242] This can, for example, mean disclosing if all reviews (positive and negative) are posted or whether reviews have been sponsored or influenced by a contractual relationship with a trader.[243] Here, too, the trader has to reveal how they attempt to influence the consumer (through ratings).

Lastly, the amendments to the Directive include new per se unfair practices related to online sales that are included in Annex I. According to the new No. 11a, "providing search results in response to a consumer's online search query without clearly disclosing any paid advertisement or payment specifically for achieving higher ranking of products within the search results" is now per se unfair. This requires traders offering search functions on their website to clearly mark paid

---

[238] *Alexander*, WRP 2019, 1235 (1238); *Duivenvoorde*, EuCML 2019, 219 (224).

[239] See Directive on Modernisation of Consumer Protection Rules, recital 23.

[240] Transparency obligations for operators of general search engines are, however, part of the Platform to Business Regulation that will be discussed in the next section.

[241] Directive on Modernisation of Consumer Protection Rules, recital 47.

[242] *Alexander*, WRP 2019, 1235 (1239).

[243] Directive on Modernisation of Consumer Protection Rules, recital 47.

advertisement in search results and payments for improving a product's ranking within the results. The new Nos. 23b and 23c address consumer reviews. It is per se unfair for a trader to state "that reviews of a product are submitted by consumers who have actually used or purchased the product without taking reasonable and proportionate steps to check that they originate from such consumers." This is clearly linked to Art. 7(6) of the Directive. In essence, it means that a trader needs to either take reasonable and proportionate steps to ensure that the reviews they provide access to originate from consumers or to clearly indicate that they do not have any such process in place. No. 23c prohibits submitting or commissioning "false consumer reviews or endorsements or misrepresenting consumer reviews or special endorsements, in order to promote products." This prohibition goes beyond Art. 7(6) and Annex No. 23b, as it includes not only product reviews but reviews in general, e.g., of the trader herself, and recommendations from consumers (e.g., on social networks).[244] Similar to the other new provisions, this can allow the consumer to better question the validity of the information that they find and has the potential to reduce one particular trader's influence over their decision.

The amendments to the Unfair Commercial Practices Directive show a strong focus on empowering the consumer not by giving them more information about the product itself or their rights but by providing them with information about the very context in which they make their decision: the consumer shall know why they see what they sees and what the underlying reasons for the trader's choice architecture are. They shall know, most importantly, whether the trader is paid for showing a specific offer in a prominent position. The trader must reveal at least some of their 'nudges'. This recognizes, on the one hand, the importance of choice architecture and, on the other hand, reflects the idea of an active consumer contributing through their decisions to the fostering of the internal market. Moreover, it recognizes that traders' and consumers' interests can diverge in cases where the trader receives compensation from a third party for influencing the consumer (e.g., payment for a better ranking): if traders always ranked offers in the way that best reflects consumers' interests, there would be no need for the new rules. However, it should be noted that it is not evident that more transparency will actually limit the respective choice architect's power. On the contrary, it appears from behavioural economic research that the transparency of a nudge does not necessarily reduce its effectiveness.[245]

---

[244] *Alexander*, WRP 2019, 1235 (1240–1241).

[245] *Bruns et al.*, Journal of Economic Psychology 2018, 41; *Congiu/Moscati*, Journal of Economic Surveys 2022, 188 (204–205); *Kroese et al.*, Journal of Public Health 2016, e133; *Loewenstein et al.*, Behavioral Science & Policy 2015, 35; *Marchiori et al.*, Social and Personality Psychology Compass 2017, e12297.

4. Ranking transparency for business users: Platform to Business (P2B) Regulation

The focus on consumer choice and autonomy in recent legislative acts is not limited to acts directly concerned with consumer protection. The so-called Platform to Business (P2B) Regulation[246] aims at increasing transparency for commercial users of online intermediaries and search engines. While not directly addressing the relationship between business and consumers, the Regulation seeks to indirectly benefit consumers (in this regard, it even uses the term 'consumer welfare') through achieving a "competitive, fair, and transparent online ecosystem where companies behave responsibly".[247] The Directive, similar to the above-described newly introduced rules in the Unfair Commercial Practices Directive, recognizes the importance of rankings on consumer decisions.[248] It also stresses the importance of the online platform economy as a potential factor that can increase consumer choice.[249] Unlike the Unfair Commercial Practices Directive, the P2B Regulation does not intervene at the level of the relationship between consumer and business but between the platform and its business users that use its intermediary services to initiate a contractual relationship with a consumer.[250] While the Regulation shall be without prejudice, inter alia, to EU competition law[251] and follows a regulatory approach, its goals, as well as the rhetoric used in the directive (e.g., 'consumer welfare' and 'fair competition'), are similar to competition law. However, the Regulation does apply to all intermediary services or search engine operators independent of their respective market position. The Regulation mainly introduces transparency obligations for online intermediation services (e.g., trading platforms such as Amazon and eBay, but also price comparison websites such as skyscanner.com or app stores such as the Google Play Store or the Apple App Store) on the one hand and, albeit to a lesser extent, online search engines (e.g., Google, Bing) on the other hand.[252] Besides certain more general rules on transparency of terms and conditions, online intermediation services under the Regulation must, in their terms and conditions, set out "the main parameters determining the ranking and the reasons for the relative importance of those main parameters as opposed to other parameters".[253] Providers of online search engines similarly must disclose the parameters "which individually or collectively are most significant in determining ranking and the

[246] Regulation (EU) 2019/11500 of the European Parliament and of the Council of 20 June 2019 on promoting fairness and transparency for business users of online intermediation services, OJ L 186, 11.7.2019, pp. 57–79.

[247] P2B Regulation, recital 3.

[248] P2B Regulation, recitals 4 and 24–27.

[249] P2B Regulation, recital 8.

[250] Art. 1(2) P2B Regulation.

[251] Art. 1(5) P2B Regulation.

[252] *Busch*, GRUR 2019, 788 (787).

[253] Art. 5(1) P2B Regulation.

relative importance of those main parameters" by providing a readily available (and comprehensible) description in this regard.[254] Both intermediation service and search engine providers must, in particular, describe how remuneration influences the ranking.[255] The Regulation aims at allowing traders to optimize their websites and products in order to achieve better rankings by making the ranking criteria more transparent.[256]

Although the P2B Regulation does not directly intervene in a consumer-business relationship, it affects what consumers ultimately see and the order in which it is presented. The Regulation's goal is, in principle, to give every undertaking an equal chance to be on the top of rankings (or at least visible) on platforms and search engines by making the ranking parameters transparent. Every undertaking shall be able to make itself visible to the consumer. The Regulation tries to enhance competition over access to the consumer through increased transparency. This is potentially enhancing consumer autonomy: while the platform or search engine operator continues to determine the criteria for what the consumer sees and in which order, increased transparency on the (commercial) user site can pressure the platform or search engine operator to use more objective criteria and reduce their power over consumers' decision-making. The underlying assumption is that business users possess some countervailing power. However, in the case of large platforms (e.g., Amazon) and search engines (e.g., Google), this assumption remains somewhat doubtful. Consequently, the direct impact on consumers is likely to be relatively modest.

5. Fair and non-discriminatory ranking: the Digital Markets Act

The Digital Markets Act ('DMA')[257] also tackles the issue of rankings, albeit limited to rankings carried out by gatekeepers. Providers of core platform services (including, inter alia, online intermediation services and online search engines)[258] shall be designated as gatekeepers if they have a significant impact on the internal market, operate a core platform service which serves as an important gateway for business users to reach end-users; and enjoy an entrenched and durable position in its operations or will foreseeably enjoy such a position in the near future.[259] These conditions are presumed to be fulfilled when certain turnover and active-users thresholds are met.[260] When it comes to rankings, gatekeepers

[254] Art. 5(2) P2B Regulation.

[255] Art. 5(3) P2B Regulation.

[256] *Busch*, GRUR 2019, 788 (793).

[257] Regulation (EU) 2022/1925 of the European Parliament and the Council of 14 September 2022 on contestable and fair markets in the digital sector and amending Directives (EU) 2019/1937 and (EU) 2020/1828, OJ L 265, 12.10.2022, pp. 1–66.

[258] Art. 2(2) DMA.

[259] Art. 3(1) DMA.

[260] Art. 3(2) DMA.

"shall not treat more favourably, in rankings and related indexing and crawling, services and products offered by the gatekeeper itself than similar services or products of a third party. The gatekeeper shall apply transparent, fair and non-discriminatory conditions to such rankings."[261]

This goes beyond the mere transparency obligation under the P2B Regulation. A focus on consumer autonomy may help to further specify what constitutes fair ranking conditions: the ranking conditions cannot be determined exclusively by the economic interest of the gatekeeper but must allow consumers to make active choices in the market, so rankings must take into account the merits of the offers.[262] In the same vein, gatekeepers

"shall allow and technically enable end users to easily change default settings on the operating system, virtual assistant and web browser of the gatekeeper that direct or steer end users to products or services provided by the gatekeeper."[263]

The Digital Markets Act thus emphasizes consumer choices that are not to be superseded (in casu: by gatekeepers). However, it does so primarily with a focus on self-preferencing.

6. *Conclusion*

The developments discussed above show that the consumer as an active market participant is at the centre of recent law and policy developments in the EU. They are not a passive bystander and mere beneficiary of the EU internal market or the weak party that needs protection.[264] Instead, they are an economic actor with an active role in the (internal) market. Recent policy statements by the Commission confirm this understanding. In the 2020 New Consumer Agenda, for example, the Commission states:

"European consumers rightly expect to benefit fully from the single market and to be empowered to make informed choices and play an active role in the green and digital transition whenever and wherever they are in the EU. They expect to have free access to goods and services across the EU and reassurance that their rights as consumers are protected, notwithstanding traditional and emerging challenges."[265]

This important role of the consumer in EU law and policy also mirrors their economic importance: consumer spending makes up 54% of the EU's GDP.[266]

---

[261] Art. 6(5) DMA.

[262] *Schweitzer*, ZEuP 2021, 503 (512–513).

[263] Art. 7(3) DMA.

[264] Hence, the term 'passive market citizen' as proposed by *Reich/Micklitz*, Europäisches Verbraucherrecht, p. 47 should be avoided.

[265] *European Commission*, New Consumer Agenda – Strengthening Consumer Resilience for sustainable Recovery, p. 1.

[266] *European Commission*, New Consumer Agenda – Strengthening Consumer Resilience for sustainable Recovery, p. 1.

The conclusion here is derived from EU secondary law instruments and hence does not allow for a direct conclusion regarding EU competition law. Nevertheless, it is relevant for this thesis as it shows a broader trend in EU law. Emphasizing and protecting the consumer's active role also through competition law against this background fits into the broader structure of EU law and policy. As the next section will show, there is also no reason to protect consumer autonomy *only* through consumer protection law rather than competition law.

III. Autonomy as a concern of consumer protection and competition law

Having established that EU consumer protection law increasingly emphasises consumer autonomy, the natural next question is: what inferences can be drawn from this for EU competition law?

The first point to consider is that the EU's consumer protection acquis primarily derives from secondary legislation, which is hierarchically subordinate to the competition rules enshrined in the Treaties. Consequently, consumer protection instruments cannot, in principle, alter the substantive scope of EU competition law. However, consumer protection is also recognised as a fundamental value of the Union, which must be taken into account when interpreting and applying competition rules.

Consumer autonomy, or the consumer's decision-making more generally, has been viewed primarily as a matter of consumer protection law rather than competition law. The core objectiveof consumer protection law is "that consumers be enabled to make rational choices to the extent that they wish to concentrate on doing so".[267] It protects the consumer's freedom of choice.[268] Consumer protection law shields the consumer from practices like coercion, deception and information deficits.[269] According to Averitt and Lande, consumer protection law seeks to ensure the consumer's "ability to choose among the available options", while competition law shall make sure that there are sufficient options to choose from (thus, they use the term 'consumer choice').[270] Averitt and Lande, however, also point out that there can be significant overlaps between competition law and consumer protection law, so a clear distinction between the two regimes is not always possible.[271] In EU law, the two regimes seem even closer aligned: in particular, they share the internal market goal as a common objective.[272] A substantial part of the European consumer protection law acquis is based on internal market competences and harmonizes national laws with the goal of increasing

[267] *Averitt/Lande*, Antitrust Law Journal 1997, 713 (171).

[268] *Grunewald/Peifer*, Verbraucherschutz im Zivilrecht, p. 1.

[269] *Grunewald/Peifer*, Verbraucherschutz im Zivilrecht, p. 1.

[270] *Averitt/Lande*, Antitrust Law Journal 1997, 713 (718); see also *Ackermann*, in: Herausforderungen für die Wettbewerbsordnung, 73.

[271] See in more detail above from p. 6.

[272] *Albors-Llorens*, Yearbook of European Law 2014, 163 (173).

cross-border trade and, in turn, consumer choice (i.e., range of options).[273] The internal market is also one of the fundamental goals of EU competition law.[274] The consumer in the EU legal and economic order does not only play an important role as an agent for the internal market but also as an agent for competition. The mere fact that consumers' decision-making autonomy is protected through consumer protection law, hence does not exclude that it is also protected through competition law. Moreover, the two regimes are increasingly converging.[275] This does not imply that competition law ought to serve as an enforcement tool for consumer protection[276], but it does highlight a certain overlapping of the normative objectives of the two frameworks.[277]

Moreover, while overlaps between the two regimes are possible, competition law is concerned with consumer decision-making for reasons that differ from those of consumer protection law. The focus is not on the individual consumer per se, but rather on the functional role that consumer choices play in ensuring the effective operation of markets and competition. This distinction will be elaborated further in the following sections.[278] At this point, it is sufficient to emphasise that, in any event, competition law is not designed to shield every consumer in every transaction from unfair or otherwise undesirable conduct. Instead, its primary task is to preserve and promote a market structure that enables consumers to exercise sufficient autonomy to fulfil their role as arbiters of competitive outcomes. In this sense, consumer autonomy is not an end in itself but a means to securing the dynamic and self-correcting nature of competitive markets.

IV. How consumer autonomy can fit in the broader structure of EU competition law

This section will examine whether and how the recognition of consumer autonomy as a relevant consideration under EU antitrust law can be reconciled with the broader structure and methodology of the field. First, this will be discussed in the context of the requirement of independence ('Selbständigkeitspostulat'). Second, it will be investigated whether the consumer's right to claim damages for breaches of competition law provide a further systematic argument in support of integrating consumer autonomy into antitrust analysis.

---

[273] Compare *Achilles*, Homo Oeconomicus, p. 378.

[274] *Mestmäcker/Schweitzer*, Europäisches Wettbewerbsrecht§ 1, para. 27.

[275] *Albors-Llorens*, Yearbook of European Law 2014, 163.

[276] See *Ackermann*, NZKart 2016, 397; *Botta/Wiedemann*, Antitrust Bulletin 2019, 428; *Thomas*, NZKart 2017, 92.

[277] See *Podszun*, SSRN 2019, p. 28.

[278] See below from p. 207.

1. Consumer autonomy as a continuum to the requirement of independence ('Selbständigkeitspostulat')

The independence of decision-making is a central concept of EU competition law. In the context of horizontal agreements between undertakings, the Court of Justice consistently emphasizes that undertakings must not relinquish their independence. This focus is most clearly articulated in Suiker Unie, where the Court held that

> "the concept inherent in the provisions of the Treaty relating to competition [is] that each economic operator must determine independently the policy which he intends to adopt on the common market including the choice of the persons and undertakings to which he makes offers or sells."[279]

Podszun has developed the idea that this notion of independence can also be extended to consumers.[280] The notion of independence is a longstanding concept of EU competition law: economic operators must make their economic decisions in the market independently. This requirement of independence (in German: 'Selbstständigkeitspostulat') has been the core argumentation of many cases on horizontal collusion.[281] As the Court of Justice puts it, restricting "undertakings' decision-making autonomy [...] is [...] liable to restrict competition".[282]

While the case law expressly refers to undertakings, the use of the broader term "economic operators", according to Podszun, suggests a potentially wider scope. Given that purchasing decisions have a clear economic impact, consumers' freedom to choose (or not choose) a particular offer forms part of the competitive process. From this perspective, consumer autonomy mirrors the independence required of undertakings and may be similarly relevant under the Selbständigkeitspostulat.

---

[279] Court of Justice, 13/12/1975, Joined Cases 40–48, 50, 54–56 111 113 114–73 Suiker Unie, ECLI:EU:C:1975:174, para. 173; also cited by *Podszun*, SSRN 2019, p. 22.

[280] *Podszun*, SSRN 2019, p. 22.

[281] Court of Justice, 14/07/1981, Case 172/90 Züchner, ECLI:EU:C:1981:178, para. 13; Court of Justice, 28/05/1998, Case C-7/95 P John Deere, ECLI:EU:C:1998:256, p. 87; Court of Justice, 31/03/1993, Joined cases C-89/85, C-104/85, C-114/85 C-116/85 C-117/85 C-125/85 to C-129/85 Ahlström Osakeyhtiö, ECLI:EU:C:1993:120, para. 63; Court of Justice, 08/06/1999, Case C-19/92 P Hüls AG, ECLI:EU:C:1999:358, para. 160; Court of Justice, 08/07/1999, Case C-49/92 P Anic Partecipazioni, ECLI:EU:C:1999:356, p. 116; Court of Justice, 02/10/2003, Case C-179/99 P Eurofer, ECLI:EU:C:2003:525, para. 42; Court of Justice, 02/10/2003, Case C-195/99 P Krupp Hoesch Stahl, ECLI:EU:C:2003:528, para. 59; Court of Justice, 02/10/2003, Case C-199/99 P Corus, ECLI:EU:C:203:531, para. 106; Court of Justice, 23/11/2006, Case C-238/05 Asnef-Equifax, ECLI:EU:C:2006:734, para. 51; Court of Justice, 04/06/2009, Case C-8/08 T-Mobile Netherlands, ECLI:EU:C:2009:343, para. 32; Court of Justice, 19/03/2015, Case C-286/13 P Dole Food, ECLI:EU:C:2015:184, para. 119; Court of Justice, 26/01/2017, Case C-609/13 P Duravit, ECLI:EU:C:217:46, para. 71.

[282] Court of Justice, 28/05/1998, Case C-7/95 P John Deere, ECLI:EU:C:1998:256, para. 88.

Moreover, a distinction needs to be made between the participating undertakings' autonomy, on the one hand, and affected third parties' autonomy, on the other hand. The concerned undertakings limit the variety of options available to themselves on how to conduct their business. Consider a price-fixing agreement: firms that agree on a certain price, take away from themselves the option to charge a different price. In this sense, competition law imposes an *obligation of autonomy* upon firms: they must not remove their ability to take decisions independently. This is reflected in the Court of Justice's case law when it emphasizes that

> "each economic operator *must* determine independently the policy which he intends to adopt on the common market including the choice of the persons and undertakings to which he makes offers or sells."[283]

This formulation clearly reflects competition law's concern with preserving the independent decision-making of undertakings. However, it does not automatically follow that competition law protects the autonomy of consumers, who are typically not parties to anticompetitive agreements and, thus, do not dispose of their own autonomy in the same manner. Nevertheless, the broad framing of independent decision-making as a concept "inherent to the Treaty" opens the door to a wider interpretation.[284] While not determinative on its own, this conceptual breadth may offer preliminary support for the view that the protection of autonomous decision-making could extend beyond undertakings to include consumers.

An additional, albeit similarly limited, argument can be made by looking at the effects of anticompetitive agreements: these agreements often restrict not only the autonomy of the parties to the agreement (the cartelists) but, more importantly, also of third parties. Horizontal agreements are often considered anticompetitive because of the effects they have on consumers or purchasers more general. While these effects can often be described as a reduction in consumer welfare, e.g., through increased prices and reduced output, this is not always the case.[285] There is a number of cases concerning horizontal agreement where the actual 'consumer harm' may also be linked to negative effects on autonomy. Even price-fixing agreements can be framed as a reduction of autonomy: products now sold at uniform prices mean fewer price options to choose from for consumers or other purchasers. This reduction in options is what the consumer choice approach would mainly look at.[286] Agreements can, however, affect consumers' decision-making more directly, often without direct effects on prices or output. One example is the US Supreme Court Case FTC v. Indiana Federation

[283] Court of Justice, 13/12/1975, Joined Cases 40–48, 50, 54–56 111 113 114–73 Suiker Unie, ECLI:EU.C.1975:174, para. 173 (emphasis added).

[284] *Podszun*, SSRN 2019, p. 24.

[285] See for consumer welfare below from p. 158.

[286] See above from p. 6.

of Dentists.[287] In this case, dentists colluded to withhold x-rays from insurance companies that demanded such x-rays in order to determine whether the treatment applied by a dentist is reimbursable. Insurers, as the affected third parties here, were harmed because information flows were limited, reducing their ability to make informed and rational decisions.[288] A similar example is the FTC's consent order against the Association of Protective Armor. This association had adopted a policy that none of its members (manufacturers of bulletproof vests) could engage in comparative advertising, in particular the (truthful) representation "that another member's vests have failed certification testing."[289] Similar concerns can also arise in tying cases where tying reduces the ability to decide by making it difficult "to evaluate the true cost of either product when they are available only as a package".[290] Grimes, in this regard, speaks of ties that reduce "consumer demand quality."[291] A tie forces the purchaser to take two decisions simultaneously regarding the tying and the tied product, which, depending on the products involved, can make the purchase decision much more complex. Tying could also harm autonomy through coercion when buyers, through the tying, are forced to buy a product they would otherwise not have purchased. Here, the buyer might be very well aware of all the relevant product characteristics but nevertheless unable to not buy the tied product. Output (of the tied product) through such practices can, even at constant prices, be increased. This was, for example, the case in Inno-B.M./Fedetab, where members of the Belgian tobacco federation agreed to require their purchasers to buy a minimum assortment of different cigarettes, including less popular "slow-moving brands".[292] The purchasers here knew very well that with some of the cigarettes they had to buy, they could make much less profit but nevertheless had to purchase them: there was no way to circumvent the tying by buying from another manufacturer since nearly all manufacturers were members of the federation. Similar concerns can arise with vertical tying agreements[293] or tying practices of dominant undertakings[294].

[287] US Supreme Court, 02/06/1986, No. 84–1809 FTC v Indiana Federation of Dentists, 476 U.S. 447.

[288] See *Newman*, Iowa Law Review 2022, 563 (583) contrasting this harm with the prevailing view (in the US) that anticompetitive conduct must reduce output.

[289] Federal Trade Commission, 17/03/1994, No. C-3481 Personal Protective Armor Association, p. 105 para. 6.

[290] US Supreme Court, 27/03/1984, No. 82–1031 Jefferson Parish, 466 U.S. 2, p. 15.

[291] *Grimes*, Antitrust Law Journal 1994, 263 (273).

[292] European Commission, 20/07/1978, IV/28.852 Inno-B.M./Fedetab, para. 87; for another example of collective tying arrangements, see European Commission, 15/05/1974, IV/400 Glass Containers.

[293] See European Commission, 11/07/1983, IV/29.395 Windsurfing International.

[294] See European Commission, 22/12/1987, IV/30.787 HILTI; upheld by Court of First Instance, 12/12/1991, Case T-30/89 HILTI, ECLI:EU:T:1991:70; Court of Justice, 03/02/1994, Case C-53/92 P Hilti, ECLI:EU:C:1994:77.

2. The right to claim damages: consumers as agents of competition law

Recognizing consumers' active role as decision-makers in the competitive landscape is also mirrored in their active role in enforcing competition law through private enforcement.[295] The Court of Justice has established that individuals have the right to claim damages for breaches of the EU competition law rules because of their direct applicability and based on the principle of effectiveness. In Courage and Crehan the CJEU held that:

"The full effectiveness of Article 85 of the Treaty [Art. 101 TFEU] and, in particular, the practical effect of the prohibition laid down in Article 85(1) [Art. 101(1) TFEU] would be put at risk if it were not open to any individual to claim damages for loss caused to him by a contract or by conduct liable to restrict or distort competition."[296]

The Court of Justice sees private actions for damages as a tool that can make a "significant contribution to the maintenance of effective competition".[297] This was confirmed by later case law[298] and eventually led to adoption of the Private Damages Directive[299]. The underlying argument is that private individuals, through their damage claims, contribute to the enforcement of EU competition law, thereby deterring anti-competitive behaviour and, in turn, contribute to the functioning of competition as such.[300] Private individuals, albeit acting in their own interest when making damage claims are hence at the same time, acting as agents for the enforcement of competition law and the maintenance of effective competition as an institution.[301] Therefore, they benefit in two ways from their private damage actions: on the one hand, they receive compensation for damages; on the other hand, they benefit indirectly from the private enforcement of competition because of its positive effect on competition. Private enforcement can serve as a useful supplement to centralized enforcement by competition agencies because, on the one hand, it safeguards against abrupt transitions in the

[295] *Podszun*, SSRN 2019, p. 25.

[296] Court of Justice, 20/09/2001, C-453/99 Courage and Crehan, ECLI:EU:C:2001:465, para. 26.

[297] Court of Justice, 20/09/2001, C-453/99 Courage and Crehan, ECLI:EU:C:2001:465, para. 27.

[298] Court of Justice, 2006, Joined Cases C-295/04 to C-298/04 Manfredi, ECLI:EU:C:2006:461, para. 59; Court of Justice, 06/11/2012, Case C-199/1 Otis, ECLI:EU:C:2012:684, para. 41; Court of Justice, 05/06/2014, Case C-557/12 Kone, ECLI:EU:C:2014:1317, para. 20.

[299] Directive 2014/104/EU of the European Parliament and of the Council of 26 November 2014 on certain rules governing actions for damages under national law for infringements of the competition law provisions of the Member States and of the European Union, OJ L 349, 5.12.2014, pp. 1–19.

[300] Expressed most explicitly in Court of Justice, 06/11/2012, Case C-199/1 Otis, ECLI:EU:C:2012:684, para. 42.

[301] See Court of Justice, 20/09/2001, C-453/99 Courage and Crehan, ECLI:EU:C:2001:465, paras. 26–27.

administration (e.g., budget cuts)[302] and mitigates budget restraints[303], and on the other hand, provides a counterbalance against tendencies of enforcement agencies to focus on particular sectors or be guided by industrial policy considerations[304]. Just as competition relies on the dispersed knowledge of market actors, so too does its enforcement benefit from the decentralized initiative of victims of competition law infringements.

The Court of Justice explicitly stated that "any individual" has the right to seek compensation for damages incurred from breaches of competition law.[305] This includes both final consumers and intermediate commercial customers.[306] It should be noted that, in particular for final consumers who often occur only very small damages, the system of private enforcement in the EU is considered relatively ineffective due to the absence of effective collective enforcement mechanisms.[307] Despite these limitations, the recognition of the right to damages as such reflects a broader principle: EU law assigns an active role to market participants, including consumers, in the enforcement of competition rules. In this regard, they act as agents not only for the enforcement of competition law but also for maintaining effective competition as an institution. Protecting consumer autonomy mirrors this procedural function for the enforcement of competition law substantively: as active market participants, consumers must be able to take autonomous decisions.[308]

3. Conclusion

EU competition law primarily focuses on safeguarding the independent decision-making of undertakings. However, an argument can be made that the autonomy and active participation of consumers in the market should also be a concern of competition law. This perspective gains traction when one considers the consumer's role not only as a passive recipient of market dynamics but as an active participant in the competitive process. The argument can also find support in consumers' right to claim damages for infringements of competition law.

---

[302] *Jones*, Private Enforcement, p. 80.

[303] *Fuchs*, in: Handbuch Private Kartellrechtsdurchsetzung, § 1, para. 74.

[304] *Fuchs*, in: Handbuch Private Kartellrechtsdurchsetzung, § 1, para. 18.

[305] Court of Justice, 20/09/2001, C-453/99 Courage and Crehan, ECLI:EU:C:2001:465, para. 26; Court of Justice, 2006, Joined Cases C-295/04 to C-298/04 Manfredi, ECLI:EU:C:2006:461, para. 61; Court of Justice, 05/06/2014, Case C-557/12 Kone, ECLI:EU:C:2014:1317, para. 21.

[306] See in this regard also Private Damages Directive, recital 3.

[307] For an analysis of the reasons therefor, in particular rational apathy, see *Krüger/Weitbrecht*, in: Handbuch Private Kartellrechtsdurchsetzung, § 19, paras. 11–17; *Ioannidou*, Competition Law Review 2011, 59 arguing for a strengthening of end consumers' role in private damage actions.

[308] *Podszun*, SSRN 2019, p. 25.

V. Freedom of contract and competition law

Competition is inherently linked to freedom of contract. It is through contracts that competition is expressed and manifests itself.[309] Freedom of contract is an essential element of any competitive market order[310] and is recognized as a principle of EU law[311].

The following paragraphs will explore how a material understanding of freedom of contract may suggest that meaningful choice depends on market structures that allow for independent decision-making. While the presumption that contracts lead to just outcomes rests on procedural safeguards, EU law does not merely assume these safeguards are in place but actively works to uphold them. Against this background, the argument can be made that competition law should also take on a role in preserving the conditions necessary for genuine contractual freedom. By ensuring a competitive market with sufficient options, competition law indirectly helps maintain the fairness and equity of contractual outcomes.

1. The contract's presumption of correctness ('Richtigkeitsgewähr')

One of the principal arguments in favour of freedom of contract is that contracts can serve as an instrument to reach the 'just' outcome without the need for authoritative regulation.[312] Paradigmatic for this view is Schmidt-Rimpler's theory of the contract's presumption of correctness (in German: 'Richtigkeitsgewähr des Vertrages').[313] According to this theory, in principle, the conclusion of a contract typically guarantees that it is not the egoistic interest of one of the contracting parties that prevails but that the contract, because both parties need to agree, leads to a compromise between the parties and hence to an outcome that corresponds to justice and expediency.[314]

Schmidt-Rimpler's most significant insight, however, is that he recognized that not every contract inherently results in a just outcome. Instead, he emphasised that certain preconditions must be met for a contract to achieve material justice, and that there are scenarios in which these preconditions are not fulfilled.[315] Consequently, it would therefore be wrong to assume the fulfilment of these conditions without further ado.[316] The task of legal policy must, therefore,

[309] Compare *Möschel*, JITE 2001, 3 (10).

[310] *Lüttringhaus*, Materialisierung, p. 340; *Mestmäcker*, AcP 1968, 235 (235).

[311] General Advocate Kokott, 17/09/2009, Case C-441/07 P Commission/Alrosa, ECLI:EU:C:2009:555, para. 225; Court of Justice, 28/04/2009, Case C-518/06 Commission/Italy, ECLI:EU:C:2009:270, para. 66.

[312] *Schmidt-Rimpler*, AcP 1941, 130 (156); see also *Biedenkopf*, Vertragliche Wettbewerbsbeschränkung, pp. 106–108.

[313] *Schmidt-Rimpler*, AcP 1941, 130.

[314] *Schmidt-Rimpler*, in: FS Nipperdey, 1 (6); *Schmidt-Rimpler*, in: FS Ludwig Raiser, 3 (5–6).

[315] *Schmidt-Rimpler*, in: FS Ludwig Raiser, 3 (6–7).

[316] *Schmidt-Rimpler*, AcP 1941, 130 (157).

be to determine the prerequisites and explore the boundaries under which a contract leads to just results.[317] Schmidt-Rimpler himself was sceptical as to the scope of the 'Richtigkeitsgewähr'.[318] A key issue he highlighted is that parties to a contract may fail to consider its impact on third parties or broader societal interests.[319] Moreover, there are several scenarios in which even the parties' own interests, or at least one of the parties' interests, are not effectively realized through the contract. Schmidt-Rimpler mentions here, inter alia, the scenario in which one party lacks the freedom to decide (in particular because of dependence from the other party or because of an inferior ability to evaluate the contract's consequences) and cases in which one side does not properly evaluate and consider the consequences (e.g., standard business terms).[320] In such scenarios, sovereign intervention can become necessary.[321] Biedenkopf, building on Schmidt-Rimpler's theory, has identified equality of the counterparties, understood in a factual and material rather than mere formal sense, as another important criterion: the contract cannot fulfil its function if the economic balance between the contracting parties is missing.[322]

Schmidt-Rimpler's theory can be characterized as a procedural theory: it is the process of concluding contracts (i.e., each party's evaluation of its advantages and disadvantages, the deliberation and negotiation) which allows the presumption that the contract's content is typically 'just'.[323] The process of concluding the contract is, therefore, an important aspect which must not be overlooked. Schmidt-Rimpler already identified the parties' autonomy as a relevant factor here: each party must be able to evaluate the advantages and disadvantages of the contract properly and must not be dependent on the other party, and their assessment must not be impaired.[324] The idea that contracts lead to good results if and only if certain requirements, including autonomy, are fulfilled can also be made applicable in the context of competition law. If one accepts Schmidt-Rimpler's argument, two conclusions must be derived from this for the law. First, mere formal freedom of contract does not always lead to 'just' outcomes. Second, the law must remedy situations where the (procedural) requirements for contracts to lead to good outcomes are not fulfilled.[325] Schmidt-Rimpler focused mainly on cases where the law refuses to recognize the validity of contracts or

[317] *Schmidt-Rimpler*, AcP 1941, 130 (157).

[318] *Schmidt-Rimpler*, AcP 1941, 130 (165); *Schmidt-Rimpler*, in: FS Nipperdey, 1 (7).

[319] *Schmidt-Rimpler*, AcP 1941, 130 (152); *Schmidt-Rimpler*, in: FS Nipperdey, 1 (7); on this problem in general, see *Atiyah*, Freedom of Contract, pp. 693–694.

[320] *Schmidt-Rimpler*, AcP 1941, 130 (158).

[321] *Schmidt-Rimpler*, AcP 1941, 130 (157).

[322] *Biedenkopf*, Vertragliche Wettbewerbsbeschränkung, p. 109.

[323] *Canaris*, AcP 2000, 273 (284); *Schmidt-Rimpler*, in: FS Ludwig Raiser, 3 (21).

[324] *Schmidt-Rimpler*, AcP 1941, 130 (158) footnote 34.

[325] This does generally not require to actually assess whether the contract's content is 'correct' according to some objective benchmark but it is enough to identify scenarios where the general procedural conditions of concluding contracts are impaired.

allows one party to contest them (e.g., deficiencies of will).[326] However, the argument can be made that the law should go beyond this and actively create and protect the very conditions surrounding the conclusion of the contract – if the law prevents errors from being made in the first place, there is less need to declare contracts void or allow their contestation.

Unlike contract law, which primarily focuses on identifying scenarios in which, for an individual contract, these requirements are not fulfilled, competition law would protect and create the general conditions which ensure that the market allows for autonomous contracts and decisions. Just like contract law must not assume that the conditions for contracts to yield good outcomes are always fulfilled, the argument can be made that competition law must not assume that the conditions for competition to function and yield good outcomes, and one of these is consumers' ability to make independent decisions,[327] are always fulfilled.[328] Notably, competition law looks also at the interconnections between different contracts: a contract between two undertakings, e.g., a horizontal price-fixing agreement, can have the effect that the purchase contract between a consumer and one of the undertakings, or even a third undertaking that purchased from the price fixer itself, does not guarantee the right outcome anymore.[329] Anti-competitive agreements, from the viewpoint of the presumption of correctness, are not problematic because of the conditions of their own conclusion but because they invalidate the presumption of the correct outcome for *other* contracts.

2. From formal to material freedom of contract

Another argument in favour of the freedom of contract is that contracts are a means of expressing individuals' self-determination. Fried, for example, argues that freedom of contract serves individual autonomy because the contract allows each individual to increase their options: by contracting with another party, they can pursue objectives that they could not reach alone.[330] Freedom of contract, therefore, increases options and choice.[331] This could tempt one to argue that autonomy is best served under a formal understanding of freedom of contract. The law's only task would then be to respect all contracts.[332] For formal freedom of contract, it is sufficient if every party under the same legal conditions can conclude contracts with others.[333] However, today it is largely recognized that

---

[326] *Schmidt-Rimpler*, AcP 1941, 130 (173–192); *Schmidt-Rimpler*, in: FS Nipperdey, 1 (10).

[327] See in more detail below from p. 148.

[328] See *Schmidt-Rimpler*, in: FS Ludwig Raiser, 3 (14).

[329] Similarly emphasizing the effect that anti-competitive agreements have on third parties *Lukes*, Kartellvertrag, p. 163.

[330] *Fried*, Contract as Promise, pp. 8, 13–14; see also *Kimel*, in: Philosophical Foundations of Contract Law, 96.

[331] *Fried*, Contract as Promise, p. 8.

[332] *Kimel*, Oxford Journal of Legal Studies 2001, 473 (474).

[333] *Drexl*, Wirtschaftliche Selbstbestimmung, pp. 294–295; *Lüttringhaus*, Materialisierung, p. 303.

freedom in a liberal legal and economic order must not be understood in a purely formal sense.[334] Unrestricted formal freedom threatens to cancel itself out.[335] While all individuals may have the equal legal freedom to conclude contracts, there are significant factual differences when it comes to the ability to exercise this freedom; these can be linked to business experience, access to relevant information or financial resources.[336] Therefore, the law must safeguard and sometimes provide for the conditions that allow for the exercise of freedoms, understood in a material or factual sense. Individual self-determination in an optimal sense can only be realized if the formation and expression of the parties' will are free not only from legal but also from factual obstacles.[337]

Contract law, in particular consumer protection law, tries to identify and remedy scenarios in which there are such factual obstacles. By doing so, it tries to protect freedom of contract for all members of our society, including weaker parties who may not otherwise be able to effectively exercise free choices. Understood in a material sense, the presumption of correctness and the goal of self-determination can be seen as complementary rather than conflicting: both aim to establish the procedural conditions under which freedom of contract should be upheld, while also setting boundaries beyond which contracts and their terms cannot be contested by state authorities.[338] The contract is a means to achieve self-determination *and* justice.[339] Where there is no self-determination, the contract cannot lead to just outcomes.[340] Therefore, legislative or judicial intervention in the formal freedom of contract to establish and protect the conditions for the factual exercise of freedoms can create, maintain and increase freedom. This understanding has been characterized as the "materialization of freedom"[341] and forms an essential element of European contract and consumer protection law.[342] For example, the Unfair Commercial Practices Directive is aimed at safeguarding the consumer's decision-making freedom.[343] This goal is apparent when it comes to the prohibition of misleading or aggressive practices, which are prohibited under the directive[344]. The former shall protect the consumer's decision-making basis understood as the formation of their will,[345] whereas the latter

[334] *Klement*, Wettbewerbsfreiheit, p. 119; *Lüttringhaus*, Materialisierung, pp. 323–324.

[335] *Fornasier*, Zwingendes Vertragsrecht, pp. 15–16; *Lüttringhaus*, Materialisierung, p. 323.

[336] *Atiyah*, Freedom of Contract, p. 6; *Lüttringhaus*, Materialisierung, p. 323.

[337] *Canaris*, AcP 2000, 273 (277); *Lüttringhaus*, Materialisierung, p. 331.

[338] *Habersack*, AcP 1989, 403 (409).

[339] *Habersack*, AcP 1989, 403 (409); *Schmidt-Rimpler*, in: FS Ludwig Raiser, 3 (9–10).

[340] *Schmidt-Rimpler*, in: FS Ludwig Raiser, 3 (13–14).

[341] *Canaris*, AcP 2000, 273 (277); *Lüttringhaus*, Materialisierung, p. 332; *Drexl*, Wirtschaftliche Selbstbestimmung, p. 208.

[342] *Lüttringhaus*, Materialisierung, pp. 331–393 with more examples.

[343] Unfair Commercial Practices Directive, recital 7; General Advocate Trstenjak, 24/03/2019, Case C-540/08 Mediaprint, ECLI:EU:C:2010:161, para. 97.

[344] Art. 5(4) Unfair Commercial Practices Directive.

[345] See regarding § 5a UWG *Alexander*, in: Münchener Kommentar Lauterkeitsrecht, § 5a UWG, para. 23.

protects the consumer's ability to act in accordance with that will[346]. Similar reasonings apply to the numerous information obligations or withdrawal rights that are part of European contract law.[347] This view finds some support in the Court of Justice judgment in case RWE/Verbraucherzentrale NRW, on a referral question on the unfairness of a clause in an energy supply contract that allowed the supplier to unilaterally raise prices but gave the consumer a right to terminate the contract for this case, the Court of Justice held that it is of fundamental importance

"[t]hat the right of termination given to the consumer is not purely formal but can actually be exercised. That would not be the case if, for reasons connected with the method of exercise of the right of termination or the conditions of the market concerned, the consumer has no real possibility of changing supplier, or if he has not been informed suitably in good time of the forthcoming change, thus depriving him of the possibility of checking how it is calculated and, if appropriate, of changing supplier. Account must be taken in particular of whether the market concerned is competitive, the possible cost to the consumer of terminating the contract, the time between the notification and the coming into force of the new tariffs, the information provided at the time of that communication, and the cost to be borne and the time taken to change supplier."[348]

Competition law itself is one of the tools that EU law deploys to protect material freedom of contract.[349] It does so by restricting the freedom of some (typically the more powerful) for the sake of protecting the freedom of others.[350] Cartels, for example, are prohibited because they reduce the buyer's freedom of contract by preventing "the buyer from being supplied at a price determined by the rules of supply and demand."[351] Contracts that restrict competition from a formal understanding of the freedom of contract would not pose any problems; they are harmful not because they restrict the participating undertakings' freedom of contract but because they restrict third parties' material freedom.[352] The General Court in Alstoff/Commission, for example, explains:

"the applicant's self-imposed restriction does not restrict *only its own freedom of action*. On the supply side, it restricts the access of [other companies] to the [...] market [...], since it limits the opportunities for these undertakings to act on that market."[353]

---

[346] See more general *Beater*, Unlauterer Wettbewerb, paras. 1567–1637.

[347] Regarding the withdrawal rights under the Off-Premises Directive, see Court of Justice, 17/12/2009, Case C-227/08 Martín Martín, ECLI:EU:C:2009:792, para. 37; for withdrawal rights under the Consumer Credit Directive, see *Eidenmüller*, AcP 2010, 67 (89); see also *Lüttringhaus*, Materialisierung, pp. 331–334 with further references.

[348] Court of Justice, 21/03/2013, Case C-92/11 RWE/Verbraucherzentrale NRW, ECLI: EU:C:2013:180, para. 54.

[349] *Klement*, Wettbewerbsfreiheit, p. 192; *Lüttringhaus*, Materialisierung, p. 334.

[350] *Klement*, Wettbewerbsfreiheit, p. 119.

[351] Court of Justice, 21/05/2015, Case C-352/13 CDC, ECLI:EU:C:2015:335, para. 43.

[352] *Mohr*, Vertragsfreiheit, p. 459; *Möschel*, JITE 2001, 3 (10); *Roth*, in: Privatrechtsgesellschaft, 179 (190).

[353] General Court, 22/03/2011, Case T-419/03 Alstoff/Commission, ECLI:EU:C:2011:102, para. 63 (emphasis added); also cited by *Lüttringhaus*, Materialisierung, p. 297.

If competition law itself serves to protect freedom of contract understood in a material sense, the argument can be made that, in turn, it shall rely on a similar material understanding of freedom and create the conditions for the effective exercise of self-determination. The argument would then be that competition law must preserve the conditions for the (material) freedom of contract at the earliest stage of the decision-making process that eventually leads (or does not lead) to a contract.[354]

3. Conclusion

Both the presumption of the correctness of contracts and a material understanding of freedom of contract may provide support to the notion that competition law protects consumers' independent decision-making. The presumption of the correctness of contracts rests on certain procedural conditions. Only where these are fulfilled can it be presumed that contracts lead to 'just' results. In line with Schmidt-Rimpler's theory that contracts lead to 'just' results where certain procedural conditions are met, EU law protects the procedural conditions to ensure that individuals can exercise their freedom of contract. EU law does not just assume that those conditions are met but actively steps in to safeguard and provide them. This may be interpreted as a material rather than a mere formal understanding of freedom of contract. Following this argument, competition can be seen an important precondition for freedom of contract understood in this material sense: only where the market structure is such as to provide meaningful and sufficient options and to allow for autonomous and independent decisions can material freedom of contract exist. In the same vein, only under these conditions can the presumption that contracts lead to 'just' results be upheld. Competition law, therefore, it can be argued, has a role to play in protecting market operators' freedom of contract. It would, in turn, rely on a similar material understanding of freedom and protect the market conditions that are necessary to allow economic actors, foremost consumers, to exercise their self-determination.

VI. Back to the roots: consumer autonomy between Hayek's discovery process and ordoliberalism

The previous section has examined how consumer autonomy can systematically fit into the structure of EU competition law. This section is concerned with a teleological but also historical interpretation, starting with an analysis of whether consumer autonomy can be an element of competition when understood as a discovery process (1.). Subsequently, it will pursue the question of whether consumer autonomy is in line with ordoliberal thinking (2.) and whether this can

[354] *Lüttringhaus*, Materialisierung, p. 339; *Mohr*, Vertragsfreiheit, p. 453.

inform EU competition law today (3.). The section will show that ordoliberal ideas can and do play a role in EU competition law, providing support for the argument that it is not only concerned with economic efficiency but also grounded in broader values which may include consumer autonomy.

1. Consumer autonomy and Hayek's discovery process

While Hayek cannot necessarily be ascribed to the ordoliberal camp, his ideas nevertheless had a significant influence on the development of ordoliberal thinking,[355] which justifies briefly describing his probably most influential contribution to competition policy here. According to Hayek, competition is to be understood as a search and discovery process without predictable results.[356] Economic science can only make 'pattern predictions' but no specific predictions for individual events. The purpose of competition is to find the best market results, which cannot be pre-determined. Competition, thus, is an experiment to discover facts that would otherwise remain unknown or unused.[357] Hayek emphasized the function of competition as a discovery process to bring together decentralized knowledge that is only available through the market and cannot possibly be predicted. This is also the very reason why competition should exist in the first place: if we knew the outcome of competition (e.g., the market result), why would we go the long and cumbersome way through competition to get there?[358] One of the most important features of competition is that it allows those who are willing and able to do so to experiment and discover new procedures and products and that it forces the rest of society to imitate the improvements found this way.[359]

Consumer autonomy, in principle, corresponds to the idea of competition as a discovery process. If the market shall serve as a discovery process to make use of dispersed knowledge and allow the pursuit of self-set individual goals, autonomous decision-making of consumers may be seen as a necessary precondition. Competition as a discovery process can only function "if the preconditions for the discovery of unknown facts are actually fulfilled."[360] The most important of these preconditions is "the freedom of the individual to make new discoveries through trial and error."[361] Otherwise, the marketplace will not fulfil this function

---

[355] For the differences between ordoliberalism and Hayek's thinking, see *Wörsdörfer*, Journal of the History of Economic Thought 2013, 291.

[356] *Hayek*, in: Rechtsordnung und Handelnsordnung, 132 (135); *Hayek*, in: Rechtsordnung und Handelnsordnung, 35 (42); *Hayek*, The Pretence of Knowledge (Nobel Prize Lecture); *Hayek*, in: Rechtsordnung und Handelnsordnung, 107 (115) emphasizing the role that competition plays in determining which goods and services are produced in the first place (rather than just bringing down costs of production).

[357] *Hayek*, American Economic Review 1945, 519.

[358] *Hayek*, in: Rechtsordnung und Handelnsordnung, 132 (132).

[359] *Hayek*, in: Rechtsordnung und Handelnsordnung, 132 (144).

[360] *Zäch/Künzler*, ZWeR 2009, 269 (279).

[361] *Zäch/Künzler*, ZWeR 2009, 269 (279).

if the results it yields are not based on autonomous thinking and acting. Protecting the pursuit of self-set individual goals without ensuring that individuals possess the capabilities and opportunities to set themselves such goals autonomously is a vain exercise. While Hayek implicitly relies on consumer decisions as part of the underlying discovery process – after all, consumer preferences need to be discovered by competition – he does not reach the same conclusion and does not put consumers or the protection of their decision-making through competition law at the centre of his thinking. Quite the opposite is true: he saw the biggest threat to individual freedom in state actions and interferences.[362] This focus may be because he developed his theories in contrast to a socialist legal and economic order.[363] In Hayek's line of thinking, freedom can only be understood in a formal rather than a material sense[364]: The state must respect any market transaction regardless of the conditions of its formation and its content.[365] Anything else would constitute pretence of knowledge. Consequently, protecting consumer autonomy under Hayek's formal understanding of freedom would not be part of the competition law analysis.[366]

2. *Consumer autonomy as an ordoliberal idea*

While sharing Hayek's focus on private liberties, ordoliberalism tends to identify not only state interference but also private economic power as a threat to these liberties.[367] The ordoliberal school of thought emerged against the background of the Nazi regime in Germany.[368] It was concerned with taming public but also private power to safeguard a free and equitable society.[369] Its early advocates had lived not only through the Nazi era but also through the previous Weimar Republic and had experienced how uncontrolled liberalism could lead to excessive concentration of private power, ultimately eliminating competition.[370] Some market participants had become so powerful that they were able to control the 'rules of the game' and deny access to others.[371] Unlimited economic freedom

[362] See *Hayek*, Law, Legislation, and Liberty, pp. 81–96.

[363] *Drexl*, Wirtschaftliche Selbstbestimmung, p. 101.

[364] See for material and formal freedom already above from p. 143.

[365] *Drexl*, Wirtschaftliche Selbstbestimmung, p. 102; Hayek, however, did express concerns for extending freedom of contract to corporations rather than only natural persons, see *Hayek*, in: Individualismus und wirtschaftliche Ordnung, 141 (128–129).

[366] *Drexl*, Wirtschaftliche Selbstbestimmung, pp. 101–103; Hayek was rather sceptical towards competition law in general, see *Hayek*, Die Verfassung der Freiheit, pp. 336–338.

[367] See *Böhm*, in: Ordnung einer freien Gesellschaft, 25; *Böhm*, Wirtschaftsordnung und Staatsverfassung, p. 30; *Eucken*, Wettbewerb, Monopol und Unternehmer, p. 12.

[368] *Behrens*, in: Consumer Choice, 123 (131); *Deutscher/Makris*, Competition Law Review 2016, 181 (186); *Gerber*, American Journal of Comparative Law 1994, 25 (28); *Möschel*, in: FS Pfeiffer, 707 (710).

[369] *Behrens*, in: Consumer Choice, 123 (131); *Klement*, Wettbewerbsfreiheit, p. 156.

[370] *Deutscher/Makris*, Competition Law Review 2016, 181 (186).

[371] *Deutscher/Makris*, Competition Law Review 2016, 181 (186).

could undermine its own prerequisites. This, so the ordoliberal view, can even spill over to democratic institutions[372] as in the case of Nazi Germany, where cartels and monopolies were ultimately brought under the control of but also colluded with the central (dictatorship) government.[373] Ordoliberals aimed to find an economic and legal order that protects personal freedoms and human dignity.[374] Inherently linked to the dignified economic and legal order, ordoliberalism is characterized by a material understanding of freedom, going beyond mere formal freedom of contract.[375] As such, an ordoliberal economic order also aims to protect and maintain the conditions for individuals to exercise their freedoms. The competitive order serves to safeguard individual freedoms and self-determination, including against private interference.[376]

Ordoliberals recognized very early that competition is the most effective means to achieve good economic outcomes, i.e., welfare.[377] In this sense, ordoliberalism, in principle, argues for a non-dilemma thesis: the guarantee and protection of individual freedoms in a competitive system inherently leads to 'efficiency', understood as the maximization of innovation, growth and an efficient allocation of resources.[378] Efficiency is, therefore, a goal of a competitive market order; it simply is not the only one and must be reconciled with other goals.[379] The procedural aspect ('competition as a process'), however, in case of conflict, must prevail over efficiency (or other result-oriented goals).[380]

Möschel, one of the more recent supporters of ordoliberalism, identifies four key elements of an ordoliberal competition policy:

(1) securing individual freedom of action as its primary goal (with economic efficiency merely as a secondary objective),

---

[372] See *Böhm*, Wirtschaftsordnung und Staatsverfassung, p. 30.

[373] *Deutscher/Makris*, Competition Law Review 2016, 181 (187).

[374] *Crane*, in: The Making of Competition Policy, 252 (253); *Drexl*, Wirtschaftliche Selbstbestimmung, p. 108; *Eucken*, Wettbewerb, Monopol und Unternehmer, p. 24; *Fikentscher*, Die Freiheit und ihr Paradox, p. 19; *Gerber*, Law and Competition, p. 240.

[375] *Eucken*, Grundsätze der Wirtschaftspolitik, pp. 275–279; *Mohr*, Vertragsfreiheit, pp. 357–360; *Möschel*, in: FS Pfeiffer, 707 (723).

[376] Compare *Drexl*, Wirtschaftliche Selbstbestimmung, p. 115; *Möschel*, in: FS Pfeiffer, 707 (712).

[377] *Deutscher/Makris*, Competition Law Review 2016, 181 (189).

[378] See *Eucken*, Wettbewerb, Monopol und Unternehmer, p. 7 who sees competition as a way to reach a 'sufficient overall supply and on this basis also of a reasonable allocation' (German original: 'zureichender Gesamtversorgung und auf dieser Grundlage auch einer vernünftigen Verteilung'); *Gröner*, in: Ordnung in Freiheit, 79 (82), referring to Eucken; *Möschel*, in: FS Pfeiffer, 707 (713).

[379] *Deutscher/Makris*, Competition Law Review 2016, 181 (189).

[380] *Böhm*, in: Cartel and Monopoly in Modern Law, 25 (33) emphasizing that freedom-oriented goals must prevail over efficiency: 'If we want freedom, we have no option but to sacrifice some advantage which we could obtain only by employing concentrated power'; *Deutscher/Makris*, Competition Law Review 2016, 181 (192); *Möschel*, in: FS Pfeiffer, 707 (715).

(2) preservation of the prerequisites of the competitive system (competition as a process),
(3) competition policy based on the rule of law, and
(4) embedding competition policy and law "in the economic order of a free and open society".[381]

Consumer autonomy, as a goal of competition law, can fit within this framework. Consumer autonomy may be understood as a fundamental prerequisite of competition itself. To preserve competition, it is necessary to protect the substantive (e.g., economic resources) and the procedural conditions for exercising these freedoms. This goal, in principle, is best to be achieved through the institution of a competitive market economy.[382] In such a market economy, however, legal rules to grant and safeguard equal freedom to consumers and producers alike are seen as constitutive elements. The consumers' important role for the functioning of competition can be traced back to the works of Ludwig Mises, who developed the idea that economic science as such is concerned with human behaviour and "characterized all human action in terms of choice."[383] Under the headline 'consumer sovereignty' he writes:

> "The direction of all economic affairs is in the market society a task of the entrepreneurs. Theirs is the control of production. They are at the helm and steer the ship. A superficial observer would believe that they are supreme. But they are not. They are bound to obey unconditionally the captain's orders. The captain is the consumer. Neither the entrepreneurs nor the farmers nor the capitalists determine what has to be produced. The consumers do that. If a businessman does not strictly obey the orders of the public as they are conveyed to him by the structure of market prices, he suffers losses, he goes bankrupt, and is thus removed from his eminent position at the helm. Other men who did better in satisfying the demand of the consumers replace him."[384]

Under thies view, consumers are 'the captains' of competition. They are the ones who give the directions in which the economy develops. The important role of consumers was later further theorized by Franz Böhm[385], one of the founding fathers of the first German Competition Act. As Behrens summarises Böhm's view, competition was the "result of individuals making use of their rights to freely engage in market transactions."[386] Böhm saw the consumer as the arbiter of

---

[381] *Giocoli*, Journal of Competition Law & Economics 2009, 747 (768–775); *Gormsen*, European Competition Journal 2007, 329 (334); *Monti*, CMLR 2002, 1057 (1059–1060); *Möschel*, in: FS Pfeiffer, 707 (707–708).

[382] *Behrens*, in: Consumer Choice, 123 (131).

[383] *Behrens*, in: Consumer Choice, 123 (128).

[384] *Mises*, Human Action, p. 270; also cited by *Behrens*, in: Consumer Choice, 123 (129–130).

[385] See for Böhm's life and work *Mestmäcker*, in: Deutschsprachige Zivilrechtslehrer, 31.

[386] *Behrens*, in: Consumer Choice, 123 (132).

the competitive process.[387] This role is based on a functional relationship between consumers, competitors and competition: the way in which consumers exercise their will is decisive for each individual economic operator's action as well as the direction of the economy as a whole.[388] This presupposes that consumers' ability to make an informed decision is not impaired or distorted – less so because of a concern for the individual consumer but rather because this would undermine competition.[389] This implies "a duty on the part of competitors to [...] keep their own offer in line with their genuine performance power and must not prevent their competitors from proceeding in the same way with regard to their offers."[390] This obligation is irrespective of other legal or moral norms that could prohibit a certain behaviour as it has to be evaluated with regard to its specific impact on competition.[391]

This function of the consumer is also relevant when considering the effects that competition has (or is supposed to have) on private power. Böhm coined the term "Entmachtungsinstrument", describing competition an instrument to reduce power.[392] Yet, it is important to recognize that competition can initially lead to an *increase* in power. The economic actor, who succeeds in the market, be it because of a better starting position or better performance, will make higher profits than their competitors. They will be able to use these profits to invest in an even better performance (e.g., through product improvements or better advertising), increasing their advantage over competitors and their power.[393] Thus, increasing power can be a natural result of competition.[394]

The counterbalance to this natural tendency for power to accumulate is not primarily found among competitors but rather on the demand side, i.e., ultimately (although sometimes indirectly) the consumers and their changing needs and preferences.[395] Consumers' ability to form and change preferences as well as to act according to these preferences is what allows competition to reduce power. Competition law serves to counterbalance the power-increasing effects of competition (e.g., preventing the acquisition of power through mergers).[396] Consequently, the argument can be made that is must also protect the power-reducing aspects of competition itself: the consumers' autonomy. Consider today's digital landscape:

[387] *Böhm*, Wettbewerb und Monopolkampf, p. 276; see also *Eucken*, Wettbewerb, Monopol und Unternehmer, p. 18.

[388] *Böhm*, Wettbewerb und Monopolkampf, p. 261.

[389] *Böhm*, Wettbewerb und Monopolkampf, p. 262.

[390] *Böhm*, Wettbewerb und Monopolkampf, p. 262.

[391] *Böhm*, Wettbewerb und Monopolkampf, p. 263.

[392] *Böhm*, ORDO 1971, 11 (20); *Böhm*, in: Cartel and Monopoly in Modern Law, 25 (42).

[393] *Klement*, Wettbewerbsfreiheit, p. 116.

[394] EU competition law implicitly recognizes this with Art. 102 TFEU, indicating that reaching a position of dominance through competition on the merits is, as such, not prohibited.

[395] *Klement*, Wettbewerbsfreiheit, pp. 116, 120.

[396] *Klement*, Wettbewerbsfreiheit, pp. 116, 118.

companies like Facebook and Google have amassed significant power. Competition law must ensure market conditions under which another firm may compete by offering the same service but better, i.e., a better social network or a better search service (for example, with less advertising). Moreover, competition law should protect market conditions that enable consumers to shift their preferences entirely and adopt different products. This dynamic is essential for de-throning dominant players not merely because another company competes on similar terms, but because consumers change their behavior – for example, spending less time online or opting for specialized search services over general ones. When consumers become cognitively locked in and lose the ability to switch, this can hence be a concern for competition law.[397]

It can also be argued that focusing on consumers' autonomy aligns with the broader ordoliberal idea that market participants (consumers and producers alike) should be active subjects rather than mere objects in the market and society.[398] According to Böhm, competition law is an integral part of an 'economic constitution'.[399] Despite high regard for free competition and scepticism towards state interference, ordoliberalism recognizes that free competition can destroy itself if monopolization and cartelization remain unchecked.[400] In the ordoliberal view, it is necessary to distinguish between competitive and anti-competitive market behaviour, setting the 'rules of the game'.[401] Only 'competition on the merits' ('Leistungswettbewerb') should be permitted, and other practices outlawed.[402] Böhm, in the context of his description of competition on the merits, already emphasized that the key element of competition is the battle for the consumer's will.[403] This will may, besides competing on price and quality, only be influenced by means of advertising, understood as emphasizing the attractiveness of one's own products.[404] Such advertising is only competition on the merits if it is truthful and uses suggestive influencing only within reasonable limits.[405] As this shows, ordoliberalism, goes beyond purely economic concerns.[406] What it pur-

[397] *Podszun*, SSRN 2019; See *Podszun*, GRUR 2020, 1268.

[398] *Behrens*, in: Consumer Choice, 123 (132–133).

[399] See *Böhm*, Wettbewerb und Monopolkampf, pp. 124–127.

[400] *Behrens*, in: Consumer Choice, 123 (134–135); *Künzler/Warlouzet*, in: Historical Foundations, 89 (7).

[401] *Behrens*, in: Consumer Choice, 123 (134–135); *Böhm*, Ordnung der Wirtschaft, p. 120; this was also the core theme of Eucken's economic vision, see *Petersen*, Rechtsordnung und Wirtschaftsordnung nach Eucken, pp. 18–28.

[402] *Behrens*, in: Consumer Choice, 123 (134–135); *Böhm*, Wettbewerb und Monopolkampf, pp. 178–187; *Eucken*, Wettbewerb, Monopol und Unternehmer, pp. 16–17; *Gerber*, Law and Competition, p. 253.

[403] *Böhm*, Wettbewerb und Monopolkampf, pp. 250–253.

[404] See also *Gerber*, Law and Competition, p. 251.

[405] *Böhm*, Wettbewerb und Monopolkampf, p. 241; *Böhm*, Ordnung der Wirtschaft, pp. 134–135.

[406] *Gerber*, Law and Competition, p. 239.

sues is a value-based competitive order. Consumer autonomy, in this sense, may be understood as an important value and, at the same time, a prerequisite for a functioning economy.

The protection of consumer autonomy would hence become an important "rule of the game". Consumer autonomy, together with and as part of economic freedom therefore can be considered to be consistent with ordoliberal principles.[407]

3. Ordoliberal influences on EU competition law

There has long been debate egarding the extent to which ordoliberalism has influenced EU competition law.[408] While a complete overview is beyond the scope of this thesis, some general observations can be made.[409]

Overall, it is widely accepted that ordoliberalism has left its mark on EU competition law which relies on a freedom-oriented approach protecting competition as an institution, a core concept of ordoliberalism.[410] One key argument is that ordoliberals played a significant role in the drafting and shaping of EU competition law.[411] Many German representatives involved in the founding of the European Communities, such as Walter Hallstein or Hans von der Groeben, had close ties with and were influenced by ordoliberalism.[412] Moreover, given that ordoliberalism was one of Europe's few ideologically and conceptually developed systems at the time, its indirect influence on the emerging EU competition law appears natural.[413] Therefore, from a historical perspective, EU competition

[407] Behrens, for example, argues that 'consumer choice' is coherent with ordoliberal thoughts *Behrens*, in: Consumer Choice, 123.

[408] For the historical development of EU competition law, see *Gerber*, Law and Competition, pp. 333–391.

[409] See in this regard *Gerber*, Law and Competition; *Pérez/Scheur*, in: Historical Foundations, 19; *Schweitzer*, in: European Competition Law Annual 2007, 119.

[410] *Behrens*, in: Consumer Choice, 123 (143–145); *Cseres*, Competition Law and Consumer Protection, pp. 91–96; *Crane*, in: The Making of Competition Policy, 252; *Deutscher/Makris*, Competition Law Review 2016, 181; *Gerber*, Law and Competition, pp. 26–365; *Giocoli*, Journal of Competition Law & Economics 2009, 747; *Hertfelder*, Consumer Welfare, p. 222; *Monti*, CMLR 2002, 1057; *Möschel*, JITE 2001, 3 (3); *Patel/Schweitzer*, in: Historical Foundations, (8, 10); *Parret*, European Competition Journal 2010, 339 (348); *Pera*, European Competition Journal 2008, 127; *Pérez/Scheur*, in: Historical Foundations, 19; *Schmitz*, University of Pennsylvania Journal of International Law 2002, 539; *Wigger/Nölke*, JCMS 2007, 487; for the opposite view, see *Akman*, Oxford Journal of Legal Studies 2009, 267; *Akman/Kassim*, JCMS 2010, 111.

[411] *Monti*, CMLR 2002, 1057 (1060); for a detailed analysis of the history of the drafting of the EU's competition provision and the ordoliberal influence thereon, see *Schweitzer*, in: European Competition Law Annual 2007, 119 (128–138).

[412] *Gerber*, Law and Competition, p. 263; *Giocoli*, Journal of Competition Law & Econom ics 2009, 747 (767, 776).

[413] *Cseres*, Competition Law and Consumer Protection, p. 92; *Gormsen*, European Competition Journal 2007, 329 (331); *Warlouzet*, JCMS 2019, 77 (81–82).

law was created, at least partly based on the will to bring ordoliberal principles on the European level (legislative intent). It should be noted, however, that this view is not without critics. For example, Akman argues that ordoliberals had far less influence on the drafting of EU competition law than is often assumed but that instead, the main goal and focus from the very beginning was 'productive efficiency'.[414] She draws extensively on the Spaak Report[415], and finds several references to efficiencies in this report. Indeed, the report sees competition policy as a part of the steps that

> "should be taken to ensure that the merging of the markets will lead to the most rational distribution of activity [and] a general raising of the standard of living [...]".[416]

However, these references can also be read in a way that aligns with the ordoliberal view: namely, that a system of undistorted competition naturally fosters efficiency, welfare, and economic progress.[417] In this sense, references to efficiency in the Spaak Report do not necessarily contradict ordoliberal principles but may instead reflect a belief in the positive outcomes of a competitive order, as promoted by ordoliberals. Akman further argues that the Spaak Report's inclusion of only a prohibition against the abuse of dominant positions – rather than a prohibition of dominance per se – does not align with early ordoliberal views "monopolies are inherently harmful and should be prohibited as such."[418] Yet, this critique overlooks the evolution of ordoliberal theory itself. While early ordoliberals held a strict stance against monopolies, this view matured over time. A more refined position later emerged, acknowledging that dominance may, in some cases, result from superior performance or innovation, and thus, should not be prohibited outright.[419] Moreover, the Spaak Report does in fact express a critical attitude toward monopolies, stating:

> "steps should be taken to prevent [...] monopoly or partial domination of the market for a product by a single enterprise, since this would do away with one of the essential advantages of a large market, namely that of reconciling the use of mass production methods and the maintenance of competition."[420]

That said, reliance on the drafting history of the Treaties may not be fully conclusive in the first place. The Member States deliberately decided not to publish the preparatory documents to allow for a functional interpretation of the Treaties

---

[414] *Akman*, Oxford Journal of Legal Studies 2009, 267.

[415] Report on the General Common Market of the Heads of Delegation to the Foreign Ministers, Brussels, 21 April 1956 ('Spaak Report').

[416] Spaak Report, p. 45.

[417] As will be explained in more detail below on p. 158, ordoliberalism does recognize efficiency as a goal.

[418] *Akman*, Oxford Journal of Legal Studies 2009, 267 (285); this view was expressed, for example, by *Böhm*, Wirtschaftsordnung und Staatsverfassung, p. 39.

[419] *Schweitzer*, in: European Competition Law Annual 2007, 119 (133–135).

[420] Spaak Report, p. 47.

rather than one based on the legislative intent, and the Court of Justice, respecting this decision, does not carry out historical interpretations of the Treaties.[421]

Looking at the issue on the more substantive side requires identifying key elements of ordoliberalism and examining whether they are reflected in EU competition law. The following paragraphs will establish that the key aspects of ordoliberalism[422] do indeed play a role in EU competition law.

First, freedom is a key value of European competition law and is frequently invoked by the European Courts and other institutions. Stylianou and Iacovides studied the rhetoric used in Court of Justice and General Court judgments, Opinions of Advocates General, Commission Decisions and Commissioner for Competition speeches from 1962–2020.[423] They found that the terms referring to "competition process", "market structure", and "freedom/competitors" were used by all institutions to quite a large extent (between 16 and 21 %). The Courts regularly emphasize freedom of action or freedom of choice of economic actors as a fundamental goal and principle of competition law.[424] Recent examples include high-profile cases such as Microsoft[425], Google Android[426] and Post Danmark[427]. The notion that economic operators must be and remain able to make independent decisions and cannot dispose of this autonomy even themselves[428] also fits into the freedom-oriented ordoliberal school of thought.[429]

Second, and related, EU competition law accepts that the 'competitive process' is an important aspect and shall be protected for its own sake.[430] This is reflected in the Court of Justice's early case law that emphasized that no direct proof of consumer harm and no evaluation of market results is necessary, but instead, any detriment to the effective competition structure is relevant[431] and has,

---

421 *Müller/Christensen*, Juristische Methodik, p. 72; *Schweitzer*, in: European Competition Law Annual 2007, 119 (124).

422 See above p. 150.

423 *Stylianou/Iacovides*, Legal Studies 2022, 620.

424 Court of Justice, 21/02/1973, Case 6–72 Continental Can, ECLI:EU:C:1973:22, para. 29; Court of Justice, 13/02/1979, Case 85/76 Hoffman-LaRoche, ECLI:EU:C:1979:36, para. 106; Court of Justice, 09/11/1983, Case 322/81 Michelin I, ECLI:EU:C:1983:313, para. 72; *Behrens*, in: Abusive Practices, 5 (14–15); *Schweitzer/Patel*, in: Historical Foundations, 207 (222–223).

425 Court of First Instance, 17/09/2007, Case T-201/04 Microsoft, ECLI:EU:T:2007:289.

426 General Court, 14/09/2022, Case T-604/18 Google Android, ECLI:EU:T:2022:541, paras. 448, 828, 1088.

427 Court of Justice, 06/10/2015, Case C-23/14 Post Danmark, ECLI:EU:C:2015:651, para. 64 finding that to assess the abusiveness of a rebate it is necessary, inter alia, 'to examine whether that rebate tends to remove or restrict the buyer's freedom to choose his sources of supply'; Court of Justice, 17/02/2011, C-52/09 TeliaSonera, ECLI:EU:C:2011:83 with the identical statement but referring to pricing practices.

428 See above p. 136.

429 *Pera*, European Competition Journal 2008, 127 (145).

430 *Deutscher/Makris*, Competition Law Review 2016, 181 (197); *Mestmäcker*, ORDO 2012, 429 (444).

431 See, inter alia, Court of Justice, 21/02/1973, Case 6–72 Continental Can, ECLI:EU:C:

despite a growing focus on consumer welfare and efficiency under a more economic approach,[432] not changed until today.[433] While antitrust rules are often applied on a case-by-case basis, taking into account economic methods, the centre of the analysis is how a conduct or agreement affects competition (e.g., excludes competitors, restricts entry) rather than directly looking at whether the outcome of the market or the conduct in question is efficient. The Court of Justice recognizes efficiency and welfare as goals of EU competition law, but without rejecting the deontological perspective that competition as such and the underlying freedoms need to be protected.[434]

Beyond interpreting how the Court of Justice understands the matter, it is equally important to examine the wording of the law itself. Monti, in this regard, offers an argument based on a systematic and grammatical interpretation of Art. 101 TFEU for why EU competition law aigns more closely with the ordoliberal tradition rather than with a consumer-welfare approach[435]: Article 101 TFEU is structured in two distinct parts: paragraph 1 prohibits restrictions of competition, while paragraph 3 allows for the justification of such restrictions under specific conditions.[436] From a consumer-welfare perspective, an agreement either harms competition (e.g., by reducing output) or it does not; once harm is established, there is no room for further balancing.[437] Moreover, the requirement that consumers must receive a 'fair share' of the benefits is incompatible with a perspective that ignores distributional concerns and cares only about allocative efficiency.[438] The structure of Art. 101 TFEU aligns more naturally with the ordoliberal thinking: a restriction of competition can be found based on limitations of economic operators' freedoms; such a restriction can then be justified. Only in

---

1973:22, para. 26; Court of Justice, 13/02/1979, Case 85/76 Hoffman-LaRoche, ECLI:EU:C:1979:36, para. 91; for more examples, see *Gormsen*, European Competition Journal 2007, 329 (339–342); *Schweitzer*, in: European Competition Law Annual 2007, 119 (140) explaining the significance of the functional approach adopted in Continental Can.

[432] See *Behrens*, in: Consumer Choice, 123 (145–146); *Schweitzer/Patel*, in: Historical Foundations, 207 (220–226); for a detailed description of what the more economic approach entails, see *Klement*, Wettbewerbsfreiheit, pp. 164–178.

[433] See most recently Court of Justice, 12/05/2022, Case C-377/20 Servizio Elettrico Nazionale, ECLI:EU:C:2022:379, para. 47: 'a competition authority discharges its burden of proof if it shows that a practice of an undertaking in a dominant position could impair, by using resources or means other than those governing normal competition, an effective competition structure, without it being necessary for that authority to prove that that practice may also cause direct harm to consumers.'

[434] *Deutscher/Makris*, Competition Law Review 2016, 181 (197).

[435] See for the consumer welfare approach below from p. 158.

[436] *Monti*, CMLR 2002, 1057 (1060); see also *Deutscher/Makris*, Competition Law Review 2016, 181 (200); *Mohr*, Vertragsfreiheit, p. 451; *Pera*, European Competition Journal 2008, 127 (147).

[437] *Monti*, CMLR 2002, 1057 (1060); see also *Deutscher/Makris*, Competition Law Review 2016, 181 (199–201).

[438] *Monti*, CMLR 2002, 1057 (1061).

the second step do efficiency considerations become relevant; still, they do not have an absolute value. Instead, they must be passed on to consumers, thus preventing a too great accumulation of wealth and power by the undertakings involved, and competition must not be eliminated "in a substantial part of the products in question", thus not suffocating other market participants' freedom of opportunity and choice.[439] This reflects a concern for distributive justice as well as skepticism toward unchecked accumulation of economic power, which are both ordoliberal ideals.[440] Finally, Art. 101(3) TFEU also may provide support for the ordoliberal view that in cases of conflict between welfare and competition, the latter must prevail: no amount of efficiency can justify the complete elimination of competition.[441] The wording and structure of Art. 101 TFEU thus also implies that restriction of competition cannot be equated with behaviour that reduces efficiency.

Third, EU competition law is grounded in the rule of law and forms part of the EU's economic constitution.[442] Art. 101 and Art. 102 TFEU have been interpreted as giving the Commission power to enforce the provisions rather than just serving as guiding administrative principles.[443] The enforcement, however, is subject to judicial review and interventions in markets must follow the rules laid down in the law itself.[444] This includes Art. 101(3) TFEU in the first place but also the block exemption regulations.[445]

Fourth, competition law does not operate in isolation but is embedded within a broader, value-based economic and societal order.[446] The most evident example is the link between market integration and competition policy, which is unique to EU competition law.[447] But even broader and in line with ordoliberal ideals, EU law provides a large array of value-based focal points for its economic order. Quite expressly, Art. 3 TEU speaks of the 'values' of the EU and mentions there, among others, a 'highly competitive social market economy'. While the term competition (which is to be protected) is not clearly defined, the vision of what kind of competition is protected and desired can be distilled from those values, namely competition as part of a humane and dignified order. This understanding has re-emerged most clearly in the recent debate on competition law and sustainability, where there is growing recognition that EU competition law is not a

---

[439] *Monti*, CMLR 2002, 1057 (1061).

[440] *Monti*, CMLR 2002, 1057 (1061).

[441] *Deutscher/Makris*, Competition Law Review 2016, 181 (201); see also *Cseres*, Competition Law and Consumer Protection, p. 248.

[442] *Cseres*, Competition Law and Consumer Protection, p. 93; *Pera*, European Competition Journal 2008, 127 (147).

[443] *Giocoli*, Journal of Competition Law & Economics 2009, 747 (777).

[444] *Giocoli*, Journal of Competition Law & Economics 2009, 747 (767–768).

[445] *Monti*, CMLR 2002, 1057 (1061).

[446] *Monti*, CMLR 2002, 1057 (1057).

[447] *Monti*, CMLR 2002, 1057 (1063).

self-contained field but must align with and contribute to the overarching values and principles of the Union.[448]

4. Conclusion

Ordoliberalism is certainly not the not the sole or all-encompassing aspect of EU competition law. However, it plays a role and cannot be ioverlooked. When it comes to consumer autonomy, ordoliberal ideas can serve as an argument that consumer autonomy can play a role in EU competition law. At the same time, consumer autonomy as a normative goal also gives support to some ordoliberal ideals. The EU's competition law regime, while certainly not ignoring it, is concerned not only with economic efficiency but with a competitive order based on certain broader values.

VII. Consumer welfare vs consumer autonomy – a dilemma?

As shown in the previous section, protecting consumer autonomy would align with the ordoliberal emphasis on safeguarding competition as an institution. However, protecting competition as an institution or the competitive process is only one of the goals discussed for antitrust law. Protecting competition as an institution can be said to be one pole in the debate on the goals of competition law, with the other being to increase consumer welfare. The following section will question whether consumer autonomy and consumer welfare are conflicting or rather complementary approaches. In this regard, it will distinguish between consumer welfare as a goal, on the one hand, and consumer welfare as a method of competition law, on the other hand. The section will show that there is no conflict of goals but only a conflict of methods.

1. Consumer welfare as a goal

The European Commission has consistently emphasized that competition law and its enforcement shall serve the consumer and their interests.[449] Paradigmatic for this is the formulation in the Guidelines on Art. 81(3) EC that competition law shall "protect competition on the market as a means of enhancing consumer welfare".[450] Similarly, in the (previous) Vertical Guidelines, the Commission sees the objective of Article 101 TFEU to prevent agreements between undertakings

---

[448] See, inter alia, *Kingston*, European Law Journal 2010, 780; *Kingston*, Greening EU Competition Law and Policy; *Nowag*, Environmental Integration in Competition and Free-Movement Laws; *Gerbrandy*, World Competition 2017, 539; *Dolmans*, SSRN 2020; *Holmes*, Journal of Antitrust Enforcement 2020, 354.

[449] *Wissing*, WuW 2020, 593; *Mestmäcker/Schweitzer*, Europäisches Wettbewerbsrecht§ 3, paras. 43–49.

[450] Communication from the Commission, Guidelines on the application of Article 81(3) of the Treaty, OJ C 101, 27.4.2004, p. 97–118, paras. 13, 33.

that "restrict competition on the market to the detriment of consumers."[451] Under this approach, consumer interests and welfare become one of the core goals of competition law and must therefore be taken into account in its interpretation and application. However, this focus does not imply that the identification of an anti-competitive practice requires the demonstration of direct consumer harm.[452] There is only one instance where the General Court appeared to adopt such an approach by requiring proof of direct consumer harm, thereby endorsing consumer welfare as a method rather than a goal.[453] In GlaxoSmithKline, it held:

"the Commission was still required to demonstrate how that provision had the effect of restricting competition to the detriment of the final consumer."[454]

This approach was explicitly rejected on appeal by the Court of Justice, which held that:

"by requiring proof that the agreement entails disadvantages for final consumers as a prerequisite for a finding of anti-competitive object and by not finding that that agreement had such an object, the Court of First Instance committed an error of law."[455]

Instead, as the Court of Justice articulated in the Post Danmark case, competition law (in casu: Art. 102 TFEU) prohibits

"not only those practices that directly cause harm to consumers but also practices that cause consumers harm through their impact on competition".[456]

Thus, the Court of Justice has acknowledged that consumer welfare (or the prevention of consumer harm) is a vital goal of competition law, but one that must be achieved by safeguarding the competitive process. It does not, however, treat consumer welfare as the sole objective. Instead, the Court of Justice continues to regularly emphasize that

---

[451] Vertical Guidelines (2010), para. 5; see also Guidance on the Commission's enforcement priorities in applying Article 82 of the EC Treaty to abusive exclusionary conduct by dominant undertakings, 2009/C 45/02 ('Art 82 Enforcement Priority Guidelines'), para. 19; Guidelines on the applicability of Article 101 of the Treaty on the Functioning of the European Union to horizontal co-operation agreements, OJ C 11, 14.1.2011, p. 1–72 ('Horizontal Guidelines'), para. 296; Guidelines on the application of Article 101 of the Treaty on the Functioning of the European Union to technology transfer agreements, OJ C 89, 28.3.2014, p. 3–50 ('Technology Transfer Guidelines'), paras. 5, 7; Guidelines on the assessment of horizontal mergers under the Council Regulation on the control of concentrations between undertakings, OJ C 31, 5.2.2004, p. 5–18 ('Horizontal Merger Guidelines'), para. 77.

[452] *Drexl*, in: Europäisches Verfassungsrecht, 905 (950).

[453] See for the distinction between consumer welfare as a method and as a goal below from p. 162.

[454] General Court, 27/09/2006, Case T-168/01 GlaxoSmithKline, ECLI:EU:T:2006:265, para. 172.

[455] Court of Justice, 06/10/2009, Joined Cases C-501/06 P, C-513/06 P, C-515/06 P C-519/06 P GlaxoSmithKline, ECLI:EU:C:2009:610, para. 64.

[456] Court of Justice, 27/03/2012, Case C-209/10 Post Danmark, ECLI:EU:C:2012:172, para. 20.

"the objective pursued by the Union's competition rules, [is] to protect not only the direct interests of competitors or consumers, but the structure of the relevant market and thus competition as such."[457]

Therefore, the Court of Justice's understanding is that, in the long term, consumer welfare is best achieved through effective competition.[458] This reflectsthe ordoliberal non-dilemma thesis.[459] Understood as a goal, consumer welfare and the protection of competition as a process are compatible with each other: if the competitive process and economic freedoms are protected, this will, at least in the long term, benefit consumers.[460] Consumer welfare can then serve as a proxy for working competition.[461] There is, however, no primacy of consumers' direct interests over competition as such.[462] The Court's approach is also compatible with incorporating economic theory and evidence. Even an effects-based approach, which requires looking at the effects of a practice or agreement on competition, is compatible with this view. The key point here is that the relevant effect that must be evaluated economically is the effect on the market (e.g., exclusionary effect, raising barriers to entry) rather than only on the final consumer (e.g., higher prices or lower output).[463] A concrete example of how this affects the application of competition law in practice is that predatory pricing in the EU – unlike in the US, where under a consumer welfare standard proof of consumer harm is required[464] – can be illegal without showing that recoupment is likely to occur.[465]

The Court of Justice's approach is coherent with a systematic reading of the Treaties. Art. 120 TFEU, in particular, appears relevant here, stating that "[t]he Member States and the Union shall act in accordance with the principle of an open market economy with free competition, favouring an efficient allocation of resources, and in compliance with the principles set out in Article 119." The

[457] Court of Justice, 04/06/2009, Case C-8/08 T-Mobile Netherlands, ECLI:EU:C:2009:343, paras. 38–39; Court of Justice, 19/03/2015, Case C-286/13 P Dole Food, ECLI:EU:C:2015:184, para. 125; Court of Justice, 14/01/2021, Case C-450/19 Kilpailu- ja kuluttajavirasto, ECLI:EU:C:2021:10, para. 34.

[458] See also *Bundeskartellamt*, European Competition Journal 2006, 211; *Gormsen*, European Competition Journal 2007, 329 (329); *Schweitzer*, in: European Competition Law Annual 2007, 119 (142).

[459] See above p. 149.

[460] See *Bundeskartellamt*, European Competition Journal 2006, 211 (218); *Hoppmann*, ZBJV 1966, 249 (253), proposing the so-called non-dilemma thesis that there is no conflict between safeguarding economic freedom and pursuing economic welfare; similar *Möschel*, JITE 2001, 3 (4); see also *Hoppmann*, Ordo 1967, 77; *Monti*, CMLR 2002, 1057.

[461] *Zimmer*, in: Competition Policy and the Economic Approach, 72 (73); compare also *Hellwig*, Preprints MPI for Research on Collective Goods 2006, pp. 27–29.

[462] *Drexl*, in: Europäisches Verfassungsrecht, 905 (943); *Schweitzer*, in: European Competition Law Annual 2007, 119 (143).

[463] *Drexl*, in: Europäisches Verfassungsrecht, 905 (925–929) arguing that this is also the key aspect of the Commission's 'more economic approach'.

[464] See above from p. 91.

[465] *Schweitzer*, in: European Competition Law Annual 2007, 119 (154–155).

'efficient allocation of resources' is here expressed as the expected result of 'free competition'.[466] This view seems once more to align well with ordoliberal perspectives on competition, freedom and efficiency.

Following this approach, there would be no conflict between pursuing consumer welfare goals and protecting consumer autonomy. On the one hand, consumer autonomy can be included in the consumer welfare goals. Consumer welfare in the EU context is typically defined broadly, encompassing low prices, high output, innovation and consumer choice and is not limited to those elements of consumer well-being that can be quantified in monetary terms.[467] The ability to make autonomous decisions is an important aspect of consumer well-being and is closely linked to consumer choice.[468] The Commission, for example, refers to welfare not only with regard to price and output but also emphasizing choice as a benchmark. The Commission regularly identifies a reduction of choice as a harm to consumers.[469] In Google Android, for example, it found that "Google's conduct is capable of harming, directly or indirectly, consumers who, as a result of Google's interference with the normal competitive process, may see *less choice* of general search services available."[470] This demonstrates that choice can be understood as a core outcome that competition is designed to foster and that competition law is meant to safeguard. While this is typically interpreted as the range of available options in the marketplace, one could argue that genuine choice can only occur when it is made autonomously. In other words, protecting a wide array of options that do not align with consumers' actual preferences would be an ineffective endeavor. Consumer welfare can only be increased through choices that consumers actually want.

On the other hand, accepting consumer welfare as a goal under this framework would not undermine the finding that consumer autonomy is an important precondition for making markets work and yield the desired results. In fact, consumer welfare is enhanced when consumers are capable of making autonomous decisions. Choice and autonomy can be understood not only as goals but

---

[466] See *Khan/Richter*, in: Geiger/Khan/Kotzur/Kirchmair, EUV/AEUV, Art. 120 AEUV, para. 3 who interpret this provision as a confirmation of the European economic constitution's ordoliberal character; see also *Wittelsberger*, in: Von der Groeben/Schwarze, Europäisches Unionsrecht, Art. 120 AEUV, para. 6 footnote 5.

[467] *Daskalova*, Competition Law Review 2015, 133; *Lianos*, in: Handbook European Competition Law, 1 (19–20); Art. 82 Enforcement Priority Guidelines, para. 19 speaking of practices that can have an adverse impact on 'consumer welfare, whether in the form of higher price levels than would have otherwise prevailed or in some other form such as limiting quality or reducing consumer choice'.

[468] *Klaus et al.*, Marketing Letters 2020, 429; for a philosophical account of the relationship between autonomy and well-being, see *Raz*, The Morality of Freedom, pp. 390–395.

[469] See in more detail the analysis of the cases from p. 168.

[470] European Commission, 18/07/2018, AT.40099 Google Android, para. 863 (emphasis added); see also European Commission, 13/05/2009, AT.37990 Intel, paras. 1598–1616; European Commission, 08/12/2017, AT.40208 ISU, para. 205.

also as conditions for functioning competition. It is therefore hardly surprising that, especially in cases where the Commission recurred to reduced choices as a harm (i.e., consequence) of certain conduct, the conduct itself was also often an interference with consumers' autonomous choices. In the Google Shopping case, for example, the abusive conduct lay in Google steering consumers to Google Shopping rather than to competing general search services, thereby interfering with their autonomous choice.[471] The harm was found in, inter alia, a reduction of choice among competing specialized search providers (since others were driven out of the market).

Hence, if one understands consumer welfare as a goal of competition law, consumer autonomy would be complementary rather than detrimental to this goal. For the purpose of this thesis, it is sufficient to demonstrate that consumer autonomy is compatible, in principle, with both perspectives: one where competition law is centered on protecting competition as an institution, and another where consumer welfare is the primary goal. This conclusion holds without the necessity of choosing one goal over the other.[472] Nevertheless, it is important to recognize that there are significant normative differences between these views. Consumer welfare is grounded in a utilitarian philosophy, while approaches that emphasize competition as a process and individual freedom are essentially rights-based, drawing on a more Kantian tradition.[473] Although both frameworks aim to protect competition, they do so for different reasons. The European tradition is likely to be somewhere in the middle between the two approaches, protecting competition based on individual freedom rights but at the same time recognizing that this is done not only for the sake of the individuals but also for the sake of overarching goals such as greater welfare.[474]

2. Consumer welfare as a method

a) The consumer welfare standard

However, consumer welfare can be understood not only as a *goal* but also as a *method* for applying competition law. Competition law under this view embodies the goal also in its application. Consequently, competition law shall then serve to protect or reach specific market outcomes. The focus is on the results rather than on the process of competition. This approach is rooted in utilitarian principles:

---

[471] The case will be discussed in more detail below from p. 170.

[472] See for the discussion on the goals of competition law, inter alia, *Lianos*, in: Handbook European Competition Law, 1; *Mestmäcker*, ORDO 2008, 185; *Mestmäcker*, ORDO 2012, 429; *Möller*, Verbraucherbegriff und Verbraucherwohlfahrt; *Schmidtchen*, ORDO 2008, 143.

[473] See *Gormsen*, European Competition Journal 2007, 329 (239–240); *Mestmäcker*, ORDO 2008, 185 (201); *Mestmäcker*, ORDO 2012, 429; *Mestmäcker*, Europäische Prüfsteine, pp. 290–291; *Monti*, CMLR 2002, 1057 (1060); *Möschel*, in: FS Pfeiffer, 707 (716).

[474] In this direction also *Mohr*, Vertragsfreiheit, p. 449.

the morality of a conduct is evaluated depending on its consequences.[475] So to evaluate whether something is good or bad, it must be assessed whether its consequences are good or bad. Welfare approaches assess conduct based on its impact on total or consumer welfare. In the EU context, it encompasses only the welfare of consumers, distinguishing it from total welfare, which also includes the welfare of producers.[476] The consumer welfare standard "looks only at the surplus that goes to the consumers, ignoring what goes to the sellers."[477] Thus, efficiency gains, for example, are relevant only insofar as they are passed through to consumers.[478] Under a consumer welfare standard, a conduct is evaluated based not on its effects on competition but directly on its effects on consumer welfare, i.e., defining restriction of competition as a measurable reduction of consumer welfare.[479] As mentioned above,[480] economists define consumer welfare as 'aggregated consumer surplus', i.e., the difference between consumers' willingness to pay for a good or service and the price.[481]

A statement of the US 7th circuit court in the case Schor v Abbot Labs can serve as an example on how the consumer welfare standard is applied: "If a manufacturer cannot make itself better off by injuring consumers through lower output and higher prices, there is no role for antitrust law to play."[482] Similarly, Schmidtchen suggests defining restrictions of competition as "those actions or conditions that cause value creation to be less than it could be."[483] Even more expressly, Bork has argued that it is the role of antitrust law "to identify and prohibit those forms of behavior whose net effect is output restricting and hence detrimental."[484] Under a consumer welfare standard, consumers' decision-making is irrelevant as it is only the outcome that matters. More purchases are good,

---

[475] *Andriychuk*, World Competition 2012, 355 (356); *Künzler*, Effizienz oder Wettbewerbsfreiheit?, p. 23.

[476] Bork used the term 'consumer welfare' when actually referring to total welfare, see *Bork*, Antitrust Paradox, p. 427; *Bradford et al.*, University of Chicago Law Review 2020, 297 (305); *Hovenkamp*, Fordham Law Review 2013, 2471 (2473); for a discussion on the use of the term, see *Orbach*, Fordham Law Review 2012, 2253 (2255–2556).

[477] *Hovenkamp*, Fordham Law Review 2013, 2471 (2472).

[478] *Salop*, Loy. Consumer L. Rev. 2009, 336 (336–337).

[479] See *Schweitzer/Patel*, in: Historical Foundations, 207 (221–222).

[480] See above p. 43.

[481] The term goes back to *Marshall*, Principles of Economics, p. 103; see also *Dworkin*, Journal of Legal Studies 1980, 191 (191–192) calling it 'individual wealth maximization'; *Foer/Durst*, Antitrust Bulletin 2018, 494 (497); *Hertfelder*, Consumer Welfare, p. 20; *Motta*, Competition Policy, p. 17.

[482] US 7th Circuit Court of Appeals, 26/07/2006, No. 05–3344 Schor v Abbot Laboratories, 457 F.3d 608 (7th Cir. 2006).

[483] *Schmidtchen*, ORDO 2008, 143 (165) original in German: 'Wettbewerbsbeschränkungen sind solche Maßnahmen oder Zustände, die bewirken, dass die Wertschöpfung kleiner ist, als sie sein könnte.'

[484] *Bork*, Antitrust Paradox, p. 122.

and fewer purchases are bad, irrespective of how and why a consumer made or did not make a purchase decision.

Consumer autonomy could hence be seen as a conflicting goal, potentially displacing consumer welfare. The following paragraphs will assess some of the criticism commonly put forward against the consumer welfare standard, which may lend support to applying competition law with a focus on consumer autonomy instead of the consumer welfare standard.

b) The difficulty of measuring consumer surplus

Naturally, it is difficult to measure consumer surplus precisely: a consumer with their purchase decision reveals that their willingness to pay is higher than the price but not by how much. Therefore, it is common to use proxies such as low prices or high output instead of directly measuring consumer surplus. If a practice leads to reduced output or higher prices, it will then constitute a restriction of competition. In the US, output often serves as the key benchmark, with some courts and scholars treating it as the exclusive test: only if output decreases does a practice restrict competition.[485] However, consumer surplus remains difficult to measure, and output or price changes are not always reliable indicators – especially where different consumer groups are affected differently or when dynamic efficiency is at stake.

In principle, the consumer welfare standard can include dynamic efficiency, since innovation increases welfare.[486] Concerted practices can either improve dynamic efficiency, e.g., a joint venture allowing two companies to collaboratively develop a new product or technique they would be unable to do independently (for example, due to economies of scale), or reduce them, e.g., reduced incentives to innovate due to greater market power. Both would be relevant under a consumer welfare standard. However, such dynamic effects are much harder to estimate than mere changes in output or prices.[487] Indeed, the very effects of market power on innovation are disputed. While in a more Schumpeterian view of competition, market power and the pursuit of it are seen as accelerators of innovation,[488] others argue precisely the opposite.[489] There is a trade-off to be made

[485] For a very detailed analysis and critique of this approach, see *Newman*, Iowa Law Review 2022, 563.

[486] *Melamed/Petit*, Review of Industrial Organization 2019, 741 (752).

[487] *Brodley*, NYU Law Review 1987, 1020 (1028–1029) comparing the measurability of production efficiency, dynamic efficiency and allocative efficiency; *Kerber*, in: Economic Theory and Competition Law, 93 (98–101); *Melamed/Petit*, Review of Industrial Organization 2019, 741 (753); *Stucke*, Boston College Law Review 2012, 551 (583) also highlighting the difficulties of distinguishing between harmful and beneficial innovations.

[488] Emphasizing this view, US Supreme Court, 13/01/2004, No. 02–682 Trinko, 540 U.S. 398, p. 7: 'The opportunity to charge monopoly prices at least for a short period is what attracts business acumen in the first place; it induces risk taking that produces innovation and economic growth.'

[489] For a nuanced view, see *Gilbert*, Innovation Policy and the Economy 2006, 159.

between consumers' (often short-term) interest in low prices versus their interest in innovation.[490] These trade-offs can also divide consumer groups – some may tolerate higher prices hoping for future benefits, others may not. Similar problems can arise with qualitative aspects,[491] which can, in principle, also be considered under a consumer welfare standard.[492] Depending on the standard of proof, competition authorities can therefore encounter difficulties in challenging anticompetitive behaviour or mergers on the ground of harm to innovation or quality. It is thus little surprise that some commentators have expressed concerns about a bias toward static harms, prices and output in particular, that come with a consumer welfare standard.[493] Similarly, predicting which trade-offs between price and quality consumers prefer is difficult.

Moreover, measuring consumer welfare can become a challenging exercise, particularly in cases where different consumers or groups of consumers are impacted differently.[494] This difficulty can be illustrated when looking at vertical agreements such as selective distribution systems: while some consumers might prefer that a product is only available in a neat store on the high street and thus receive a higher surplus from the product sold under such restraints, others might not be able to afford the higher prices and thus lose their surplus from the purchases that would have incurred absent the agreements.[495] In a scenario where a practice positively affects some consumers while it harms others, effects-based approaches do require an interpersonal comparison of utility.[496] In the example of service-enhancing selective distribution, one would have to compare the loss in utility for those that, due to the selective distribution system, are unable to buy the product with the higher price and forego a purchase with those that have now a greater utility because of the better service and/or image that comes with the agreement. Here, output as a proxy for surplus reaches its limits.

Welfare analysis remains a challenging task that does not always allow clear conclusions. Against this background, the EU approach that does not require showing direct consumer harm appears sensible over the application of a consumer welfare standard.

---

[490] *Brodley*, NYU Law Review 1987, 1020 (1037).

[491] *Künzler*, in: Goals of Competition Law, 182 (186); *Zäch/Künzler*, ZWeR 2009, 269 (272–273).

[492] This is different under a so-called 'price standard', see *Renckens*, Journal of Competition Law & Economics 2007, 149 (155).

[493] *Newman*, Iowa Law Review 2022, 563; *Wu*, CPI 2018, pp. 5–6.

[494] *Drexl*, in: Competition Policy and the Economic Approach, 311 (319–320); *Hovenkamp*, Fordham Law Review 2013, 2471 (2480–2492).

[495] *Comanor*, Harvard Law Review 1985, 983 (990–998); *Newman*, Iowa Law Review 2022, 563 (589–591).

[496] *Zäch/Künzler*, ZWeR 2009, 269 (274). Cf. Regard interpersonal comparison of utilities *Glick*, Antitrust Bulletin 2018, 455 (462–463); *Robbins*, Economic Journal 1938, 635; *Scitovsky*, American Economic Review 1951, 303 (304–305).

c) Revealed preferences and autonomy

However, commentators have raised a more fundamental problem relating to the consumer welfare standard which is its reliance on revealed preferences. The consumer welfare standard assumes that consumers reveal their true preferences through their purchasing behavior.[497]If a consumer buys good G at price P, their willingness to pay is presumed to be higher than P. A lower price is therefore seen as welfare-enhancing, as more consumers will choose to buy G below P. Under such an approach, higher prices, lower output but also reduced innovation are possible adverse welfare effects. Higher prices reduce surplus, as consumers must pay more to satisfy their preferences. Lower output similarly reduces consumer surplus because fewer preference-satisfying transactions occur. The same holds for reduced innovation because innovation can, on the one hand, reduce prices (thus increasing consumer surplus) or create new products that consumers can buy to satisfy their (new or old) preferences.

The critique of the consumer welfare standard as a method centers on its reliance on consumer choices without considering how those choices are formed. The consumer welfare standard "links actions to choices, choices to preferences and preferences to welfare."[498] It assumes that satisfying preferences through (consumption) choices constitute well-being.[499] This creates a conflict between measuring competition restrictions via decreases in consumer welfare – based on revealed preferences – and an approach that also seeks to protect consumer autonomy.The revealed preference approach, in principle, prevents usfrom questioning consumer decisions. The process behind such decisions is irrelevant. Why a consumer chooses to buy product B over product C does not matter. On the other hand, protecting consumer autonomy would, in principle, ask precisely this question: do we believe that the consumer chose B over C based on an autonomous decision?

Critics of the consumer welfare standard highlight that the revealed preference approach fails to explain *why* we should believe a consumption decision reflects a true preference. Is there really the supposed link between choices, preference and welfare? Indeed, behavioural economics teaches that, at least in some scenarios, this link is broken.[500] Behavioural economic literature[501] suggests that

> "preferences are constructed and not just revealed in the process of choice [...], meaning that preferences are often not consistent across different choice environments [...]".[502]

[497] *Bork*, Antitrust Paradox, pp. 90–91; *Wright*, Yale Law Journal 2012, 2216 (2237).

[498] *Lianos*, in: Handbook European Competition Law, 1 (8); see also *Glick*, Antitrust Bulletin 2018, 455 (478).

[499] *Lianos*, in: Handbook European Competition Law, 1 (8).

[500] *Lianos*, in: Handbook European Competition Law, 1 (10–11); *Siciliani*, Consumer Theories of Harm, pp. 81–92.

[501] See above from p. 10.

[502] *Dhar/Gorlin*, Journal of Consumer Psychology 2013, 528 (528).

Consumption decisions, therefore, do not necessarily reflect true preferences. To illustrate the problem, take vertical agreements: according to the above-described economic arguments[503], they can be efficiency-enhancing in that they can cater to consumer demand for non-price competition, e.g., pre-sale services. If, for example, a (qualitative) selective distribution system leads to higher prices but simultaneously increases output, Posner, an outspoken proponent of the consumer welfare standard, would consider this to increase welfare.[504] His conclusion is based on the assumption that output is increased because consumers prefer the product with the restrictions (e.g., the increased service). This assumption relies on the revealed preference doctrine – because consumers buy more of the product, they *must* prefer it to be sold under vertical restrictions. But this argument weakens if we move away from the rational consumer model. If purchases don't reliably reflect true preferences, the output test loses its foundation. Against this background, some proponents of the consumer welfare standard have expressed concerns about taking into account behavioural economic insights in the consumer welfare analysis: if consumers do sometimes behave irrationally and therefore, their consumption decisions do not necessarily reflect their true preferences, as Werden et al. reflect, this has the potential to "destroy the analytic basis of welfare economics."[505] Their response, essentially, is to overlook the fact that consumers do not always make rational choices because it complicates welfare analysis. That the consumer welfare standard based on output and prices can lead to clear and predictable results, of course, does not make it useful if those results are not real measurements of welfare. As Morell puts it:

> "We do not conduct welfare analysis for the fun of it but because we (try to) believe that it actually tells us something about the well-being of consumers."[506]

The revealed preference approach may thus be seen as a limited tool for measuring consumer surplus and even more so for capturing consumer welfare in a broader sense. This weakens the case for using the consumer welfare standard as a method for applying competition law – at least if it defines restrictions of competition strictly as measurable reductions in consumer surplus. Still, the proxies typically used under this standard, i.e., changes in output and prices, can serve as helpful indicators; they simply should not be given absolute weight. For instance, if a new product enters the market and quickly gains market shares from competitors, it's reasonable to infer that consumers prefer it. If a consumer has the choice between products A and B and chooses product B, at least at this moment, they likely prefer B over A. But, unlike the traditional consumer welfare standard, competition law should not ignore *how* these choices are made. If consumer decisions are not made autonomously, for example, because firms

---

503 See above from p. 44.
504 *Posner*, University of Chicago Law Review 1981, 6 (21).
505 *Werden et al.*, JITE 2011, 126 (137).
506 *Morell*, JITE 2011, 143 (146).

exploit their behavioural biases, we cannot assume that they lead to an efficient allocation of resources.[507] In such cases, the link between choices, preferences, and welfare breaks down. A consumer welfare standard that ignores the question of whether decisions are made autonomously risks failing on its own terms: it does not (necessarily) measure true consumer welfare.

VIII. Consumer autonomy in the decisional practice

The Court of Justice (as well as the General Court) and the European Commission, in several decisions mainly outside of the realm of vertical agreements, taken into account consumer autonomy. The same is true for national competition authorities and courts. The following paragraphs will discuss some exemplary cases in that regard. This is relevant for this thesis for two reasons: first, if consumer autonomy plays a role in other antitrust cases, this provides additional support for this Chapter's normative conclusion that it may be a relevant goal of EU competition law. Second, it can help to clarify how consumer autonomy is made applicable in practice.

1. Microsoft

A first important case here is the Commission's 2004 Microsoft decision.[508] The case concerned the interoperability of Microsoft work group server operating systems with third-party software on the one hand and tying the Windows Media Player into the PC operating system Windows on the other hand. Microsoft had a dominant position in both relevant markets. Concerning work group server software, Microsoft did not provide the necessary information for other software developers to program server software that could neatly be integrated into a Microsoft group server environment. The Commission held that:

> "Microsoft's refusal to supply has the consequence of stifling innovation in the impacted market and of diminishing consumers' choices by locking them into a homogeneous Microsoft solution."[509]

Similarly, the tying accusation was based, inter alia, on its negative effect on consumer decisions. Microsoft required Original Equipment Manufacturers ('OEMS') that wished to pre-install windows on their computers to also pre-install Windows Media Player, Microsoft's multimedia software. The Commission considered this practice abusive under Art. 102 TFEU, inter alia, because it deprived consumers of the real choice between competing multimedia players.[510] The decision in its main elements was upheld by the Court of First Instance in a

[507] *Huffman/Heidtke*, William & Mary Policy Review 2012, 77 (83).
[508] European Commission, 24/05/2004, AT.37792 Microsoft.
[509] European Commission, 24/05/2004, AT.37792 Microsoft, para. 782.
[510] European Commission, 24/05/2004, AT.37792 Microsoft, paras. 826–834.

2007 judgement, similarly stressing consumer choice.[511] Concerning the tying of the Windows Media Player, for instance, the Court of First Instance held:

> "In the present case, it is beyond dispute that Microsoft does not give customers the choice to acquire Windows without Windows Media Player. Furthermore, the tying at issue has a direct influence on third parties and therefore interferes with their free choice [...]."[512]

While Nihoul cites this case as an example of a consumer choice approach,[513] it also fits within the broader concept of consumer autonomy. In principle, consumers could still install another media player alongside the pre-installed Windows Media Player. However, they would generally not do so but instead just use the pre-installed software without an active choice, so the argument of the Commission.[514] Windows Media Player's success was therefore not linked to consumers exercising their preferences anymore. Access to Microsoft's APIs, on the other hand, had only to be granted on the basis of the stricter essential facilities doctrine.[515] The different approach is justified because, regarding APIs, Microsoft was not in a position to steer consumers towards a particular choice.

2. Google Android

One of the most prominent cases relating to consumer autonomy is Google Android.[516] In this case, the Commission fined Google for tying the Google Search App and the Google Chrome Browser to must-have-Android Apps such as the Google Play Store. Similar to the Microsoft case, Google required pre-installation of the tied apps. This tying resulted in Google Search and the Google Chrome Browser being pre-installed on nearly every Android smartphone. Consumer decisions were hence superseded: due to status quo bias, most users stuck with the pre-installed apps.[517] While consumers could theoretically switch to alternative browsers or search engines, in practice, they rarely did. On the level of the OEMs, the tying practice was coercive in the way that OEMs who were dependent on the use of the Google Play Store were coerced into pre-installing the Google Search App and the Google Chrome Browser. For consumers, the effect was manipulative: the default settings shaped user behavior, meaning most did not make an active choice.

---

[511] Court of First Instance, 17/09/2007, Case T-201/04 Microsoft, ECLI:EU:T:2007:289.

[512] Court of First Instance, 17/09/2007, Case T-201/04 Microsoft, ECLI:EU:T:2007:289, para. 1013.

[513] *Nihoul*, in: Consumer Choice, 9 (13–15).

[514] European Commission, 24/05/2004, AT.37792 Microsoft, paras. 845–877.

[515] European Commission, 24/05/2004, AT.37792 Microsoft, paras. 546–692.

[516] European Commission, 18/07/2018, AT.40099 Google Android, the decision was largely upheld under appeal by the General Court, 14/09/2022, Case T-604/18 Google Android, ECLI:EU:T:2022:541.

[517] European Commission, 18/07/2018, AT.40099 Google Android, paras. 778–803.

The Google Android case highlights that competition relies on the role of the consumer as an active market participant. When dominant firms prevent consumers from making active decisions – as in Google Android – competition falters: even superior rivals may not be able to succeed, and consumers may not even realize alternatives exist. Consumer autonomy hence becomes relevant for competition law, at least where otherwise there is a risk of market foreclosure. Such protection of consumer autonomy is also preserving consumer choices in the long term. While initially, consumers may still have the theoretical choice between different options, where an agreement or practice prevents them from effectively exercising this choice, in the long run, the number of available options will diminish as competitors will be excluded from the market. The Google Android case also shows that behavioural economics can play a role in the competition law analysis. Based on a perfectly rational, surplus-maximizing consumer, no competitive concerns would have been found: the consumer would disregard any default options and pre-installations and choose the search engine and browser that best fit their preferences. This was clearly not the case in Google Android. It should be noted, however, that the Commission did not identify consumer harm in the very fact that consumers' status quo bias was 'exploited' but instead that this strategy could eliminate competitors. The exploitation of the bias gave rise to exclusionary abuse. By reducing active choice and limiting consumer autonomy, Google shielded itself from competitive pressure.

3. Google Shopping

The Google Shopping case[518] follows a similar pattern. Google systematically gave prominent placement to its own comparison-shopping service while demoting rivals in generic search results. Considering their choice between different comparison-shopping websites, the Commission found that consumers typically look only at the first results, with more than 30% clicking on the very first result.[519] Google here 'exploited' consumers' reliance on defaults (presented by the top search results) and, by doing so, superseded active consumer decisions with the result that consumers stuck with Google Shopping rather than looking for a competing comparison-shopping website. The Google Search decision interestingly involves fewer references to consumer choice than the later Google Android decision. The Commission, in this case, relied on a somewhat novel theory of self-preferencing as abusive conduct. In the aftermath and already during the investigation, this sparked a debate on whether self-preferencing can fall under Art. 102 TFEU. Opponents argued that a prohibition of self-preferencing contradicts the strict requirements for access to a dominant undertaking's infrastructure developed under the essential facilities doctrine and that consum-

[518] European Commission, 27/06/2017, AT.39740 Google Shopping.

[519] European Commission, 27/06/2017, AT.39740 Google Shopping, paras. 543–567.

ers would ultimately benefit from Google's allegedly anticompetitive practices.[520] One of the main issues was the idea that Google offered an integrated product and, by promoting Google Shopping, improved Google Search. Proponents countered that self-discrimination could amount to an abuse of dominance where it prevents competitors from entering the market.[521]

Seeing the case from the angle of autonomy offers an additional basis for the decision: Google's behaviour was not anti-competitive *just* because it was self-preferencing but because it shielded itself from competition by overriding consumer choices. It effectively prevented consumers from making an autonomous decision regarding their comparison-shopping website, thereby excluding competitors and new entrants. The prohibition of self-preferencing was justified by the passivity of consumers who, at least to a large extent, would take whatever Google served them and the related lack of disciplining Google through competition.[522] This is also reflected in the General Court's judgment upholding the Commission's decision.[523] More explicitly than the Commission, the Court recognised Google's power to steer consumers and noted:

"the promotion on Google's general results pages of one type of specialised result – its own – over the specialised results of competitors involves a certain form of abnormality."[524]

The Court thus echoes the Metro judgment, excepting some level of neutrality from certain operators.[525] Moreover, while the case was concerned only with self-preferencing, the judgment can be interpreted more broadly. The 'abnormality' of preferring one type of results over another (absent an objective justification) would have also occurred if the promoted results were not those of a Google product but of another company.[526] The Court of Justice dismissed Google's appeal against the General Court's judgment, rendering the decision final.[527]

Naturally, undertakings like Google, whose business model relies on gaining consumer attention and influencing their decision-making, face more antitrust obligations than companies in more traditional sectors of the economy from the viewpoint of consumer autonomy. This may help explain why the self-preferencing doctrine has not developed earlier. The Google cases may also be relevant to give substance to the concept of competition on the merits: a dominant undertaking that succeeds in the market not because consumers actively choose its offer

---

[520] *Bork/Sidak*, Journal of Competition Law & Economics 2012, 663; *Brauneck*, GRUR Int. 2018, 103; *Kokkoris*, Antitrust Bulletin 2017, 313; *Vesterdorf*, CLPD 2015, 4.

[521] *Valdivia*, World Competition 2018, 43.

[522] Compare *Schweitzer et al.*, Modernisierung der Missbrauchsaufsicht, p. 128.

[523] General Court, 10/11/2021, T-612/17 Google Shopping, ECLI:EU:T:2021:763.

[524] General Court, 10/11/2021, T-612/17 Google Shopping, ECLI:EU:T:2021:763, para. 176.

[525] See above from p. 102.

[526] For this type of reasoning see the discussion of Netdoktor v. Google/Ministry of Health below from p. 174.

[527] Court of Justice, 10/09/2024, C-48/22 P Google Shopping, ECLI:EU:C:2024:726.

but because they don't choose at all is not competing on the merits.[528] Both Google Shopping and Google Android bear strong similarities to the earlier Microsoft case, where consumer decisions were likewise overridden. The Microsoft case also allows to distinguish self-preferencing from the stricter essential facilities doctrine: the reason why Microsoft had to grant access to its APIs only based on the strict essential facilities doctrine can be explained by the fact that Microsoft, when it comes to work group server software (unlike Google when it comes to search results), was not in a position capable of steering consumers towards a particular choice.[529]

4. Allianz Hungaria

Another interesting case concerning consumer autonomy is the 2013 Allianz Hungaria judgment[530]. The case concerned the vertical relationship between car insurers and car repair shops that were, at the same time, car dealers and insurance brokers. Essentially, the agreement at issue provided higher hourly pay for repair shops that reached a certain number and percentage of insurance policies sold by the insurance company. While leaving it to the referring court to decide, the Court of Justice indicated that in assessing whether the agreement can constitute a restriction of competition by object the national court should assess whether by (national) law, the insurance brokers are required to be independent of the insurance companies.[531] This statement somewhat mirrors the notion in Metro that companies on the higher level of the value chain (e.g., manufacturers) shall, in principle, not interfere with how the lower level (e.g., retailers) provide options and advice to the consumer. The underlying assumption appears to be that insurance brokers are better able to give advice to consumers where they are independent of the insurance companies. The agreement's effects on consumers' decision-making were hence relevant to assess whether it constitutes a restriction of competition, albeit in this case only indirectly through considering other laws intended to protect consumers' decision-making.

5. Facebook (Bundesgerichtshof)

The German Bundesgerichtshof's ('BGH') Facebook case[532] also can be read with a focus on consumer autonomy.[533] The centre of the court's argumentation was consumer choice (understood in terms of variety of options), underpinned by fundamental rights considerations. The abusive conduct consisted of Facebook

[528] See below from p. 208.
[529] See already above p. 169.
[530] Court of Justice, 13/03/2013, C-32/11 Allianz Hungaria, ECLI:EU:C:2013:160.
[531] Court of Justice, 13/03/2013, C-32/11 Allianz Hungaria, ECLI:EU:C:2013:160, para. 47.
[532] Bundesgerichtshof, 23/06/2020, KVR 69/19 Facebook, GRUR 2020, 1318.
[533] See *Podszun*, SSRN 2019; *Podszun*, GRUR 2020, 1268; *Scheele*, JECLAP 2021, 34.

making the use of the social media platform for its users dependent on their consent to use and combining user data collected not only on Facebook but also on third-party websites (off-Facebook data). While the Bundeskartellamt initially used data protection rules as a benchmark to determine the inappropriateness of Facebook's data use and its compatibility with competition law, the BGH found an abuse in an "imposed service extension": users were forced to accept a very personalized social network experience they had to 'pay' for with their personal data. According to the BGH, Facebook's behaviour was anti-competitive because of its exploitative nature and because of its effect to hinder competition.[534] The court emphasized that consumers are, to a large extent, dependent on the use of Facebook for participation in social life and public discourse.[535] Further, the BGH argued that the constitutional right to informational self-determination in its indirect horizontal effect through the interpretation of the competition rules must be taken into account.[536] The right to self-determination requires, inter alia, that individuals have

> "the possibility of influencing, in a differentiated manner, the context and the way in which their personal data are made available to and used by others. In other words, individuals are guaranteed the right to be substantially involved in the decision as to which characteristics can be ascribed to them [...]".[537]

The argument also rested on the critical role Facebook plays in public communication, which amounted to a position similar to an infrastructure provider which cannot be bypassed if one wants to participate in public discourse. Consumers who wanted their data protected had to either agree to Facebook's condition or forego participating in a large part of the public discourse.[538] According to the BGH, Facebook's practice of collecting off-Facebook data was not linked to consumer preferences. The court held that this in itself can be an important criterion in establishing an abuse of dominance.[539] The BGH considered Facebook's conduct exclusionary: Facebook's increased data power can have exclusionary effects.[540] In particular, through the ever-increasing collection of data, Facebook can improve its offer up to a point where competitors cannot match it.[541] Making one's product better and thereby outcompeting competitors in itself

---

[534] Bundesgerichtshof, 23/06/2020, KVR 69/19 Facebook, GRUR 2020, 1318, para. 64.

[535] Bundesgerichtshof, 23/06/2020, KVR 69/19 Facebook, GRUR 2020, 1318, para. 102.

[536] Bundesgerichtshof, 23/06/2020, KVR 69/19 Facebook, GRUR 2020, 1318, paras. 103–111.

[537] Bundesgerichtshof, 23/06/2020, KVR 69/19 Facebook, GRUR 2020, 1318, para. 104 (courtesy translation by the Bundeskartellamt, available at https://www.bundeskartellamt.de/SharedDocs/Meldung/EN/AktuelleMeldungen/2021/11_06_2021_BGH_KVR-69-19.html?nn=4136442) (accessed: 11 March 2025).

[538] Bundesgerichtshof, 23/06/2020, KVR 69/19 Facebook, GRUR 2020, 1318, para. 102.

[539] Bundesgerichtshof, 23/06/2020, KVR 69/19 Facebook, GRUR 2020, 1318, para. 87.

[540] Bundesgerichtshof, 23/06/2020, KVR 69/19 Facebook, GRUR 2020, 1318, paras. 92–96.

[541] Bundesgerichtshof, 23/06/2020, KVR 69/19 Facebook, GRUR 2020, 1318, para. 94.

is no concern of competition law. It usually constitutes competition on the merits. This is, however, not the case if the product improvement is based on non-autonomous consumer behaviour. Facebook only improved its product at the expense of consumer autonomy and, thereby, not through competition on the merits.

Overall, the judgment is guided by the desire to protect autonomous consumer decisions.[542] This is also reflected in the remedy which the Bundeskartellamt had imposed and which the BGH upheld: Facebook must give its users a 'real' choice to refuse or withdraw consent to Facebook's use of off-Facebook data without suffering any disadvantages.[543]

The Court of Justice in its Facebook judgment, concerning the same case, held that in the context of examining an abuse of a dominant position, competition authorities may examine the compliance of the dominant company's behaviour with rules other than those relating to competition law, such as those on the protection of personal data.[544] In this regard, the Court emphasized that access to personal data is a significant parameter of competition in the digital economy.[545] While the judgment is less explicit, it confirms that consumers' decisions (e.g., regarding the protection of their data) and how undertakings influence or undermine these decisions, can be a consideration in the competition law analysis.

6. Netdoktor v. Google/Ministry of Health (Landgericht München I)

Another interesting case to illuminate how courts apply ideas of consumer autonomy is the case Netdoktor v. Google and the German Ministry of Health, which led to two decisions by the Regional Court Munich I ('LG München I').[546] Google and the German Ministry of Health had entered into (an informal)[547] agreement that Google would prominently display an info box with information provided by the ministry's National Health Portal as well as a link to this portal when users search for health-related information (e.g., specific diseases) on Google. Users would find some useful information related to their search query already in this box, so they would not need to click their way to other websites. The court ordered the cooperation to be stopped on competition law grounds. It argued that the info box that took over the most prominent position within the Google Search results reduces the visibility of other offers (e.g., private providers

[542] *Podszun*, GRUR 2020, 1268.

[543] Bundesgerichtshof, 23/06/2020, KVR 69/19 Facebook, GRUR 2020, 1318, paras. 125–131.

[544] Court of Justice, 04/07/2023, Case C-252/21 Facebook, ECLI:EU:C:2023:537, para. 48.

[545] Court of Justice, 04/07/2023, Case C-252/21 Facebook, ECLI:EU:C:2023:537, para. 51.

[546] Landgericht München I, 10/02/2021, 37 O 15720/20 and 37 O 15721/20 Netdoktor/Google; for a detailled discussion of the case, see *Persch*, JECLAP 2021, 694.

[547] They held a common press conference announcing their collaboration.

of health portals such as the claimant in the case). Typical Google Search users would either be already satisfied with the information in the info box and not click further or would at least click on the link in the info box and be directed to the National Health Portal. The arrangement would thus close out private competitors. Google's interest in the arrangement was merely financial: taking information from the National Health Portal and showing it directly in the search results lets users stay longer on Google, increasing its ad revenue. As a publicly financed offer, the National Health Portal was the ideal partner because it was not dependent on any ad revenue itself.

The case is similar in many respects to the Google Sjopping case, as in both, Google used its power to direct consumer attention. There is, however, one significant difference here. Unlike in Google Shopping, Google did not give preferential treatment to its own offer (Google was not active in the market for health portals) but to another undertaking's (the National Health Portal)[548] offer. There was, therefore, no leveraging of market power to gain a competitive advantage in another market. Consumers, it would seem at first sight, were not harmed since the arrangement made it easier for them to find the information they were looking for. Unlike in Google Shopping, the arrangement relatively clearly led to more precise search results. The restriction of competition must therefore lie somewhere else. The most plausible explanation is that the arrangement superseded consumer decisions. Ultimately, two undertakings here decided which offer would most likely prevail. The conduct harmed competition in a market that Google was not active in by superseding consumer choice and determining the winner in the market. Under a consumer welfare standard, the conduct would most likely not have raised concerns: users looking for health-related information were not directly harmed (in the sense of reduced consumer surplus). The arrangement neither led to higher prices (in the form of more advertising) nor reduced quality. After all, consumers would find the information they were looking for easier.

Competition was not harmed because of reduced consumer welfare but because the agreement circumvented autonomous consumer decisions and determined the winner in a market without consumer involvement through active decisions. As with the other cases discussed, such conduct produced exclusionary effects.

7. Hard-wearing floor covering manufacturers (Autorité de la Concurrence)

In a recent case against hard-wearing floor covering manufacturers, the French competition authority also looked specifically at the impact of an agreement on

[548] Based on the functional definition of 'undertaking', the National Health Portal was considered an undertaking notwithstanding that it was operated by the Ministry of Health.

consumers.[549] Several companies had agreed, among other measures, to limit the advertising of their individual environmental performance. The likely effect, or at least the goal of the agreement, was to shift consumer decisions away from the environmental impact of their purchase decision, possibly leading to a higher (or, despite changing preferences constant) demand. The agreement, therefore, was essentially an attempt to decouple demand from consumers' preferences by reducing transparency regarding the product's environmental impact.

8. Conclusion: distinguishing exclusionary and exploitative restrictions of autonomy

A general principle can be derived from the case law that one of the tasks of competition law is to preserve market conditions that guarantee independent decision-making for all economic actors, including consumers.[550] In this light, any impediment to consumers' decision-making can form part of a normative theory of harm.[551]

One aspect that catches the eye when looking at the decisions is that most of them deal with the *exclusionary effects* that restrictions of autonomy have. They focus on the importance of autonomy for the functioning of markets: only when consumers are able to take autonomous decisions and are active agents in the market can they, through their decisions, provide for dynamic competition by choosing offers from other undertakings than the incumbent dominant player. Superseding or limiting consumers' decisions is part of the applied theory of harm, where it prevents other companies from reaching the consumer with their offer, thereby raising entry barriers and foreclosing competitors. When the link between a company's success in the market and consumer choices is broken through a company's behaviour, and this excludes competitors, this is not competition on the merits.[552] Competition law, therefore, serves to protect consumers' decision-making mainly because of its functional relationship with the market instead of protecting individual consumers from making errors. A restriction of competition, therefore, requires an aggregate effect that influences the market structure (e.g., by raising entry barriers or foreclosing competitors).

The only case that also considered *exploitative effects* is the Facebook case by the German Bundesgerichtshof. This was driven by recourse to the importance of fundamental rights in interpreting German competition law. While the decision hence cannot be directly transferred to EU law, it nevertheless indicates when reductions in consumer autonomy may be considered exploitative: when they concern an area of particular significance for the exercise of consumers' funda-

---

[549] Autorité de la Concurrence, 19/10/2017, Décision 17-D-20 Hard-wearing floor covering.

[550] *Podszun*, SSRN 2019, p. 25.

[551] *Podszun*, SSRN 2019, p. 26.

[552] See in more detail below from p. 208.

mental rights. There is a strong argument to draw a distinction between the products and services concerned by a practice when it comes to exploitative effects. Only few services or products appear to be of comparable importance to Facebook for the exercise of one's fundamental rights. For example, one could think of access to the internet or other information sources, potentially including search engines. Following this approach, exploitative cases would be rather exceptional. Vertical agreements that restrict the sale of products online typically do not concern products that are of great importance for the exercise of fundamental rights.[553] Consequently, the remainder of this thesis will focus on their exclusionary rather than any exploitative effects.

§ 3 Conclusion

[1] The relationship between consumer autonomy and competition can be described as dialectic: consumers, through their choices, play an important part in the competitive process, and their decisions are a substantial element of competition as a coordinating process.
[2] Competition, on the one hand, serves consumers by providing them with a variety of choices.
[3] Protecting consumer autonomy appears, in principle, compatible with the goals of EU competition law.
[4] However, such protection would be concerned primarily with aggregate consumer decisions rather than individual transactions.
[5] The existing case law that considers and protects consumers' independent decision-making is mainly concerned with exclusionary practices.

[553] Previous cases in this regarded concerned, e.g., cosmetic products, shoes and other everyday goods. Fundamental rights could play a role, for example, in a hypothetical scenario where a certain phone producer sells only in stores and their phone is the only way to access an important platform such as Facebook.

Chapter 3

Making autonomy workable in the context of vertical agreements

Consumer autonomy has played a role in the case law and decisional practice on vertical agreements and may be considered a normative goal of EU antitrust law. However, it is a concept that is difficult to make operable. While the Court of Justice's reasoning, to some extent, relies on the goal of protecting consumers' decision-making in the context of vertical agreements, it does not do so in an unequivocal and clear fashion. The fundamental question remains how to properly distinguish between procompetitive (or neutral) and anti-competitive vertical agreements that influence consumers' decision-making. To approach this question, this Chapter will first explore how vertical agreements can and do influence consumer decisions and show that competition law does not protect individual consumers' autonomy but safeguards consumers' role in the competitive process (§ 1). Subsequently, it will develop a theory of harm to assess under which circumstances vertical agreements may be considered restrictive of competition because of their influence on consumer decisions (§ 2). Next, it will demonstrate that while consumer autonomy may be a valid normative concern, it does not provide a justification for the current treatment of online sales restrictions under EU competition law (§ 3). Finally, the Chapter concludes (§ 4).

§ 1 How can vertical agreements influence consumer decisions?

This section examines how vertical agreements can affect consumers' decision-making and considers which of these effects may be relevant under competition law. Vertical agreements, inter alia, can change retailer incentives to promote specific products, impact search costs, or ensure better consumer advice. They can also influence consumer preferences, for example, through horizontal product differentiation. This section provides an initial overview of vertical agreements' effects on consumers' decision-making and to what extent these effects may be relevant for the competition law analysis. The subsequent section will establish a theory of harm to find a restriction of competition based on these effects.

I. Changing incentives for retailers and transferring power to the manufacturer

Being able to shape the context and parameters of consumer choice is a powerful position. It allows one to steer the consumer in a particular direction and make some (purchase) decisions more likely than others. For most purchases, it is the retailer who holds this position. The retailer is in direct contact with consumers and has, therefore, some immediate influence on their decision-making.[1] They decide which products to stock, how to arrange them, which prices they ask, if they offer individual advice to customers, where the store is located (e.g., on the high street or a cheaper side street) and how it is designed, which music is played etc. Using the words of Thaler and Sunstein, they are in the role of the choice architect[2]. Take the example of a classic brick and mortar retail store: The retailer can place certain items on top-shelve to trigger availability heuristics[3], they can set an anchor[4] by showing or not showing specific prices in a visible manner or they can use decoy effects[5] by placing certain products next to each other. In this way, they can steer consumers to certain products. This is also the case where a salesperson is present who can, for example, tell the consumer about the positive features of products and omit the negative ones (thus possibly triggering the representativeness heuristic[6]).

In the absence of vertical agreements, retailers are primarily driven to maximize their overall profits, not the sales of specific brands. The retailer's incentive lies in promoting products with the highest retail margin, i.e. the highest difference between wholesale price and resale price. For example, a retailer sells two types of television sets. The first one from brand A has a wholesale price of 100 EUR, the second of brand B of 150 EUR. If the retailer can sell each for the price of 160 EUR to the final consumer, they will prefer to sell the brand A item (where the retail margin is 60 whereas for brand B it is only 10 EUR). The wholesale price is influenced, inter alia, by the distribution of negotiation power between retailer and wholesaler. Manufacturer of well-known brands in this regard may have an advantage and can be able to demand higher wholesale prices, reducing the retailers' margin compared to less well-known brands.[7] The retailer thus has an incentive to promote other products, e.g., of manufacturers that are less well-known and have less negotiation power because of the higher retailer margins.[8]

[1] *Sullivan/Grimes*, Law of Antitrust, p. 353.

[2] *Thaler*, Nudge, pp. 13–16.

[3] For the availability heuristic see above p. 15.

[4] For anchor effects see above p. 16.

[5] For decoy effects see above p. 17.

[6] See above p. 15.

[7] *Steiner*, Reprints for Antitrust Law and Economics 1990, 143 (151–152); for a formalization, see *Hunold/Muthers*, RAND Journal of Economics 2017, 3 (15–16).

[8] *Grimes*, California Law Review 1992, 815 (839); *Hunold/Muthers*, RAND Journal of Economics 2017, 3 (15–16).

There is an inverse relationship between retailer and manufacturer margins: higher manufacturer margins typically go hand in hand with lower retailer margins.[9]

The more competition there is between retailers regarding the sale of a specific product, the lower the retailer margins are. The more intra-brand competition there is, the closer the retailer margin is to zero. If there is competition between retailers for all the products they sell, they will, consequently, have very low margins for all those products. In this case, there are likely no substantial differences between the retailer margins for specific products. If a retailer sells toothpaste from three different manufactures but faces high competition from other retailers which also sell the same brands, for all three toothpastes the retailer will be able to charge a price only slightly above their wholesale price. Because the margin is hence similar (low) for all toothpastes, the retailer does not earn more if they sell toothpaste A compared to toothpaste B. Intra-brand competition can thus be said to have an equalizing effect on retailer margins across brands and, therefore, to make retailers less likely to promote a certain brand.[10] As a result, retailers have, in principle, no strong financial incentive to push one brand over another and are more likely to focus on satisfying consumer needs through neutral, quality advice, rather than steering choices based on margin differences.

Vertical agreements can change these incentives. Sullivan and Grimes argue that vertical agreements can essentially work like a bribe to the retailer for pushing the manufacturer's product, going beyond just recommending it where it best fits the consumers' needs and preferences.[11] Carstensen similarly stresses that vertical agreements can be used by the manufacturer to buy "access to and/or facilitating exploitation of dealer relational power".[12] A retailer that for some of the products they sell faces no or less intra-brand competition, earns a higher margin for those product. In the toothpaste example above, imagine that the retailer sells toothpastes A, B and C but for toothpaste C, the manufacturer imposes a minimum retail price of 10 EUR on all retailers. A and B toothpaste manufacturers, on the other hand, can be sold at any price and because of high intra-brand competition, retailers sell them at a price of 5 EUR. If wholesale prices for the three toothpastes are similar (let's say 3 EUR), the retailer will have a higher margin for the sale of toothpaste C (7 EUR, compared to 2 EUR). The retailer will hence prefer to sell more of toothpaste C compared to A and B and may try to steer consumers to buying toothpaste C (despite its higher price). The higher retailer margin due to limited intra-brand competition, hence, may incentivise retailers to promote particular products.[13] This may be particularly success-

---

[9] *Steiner*, Review of Industrial Organization 1993, 717.

[10] *Grimes*, Southwestern University Law Review 1992, 1285 (1307); *Grimes*, Antitrust Law Journal 1995, 83 (99); *Sullivan/Grimes*, Law of Antitrust, p. 335.

[11] *Sullivan/Grimes*, Law of Antitrust, pp. 312–313, see also *Areeda/Hovenkamp*, Antitrust Law, Vol. 8, para. 1614c.

[12] *Carstensen*, Antitrust Law Journal 2001, 569 (582).

[13] *Carstensen*, Antitrust Law Journal 2001, 569 (583).

ful where retailer has some relation power over the consumer because the consumer is not informed or where the product is complex.[14]

Intra-brand competition alone does not necessarily prevent this. Carstensen argues that the typical reaction of the manufacturer's competitors is to engage in the same conduct and also restrict intra-brand competition to get their products promoted.[15] In the toothpaste example that would mean that manufacturers of toothpaste A and B once they see that consumers buy more and more toothpaste C because retailers steer them towards that choice, will also try to give retailers a higher margins to make them promote their products. This dynamic can result in higher overall prices and may exclude competitors who choose not to adopt similar practices.[16] Hunold and Muthers have formalized the thoughts of Sullivan/Grimes and Carstensen in a 2016 paper, essentially confirming their findings.[17]

Manufacturers with market power can use restrictions on intra-brand competition to block market access for new entrants. The manufacturer with market power through high retailer margins can incentivise the retailer not to sell products of newcomers that may challenge the incumbent.[18] To guarantee high retailer margins, the manufacturer needs to limit intra-brand competition (e.g., reduce the number of retailers, set a minimum retail price). Simply setting a low wholesale price would not achieve the same result. The reason is that when there is intra-brand competition, the lower wholesale price is likely going to be competed away, so the retailer will have to ultimately pass down the lower price to the consumer – eliminating their incentive to push the manufacturer's products over others.[19] This reasoning also applies to upfront access payments, such as slotting allowances.[20]

To conclude, strong intra-brand competition encourages retailers to provide more neutral advice, which may lead to better consumer decisions.[21] This aspect would be difficult to take into account from a consumer welfare point of view: if consumer welfare is measured by consumer surplus, and output and prices are used as proxies for surplus, at least short-term, no measurable effects of an agreement that limits competition among retailers appear likely. Output would likely remain unchanged.[22] Nevertheless, it appears difficult to argue that this

---

[14] *Carstensen*, Antitrust Law Journal 2001, 569 (582–583).

[15] *Carstensen*, Antitrust Law Journal 2001, 569 (584).

[16] *Hunold/Muthers*, RAND Journal of Economics 2017, 3 (6) arguing that RPM leads to a prisoner's dilemma for competing manufacturers.

[17] *Hunold/Muthers*, RAND Journal of Economics 2017, 3.

[18] *Carstensen*, Antitrust Law Journal 2001, 569 (587–588).

[19] *Areeda/Hovenkamp*, Antitrust Law, Vol. 8, para. 1614c.

[20] For the treatment of upfront access payments, see Vertical Guidelines, para. 379; for a brief overview on the economic effects of slotting allowances, see *Desai et al.*, in: Encyclopedia of Strategic Management, 1572.

[21] *Sullivan/Grimes*, Law of Antitrust, p. 312.

[22] *Areeda/Hovenkamp*, Antitrust Law, Vol. 8, para. 1603 footnote 17.

increases consumer welfare.[23] Imagine a consumer visiting a store in search of a new laptop. Based on the consumer's particular needs and preferences, laptop A (priced at 1100 €) and B (priced at 1000 €) would suit them equally well. If the retailer, due to limited intra-brand competition for laptop A and higher margins, persuades the consumer to choose A over B, this may ultimately harm the consumer by leading them to spend more without receiving additional value.[24]

The natural question that arises is whether consumers wouldn't simply turnto a different retailer offering more neutral advice. Depending on the market situation, few such retailers might be available if the restraint covers a large part of the market. But even where it doesn't, consumers are not necessarily able to detect this behaviour. As Grimes puts it:

> "Individual purchasers may never realize that they have been steered to a high-profit item if the product performs within the normal range. Unless the product is a lemon, a common psychological reaction of many buyers of big ticket items is to justify their purchase regardless of its objective worth."[25]

The psychological reaction described by Grimes can be explained by the consumers' desire to avoid cognitive dissonance. Humans try to avoid conflicting beliefs and are therefore likely to disregard information that contradicts what they learned about a product they have previously acquired.[26] Cognitive dissonance suggests that the retailer has a powerful position over the consumer's decision-making. The potential effect that vertical agreements have on retailers' incentives must hence be taken seriously. The next paragraphs will examine how specific vertical agreements can affect consumers' decision-making by changing retailer's incentives.

1. Resale Price Maintenance

Most commentary on how vertical agreements affect retailer incentives focuses on on (minimum) RPM, which directly increases the retailer's margin for the covered products as it limits the ability of other retailers to compete on price. Therefore, the price level will be higher than for similar products for which retailers can freely set the retail prices, granting the retailer an additional profit each time they manage to steer a consumer to the covered products. This provides support for the strict treatment of RPM under European law and the importance of price competition which, as the Court of Justice puts it, is so important that it can never be eliminated.[27] The European Commission in the Vertical Guidelines explicitly recognizes this additional harm of RPM, stating:

[23] *Areeda/Hovenkamp*, Antitrust Law, Vol. 8, para. 1614c.

[24] Applying the consumer welfare standard, such conduct would have to be praised: because the consumer chose the more expensive laptop, they *must* have preferred to pay more.

[25] *Grimes*, California Law Review 1992, 815 (832).

[26] *Festinger*, Cognitive Dissonance; *Künzler*, Restoring Consumer Sovereignty, p. 152.

[27] Court of Justice, 25/10/1977, Case 26–76 Metro I, ECLI:EU:C:1977:167, para. 21.

"The increased margin that RPM may offer distributors, may entice the latter to favour the particular brand over rival brands when advising customers, even where such advice is not in the interest of these customers, or not to sell these rival brands at all."[28]

2. Quantitative and qualitative selective distribution

The distinction between quantitative and qualitative selective distribution criteria is based on the idea that the former may give the retailer the adverse incentive to steer consumers to one particular product regardless of its merits.[29] Quantitative criteria, according to the Court of Justice, can provide the retailer with the incentive to deviate from their neutral role and to promote the products of a particular manufacturer.[30] Quantitative restrictions include, inter alia, an adequate turnover, obligations to keep a certain level of stocks or a limitation on the number of dealers.[31] Limiting the number of dealers, just like RPM, will reduce competition between retailers. The purpose and effect of quantitative criteria is, therefore, often to ensure a certain level of profit for the retailer.[32] In itself this is not a legitimate goal.[33] Imagine a simple market with five brands of shoes and 20 retailers. One of the brands' manufacturers (A) allows only five retailers to sell shoes of their brand. Those five retailers also sell the other brands, but they will have an incentive to push for the sale of brand A shoes as there is less intra-brand competition here (if one of the outsiders is more efficient, this does not affect their sales of brand A), so their margins are higher for brand A. The effects are hence similar to RPM. Because of cognitive dissonance, the affected consumers might not discover that they are being deprived of an objective choice and neutral advice. If other manufacturers react and adopt similar practices, at some point, no retailer might give the consumer neutral advice anymore, and the price level will overall become higher. Consumers may, therefore, not only be deprived of the ability to receive impartial advice, but they also must pay higher prices. Similar effects can occur for other quantitative criteria, such as minimum annual purchases or minimum stock requirements. Suppose the retailer must sell a certain amount of a specific manufacturer's products. In that case, they are incentivised to promote those products over other products to reach the agreed-upon sales amount.

Qualitative criteria, on the other hand, increase the retailer's costs on the sale of all products. As a result, when a retailer sells both selectively distributed products and others, they may have an incentive to steer consumers toward the higher-cost, selectively distributed items in order to protect their margins because the retailer faces higher price competition for those products that are openly

---

[28] Vertical Guidelines, para. 196(f).

[29] See above p. 104.

[30] Court of Justice, 25/10/1977, Case 26–76 Metro I, ECLI:EU:C:1977:167, para. 40.

[31] See above from p. 70.

[32] *Lang*, Fordham International Law Journal 1984, 323 (337).

[33] *Lang*, Fordham International Law Journal 1984, 323 (338).

distributed. To illustrate this, let's look at the example of Metro I: SABA retailers had to fulfil certain qualitative criteria, including the requirement to have "qualified staff to give proper advice and supply technical service to customers".[34] If a SABA retailer also sold products of other manufacturers who do not attach similar requirements to the sale of their products, the retailer's margin for the latter would potentially be lower because other retailers of those products (if they don't also sell SABA products) would not have to fulfil similar qualitative requirements. Qualitative criteria, therefore, can also change retailers' incentives and make them steer consumers to a particular manufacturer's products. Nevertheless, the risk that this happens is lower than for quantitative criteria because, unlike quantitative criteria, qualitative criteria directly require the retailer to provide certain services. When competition among the different authorised retailers is strong, they will not have a high margin because the margin is going to be competed away. Qualitative criteria, hence, do not eliminate the margin-equalizing effect of intra-brand competition. While this can mean that a retailer that participates in a selective distribution system might not stock certain products whose price is low, among the products they stock and sell, those sold under selective distribution do not necessarily come with a higher margin. Thus, they are likely to give the consumer relatively neutral advice.

3. Exclusive distribution

Exclusive distribution, like selective distribution, can restrict the number of retailers that sell a particular product. Exclusive distribution thus also has the potential for changing retailers' incentives to push the sales of a specific brand. However, exclusive distribution only protects against active selling from outside the exclusive territory, whereas in a selective distribution system, the retailer is protected from active and passive sales by unauthorised distributors.[35] Selective distribution systems are closed systems, making it impossible for non-authorised distributors to obtain the products.[36] This is not the case for exclusive distribution, where a retailer may, in principle, sell the product also to other retailers that follow different business models.[37] This also means that exclusive distribution is less likely to hinder pressure by price discounters or new forms of distribution on the retailer's margin than selective distribution.[38] Consequently, the risk of altering retailer incentives appears lower with exclusive distribution than with selective distribution.

[34] Court of Justice, 25/10/1977, Case 26–76 Metro I, ECLI:EU:C:1977:167, para. 34.
[35] Vertical Guidelines, para. 145.
[36] Vertical Guidelines, para. 154.
[37] Vertical Guidelines, para. 154.
[38] Vertical Guidelines, para. 154.

4. Category management

Category management is defined in the Vertical Guidelines as agreements "by which, within a distribution agreement, the distributor entrusts the supplier (the 'category captain') with the marketing of a category of products."[39] Here, the agreement does not change the retailer's incentive to promote or push for the sale of specific products but rather directly transfers the power to do so to the supplier who is selected as category captain. Such agreements, according to the Vertical Guidelines, may "result in anticompetitive foreclosure of other suppliers, if the category captain is able, due to its influence over the marketing decisions of the distributor, to limit or disadvantage the distribution of products of competing suppliers."[40] The Vertical Guidelines, therefore, recognize that agreements through which the retailer confers some of their power over the consumer's decision-making to the manufacturer can be anti-competitive. As always, there are efficiencies that can go hand in hand with such conduct, for example, economies of scale or better use of the supplier's marketing expertise.[41]

The French Competition Authority has published a guidance document on category management agreements in which it identifies the referral of decision-making power from the distributor to the supplier as a risk to competition.[42] Based on data provided by operators using category management partnerships, the authority found little evidence of efficiency gains. In particular, it did not find an increase in quantities over the product category that category captains managed, although promoting growth for the entire category is one of the main arguments for category management.[43] Under category management, the retailer typically sources out some of its power over the retail context to the category captain. The competitive concern here is the transfer of retailer power over the consumer's decision-making process to a supplier.

In the USA, the 6th Circuit Court in Conwood v. United States Tobacco found a violation of antitrust law in a snuff tobacco company's usage of category management agreements to remove a competitor from supermarket shelves (through providing misleading information to retailers, removing racks and product placements and interfering with the competitor's in-store advertising).[44] In the European Union, a Dutch court had the opportunity to issue a ruling on a category management case in Mars v. Nestlé.[45] The case concerned a promotional pro-

---

[39] Vertical Guidelines, para. 385; see for the discussion on category management also *Metzlaff*, ZVertriebsR 2012, 138.

[40] Vertical Guidelines, para. 386.

[41] Vertical Guidelines, para. 288.

[42] *Autorité de la Concurrence*, Opinion No 10-A-25 on 'Category Management' Agreements between Retail Grocery Operators and Some of the Suppliers thereof, paras. 79–98.

[43] *Autorité de la Concurrence*, Opinion No 10-A-25 on 'Category Management' Agreements between Retail Grocery Operators and Some of the Suppliers thereof, paras. 56–66.

[44] 6th Circuit Court, 15/05/2002, 290 F.3d 768 Conwood, 123 S. Ct. 876 (2003).

[45] Rb. Oost-Brabant, 07/08/2013, 232816/HA ZA 11–1168 Mars, ECLI:NL:RBOBR:2013:4356; for an English Summary, see *Graham*, JECLAP 2014, 85.

gram of the snack producer Mars for independent petrol stations. The company gave the stations compensation and bonuses if they set up their shelves as defined by Mars, e.g., prominently displaying Mars products. The court found that the conduct had the effect of excluding competitors who were not able to set up similar programs.

II. Collusion with intermediaries

Intermediaries can wield significant influence over consumer decisions.[46] A prime example is Google: where and how Google presents search results influences what users click on and, when it comes to shopping decisions, what they ultimately purchase. The same holds true for online marketplaces such as Amazon. This kind of influence over consumer choices can be monetized not only through advertising but also through selling off (some) influence over the results and rankings on such websites. Intermediaries can, for example, offer to show false customer reviews in favour against remuneration (e.g., for retailers or hotels). Here, the problem is not the individual behaviour of the intermediary, as would be the case, for example, where the intermediary does not take steps to prevent false or misleading reviews (which could be a concern of consumer protection law)[47] or a unilateral promotion of their own products[48] but rather a form of collusion between the intermediary and the product or service providers that they intermediate with. Collusion with intermediaries can, however, also take more subtle forms such as paying for a better ranking or demoting competitors in the ranking. This type of collusion with intermediaries is what happened in the Netdoktor/Google case.[49] Based on an agreement with the German Ministry of Health, Google promoted the search results of a particular website (the National Health Portal) with the result that users stayed longer on Google. This had the potential to exclude the national health portal's rivals. This collusion is distinct from self-preferencing, as it involves promoting another company's offerings rather than the intermediary's own products. Reports of similar preferential treatment for certain sellers on Amazon further underline the potentially broader issue of such intermediary collusion.[50]

---

[46] See *Patterson*, Antitrust Law in the New Economy.

[47] For example, the Italian Competition and Consumer Protection Authority fined TripAdvisor for the inadequacy of how the company monitored its reviews and presented those as more reliable than they were, see AGCM, 19/12/2014, PS9345 Tripadvisor.

[48] Such conduct, however, can fall under Art. 102 TFEU as the Google shopping case shows, see above p. 170.

[49] See above p. 174.

[50] *US Congress Antitrust Subcommittee*, Investigation of Competition in Digital Markets – Majority Staff Report and Recommendations, p. 242; in the EU, this was subject of an investigation and commitment decision, see European Commission, 20/12/2022, Cases AT.40462 and AT.40703.

Considering recent efforts to prohibit self-preferencing through competition law but also new regulatory acts like Digital Markets Act, this type of collusion may become more frequent. Intermediaries facing increased scrutiny might respond not by offering more objective choices to consumers but by actively steering them toward the highest-paying partner. In effect, rather than leveraging their own market power in an adjacent market, they can try to 'crown the king' (another company) in such a market and demand a share of this company's monopoly profits.[51] Aghion and Bolton have developed a model in which a dominant firm can compensate their buyers for signing long-term contracts, which preclude the entry of more efficient competitors.[52] Crowning the king is somewhat similar: the newly crowned 'king' will have to share some of their excess profits with the intermediary to make sure that the intermediary does not dethrone her. The harm to competition is the same as in the case of self-preferencing: success in the market is detached from consumer decisions.

This type of third-party preferencing played a role in the context of the Bundeskartellamt's Google News Showcase investigation. In this service, Google shows news from certain publishers (that receive a remuneration from Google) in so-called 'story panels'. The risk here is that Google prominently shows only a few offers and thus excludes other news publishers. Google's interest in 'crowning' a king would be that a monopolist news publisher could then share their excess profits with Google in the form of a lower price that Google has to pay to show the news. The Bundeskartellamt conducted an investigation in this regard, looking at whether Google ensures non-discriminatory access to the Google News Showcase for publishers.[53] Such a requirement could ensure that Google cannot crown a king in adjacent markets. In December 2022, the Bundeskartellamt concluded the investigation without a formal decision after Google implemented a series of changes to the News Showcase to the advantage of publishers.[54] In particular, Google abandoned the plan to include the News Showcase in its general search results and is "working towards providing non-discriminatory access to the platform."

Collusion could also occur through agreements between intermediaries and retailers that provide for a better ranking if retailers don't offer better prices at other intermediaries. For instance, Amazon, Booking.com, and Expedia have been reported to demote search results if consumers can obtain a better deal

---

[51] I have already made this argument elsewhere, see *Persch*, JECLAP 2021, 694.

[52] *Aghion/Bolton*, American Economic Review 1987, 388.

[53] *Bundeskartellamt*, 12/01/2022, Press release of 12/01/2022, Google News Showcase, available at https://www.bundeskartellamt.de/SharedDocs/Meldung/EN/Pressemitteilungen/2022/12_01_2022_Google_News_Showcase.html (accessed: 11 March 2025).

[54] *Bundeskartellamt*, 21/12/2022, Press release of 21/12/2022, Improvements for Publishers using Google News Showcase, available at https://www.bundeskartellamt.de/SharedDocs/Meldung/EN/Pressemitteilungen/2022/21_12_2022_Google_News_Showcase.html?nn=3591568 (accessed: 11 March 2025).

elsewhere.[55] Although such practices often arise unilaterally and are mostly a concern of Art. 102 TFEU[56], they could also be implemented vertical agreements. Another potentially harmful practice is the application of choice pressure: this refers to mechanisms that pressure the consumer to take a hasty or not thought-through decision, such as scarcity or (false) popularity claims (e.g., notices that only one more room is available for a hotel booking).[57] A vertical agreement in this regard could take place, for example, between an online booking platform and a hotel chain, requiring the former to always mark the chain's hotel rooms as scarce. Similarly, intermediaries could agree to mark certain results as exclusive to prevent consumers from looking for a better deal elsewhere.[58]

III. Increasing search costs

This section will explore another potential harm of vertical agreements: increasing search costs. While the consumer welfare effects of increasing search costs are disputed[59], high search costs can have negative effects on consumers and their autonomy. Ellison and Ellison, for example, identify the following three ways that search costs may harm consumers: (1) consumers must spend time and resources on searching which they would otherwise spend on leisure and consumption, (2) if they do not invest in search, they are likely to buy imperfect consumption bundles, (3) the prices are higher because of the softened competition, so there is a deadweight loss and a lower consumer surplus.[60] The higher the search costs for consumers, "the more likely they will make a less than optimal transaction."[61] Search costs can also lead to an overall higher price level: if, for example, costs for searching for an alternative product (or the price of the product) are high, competitors of a high-priced item have little incentive to offer a cheaper product as they might not be rewarded with extra demand. While search costs have been discussed in economic literature[62] for quite some time, the recent rise of behavioural economic literature has put a new light on the phenomenon. This includes how firms can raise search costs through the design of their stores and

---

[55] For Booking.com and Expedia, see *Hunold et al.*, Marketing Science 2020, 92; for Amazon, see *Weise*, The New York Times, 19/12/2019, Prime Power: How Amazon squeezes the Businesses behind its Store, available at https://www.nytimes.com/2019/12/19/technology/amazon-sellers.html (accessed: 11 March 2025).

[56] Amazon's behaviour in this regard has been investigated by the European Commission, the investigation was concluded with a commitment decision, European Commission, 20/12/2022, Cases AT.40462 and AT.40703.

[57] See *Bundeskartellamt*, Sektoruntersuchung Vergleichsportale, pp. 99, 107–108; *Competition and Markets Authority*, Online Choice Architecture, p. 21.

[58] See *Bundeskartellamt*, Sektoruntersuchung Vergleichsportale, p. 100.

[59] See above p. 54.

[60] *Ellison/Ellison*, Innovation Policy and the Economy 2018, 1 (16).

[61] *Hovenkamp*, Federal Antitrust Policy, p. 14 footnote 11.

[62] See in this regard above from p. 54.

framing their prices and product offerings. The latter has often been emphasized in the context of complex pricing schemes, which directly increase search costs and can soften competition.[63] While higher search costs do not necessarily lead to higher prices in each market, and thus a consumer welfare analysis might not always condemn them, raising search costs is typically considered detrimental to effective competition. As Bar-Gill puts it: "For competition to work well, consumers must be able to compare the benefits and costs of different products and choose the ones that provide the best value, given the consumer's tastes and needs. [...] Less information implies weaker competition."[64] The following paragraphs will discuss how vertical agreements can increase search costs.

1. Vertical obfuscation agreements

Firms can be interested in making decisions more difficult for consumers by adopting strategies that make comparing products harder.[65] Obfuscating products and prices may limit competition and result in higher profits.[66] Obfuscation can be achieved, for example, by adding attributes to the product[67] or by making the pricing structure itself artificially complex[68].[69] For instance, firms can add extraneous attributes to a product or design a pricing structure that initially reveals only part of the total price, with additional fees and costs added later. This is common in the hotel industry where in some jurisdictions (where this is not prohibited), often a 'resort fee', 'amenity fee', or 'convenience fee' is added to the final price.[70] A larger number of firms in a market may not necessarily provide relief to obfuscation; such market circumstances can, on the contrary, even increase the incentive to obfuscate prices.[71]

Obfuscation strategies can also be employed in online stores. Ellison and Ellison, for example, find that many firms online aggressively promote a low-quality/low-price version of products to attract consumers to their website and then, through their website's design, lure them into upgrading the initial low-cost product.[72] This strategy can lead to a deadweight loss plus a wealth transfer between different consumer groups (those who end up purchasing the advertised option will be 'subsidized' by those who go for the add-on).[73] There are numerous

[63] *Huck et al.*, Consumer Behavioral Biases, p. 37.

[64] *Bar-Gill*, NYU Law and Economics Research Paper 2011, (14).

[65] *Huck et al.*, Consumer Behavioral Biases, p. 32.

[66] *Fehr/Wu*, University of Zurich Working Paper Series 2021.

[67] *Ellison/Ellison*, Econometrica 2009, 427; *Gabaix/Laibson*, Quarterly Journal of Economics 2006, 505.

[68] *Carlin*, Journal of Financial Economics 2009, 278; *Wilson*, International Journal of Industrial Organization 2010, 496.

[69] *Hamilton et al.*, Annual Review of Resource Economics 2020, 87 (99).

[70] *Stucke/Ezrachi*, Competition Overdose, p. 73.

[71] *Huck et al.*, Consumer Behavioral Biases, pp. 37–38.

[72] *Ellison/Ellison*, Econometrica 2009, 427.

[73] *Ellison/Ellison*, Innovation Policy and the Economy 2018, 1 (14).

studies and experiments that show that obfuscation practices do occur and that they can be harmful.[74]

Competition does not necessarily resolve these issues. Competitors often cannot simply ignore consumer biases but must exploit them to stay in the market.[75] Hence, an often-observed reaction to competitors' obfuscation strategies is to copy those very strategies. For example, the American event-ticket reseller StubHub tried to increase transparency by shifting to 'all in'-pricing and saw its market share decline afterwards. Ultimately, the company retreated to its previous system, where consumers only see the final ticket price at the end of their purchase.[76] Stubhub did not manage to keep its 'all-in' price policy next to competitors that engaged in drip pricing. A similar story concerns the Caesar's Hotel in Las Vegas: while other hotels charged hidden resort fees, Caesar's initially resisted this development and kept a 'no resort fee' policy. However, eventually, it followed suit, similarly charging resort fees.[77] As Sullivan, in a report prepared for the FTC on the issue of resort fees in the hotel industry, explains:

> "firms cannot quit using drip pricing when other firms use drip pricing or their prices would look higher than their competitors' prices and consumers would not buy their product."[78]

Most research on obfuscation has focused on retailers' unilateral obfuscation efforts. Manufacturers typically have a less direct influence over the consumer but can nevertheless obfuscate or at least aid the retailer in their obfuscation efforts through measures such as product design, packaging and selective product information,[79] and measures of product differentiation by vertical means. Richards et al., for example, studied product packaging as a form of strategic obfuscation for soft drinks in France and for coffee in Germany.[80] They came to the conclusion that retailer-specific product packaging and size for these products typically came with a higher price (per kg/litre).[81] Unique packaging formats for one particular retailer led to a higher price and retailer markup than formats largely available to all retailers.[82] This example shows that manufactur-

---

[74] For a literature review, see *Ellison*, in: Handbook Economics of Retailing and Distribution, 287; *Grubb*, Review of Industrial Organization 2015, 247; *Huck et al.*, Consumer Behavioral Biases.

[75] *Bar-Gill*, NYU Law and Economics Research Paper 2011, (3); *Spiegler*, Theoretical Economics 2006, 207.

[76] *Smith*, Wallstreet Journal, 31/08/2015, StubHub Gets Out of 'All-In' Pricing, available at http://www.wsj.com/articles/stubhub-gets-out-of-all-in-pricing-1441065436 (accessed: 11 March 2025).

[77] *Stucke/Ezrachi*, Competition Overdose, pp. 79–80.

[78] *Sullivan*, Hotel Resort Fees, p. 15.

[79] *Rao*, SSRN 2022, concerning advertising with the 'no High Fructose Corn Syrup' label by low quality brands to hide negative attributes.

[80] *Richards et al.*, Review of Industrial Organization 2020, 859.

[81] *Richards et al.*, Review of Industrial Organization 2020, 859.

[82] *Richards et al.*, Review of Industrial Organization 2020, 859.

ers, through their product and packaging design, can make price comparisons across retailers more difficult, limiting intra-brand competition.[83] The FTC's case against Toys 'R Us ('TRU') was in part based on such conduct: as a response to the emergence of wholesale clubs (such as Costco), a type of discount retailers, TRU had agreed with manufacturers that they would "develop a special line of differentiated products for the clubs".[84] This 'special line' included combination packs but also individually packaged toys "redesigned to make them visually distinct from the items sold at TRU and other traditional retailers."[85] TRU's goal was

> "to prevent consumers from comparing the price and quality of products in the clubs to the price and quality of the same toys displayed and sold at TRU, and thereby to reduce the effectiveness of the clubs as competitors."[86]

In this case, TRU's vertical arrangement was built on the promise that essentially all manufacturers would enter into the same agreement.[87]

In light of these considerations, agreements between manufacturers and retailers that provide for retailer-specific product packaging and/or naming can raise antitrust concerns if they make comparison harder for consumers. If an identical or very similar product is sold under the same brand but in different quantities and this is based on an agreement between the retailer and manufacturer, this should raise concerns. The same applies to agreements allowing the retailer to sell the product under an 'exclusive name' without any substantial differences. Similar to changing the product packaging, manufacturers and retailers can increase consumer search costs by agreeing to market a product under a different name for each retailer, making price comparison across retailers artificially more difficult. This seems to be a phenomenon, for example, in the US mattress market where identical mattresses are sold under different names (but the same brand) in different stores: the 'Beautyrest Recharge Allie' at Macy's is the same product as the 'Beautyrest Recharge Devonwood Luxury' at Sears or the 'Beautyrest Signature Select Hartfield' at Mattress Firm.[88] This vertical differentiation is to be distinguished from brand/product differentiation as such between identical products, for example, through the use of different trademarks. Bernitz discusses in this regard the case of a Swedish paint manufacturer who sold the identical paint as a plain version and, in a different package and under a different name and trademark, also as paint for boats (for which it was similarly

---

83 *Richards et al.*, Review of Industrial Organization 2020, 859.

84 Federal Trade Commission, 18/10/1998, No. 091 0082 Toys R' Us.

85 Federal Trade Commission, 18/10/1998, No. 091 0082 Toys R' Us.

86 Federal Trade Commission, 18/10/1998, No. 091 0082 Toys R' Us, p. 1.

87 Federal Trade Commission, 18/10/1998, No. 091 0082 Toys R' Us, pp. 27–36.

88 *Lee*, Vox, 05/03/2015, Mattress stores want to rip you off. Here's how to fight back., available at https://www.vox.com/2015/3/5/8151607/mattress-buying-tips-savings (accessed: 11 March 2025).

suitable).[89] While this, prima facie, raises similar issues, only 'competition' between products of the same manufacturer (at the same retailer) will be affected rather than competition between retailers or between manufacturers.

Similar to RPM, agreements which raise search costs concerning different retailers' prices and services can lead to limited intra-brand competition and higher retail margins and thus give the retailer an incentive to push for the sale of the specific product over other products. Therefore, agreements that "deliberately make comparison difficult" prima facie may raise competition law concerns.[90]

2. *Other informational restraints*

Vertical agreements can restrict retailers from advertising more generally, for example, through minimum advertised prices ('MAPs') or by prohibiting comparative advertising. Such restrictions can increase search costs for consumers because they prevent the retailer from advertising with prices and/or product information. Consequently, these restrictions can make it harder for consumers to compare offers and reduce intra-brand competition, while also incentivizing retailers to promote products covered by such agreements (due to higher retail margins), yielding effects similar to those of RPM.

Vertical agreements can also require retailers to engage in tactics that discourage search. The retailer, for example, can offer bargain assurances, such as a price match guarantee, that gives the consumer the impression that they cannot make a better deal elsewhere.[91] If such assurances are part of a vertical agreement, this could have effects similar to RPM. The same is true for recommended retail prices if retailers are obliged to point them out to consumers because consumers often misinterpret them. For example, consumers can believe that recommended resale prices represent the price at which competitors sell the product or the wholesale price.[92] This interpretation can discourage them from searching for a better bargain.

Informational restraints can be retailer- or manufacturer-induced. Retailers may favor higher search costs because this enables them to use obfuscation strategies that limit consumers' ability to compare products, thereby protecting their margins. However, manufacturers can also be genuinely interested in raising inter-brand search costs. One scenario where manufacturers do not want consumers to engage in too much search is when they are afraid of the possible results of such search. Grimes gives the anecdotal example of 'Classic Car Wax', which branded itself as a high quality and superior product despite receiving quite an average rating in Consumer Reports.[93] Of course, if more consumers knew about

[89] *Bernitz*, Journal of Consumer Policy 1981, 21.

[90] *Patterson*, Antitrust Law in the New Economy, p. 149.

[91] See *Lindsey-Mullikin/Petty*, Journal of Business Research 2011, 67.

[92] *Compeau et al.*, Journal of Consumer Affairs 2004, 178 (184); *Lindsey-Mullikin/Petty*, Journal of Business Research 2011, 67 (69).

[93] *Grimes*, California Law Review 1992, 815 (833–834).

the average rating before their purchase, this would likely contradict the marketing campaign. It should, in this regard, be noted that many high-priced items in quality rankings do not actually fare much (or at all) better than standard or white brands.[94] The most obvious example is pharmaceutical products, where generics often have the same ingredients and effects as incumbent brands, and nevertheless, the latter can charge a significantly higher price. Bronnenberg et al., for example, found that Bayer Aspirin is more than three times higher priced than the identical CVS aspirin.[95] They show in a study that more informed buyers (in this case, pharmacists, physicians and healthcare workers who know more about the active ingredients in the drug) are much less likely to purchase the national brand. They find similar (but to a lesser extent) effects for pantry staples (salt, sugar, and baking soda) when comparing the purchase decisions of chefs (who opted for the store brand compared to the national brand to 77 %) and average consumers (60 % store brand). They reach the conclusion that "misinformation explains a sizable portion of the brand premium in many health categories, as well as in certain food categories (such as pantry staples) with little physical variation across brands."[96]

Another scenario where a lack of consumer information could play a role is where a specific manufacturer or service provider has gained a reputation as being typically among the cheapest options and, harnessing this reputation, shies away from being compared with other products. This strategy may help explaining why the low-cost airline Ryanair, for example, is reluctant to cooperate with and allow online travel agencies to cooperate with meta-comparison websites.[97] Such comparison websites for an established low-cost airline bear the risk that consumers find competitors' lower prices on some routes and dates, considering not only the initial flight price but also potential add-ons (such as additional luggage fees).[98] One could, in this regard, also think of restrictions on original equipment manufacturers ('OEMs') to advertise spare parts that they sell separately as being equivalent (or identical) to those sold by the manufacturer of the final product. Suppose the OEM of Mercedes rear view mirrors that are purchased and incorporated by Mercedes into their cars sells them as replacement parts independently of Mercedes. In that case, if the OEM cannot advertise them as being identical to the ones that Mercedes sells or uses, this is an informational

[94] *Apelbaum et al.*, Journal of Product & Brand Management 2003, 154 finding that national brands that are qualitatively superior to store brands charge premiums also over store brands with the same quality; *Boyle et al.*, Journal of Product & Brand Management 2018, 647; *Caves/Greene*, International Journal of Industrial Organization 1996, 29 finding some correlation between quality and prices but none between quality and advertising; *Grimes*, Antitrust Bulletin 2010, 101 (116–117) footnote 31; *Trevena et al.*, Nutrients 2015, 7027.

[95] *Bronnenberg et al.*, Quarterly Journal of Economics 2015, 1669.

[96] *Bronnenberg et al.*, Quarterly Journal of Economics 2015, 1669 (1674).

[97] See *Bundeskartellamt*, Sektoruntersuchung Vergleichsportale, p. 63.

[98] See *Bundeskartellamt*, Sektoruntersuchung Vergleichsportale, p. 64.

restriction. Mercedes would be interested in such a restriction, allowing itself to sell spare parts at a higher price since consumers would not know that identical spare parts are available.[99]

Manufacturers' and consumers' interests are not always aligned. While for the consumer, having the best available information and making an informed decision is typically desirable; this can run counter manufacturers' interests. Especially in scenarios where there are significant price differences among largely similar products, manufacturers of more expensive goods can have the incentive to raise search costs. Raising search costs can be achieved, for example, through the before-mentioned vertical obfuscation agreements, directly making product comparison more difficult. It can, however, also be done by limiting consumers' access to information provided by third parties. Where there are search frictions, intermediaries, such as advisors, platforms, or recommender systems, can reduce consumers' search costs.[100] Vertical agreements can prevent the use of intermediaries. In the brick and mortar world, a manufacturer could, for example, try to prevent their retailers from collaborating with (or even selling to) product testers.[101] In the online context, such informational restrictions could take the form of bans on providing information to or making websites interoperable with intermediaries such as price comparison websites or search engines. These specific online restrictions will be discussed in more detail later.[102]

IV. 'Spurious' brand and horizontal product differentiation

Vertical agreements can be used to differentiate products[103] and brands.[104] If a manufacturer's products are only available for sale in a specific atmosphere, such as a trendy store on the high street, this might make them distinct in the eye of the

[99] In the same vein, Art. 5 point (c) of the Motor Vehicle Block Exemption Regulation ('MVBER') (Commission Regulation (EU) No 461/2010 of 27 May 2010 on the application of Article 101(3) of the Treaty on the Functioning of the European Union to categories of vertical agreements and concerted practices in the motor vehicle sector) qualifies as hardcore restriction the "agreement between a manufacturer of motor vehicles which uses components for the initial assembly of motor vehicles and the supplier of such components, of the supplier's ability to place its trade mark or logo effectively and in an easily visible manner on the components supplied or on spare parts." This shall serve to increase consumer choice, see *European Commission*, Supplementary guidelines on vertical restraints in agreements for the sale and repair of motor vehicles and for the distribution of spare parts for motor vehicles, OJ C 138, 28.5.2010, p. 16–27, para. 24.

[100] *Gavazza/Lizzeri*, in: Handbook Industrial Organization, 433 (466).

[101] However, no instances of such attempts are known and indeed this appears very difficult to implement in practice.

[102] See below from p. 229.

[103] See regarding 'meaningless product differentiation' already above from p. 18.

[104] *Areeda/Hovenkamp*, Antitrust Law, Vol. 8, para. 1612b; for an appraisal of brand differentiation through vertical restraints as a mechanism of signaling, see *Ahlert et al.*, Vielfalt durch Gestaltungsfreiheit, pp. 159–184.

consumer. The vertical agreement, in these cases, aims at improving the product's and brand's image. The importance of brands as a topic of antitrust law has only relatively recently been discovered. However, several contributions discuss how brands relate to competition and antitrust law.[105] Brands, similar to advertising[106], are considered to serve two functions: (1) an informative function and (2) product differentiation and persuasion.[107] It is widely argued that the informative function should be embraced by competition law.[108] Essentially, the argument behind is the following: a brand may signal certain product characteristics or a certain level of quality.[109] Building and maintaining a good brand reputation is costly, and investing in this reputation could backfire if consumers' quality expectations are not fulfilled.[110] Cognitive dissonance might mitigate some of the negative effects of these costs (the consumer, in some cases, might ignore a deviation from the expected quality), but there remains some incentive for a manufacturer with a good brand image to invest in a more or less consistent (not necessarily high) quality. It should be noted that the manufacturer, in this regard, is facing a trade-off between saving costs by lowering quality and not damaging their reputation.[111] As Aldred puts it, the firm's self-interest is "building a good reputation at least cost."[112] In some instances, it can be cheaper to invest in marketing than in high-quality products, and the effects on the firm's reputation may be similar.[113] Therefore, the positive effects that branding can have on consumer decisions should not be overestimated.[114] The effects of product differentiation and persuasion are considered more critically.[115] In his seminal book "The Theory of Monopolistic Competition", Chamberlin identified product differentiation as a concern for competition. He describes how more differentiated products change the marketplace, coining the term 'monopolistic competition':

> "Where there is any degree of differentiation whatever, each seller has an absolute monopoly of his own product, but is subject to the competition of more or less imperfect substitutes. Since each is a monopolist and yet has competitors, we may speak of them as 'competing monopolists', and, with peculiar appropriateness, of the forces at work as those of 'monopolistic competition'."[116]

---

[105] See for a collection *Desai et al.*, Brands, Competition Law and IP.

[106] For a critical perspective on advertising, see *Dixit/Norman*, Bell Journal of Economics 1978, 1.

[107] *Davis/Edwards-Warren*, in: Brands, Competition Law and IP, 13 (13–14).

[108] *Grimes*, in: Brands, Competition Law and IP, 138 (138–141).

[109] *Davis/Edwards-Warren*, in: Brands, Competition Law and IP, 13 (18).

[110] *Griffiths*, in: Trade Marks and Brands, 241 (252).

[111] *Aldred*, in: Trade Marks and Brands, 267 (270).

[112] *Aldred*, in: Trade Marks and Brands, 267 (270).

[113] *Aldred*, in: Trade Marks and Brands, 267 (270–271).

[114] *Areeda/Hovenkamp*, Antitrust Law, Vol. 8, para. 1612c2.

[115] See *Comanor*, Harvard Law Review 1968, 1419 (1424–1423).

[116] *Chamberlin*, Monopolistic Competition, p. 9; see *Desai/Waller*, in: Brands, Competition Law and IP, 75 (84).

The idea of monopolistic competition is an important insight: product and brand differentiation can serve as a source of market power because they reduce demand elasticity.[117] Hence, from the outset, vertical agreements that increase product differentiation do not increase but *decrease* inter-brand competition.[118] This is also reflected in the Vertical Guidelines, which state that "the degree of product differentiation can […] be a relevant indicator for the presence of market power. Branding tends to increase product differentiation and reduce the substitutability of the product, leading to reduced elasticity of demand and an increased possibility to raise price."[119]

However, from a consumer welfare perspective, brand differentiation is generally welcomed: if a brand with a good image makes consumers pay more for a product, it *must* be that they value the branded product more.[120] Therefore, it is argued that brand differentiation must be welcomed by antitrust law as an increase in consumer welfare.[121] Moreover, any critique of this approach is often rejected with the argument that there is no 'objective theory of value' – antitrust courts and regulators are not equipped to establish in each case "what things are really worth and what attributes are more valuable than others".[122] As a result, proponants of the consumer welfare standard[123] tend to see no problem with brands and even less with vertical agreements that increase brand promotion and differentiation.[124] From their standpoint, any increase in consumers' willingness to pay is evidence of enhanced value and should be embraced.[125] There is some evidence from neurosciences that seems to support this argument: in the context of wine consumption, for example, higher stated prices (for identical wines) led to higher involvement of the brain areas associated with pleasure.[126] This could indicate that higher willingness to pay may correspond to higher pleasuree in consumption.

---

[117] *Comanor*, Harvard Law Review 1968, 1419 (1423); *Griffiths*, in: Trade Marks and Brands, 241 (252).

[118] *American Bar Association*, Vertical Restrictions, pp. 64–65; *Comanor*, Harvard Law Review 1968, 1419 (1424–1427).

[119] Vertical Guidelines, para. 282.

[120] See *Crane*, in: Brands, Competition Law and IP, 128 (132); *Posner*, University of Chicago Law Review 1981, 6 (21).

[121] Compare *Posner*, Antitrust Law & Economics Review 1968, 47.

[122] *Areeda/Hovenkamp*, Antitrust Law, Vol. 8, para. 1612c2; *Crane*, in: Brands, Competition Law and IP, 128 (134); *Orbach*, Antitrust Bulletin 2010, 277 (302–303); for a similar argument regarding advertising, see *Stiglitz*, in: Handbook Industrial Organization, 769 (842).

[123] See above p. 162.

[124] See *Posner*, University of Chicago Law Review 1981, 6; *Posner*, Antitrust Law & Economics Review 1968, 47.

[125] *Litman*, Yale Law Journal 1999, 1717 (1725) in the context of trademark protection, criticizing that '[w]hat consumers are willing to pay has become synonymous with value.'

[126] *Plassmann et al.*, Proceedings of the National Academy of Sciences 2008, 1050.

There is, however, no consensus on the welfare effects of product differentiation. In this regard, it must be noted that a higher willingness to pay does not in all cases lead to higher consumer welfare. Döpper et al., for example, investigated the evolution of markups in consumer products in the US from 2006 to 2019. In this period, there was a decrease of marginal costs (of production) but nevertheless prices remained largely unchanged.[127] Cost reductions over this period were not fully passed on to consumers. The study's authors attribute this, to a large extent, to a reduction in consumers' price sensitivity.[128] So while consumers' willingness to pay has increased (higher surplus), this has also prevented prices from falling with falling marginal costs (lower surplus). They found that the median Lerner index[129] for those products has increased from around 0.45 to over 0.60 in this period.[130] Overall, Döpper et al. find that in a counterfactual scenario with equal markups compared to 2006, consumer surplus would have increased greater (almost 14 % more).[131] This highlights a tension between two opposing effects: on one hand, a higher willingness to pay may signal increased consumer surplus; on the other hand, it can also enable firms to achieve higher markups and prices. This makes it difficult to grasp the full effects of an increased willingness to pay on consumer surplus.

Some scholars criticize the unequivocal embracement of brand and product differentiation through vertical agreements on a more fundamental level.[132] Comanor, for example, contemplates: "when product differentiation is achieved not by 'superior skill, foresight, and industry', but rather by imposing customer and territorial restrictions – agreements which expressly restrict the behavior of independent firms – the offending firm becomes subject to antitrust attack."[133] Luxury products are the most typical example of products whose image is, at least in part, created or fostered through vertical agreements. The manufacturer tries to convince the consumer to buy their products not by making them as widely available as possible but by creating an artificial scarcity of supply on the one hand and a unique shopping experience on the other hand. One way to look at a product's luxury image is that it creates a want in the consumer. If, as a result, the consumer buys the product, in some sense, they are not better off than had the want not been created and the consumer not bought the product.

---

[127] *Döpper et al.*, SSRN 2022, p. 18.

[128] *Döpper et al.*, SSRN 2022, pp. 24–32.

[129] The Lerner index measures a firm's markup by calculating the difference between price and marginal costs (in percent). Formula: L=(P–MC)/P. Example: a gadget is priced at 10 EUR and the marginal costs to produce the gadget are 8 EUR, the Lerner index is 0,2 ((10–8)/10).

[130] *Döpper et al.*, SSRN 2022, p. 16.

[131] *Döpper et al.*, SSRN 2022, p. 31.

[132] See also above p. 18 for a behavioural economics perspective on irrelevant product attributes.

[133] *Comanor*, Harvard Law Review 1968, 1419 (1424).

For illustration, take the following scenario: a consumer is taking a walk on the main street, sees a fancy store that sells luxury watches and looks at the shop windows where some particularly expensive models are showcased. They go inside the shop, where nice smells, comfortable music, attentive sales personnel, and an overall atmosphere of luxury surround her. As a result, they decide to buy a watch for € 1000. Now it could be argued that their desire to buy the watch had just been created. By buying the watch, they just fulfil the newly created want, leaving them without any net benefit from having discovered the store and watch in the first place. Moreover, other consumers might walk past the store and see the watch – leading to a similar desire to buy it – but do not have the money to do so. Those consumers could then be worse off as there is something they want but that they cannot get. Galbraith was the first to make this point: if wants are created by production, one cannot say that production (and consequently purchases of produced goods) is increasing welfare:

> "it can no longer be assumed that welfare is greater at an all-round higher level of production than at a lower one. It may be the same. The higher level of production has, merely, a higher level of want creation necessitating a higher level of want satisfaction."[134]

Products with a luxury image seem to be the very culmination of this idea: the want becomes the very product itself. Some categories of products are not bought because of any intrinsic 'objective' characteristic or usefulness but solely because of their image. In other words: while one cannot argue that there is no want for luxury products once they exist, it is unclear whether there was harm if they did not. The very way of creating the products is to create the want for them.

Taking Galbraith's approach seriously would suggest that all efforts to persuade consumers harm their autonomy. Almost every purchase decision, except perhaps of some basic needs like food or shelter, would not be the result of the consumer's autonomous choice but of persuasion and manipulation, i.e., of want-creation. There are some examples of products that make Galbraith's argument look appealing at a first glance. One is so-called 'decorative books'. Those are paper squares with a brand logo, resembling a book but without actual pages (sometimes sold at prices that exceed the price of an actual book).[135] Yet, distinguishing between wants created by advertising (including those shaped by vertical agreements) and other forms of desire is inherently difficult. This is a general problem when faced with the distinction between *good* and *bad* product differentiation.[136] As Hovenkamp puts it, "even if we admit that some amount of product differentiation may be 'excessive', it is impossible to tell when it becomes

[134] *Galbraith*, The Affluent Society, p. 131; see also *Kahneman/Krueger*, Journal of Economic Perspectives 2006, 3 for an overview of measurements of well-being that cast doubt on consumption as a valid indicator of well-being.

[135] Bellari Home, Decorative Books, available at https://www.bellarihome.com/products/decorative-books-collection-i (accessed: 11 March 2025).

[136] See *Posner*, Antitrust Law & Economics Review 1968, 47 (49).

so."[137] Unlike some of the other practices described above, horizontal product differentiation will typically change consumers' actual preferences and thus lead to a rather long-term shift in the demand curve. Because it affects preferences rather than merely influencing immediate choices, such differentiation is generally not seen as undermining consumer autonomy.[138]

A similar debate takes place in context of trademark law which some authors have drawn from also in the competition law context. Trademark law is criticized sometimes overly protecting trademarks as anti-dilution instruments: It is argued that where consumers value 'atmospheric' elements of products (such as a Batman picture on breakfast cereals), this does not mean that this value can be entirely exploited by and assigned to the trademark owner as a property right.[139] Litman argues that

> "[i]f the thing itself is valuable, if it is in some sense itself a product, then we want other purveyors to compete in offering it to consumers in their own forms and on their own terms. Competition is, after all, the premise of the system."[140]

In the same vein, Sheff posits that the trademark protection of goods for the status they confer amounts to "governmental regulation of social expression."[141] In another article, he even goes one step further and puts forward that brands can be used to bias consumers.[142] Schwaderer[143] and also Künzler[144] make the argument that these thoughts can be transferred to antitrust law and that there, too, the law is overly protective of artificially created scarcity and preventing dilution.

However, vertical agreements and trademark protection are two pairs of shoes: trademark law grants protection to the trademark owner without further ado just for having the trademark.[145] they can intervene and bring legal action against anyone allegedly infringing their trademark.[146] The situation is, however, different for a vertical agreement that serves to prevent dilution. Here, the manufacturer must actively establish and maintain a distribution system designed to create or preserve a desired image. In this respect, the situation is more akin to Walt Disney inventing Micky Mouse nearly a century ago than to the Disney Company suing someone for creating a Micky Mouse story today without asking

137 *Areeda/Hovenkamp*, Antitrust Law, Vol. 8, para. 1612c2.

138 *Huffman/Heidtke*, William & Mary Policy Review 2012, 77 (84).

139 *Litman*, Yale Law Journal 1999, 1717 (1728–1731); see also *Ramello/Silva*, Industrial and Corporate Change 2006, 937.

140 *Litman*, Yale Law Journal 1999, 1717 (1730–1731).

141 *Sheff*, Minnesota Law Review 2012, 769 (832).

142 *Sheff*, Cardozo Law Review 2010, 1245 (1277–1295).

143 *Schwaderer*, Resale Price Maintenance, pp. 162–171.

144 *Künzler*, Restoring Consumer Sovereignty, pp. 23–86.

145 See Directive (EU) 2015/2436 of the European Parliament and of the Council of 16 December 2015 to approximate the laws of the Member States relating to trade marks, OJ L 336, 23.12.2015, p. 1–26 ('Trademark Directive'), Art. 10 (1).

146 See Art. 10(2) Trademark Directive.

for permission. Competition law, unlike trademark law, does not protect anything here; it simply refrains from intervening in the manufacturer's own effort to create or preserve an image.

Against this background, a vertical agreement should not be condemned as anti-competitive solely *because* it has the goal or effect of horizontally differentiating brands or products.[147] However, given the ambiguous effects that product differentiation can have, this should not shield the respective vertical agreements from being anti-competitive for *other reasons*. Grimes brings it to the point, arguing that "if the primary goal or effect of the brand promotion is non-informational (such as image or status enhancement), that is a far less compelling justification for the restraint."[148] While some negative effects of product differentiation might be unavoidable, there is no reason to make such differentiation a universal justification for vertical agreements. Moreover, given the ambiguous welfare effects of product differentiation, there appears to be relatively little risk of overenforcement.[149] This is also true when looking at consumer autonomy: on the one hand, a brand image can give a consumer more information about a product's quality and characteristics (although they might not always be 100 % accurate). Neither the positive nor the negative aspect should thus be the primary focus of antitrust law. While a vertical agreement should not be condemned simply because it leads to horizontal product differentiation and/or improves a product's image, if the same agreement for other reasons raises competition concerns, it should not be justified based only on the manufacturer's desire to raise consumers' willingness to pay. In this light, the Court of Justice was at least partly right in Pierre Fabre: maintaining a prestigious image is not a legitimate aim for restricting competition.[150] The Court of Justice just went too far in its assessment because it did not explain why competition was restricted in the first place.

V. Reducing 'subconscious reflection' – debiasing through intra-brand competition?

Adrian Künzler, in his book "Restoring Consumer Sovereignty"[151] and two articles[152], argues that intra-brand competition[153] plays an important role in the

[147] Product differentiation or product design can, however, be a concern for horizontal collusion and abuse of dominance cases, see *Petty*, Journal of Consumer Affairs 2018, 252.

[148] *Grimes*, in: Brands, Competition Law and IP, 138 (141).

[149] Compare *Areeda/Hovenkamp*, Antitrust Law, Vol. 8, para. 1601n.

[150] Court of Justice, 13/10/2011, Case C-439/09 Pierre Fabre, ECLI:EU:C:2011:649, para. 46.

[151] *Künzler*, Restoring Consumer Sovereignty.

[152] *Künzler*, Oxford Journal of Legal Studies 2017, 75; *Künzler*, in: Goals of Competition Law, 182.

[153] Künzler uses the term intratype competition but understands intra-brand competition as a subcategory if this term, see *Künzler*, Restoring Consumer Sovereignty, p. 17.

competitive process as it allows consumers to make better decisions through reducing influence on consumers' 'subconscious reflection':

"A different purchasing environment, a different price, different terms and conditions, and the consumer's ability to compare similar goods next to each other all may calm the subconscious impressions, anxieties, and fears that render it difficult for the consumer to make any alternative decision."[154] Therefore, "[i]ntratype competition may [...] be a pre-condition for consumers to search and may mitigate a product manufacturer's effort to manipulate consumer preferences based on subconscious appeal and affect-driven emotions."[155]

Essentially, the argument is that in a world of non-rational consumers, "intratype competition mitigates behavioral biases and counteracts the externalities of such biases on consumer balance sheets."[156] If the consumer sees and experiences a good in different contexts, at different prices etc., they will be better able to make an independent decision that is less dependent on the manufacturer's advertising or other forms of influence.[157] This leads Künzler to the conclusion that

"a free riding defence that solely intends to avert the dilution of subconscious appeal of a particular good or service could no longer (on its own) constitute a legitimate business justification for allegedly anticompetitive conduct."[158]

Künzler here is referring to the argument that resale price maintenance, selective distribution or other vertical restraints may be necessary so that all retailers present the product in a certain (e.g. luxurious) way and prevent consumers from perceiving the product in a different atmosphere. Künzler's arguments should be taken seriously. It is broadly accepted that consumers are not always rational actors but that they do make mistakes and are guided by certain biases in their decision-making. Moreover, those biases can be used by those who can control the decision-making context to steer consumers towards a particular choice.[159] Künzler argues that more intra-brand competition will ultimately lead to better consumption decisions not because retailers are necessarily the better choice architects from the consumer's perspective but simply because greater intra-brand variety will allow consumers to arrive at better decisions. This, in turn, makes sure that consumers are the arbiters of the competitive process and the one that give the orders to producers rather than vice versa.[160]

The key insight from Künzler's work is that intra-brand competition has value for consumers' decision-making by making consumers less dependent on the influence and information of a particular manufacturer or retailer. While vertical

---

[154] *Künzler*, Restoring Consumer Sovereignty, p. 165.
[155] *Künzler*, Restoring Consumer Sovereignty, p. 166.
[156] *Künzler*, Restoring Consumer Sovereignty, p. 174.
[157] *Künzler*, Restoring Consumer Sovereignty, p. 178.
[158] *Künzler*, Restoring Consumer Sovereignty, p. 256.
[159] See above from p. 15.
[160] *Künzler*, Restoring Consumer Sovereignty, p. 270.

agreements may indeed improve the image of a product, they may at the same time limit the consumer's ability to inform herself about the price, quantity and quality attributes.[161] In particular, subconscious decision-making may be affected by greater intra-brand variety: where a manufacturer cannot control the distribution, their products will be available under different purchasing contexts, grouped with different products and at different prices.[162] This may lead consumers to subconsciously change their perceptions of a product's relative price and quality.[163] For example, a consumer who encounters a high-priced product only among other expensive items in a luxury store will assess its price-quality ratio differently than if they also see it in another store alongside lower-priced products. Against this background, Künzler argues that dilution prevention should not justify anticompetitive conduct. Vertical agreements that mainly influence consumers' decision-making by improving a product's image or preventing dilution, against this background, can, in principle, not be considered anticompetitive for that reason. However, on the other hand, dilution prevention or improving a product's image is not in itself sufficient to qualify an agreement as anticompetitive either. As explained in the context of product differentiation, the effects in this regard are ambiguous.[164]

VI. Information and misinformation through prices

When it comes to price restraints, in particular minimum RPM, Schwaderer suggests that they can have two diverging effects on how consumers make decisions.[165] First, prices can work as a quality signal. Second, prices can be used to bias consumers.

1. Price as a quality signal

Schwaderer's arguments relating to the price as a quality model are based on the work of Inderst et al.[166] The model is related but not identical to the image-certification model discussed in Chapter 1[167]. The difference is that under Inderst's model, the relevant parameter is not the provision of retailer image certification but the price as such. Based on marketing literature, Inderst argues that prices serve as an indicator of a product's quality.[168] His model is linked to Akerlof's

[161] *Künzler*, Oxford Journal of Legal Studies 2017, 75 (91).

[162] *Künzler*, Oxford Journal of Legal Studies 2017, 75 (102–103).

[163] *Künzler*, Oxford Journal of Legal Studies 2017, 75 (103).

[164] See above from p. 200.

[165] *Schwaderer*, Resale Price Maintenance, pp. 123–182, Schwaderer also distinguishes a third, 'price as utility', model. This one appears less relevant for the consumer decision, however. It is equivalent to the image creation model, discussed in Chapter 1.

[166] *Inderst*, Price Ownership; *Inderst/Maier-Rigaud*, CPI 2015; *Inderst/Pfeil*, SSRN 2013.

[167] See above p. 47.

[168] *Inderst*, Price Ownership, p. 12.

market for lemons[169]: if the manufacturer can credibly signal high quality through high prices, there is no race to the bottom where only low-quality products are offered.[170] This mechanism works through several incentives for the manufacturer to provide high quality at high prices: (1) they receive a higher margin on the products and has thus more to lose from a drop in demand due to disappointing quality expectations ('margin effect'); (2) the manufacturer occurs lower overall costs for a quality increase because their demand is lower (due to higher prices) ('cost effect'); (3) demand effects on quality changes are greater at higher prices because of a different composition of the consumer base (the inframarginal consumer now values quality more) ('elasticity effect').[171] From the manufacturer's perspective, retailers can set the price too low: if one retailer asks a high price (thereby indicating high quality), other retailers could free-ride on the induced high-quality perception and take sales away by charging a lower price. RPM could thus maintain the manufacturer's incentive to provide high-quality products. While the model was developed for RPM, it could also apply to online sales bans: lower online retail prices could lower the overall price level, reducing the manufacturer's incentive to produce high-quality products.[172] Rational consumers will anticipate the manufacturer's incentives to provide high quality at high prices.[173] Therefore, high prices can help consumers to make an informed decision regarding high quality.

Inderst claims that his model is particularly relevant for new products or little-known brands as there, consumers have few other alternative cues regarding the quality.[174] Where consumers can observe the true level of quality easily, high prices cannot be explained by his model.[175]

2. Price as bias-inducing anchor

Schwaderer, building on the work of Künzler[176], suggests that minimum RPM can be used to bias consumers by creating an arbitrarily high initial anchor through a high and uniform retail price.[177] Once this anchor is set, consumers can be locked into believing the product is of high intrinsic quality even when confronted with information that indicates the opposite.[178] Without RPM, there is a

---

[169] *Akerlof*, Quarterly Journal of Economics 1970, 488.

[170] *Inderst*, Price Ownership, p. 14; *Inderst/Maier-Rigaud*, CPI 2015, p. 6.

[171] *Inderst*, Price Ownership, pp. 18–24; for a brief summary, see *Inderst/Maier-Rigaud*, CPI 2015, p. 8.

[172] Compare *Inderst/Maier-Rigaud*, CPI 2015, p. 3 footnote 5.

[173] *Inderst*, Price Ownership, p. 28.

[174] *Inderst*, Price Ownership, pp. 16–17.

[175] *Inderst*, Price Ownership, pp. 28–29.

[176] See above from p. 201.

[177] *Schwaderer*, Resale Price Maintenance, pp. 172–175.

[178] *Schwaderer*, Resale Price Maintenance, p. 173.

risk that retailers do not set uniform prices because they don't consider overall demand.[179] Schwaderer argues that in such cases,

> "if the consumer were rational and not biased through the setting of the strong initial anchor, the consumer would have made a different purchase decision."[180]

This would be detrimental to welfare as measured through the consumer's hypothetical choice "had [they] been able to make a rational decision".[181] The obvious criticism of this is that it is near impossible to find out what the consumer's hypothetical choice would have been absent of the restraint. Schwaderer's approach, nevertheless, is highly relevant as it puts the consumers' decision-making at the centre of the analysis. However, misinformation, irrespective of a concrete welfare loss, may pose a problem because it harms consumers' autonomy and their ability to function efficiently as arbiters of the competitive process. Therefore, Schwaderer's argument remains important even in the face of the difficulties that come with measuring welfare in these cases.

However, Schwaderer goes too far in the conclusions she draws.[182] She finds that the possibility of using RPM to bias consumers is sufficient to justify the treatment of RPM as by object restriction under EU competition law because, in light of the bias effect, "the elimination of intra-brand competition cannot be considered to be outweighed by inter-brand competition."[183] She thereby fails to distinguish between restriction of competition and efficiency defence: while a restriction of competition should not be justified because the manufacturer wants to make consumers pay a higher price due to anchoring, this does not mean that every such attempt is a restriction of competition in the first place. As already indicated in the previous Chapter and as will be discussed in more detail in § 2, competition law is concerned with effects on the consumers' decision-making only where they risk influencing market-wide outcomes.[184] Where only one manufacturer manages to bias consumers through a high price anchor, this should a priori, not necessary raise competition law concerns.

VII. Better advice and information services by retailers

On the positive side, vertical agreements can help consumers to make better decisions when they induce retailers to provide better sales advice. This is, to a large extent, what has guided the original Metro case law on qualitative selective distribution.[185] It is based on Telser's free-riding theory.[186] Qualitative criteria in

---

[179] *Schwaderer*, Resale Price Maintenance, p. 175.
[180] *Schwaderer*, Resale Price Maintenance, p. 178.
[181] *Schwaderer*, Resale Price Maintenance, pp. 178–179.
[182] *Schwaderer*, Resale Price Maintenance, p. 2011.
[183] *Schwaderer*, Resale Price Maintenance, p. 203.
[184] See below from p. 212.
[185] See above from p. 25.
[186] See above from p. 45.

selective distribution can require the retailer to give better advice to the consumer when it comes to complex products. This can include, inter alia, the presence of trained personnel, opportunities to test and try the product or professional presentations. The rationale behind this is that complex products might require specialist retailers to properly explain the product characteristics and its use to the consumer. Vertical agreements could also require the retailer *not* to engage in certain practices to influence the consumer. A manufacturer could, for example, require their retailers not to engage in drip pricing or other obfuscation strategies or to not cooperate with intermediaries who engage in such practices. Similarly, an intermediary could require the same from retailers that offer goods or services on their platform, potentially also requiring the same for their offers on other platforms. This would make sure that there is no race-to-the-bottom obfuscation competition where every retailer has the incentive to obfuscate more than their competitors. Unlike most favoured nation clauses,[187] this would not preclude making better offers on other platforms; it would just ensure that those offers are easily comparable and, thus, actually better. Firms' efforts to improve consumer decisions, like in the above-mentioned case of StubHub,[188] might then become more successful.

VIII. Summary

Vertical agreements can influence consumers' decision-making in a variety of ways. In some instances, they can improve consumers' decisions when they lead to retailers providing better advice. This will typically relevant for complex products for which outside information is difficult to obtain. With today's widespread access to online information and lower search costs, the importance of such benefits may have diminished. Vertical agreements can also help to eliminate or reduce obfuscation strategies by retailers or intermediaries. In other instances, vertical agreements can have negative effects on consumers' decision-making. This is particularly the case where agreements incentivise the retailer to promote a manufacturer's products irrespective of their merits. The risk of such incentives is the highest for RPM and quantitative selective distribution. Similar problems can arise when retailers collude with intermediaries such as search engines or platforms to promote their products. Vertical agreements can also increase consumers' search costs through obfuscation agreements or other informational restrictions. Examples here include bans on price comparison websites or advertising bans. Where negative effects prevail, this can, in principle, be relevant for the evaluation of an agreement as anti-competitive, although – as will be discussed in more detail in the next section – this is not in itself sufficient. Vertical agreements can further lead to horizontal product differentiation and reduce

[187] See Vertical Guidelines, paras. 356–378.

[188] See above from p. 191.

consumers' subconscious reflection. However, the effects in this regard are ambivalent, and there are no workable criteria to distinguish positive from negative effects. Therefore, these aspects should, a priori, not be a concern for competition law. An agreement with the goal or effect of horizontal brand/product differentiation or reducing subconscious reflection should not be considered restrictive of competition for that reason alone. At the same time, however, where it restricts competition for other reasons, it should not be justified[189] solely on this basis either.

§ 2 When do vertical agreements restrict competition based on consumer autonomy?

The previous section has shown that vertical agreements can influence consumers' decision-making. However, the effects in this regard are ambivalent: they can be positive or negative, and it is not always easy to distinguish between the two. Including concerns for the consumer's decision-making in the antitrust analysis of vertical agreements, therefore, risks bringing about legal uncertainty and an inconsistent application of the law.

While courts and competition authorities have looked at consumer autonomy when evaluating vertical agreements, they have yet failed to develop a coherent theory of harm to distinguish anti-competitive from pro-competitive or neutral agreements on this basis.[190] Although, at least to some extent, this is mitigated by the fact that many agreements are exempted under the VBER, it is nevertheless unsatisfying. For hardcore restrictions (for which the VBER does not apply) as well as for agreements between undertakings that do not fall within the VBER's market share threshold, the question of when an agreement restricts competition in the first place remains highly relevant.[191] This section tries to fill this gap and develop a theory of harm that can be applied to find under which conditions a vertical agreement constitutes a restriction of competition based on its effects on consumers' decision-making.

I. Protecting noble rather than race to the bottom competition

As a first step before a theory of harm can be developed, it is necessary to determine the substantive reach of competition law in the context of consumer

[189] This refers to both, a Metro style inherent exception to Art. 101(1) TFEU and a justification under Art. 101(3) TFEU.

[190] See above from p. 99.

[191] As discussed in Chapter 1, hardcore restrictions are treated as restrictions of competition by object. However, it is not in all cases clear why they restrict competition in the first place, see above from p. 41.

autonomy also compared to other fields of law. This will be done on the following pages.

1. Art. 101 TFEU as a general clause and the concept of competition on the merits

Art. 101 TFEU and Art. 102 TFEU are general clauses consisting of indeterminate legal terms requiring interpretation and development by courts and competition authorities.[192] They must be interpreted, taking into account their goals.[193] The natural question arising from this is how a normative concern of protecting consumer autonomy may be included in the practical application of the law. One possible way of doing so is recurring to the concept of 'competition on the merits' ('Leistungswettbewerb') used by the Court of Justice to distinguish anti-competitive and pro-competitive behaviour[194]. While the concept of competition on the merits is mostly mentioned in the context of Art. 102 TFU, it can also be made applicable under Art. 101 TFEU, as both provisions share the same normative goals[195]. 'Leistungswettbewerb', as Vanberg puts it,

> "denotes the ideal of a market order framed by rules that aim at making producers responsive to consumer interests [...]. To establish an order of *Leistungswettbewerb* means to adopt rules for the market game that make consumer preferences the ultimate controlling force in the process of production."[196]

[192] See regarding German competition law Bundesverfassungsgericht, 03/06/2022, 1 BvR 2103/16 Pechstein, NJW 2022, 2677, para. 33; Bundesgerichtshof, 23/06/2020, KVR 69/19 Facebook, GRUR 2020, 1318, para. 55; regarding EU law *Botta/Wiedemann*, Antitrust Bulletin 2019, 428 (441); *Fuchs*, in: Immenga/Mestmäcker, Art. 102 AEUV, para. 133; *Oppermann/Chmeis*, in: Consistent Application, 195 (206); *Schröter*, in: von der Groeben/Schwarze, Europäisches Unionsrecht, Art. 101 AEUV, para. 4.

[193] *Fuchs*, in: Immenga/Mestmäcker, Art. 102 AEUV, para. 199.

[194] The Court uses various terms interchangeably, see Court of Justice, 13/02/1979, Case 85/76 Hoffman-LaRoche, ECLI:EU:C:1979:36, para. 90: 'normal competition in products or services on the basis of the transactions of commercial operators'; Court of Justice, 11/12/1980, Case 31/80 L'Oréal, ECLI:EU:C:1980:289, para. 27: 'normal competition'; Court of Justice, 09/11/1983, Case 322/81 Michelin I, ECLI:EU:C:1983:313, para. 70: 'normal competition [...] based on traders' performance'; Court of Justice, 03/07/1991, Case C-62/86 Akzo, ECLI:EU:C:1991:286, para. 70: 'competition on the basis of quality'; Court of Justice, 15/03/2007, C-95/04 P British Airways, ECLI:EU:C:2007:166, para. 241: 'normal competition'; Court of Justice, 02/04/2009, Case C-202/07 P France Télécom, ECLI:EU:C:2009:214, para. 106: 'competition on the basis of quality'; Court of Justice, 16/07/2015, Case C-170/13 Huawei, ECLI:EU:C:2015:477: 'normal competition'; Court of First Instance, 10/07/1990, Case T-51/89 TetraPak, ECLI:EU:T:1990:41, para. 23: 'normal competition'; Court of First Instance, 17/07/1998, Case T-111/96 ITT Promedia, ECLI:EU:T:1998:183, para. 138: 'normal competition'; Court of First Instance, 23/10/2003, Case T-65/98 Van den Bergh Foods, ECLI:EU:T:2003:281, para. 157: 'normal competition'; General Court, 12/06/2014, Case T-286/09 Intel, ECLI:EU:T:2014:547, para. 205: 'competition on the merits'.

[195] Court of Justice, 21/02/1973, Case 6–72 Continental Can, ECLI:EU:C:1973:22, para. 25; Court of First Instance, 10/07/1990, Case T-51/89 TetraPak, ECLI:EU:T:1990:41, para. 22.

[196] *Vanberg*, in: Competition Policy and the Economic Approach, 44 (56) (emphasis in original).

The question to be asked is whether a practice is benefitting an economic actor because they are just performing better than their competitors. Only performance-based gains in profit and market share are legitimate: undertakings shall compete to best cater to consumers' needs and preferences. The concept of competition on the merits is as such not a positive prescription but serves to "filter out those business strategies which are incompatible with the ordering principles of a competitive society."[197]

Behrens, advocating for a consumer choice standard under EU competition law, suggests using the concept 'competition on the merits' to identify

> "a restraint of competition [...] wherever (1) the number of freely competing producers is artificially reduced in ways that do not result from the normal process of competition itself, and (2) where this reduces the scope of alternatives among which consumers may freely choose."[198]

He emphasizes that consumers should have the chance to decide for themselves in the market and that this is part of their economic freedom protected by competition law.[199] In his view, the market structure is of particular importance here:

> "Consumers' freedom (or consumers' sovereignty [...]) to choose between alternative products or services offered in the market is dependent upon the degree of decentralization of production."[200]

Concentration in a market, therefore, reduces consumer choice. The reduction in consumer choice can only be justified when it results from legitimate competition (on the merits). Behrens here understands consumer choice purely in terms of variety of options: any reduction of variety is anti-competitive if it is not based on competition on the merits. However, Behrens does not consider the process of choosing. If the consumer is the arbiter of the competitive process[201], this does not only require that there are options that they can choose from (variety) but also that they can make their choice according to their preferences and needs. The process of choosing hence becomes relevant. Only if this process is not unduly impaired can the consumer's choice be the relevant benchmark to determine success or failure in the market. If consumers don't choose the best product from the most efficient or innovative company but instead the product from the company that has best manipulated consumers' decisions, competition does neither lead to increased welfare, nor can it discover unknown facts.

One can therefore make the argument that is not only the range of options that competition law needs to protect but also "the ability or freedom of consumers by exercising their choice to ensure that markets deliver the products and services

---

197 *Mohr*, Vertragsfreiheit, p. 388 (translation from German by the author) referring to Böhm's understanding of 'Leistungswettbewerb'.

198 *Behrens*, in: Consumer Choice, 123 (142).

199 *Behrens*, in: Consumer Choice, 123 (142); see also *Ulmer*, GRUR 1977, 565.

200 *Behrens*, in: Consumer Choice, 123 (142).

201 *Böhm*, Wettbewerb und Monopolkampf, p. 276.

that meet their preferences."[202] Only if the consumer can select the best offer in the market can she, on the one hand, indirectly stimulate the competitive process (forcing suppliers and manufacturers to compete fiercely on quality, price and innovation) and, on the other hand, "appropriate the gains from competition."[203] Practices that reduce consumer autonomy can lead to consumer mistakes (e.g., biases) that can diminish the positive effects competition is supposed to bring: when consumers do not properly evaluate prices or quality, the market will not bring prices down and quality up.[204] Consumers' ability to compare prices and product attributes are important factors in the competitive process. If consumers overvalue a product, this product will be oversupplied, inducing social harm through the inefficient use of resources.[205] As Huck et al. describe it:

> "biases and the cross subsidies they generate may lead to overproduction of goods that in the end will be thrown away or suboptimal design of products that may have too much of one attribute and too little of another."[206]

Another possible harm is that firms can have an incentive to invest in consumers' perception of the products rather than in innovation and quality, risking a race to the bottom competition. The process of choosing must is therefore important, providing support for making consumer autonomy a necessary precondition of competition.[207] Moreover, Behrens' approach does not give any answer to the question of what competition on the merits is, making it difficult to identify those reductions of consumer choice that do not "result from legitimate competition."

Drexl has suggested a more promising approach. He argues that protection of freedom requires not only protection from economic power, understood as passive freedom but must be understood in an active sense as the freedom to pursue self-set goals on the market notwithstanding their economic or other nature.[208] The law's task, according to Drexl, must be to ensure that consumers can bring to bear all their autonomously set concerns in the market. This must include purely egoistic rational preferences but similarly altruistic preferences such as environmental protection. The law must create the basic conditions for consumers' self-determination through autonomous decisions in the market.[209] In particular, in the context of competition law, Drexl argues that while the law shall not have the function of evaluating autonomous goals but solely to create and protect the conditions for autonomous goal-setting, competition law interferences in market

[202] *Graef*, CMLR 2021, 471 (478).

[203] *Wilson/Price*, Oxford Economic Papers 2010, 647 (647).

[204] *Huffman/Heidtke*, William & Mary Policy Review 2012, 77 (83); *Kőszegi/Heidhues*, in: Handbook Behavioral Economics, 517 (588).

[205] Compare *Kőszegi/Heidhues*, in: Handbook Behavioral Economics, 517 (530).

[206] *Huck et al.*, Consumer Behavioral Biases, p. 7.

[207] *Glöckner*, Europäisches Lauterkeitsrecht, pp. 282, 468; *Siciliani*, Consumer Theories of Harm, p. 57.

[208] *Drexl*, Wirtschaftliche Selbstbestimmung, pp. 176–181.

[209] *Drexl*, Wirtschaftliche Selbstbestimmung, p. 181.

conduct can be justified by the restriction of private decision-making freedoms by third parties (undertakings).[210] Autonomy under this approach becomes a core element of competition law as part of a humane and dignified order.

This focus would allow an approximation of the term 'restriction of competition': any restriction of decision-making autonomy may be an element of (but is not in itself sufficient) a restriction of competition.[211]

This approach also adds some flesh to the concept of competition on the merits. Conduct that harms consumers' autonomous decision-making is not competition on the merits. If such conduct influences the market structure, e.g., by foreclosing market entry or excluding competitors, it should be considered prima facie anti-competitive. In this sense, the 'range of options' is only indirectly relevant. Where the range of options (through the influence on the market structure) is reduced by diminishing the consumer's ability to make an independent and informed decision, this range of options becomes inadequate. The adequacy of the range of options is, therefore, only a result of the effective application of competition law rather than itself a criterion that must be measured and evaluated by courts and competition authorities. It should be noted that, in principle, competition preserves autonomy and self-determination. The task of courts and competition authorities is to identify situations in which economic operators abrogate other actors' self-determination. As the examples above show, companies' attempts in this regard are frequent.

Ultimately, courts and competition authorities must determine the precise boundaries of how far companies can go in influencing consumers' decision-making. The judgments and decisions mentioned above indicate that they have already set out to do this.[212] Behavioural economic insights are an important tool in this regard, not only in digital markets. While digital companies like Google have certainly advanced the use of behaviourally informed market (and abuse) strategies, they are not the only ones using them. If users click mainly on the first three to five search results and pay no attention to the remaining results when conducting a search online, irrespective of their merits,[213] it is safe to assume that in traditional brick and mortar stores, similar product placement strategies can work.

Like every indeterminate legal term, the understanding of 'competition on the merits' is subject to changes depending on the accepted moral standards in society as well as new scientific findings. Nipperdey, who was among the first to use the term in the legal discourse, for example, in 1930, argued that price-cutting by a cartel to drive a cartel outsider out of business constitutes 'Leistungswettbewerb'.[214] Economic evidence and theory have certainly overhauled this idea, and

[210] *Drexl*, Wirtschaftliche Selbstbestimmung, p. 182.
[211] *Drexl*, Wirtschaftliche Selbstbestimmung, p. 184.
[212] See above from p. 168.
[213] European Commission, 27/06/2017, AT.39740 Google Shopping, para. 455.
[214] *Nipperdey*, Kartell-Rundschau 1930, 127.

no one today would defend Nipperdey's position. This example shows that the vagueness of the term can also constitute a benefit as it allows a constant update to new scientific evidence and, often relatedly, changing societal moral views.[215] As Köhler puts it: "The assessment of what is anti-competitive is, however, subject to the prevailing but ever-changing socio-political and economic views."[216] Findings from behavioural economics have recently played an important role in the scientific and public discourse.[217] They can also inform our understanding of what constitutes competition on the merits.

Critique against the concept of competition on the merits postulates that the term by itself is too vague to distinguish pro- from anti-competitive behaviour.[218] One of the points of critique brought forward against the concept of competition on the merits is that what constitutes competition on the merits shall be for consumers themselves to decide.[219] However, the normative underpinning of competition on the merits is exactly to give consumers this opportunity in a material sense. Moreover, competition on the merits need not be understood as the exclusive element of a restriction of competition but rather as only one of several puzzle pieces, notably the market circumstances and the effects of the practice or agreement on the market being additional elements. This understanding is also how the Court of Justice uses the concept.[220] The additional requirement of a market-structure effect mitigates the risk of errors. While the concept remains imperfect due to its inherent vagueness, it appears nevertheless justified to uphold it.[221] In light of ever-changing business practices, new market developments, as well as changing scientific findings and societal views, a general clause is necessary to provide the required flexibility for competition law to respond to these changes.[222]

2. Market effect: protecting 'noble' competition

Consumer autonomy can be a concern for antitrust law because of its potential effects on competition.[223] Consumer autonomy is central to competition law

[215] Compare *Ulmer*, GRUR 1977, 565.

[216] *Köhler*, WRP 2005, 645 (646) (translation by the author).

[217] See *Geiger*, Social Science History 2017, 555.

[218] *Geradin*, JECLAP 2014, 344; *Pichler*, Kartell- und Lauterkeitsrecht, pp. 121–123; *Wurmnest*, Marktmacht und Verdrängungsmissbrauch, p. 347; see also *Glöckner*, Europäisches Lauterkeitsrecht, p. 24; *Sosnitza*, Wettbewerbsbeschränkungen, pp. 81–82.

[219] *Sosnitza*, Wettbewerbsbeschränkungen, p. 82.

[220] Court of Justice, 13/02/1979, Case 85/76 Hoffman-LaRoche, ECLI:EU:C:1979:36, para. 6; *Eilmansberger*, CMLR 2005, 129 (149).

[221] *Eilmansberger*, CMLR 2005, 129; *Glöckner*, Europäisches Lauterkeitsrecht, p. 244; *Grewe*, Missbrauchsverbot, p. 178; *Ulmer*, GRUR 1977, 565; see also *Hetmank*, GRUR 2014, 437 (439–440) regarding the parallel debate in the context of the law on unfair competition.

[222] Compare, in the context of unfair competition law, *Bundeskartellamt*, Sektoruntersuchung Vergleichsportale, p. 138.

[223] See above from p. 148.

mainly because of its functional relationship with competition: only competition based on autonomous consumer decisions promises to bring desirable results. Hence, competition law is not as such protecting every individual consumption decision from being influenced in an undesirable way. This understanding is compatible with the view that individual market actors and consumers are not protected for their own sake[224] but rather for the sake of their functional relationship with the market.

However, when a distortion of consumer autonomy threatens to influence market-wide outcomes, it can become a matter for competition law.[225] Competition law, in this sense, can go beyond the traditional revealed preference paradigm[226] and actively protect consumers' autonomous decision-making for the sake of the functioning of the market. A restriction of competition needs to be able to influence the market-wide outcome in a detrimental way. This includes traditional exclusionary practices: another company is driven out of the market through means other than competition on the merits. However, market-wide effects that distort consumers' role as arbiters in the competitive process can also occur in a separate scenario. When one company adopts obfuscation or other strategies that harm consumers' autonomy, a possible reaction of competitors is to copy this very strategy.[227] Therefore, one could argue that in such a situation, exclusion is unlikely, and hence the conduct or agreement is not anti-competitive. As long as competitors can replicate the same practice, they will not be excluded. However, it can be argued that competition law does not protect just any form of competition but only competition on the merits. Accepting practices that harm consumer autonomy but are replicable by competitors (and thus do not exclude them) would mean accepting a form of competition that is nothing more than a race to the bottom. While competitors would not necessarily have to leave the market, competition would nevertheless be distorted if firms did not have to invest in the merits of their products.[228]

The question thus must be whether competition law also protects those (hypothetical) competitors who are not willing to engage in the same harmful conduct. If, for example, one manufacturer engages in RPM, and hence their retailers start to promote their products over those of other manufacturers, e.g., through always placing them on the top shelf in their stores, another manufacturer might see herself forced to similarly adopt RPM. Otherwise, his other manufacturer risks that every retailer promotes only their competitor's products. Not following

[224] *Morell*, (Behavioral) Law and Economics im Europäischen Wettbewerbsrecht, p. 197.

[225] Compare *Huffman/Heidtke*, William & Mary Policy Review 2012, 77 (102); *Huffman*, Antitrust Law Journal 2012, 105 (131); *Morell*, (Behavioral) Law and Economics im Europäischen Wettbewerbsrecht, p. 213.

[226] See in this regard also above from p. 158.

[227] See *Gabaix/Laibson*, Quarterly Journal of Economics 2006, 505; *Huffman/Heidtke*, William & Mary Policy Review 2012, 77 (106).

[228] *Competition and Markets Authority*, Online Choice Architecture, para. 14.

may even lead to being excluded from the market. Therefore, the question to be asked is what kind of competitor should be looked at to establish an exclusionary effect: the one who copies the first firm's harmful practice or the competitor who continues to leave a more neutral choice to consumers. The question of which kind of competitor is relevant to establish an exclusionary effect is not exclusive to the realm of vertical agreements. In the realm of predatory pricing, for example, this is typically the 'as efficient competitor'.[229] This test serves to determine whether

> "a competitor that is as efficient as the dominant undertaking allegedly responsible for those pricing practices, and which, in order not to be driven immediately from the market, would charge its customers the same prices as those charged by that undertaking, would have to do so at a loss and accentuating that loss, causing it to leave the market in the longer term [...]".[230]

So only the (potential) exclusion of a competitor which is at least as efficient as the dominant firm is relevant for certain pricing practices under Art. 102 TFEU.[231] In the context of agreements that make consumer decisions more difficult, the question is whether the exclusion of a competitor who herself is refraining from similar practices is sufficient. The reaction of competitors can often be to copy the same harmful practices, resulting in an obfuscation equilibrium.[232] Firms in many markets have the incentive to exploit consumers' behavioural biases and information gaps even if there is competition. Indeed, the very fact that there is competition may force firms to adopt those practices to not be outcompeted.[233] Can the exclusion of rivals that do not copy the same practice be nevertheless relevant for competition law?

In the argument put forward here, in certain cases, the answer is yes. Competition law tries to preserve 'competition on the merits' and not a race to the bottom competition. As discussed above, manipulating consumers and superseding their choice cannot be considered competition on the merits. Consumers must be active and empowered market participants. Further, where consumer decisions are not made autonomously, competition cannot be said to enhance consumer welfare (even though this might not be measurable under the revealed preferences approach)[234]. Therefore, excluding rivals that do not engage in similar practices or agreements can be a concern for antitrust law. If the only possible reaction to a vertical agreement that leads to obfuscation or other harms to the

---

[229] See *Kellerbauer*, EuZW 2015, 261.

[230] General Court, 10/11/2021, T-612/17 Google Shopping, ECLI:EU:T:2021:763, para. 538; Art. 82 Enforcement Priority Guidelines, paras. 23–27.

[231] This test, however, is not a generally applicable test for all exclusionary practices, see General Court, 10/11/2021, T-612/17 Google Shopping, ECLI:EU:T:2021:763, para. 538.

[232] See above from p. 180.

[233] *Bar-Gill*, Seduction by Contract, p. 24; *Bar-Gill*, NYU Law and Economics Research Paper 2011; *Patterson*, Antitrust Law in the New Economy, p. 151.

[234] See for the revealed preference approach above p. 166.

consumers' decision-making is to copy the same agreement, this could then amount to the exclusion of those rivals that are 'noble' enough to not follow ('noble rivals'[235]). Another related way to examine the issue is to consider firms' behaviour vis-á-vis consumers' decision-making as an element of quality competition.[236] Where practices that diminish consumers' ability to make independent decisions are prevalent in a market, this can hence be a problem to be addressed (also) by competition law.

3. Law against unfair competition vs competition law

The concept of competition on the merits is not unique to competition law, but it is also used in the law against unfair competition ('fair trading law'),[237] in the EU based on the Unfair Commercial Practices Directive and various laws of the Member States[238]. The Unfair Commercial Practices Directive prohibits 'unfair commercial practices', including 'misleading actions or omissions', 'aggressive commercial practices' and the 'use of harassment, coercion and undue influence'. It applies without prejudice to the EU competition law rules.[239] There are some parallels between the approach advocated here and unfair trading law. Under German law against unfair competition, the case law even recognizes 'general market obstruction' as a specific category of violation. Under this category, conduct which, although not unfair per se, is nevertheless questionable, where alone or in combination with similar measures by competitors, it gives rise to a serious risk that competition based on entrepreneurial performance will be restricted to a considerable extent.[240] The Bundesgerichtshof, for example, in a 1976 case, ruled that an agreement between a manufacturer and their retailers in which the latter agreed to 'rent' parts of their shopwindow to the manufacturer for the presentation of their products, could violate the law against unfair competition because of the risk of this practice towards a general market trend in which retailers influence their customers in an "unobjective manner".[241] Today, the main areas where general market obstruction is discussed are the supply of

[235] The term 'noble' here is inspired by the concept of noble competition developed by *Stucke/Ezrachi*, Competition Overdose, pp. 255–292.

[236] *Siciliani*, Consumer Theories of Harm, pp. 57–58.

[237] *Hetmank*, GRUR 2014, 437 (439–440).

[238] See *Glöckner*, Europäisches Lauterkeitsrecht, pp. 329–507; for an overview of different enforcement approaches in the Member States, see *Podszun et al.*, Behördliche Durchsetzung des Verbraucherrechts?, p. 67.

[239] Unfair Commercial Practices Directive, recital 9.

[240] Bundesgerichtshof, 29/10/2009, I ZR 180/07 Stumme Verkäufer II, GRUR 2010, 455, para. 20.

[241] Bundesgerichtshof, 03/12/1976, I ZR 34/75 Schaufensteraktion, GRUR 1977, 257, similar: OLG München, 21/05/1992, 6 U 4016/91 Besonders plazierte Arzneimittel, GRUR 1992, 712; see *Köhler*, in: Köhler/Bornkamm/Feddersen, UWG, § 4 UWG, para. 4.60, arguing that this finding cannot be upheld today.

goods or services free of charge and sales below costs.[242] In its current interpretation, general market obstruction is hence not focused on practices that influence consumers' decision-making.[243] It should, however, be noted that the category is disputed, and since it is not enshrined in the text of the law, many argue to abandon it completely exactly because of its potential overlap with competition law and the limited capabilities of civil proceedings to analyse market conditions and effects.[244] In particular, it is argued that an evaluation and prognosis of market effects can be carried out much better with the competencies and tools of a competition authority.[245]

As the example of general market obstruction shows, overlaps between competition law and fair trading law can occur. Competition law and fair trading law are largely understood as complementary sets of rules sharing the same objectives.[246] Because of the converging goals of the two regimes, there is no principled conflict between them.[247] Instead, fair trading law can provide indications regarding the evaluation of agreements also under competition law.[248]

4. Consumer protection vs competition law

A similar objection could be that consumer autonomy and preventing a race to the bottom competition should be a concern for consumer protection law rather than competition law.[249] And indeed, consumer protection law in many jurisdictions tries to address some of the issues mentioned above. In the European Union, drip pricing is illegal in many cases, for example.[250] However, there are sev-

---

[242] *Beater*, Unlauterer Wettbewerb, paras. 2284–2295; *Dreher/Kulka*, Wettbewerbs- und Kartellrecht, para. 494; *Heermann*, in: Münchener Kommentar Lauterkeitsrecht, B. Allgemeine Marktbehinderung, paras. 23–51; *Köhler*, in: Köhler/Bornkamm/Feddersen, UWG, § 4 UWG, para. 5.17.

[243] *Ohly*, in: Ohly/Sosnitza, § 4 UWG, IV. Anhang: Allgemeine Marktstörung, para. 4/96.

[244] *Heermann*, in: Münchener Kommentar Lauterkeitsrecht, B. Allgemeine Marktbehinderung, para. 2; *Köhler*, in: Köhler/Bornkamm/Feddersen, UWG, § 4 UWG, para. 5.2; *Ohly*, in: Ohly/Sosnitza, § 4 UWG, IV. Anhang: Allgemeine Marktstörung, para. 4/97; *Pichler*, Kartell- und Lauterkeitsrecht, pp. 341–349; for a retention *Beater*, Unlauterer Wettbewerb, paras. 2282–2283; see also *Dreher/Kulka*, Wettbewerbs- und Kartellrecht, para. 497 arguing that in any case competition law could be applicable at the same time.

[245] *Lux*, Allgemeine Marktbehinderung, pp. 376–380; *Heermann*, in: Münchener Kommentar Lauterkeitsrecht, B. Allgemeine Marktbehinderung, para. 8.

[246] *Albors-Llorens*, Yearbook of European Law 2014, 163 (176–177); *Drexl*, Wirtschaftliche Selbstbestimmung, p. 299; *Grewe*, Missbrauchsverbot, pp. 172–186; *Köhler*, in: Köhler/Bornkamm/Feddersen, UWG, Einleitung, para. 6.11; *Köhler*, WRP 2005, 645; *Pichler*, Kartell- und Lauterkeitsrecht, pp. 181–184; for a historical perspective, see *Glöckner*, Europäisches Lauterkeitsrecht, pp. 204–218.

[247] *Köhler*, in: Köhler/Bornkamm/Feddersen, UWG, Einleitung, para. 6.13.

[248] *Mestmäcker/Schweitzer*, Europäisches Wettbewerbsrecht, § 11, para. 105.

[249] In this direction *Ackermann*, NZKart 2016, 397; *Franck*, ZWeR 2016, 137.

[250] The Consumer Rights Directive, for example, in its Art. 22 requires the trader to seek the consumer's express consent – contrary to using default options – to any extra payment.

eral arguments that speak in favour of including the issue (also) in the realm of competition law.[251] The first is that antitrust law is typically more flexible than consumer protection law. Reacting to ever new obfuscation strategies by new consumer protection laws is not always feasible in terms of timing and effectiveness. Moreover, while consumer protection law typically prescribes certain positive or negative obligations, competition law can prevent market conditions that give companies the incentive to harm consumers' autonomy. In this regard, competition law can more effectively address subtle forms of influencing by preventing incentives to harm consumer autonomy in the first place. The second argument is a normative one. Competition law is concerned with the market structure rather than individual market participants. Where certain practices or agreements have the potential to effectively change the market structure and lead to a different market equilibrium, this must thus be a concern of competition law.[252] In such scenarios, about more than just an individual transaction with a sub-optimal outcome for an individual or a small number of consumers.[253]

Competition law also offers intervention opportunities that are less restrictive of the free market in that it typically does not prescribe positive obligations ("this is the information you have to provide")[254] but rather sets out negative rules of prohibited behaviour but leaves it to the market participants how to best comply. Take, for example, intermediaries such as consumer reports or comparison websites that aid consumers in their decision-making.[255] Preventing the exclusion of such intermediaries through vertical agreements (antitrust intervention) is a much less strong interference in the market as prescribing positive rules on how information must be presented to consumers. Moreover, addressing these issues through consumer protection law is more restrictive as competition law applies only where there is a potential exclusionary effect (including of noble rivals). It does not, as such, outlaw influencing the consumer's decision-making and using behaviourally informed advertising, marketing, or sales strategies.[256]

---

[251] See *Huffman/Heidtke*, William & Mary Policy Review 2012, 77 (105).

[252] *Cseres*, Competition Law and Consumer Protection, p. 408.

[253] This is the core concern of consumer protection law, see *Huffman*, European Competition Journal 2010, 7 (10).

[254] Moreover, it should be noted that mandated disclosure is criticized as a relatively ineffective way of consumer protection, see *Ben-Shahar/Schneider*, More Than You Wanted to Know.

[255] *Issacharoff*, JITE 2011, 56; *Patterson*, Antitrust Law in the New Economy, p. 161.

[256] Compare *Huffman/Heidtke*, William & Mary Policy Review 2012, 77 (90) making the argument that 'consumer-protection-based regulation is inherently disempowering' compared to antitrust law.

II. Developing a theory of harm based on consumer autonomy

The following paragraphs will develop a theory of harm that can potentially be applied to find a restriction of competition based on a vertical agreement's effects on consumers' decision-making. The goal is to define precise and workable criteria corresponding to the normative scope of competition law.

1. Diminish consumers' ability to make independent and informed decisions

Incorporating the notion of competition on the merits[257], the agreement must diminish consumers' ability to make independent and informed choices. This can take two distinct forms:

First, an agreement may incentivize the retailer to exploit consumer information gaps and not offer 'neutral' advice. One possible objection against this is that there is no objective or neutral advice. After all, behavioural economic insights teach us that choice architecture can never be truly neutral.[258] This, however, should not be used as an argument for a laissez-fare approach. Just because, for example, a retailer in presenting products to the consumer cannot *not* influence the consumer's decision, this does not give them an unlimited right to do so. Neutral advice must be understood from the consumer's perspective and expectations. The retailer, from this perspective, is neutral if they earn a relatively similar margin on the different items they sell.[259] Retailers typically have the incentive to push for the sale of a particular product where a limitation of intra-brand competition leads to a higher retailer margin for a specific manufacturer's products. Retail price maintenance is the most likely to have this result. Where a limitation of intra-brand competition goes together with direct requirements as to the services or quality, the retailer must provide, as typically the case for selective distribution, there is less risk of such incentives. The higher prices that come with such requirements are often consumed away by the higher costs which the retailer must incur to provide the services. Therefore, from this perspective, vertical agreements that do not lead to a higher retail margin, irrespective of the quality and services the retailer provides, will, in most cases, not be harmful.

Second, vertical agreements can directly affect the consumer's decision-making and complicate consumer decisions. This can apply to any interference with the retailer's 'choice information' and 'choice structure'. Choice information refers to the type and amount of information provided to consumers.[260] Choice structure refers to

---

[257] See above from p. 208.
[258] See *Thaler*, Nudge, p. 2.
[259] See above p. 181.
[260] *Competition and Markets Authority*, Online Choice Architecture, p. 20.

"how choices are structured, including which options consumers can or are likely to see, how cognitively challenging or time consuming it is to make a choice, how different options are ranked or presented, and what happens once a consumer has chosen."[261]

Finding the exact demarcations of what kind of influence is still permissible and what goes too far is a difficult exercise. Certain categories can, however, in principle, be identified. The first category of agreements covers agreements that violate other laws which are intended to protect consumers' decision-making, such as consumer protection laws or data protection laws. While competition law does not generally serve as an instrument to enforce other laws, because of the importance of independent and informed consumer decisions for the functioning of competition, rules that pursue to protect consumers' decision-making can serve as a benchmark for what does not constitute competition on the merits.[262] This category is in line with the Court of Justice's approach in Allianz Hungaria[263].[264] It was also relevant in the context of the Facebook decision where one of the elements to find that Facebook's behaviour did not constitute competition on the merits was a violation of data protection law.[265]

A second category of agreements could be those that lead to the exploitation of known biases in decision-making.[266] The Google Shopping[267] case, for example, may serve as a blueprint. The key question is whether the agreement decouples success in the market from active consumer decisions. In Google Shopping, the Commission established that Google Shopping's success was decoupled from consumer decisions based on an assessment that the ranking on Google leads to a higher click rate, largely irrespective of the relevance of the underlying website.[268] A similar analysis can be applied in offline contexts. For instance, empirical research could assess whether specific product placements in physical stores result in disproportionately higher sales, regardless of a product's intrinsic merits.[269] Where this is the case, an agreement facilitating such placement can be said

---

[261] *Competition and Markets Authority*, Online Choice Architecture, p. 17.

[262] See *Grewe*, Missbrauchsverbot, p. 142, arguing that such laws are relevant in the competition law analysis that are 'precondition for the functioning of the relevant market'; in the same direction *Glöckner*, Europäisches Lauterkeitsrecht, pp. 279–284; in the same direction *Lettl*, WuW 2016, 214; see also *Buiten*, Journal of Antitrust Enforcement 2021, 270, discussing data protection and competition law.

[263] See above p. 172.

[264] See also *Grewe*, Missbrauchsverbot, p. 179.

[265] See above from p. Error! Bookmark not defined..

[266] The term 'behavioural exploitation' for antitrust purposes has been coined by Huffman, see *Huffman*, Antitrust Law Journal 2012, 105 (141–144); *Huffman*, European Competition Journal 2010, 7 (16–17); *Huffman/Heidtke*, William & Mary Policy Review 2012, 77 (80).

[267] See above p. 170.

[268] European Commission, 27/06/2017, AT.39740 Google Shopping, paras. 454–501.

[269] Such conduct would typically not be covered by the law against unfair trading practices. The Unfair Commercial Practices Directive in its rectial 6 explicitly states that it does not affect "advertising and marketing practices, such as legitimate product placement, brand

to impair consumers' ability to make independent and informed decisions. The concerns regarding collusion with intermediaries are also relevant here.[270] Agreements that prevent a retailer, manufacturer, or third party from providing consumers with objective and relevant information fall into this category. While this does not prescribe positive obligations on anyone to provide information, actively preventing someone else from providing information relevant to consumers is not competition on the merits. This may apply, for example, if a retailer is restricted from cooperating with information intermediaries such as price comparison websites or search engines. More extreme examples could include agreements that prevent a retailer from informing the consumer about known defaults of a product or about the advantages of competing products.

Third, attempts to deliberately make comparisons across retailers more difficult for consumers may also fall under this criterion. The Toys 'R Us case[271] illustrates that vertical agreements between manufacturers and retailers about product differentiation can make price comparison more difficult across retailers.

2. Exclusionary effect

To find a restriction of competition, a market-wide effect must be established.[272] This can take the form of classical exclusion (a) or the exclusion of noble competitors (b).

a) Classical exclusion

Classical exclusion refers to a situation where competitors are excluded or markets are foreclosed. Where exclusion takes place through distorting or superseding consumer choices, it is not based on competition on the merits ('Leistungswettbewerb') and, thus, in principle, anti-competitive. This type of exclusion has been the core accusation in a number of recent competition law cases, mainly in the digital sector.[273] Most of them were abuse of dominance cases, but with Google/German Ministry of Health[274], there is also an example of a vertical agreement that led to the exclusion of competitors because it superseded consumer choices. Foreclosure or exclusion can occur both on the retail and the manu-

---

differentiation or the offering of incentives which may legitimately affect consumers' perceptions of products and influence their behaviour without impairing the consumer's ability to make an informed decision."

[270] See above p. 187.

[271] See above p. 192.

[272] See above from p. 212.

[273] Court of First Instance, 17/09/2007, Case T-201/04 Microsoft, ECLI:EU:T:2007:289; Landgericht München I, 10/02/2021, 37 O 15720/20 and 37 O 15721/20 Netdoktor/Google; Bundesgerichtshof, 23/06/2020, KVR 69/19 Facebook, GRUR 2020, 1318; European Commission, 27/06/2017, AT.39740 Google Shopping; *Podszun*, SSRN 2019.

[274] See the cases explained above from p. 168.

facturing level. Exclusion on the manufacturer level was a concern, for example, in the category captain case against Mars in the Netherlands or Conwood v. United States Tobacco in the US.[275] On the retail level, exclusion should matter only as far as the retail market as such is concerned rather than only competition among one manufacturer's retailers is limited. It would not amount to exclusion, for example, if a retailer cannot sell phones of brand A (for example, because of exclusive distribution) but can sell other brands. An example of exclusion on the retail level is the already-mentioned Toys 'R Us case.[276] By agreeing with manufacturers that they will only sell products which are difficult to compare regarding prices with similar products sold at Toys 'R Us to competing retailers, the company made the market entry on the retail level for toys (in general) more difficult. In cases of classical exclusion, the theory of harm suggested here can help to precisely identify the restriction of competition and the anti-competitive behaviour or agreement.

As previously discussed, a common reaction of rivals to such practices may be to adopt the same strategies themselves. In some instances, such imitation may indeed be the only way for a competitor to survive in the market.[277] Finding an exclusionary effect often involves assessing whether rivals can profitably replicate the alleged anti-competitive agreement or practice.[278] If they can, traditional notions of exclusion may not apply.

b) Exclusion of noble rivals

A novel element of the potential theory of harm suggested in this thesis concerns precisely this situation, i.e., the exclusion of 'noble rivals'. Where the agreement or conduct diminishes consumers' ability to make an independent and informed decision, replicability may *not* be considered positive. Quite the opposite is true: if competitors can replicate the conduct, there is a risk that this triggers a race to the bottom competition. Therefore, an agreement that has the objective or effect of diminishing consumers' ability to make independent and informed decisions, this may raise concerns if the only viable reaction of competitors is the adoption of similarly harmful practices. Whether this is the case or not depends on the specific market circumstances, particularly the participating undertakings' market position and how widespread similar agreements are. It should be noted that the concept of 'noble rivals' is purely fictional for the purposes of applying competition law. There is no need to show that any competitor had the noble intention

[275] See above p. 186.

[276] See above from p. 212.

[277] See above from p. 191.

[278] See Court of Justice, 12/05/2022, Case C-377/20 Servizio Elettrico Nazionale, ECLI: EU:C:2022:379, para. 82; Art. 82 Enforcement Priority Guidelines, para. 54; *Graham*, JECLAP 2014, 85 (86). It should be noted that this method to find exclusionary effect is typically applied in the context of Art. 102 TFEU. As a method to find an exclusionary effect, however, there appears no reason why it cannot be applied also in the context of Art. 101 TFEU.

of not adopting a similar practice. Just like for the as-efficient competitor test, the as-efficient competitor is purely hypothetical.[279]

3. Significant contribution to the exclusionary effect

A too-broad application of competition law risks condemning market participants for conduct that is essentially beyond their control. Even worse, it may lead to the exit of competitors from the market: if one powerful company engages in a practice that harms consumer autonomy and the competitors do *not* follow their example because of competition law concerns, they can be driven out of the market. Competition law, in this case, could unwillingly exacerbate exclusionary effects. Therefore, limiting factors must be found to identify the real 'villain' in such a scenario and distinguish them from the mere copiers. Here, the criteria established by the Court of Justice in Delimitis for exclusive contracts can serve as a blueprint: to find an undertaking liable under competition law for excluding competitors, it must significantly contribute to the exclusion of rivals.[280] An undertaking can, therefore, only be held liable if their conduct significantly contributes to either the classical exclusion of rivals or the exclusion of noble competitors. As often, this will depend mainly on the position in the market. Undertakings with only unimportant market positions will typically not be able to contribute to the exclusionary effect significantly. Parallels can also be drawn to the cumulative effects of vertical agreements for which the Commission considers that an individual supplier with a market share not exceeding 5% will generally not contribute significantly.[281]

III. Summary: a theory of harm based on consumer autonomy

To find a restriction of competition based on harms to consumer autonomy, three conditions need to be fulfilled:

First, the agreement must diminish consumers' ability to make independent and informed choices. An agreement can have this effect either by incentivizing retailers to exploit consumer information gaps and not offer neutral advice or by directly interfering with the retailer's choice information or structure, thereby directly affecting consumers' decision-making. This can include (1) agreements that violate other laws intended to protect consumers' decision-making, (2) agreements that lead to the exploitation of known biases in decision-making, (3) agreements that prevent retailers, manufacturers or third parties from providing objective and relevant information to consumers and (4) attempts to deliberately

---

[279] See General Court, 12/06/2014, Case T-286/09 Intel, ECLI:EU:T:2014:547, para. 30; European Commission, 13/05/2009, AT.37990 Intel, para. 1004; *Kellerbauer*, EuZW 2015, 261 (263).

[280] Court of Justice, 28/02/1991, C-234/89 Delimitis, ECLI:EU:C:1991:91, paras. 24–26.

[281] Vertical Guidelines, para. 156.

make comparison across retailers more difficult, for example, through retailer-specific product differentiation. The focal point of the assessment must be the consumers' functional role as arbiters in the competitive process. Therefore, the comparability of product attributes and prices, both inter- and intra-brand, is an important consideration.

Second, the agreement must have an exclusionary effect. This can either be understood in a traditional sense (driving competitors out of the market) or as the exclusion of 'noble rivals', that is, (hypothetical) competitors unwilling to copy the practice. For the latter case, a risk must be established that the agreement will likely lead to a new equilibrium in the market where nearly all competitors will adopt similar agreements.

Third, to find a vertical agreement restrictive of competition and hold individual companies liable on this basis, it must be established that the agreement in question significantly contributes to the exclusionary effect.

IV. Justification under Art. 101(3) TFEU

The theory of harm developed above does not, in principle, say anything about whether such agreements can be justified under Art. 101(3) TFEU, as it focuses only on the restriction of competition in the first place. Justifications would remain possible. As discussed above, the mere improvement of a product's image or dilution prevention should not be relevant here.[282] There can, however, be other valid business reasons, depending on the specific type of agreement. For example, product differentiation that makes price comparison across retailers harder could serve to accommodate space restrictions of a particular retailer (smaller stores and thus limited shelf space) or different customer needs (for example, city centre stores where customers are better served with smaller packs if they typically do not go there by car).[283]

§ 3 Implications for EU competition law

As discussed in Chapter 1, EU competition law when it comes to vertical agreements is criticised by economic literature.[284] This is true, particularly for selective distribution agreements and online sales restrictions. Selective distribution agreements under EU competition law are typically considered restrictions by object except where the Metro conditions are fulfilled. Similarly, hardcore restrictions (Art. 4 VBER) are typically considered restrictions of competition by object, notably restrictions that have the object of preventing the effective use of

[282] See above from p. 195.

[283] See *Richards et al.*, Review of Industrial Organization 2020, 859 (9–10).

[284] See above from p. 68.

the internet.[285] Qualifying an agreement as a restriction by object has far-reaching consequences for undertakings and thus deters them from entering into such agreements.[286] Chapter 2, however, has shown that the law on vertical agreements may not be based purely on economic considerations but that consumer autonomy as a goal may provide for an additional pathway to understand the EU's treatment of vertical agreements. Practices that risk influencing the market-wide outcome and harm consumer autonomy can, under this view, be anti-competitive for that reason. The previous sections have developed a theory of harm that would help to find a restriction of competition based on consumer autonomy. Against this background, the legal standard for finding a restriction of competition by object (I.) will be discussed to subsequently assess whether the Metro case law (II.), as well as the law on vertical agreements as applied to different variants of online sales bans (III.) can be justified when taking into account consumer autonomy as a normative concern.

I. Benchmark: the requirements to find a restriction of competition by object

The Court of Justice has defined restrictions by object as those that "can be regarded, by their very nature, as being injurious to the proper functioning of normal competition".[287] For an agreement to be considered a restriction by object, it is necessary that it "reveals in itself a sufficient degree of harm to competition."[288] Other formulations used by the Court of Justice are that the agreement must have a "sufficiently deleterious effect on competition"[289] or by its "very nature be injurious to the proper functioning of normal competition."[290] The most established restrictions of competition by object include hardcore cartels (such as price fixing, market division, output restrictions or bid rigging).[291] In the wBudapest Bank case, the Court of Justice has emphasized that restrictions of competition by object must be interpreted restrictively[292] and that agreements for which there are strong indications of procompetitive rationales cannot be consid-

[285] Vertical Guidelines, paras. 179, 203.

[286] See above from p. 23.

[287] Court of Justice, 12/12/2012, Case C-226/11 Expedia, ECLI:EU:C:2012:795, para. 37.

[288] Court of Justice, 11/09/2014, Case C-67/13 P Cartes Bancaires, ECLI:EU:C:2014:2204, para. 57.

[289] Court of Justice, 30/06/1966, Case 56–65 STN, ECLI:EU:C:1966:38, p. 249.

[290] Court of Justice, 13/03/2013, C-32/11 Allianz Hungaria, ECLI:EU:C:2013:160, para. 35.

[291] *Mestmäcker/Schweitzer*, Europäisches Wettbewerbsrecht§ 11, para. 25.

[292] Court of Justice, 02/04/2020, Case C-228/18 Budapest Bank, ECLI:EU:C:2020:265, para. 54; see also Court of Justice, 11/09/2014, Case C-67/13 P Cartes Bancaires, ECLI:EU:C:2014:2204; Maxima Latvija, 26/11/2015, Case C-345/14 Maxima Latvija, ECLI:EU:C:2015:784, para. 18.

ered a restriction of competition by object[293]. There must be "sufficiently reliable and robust experience" regarding the expected harms to find a restriction by object.[294] In the same vein, in the Generics judgment, the Court of Justice emphasized that procompetitive rationales brought forward by the party can play a role regarding the nature of an agreement as restriction of competition by object.[295] However, the possibility of procompetitive effects "cannot as such preclude characterisation as a 'restriction by object'."[296] Colomo takes the two judgments as an occasion to argue that neither selective distribution nor RPM agreements deserve to be treated as restrictions by object.[297] While the Generics and Budapest Bank judgments were concerned with horizontal agreements, the Court of Justice, in the subsequent Visma judgment, also emphasized the need for a rather strict approach in the context of vertical agreements finding that they are typically less harmful than horizontal agreements.[298] This was recently confirmed in Super Bock Bebidas where the Court of Justice held that to find an agreement (the case was concerned with a vertical resale price maintenance agreement) to constitute a restriction of object,

> "regard must be had to the content of its provisions, its objectives and the economic and legal context of which it forms a part. When determining that context, it is also necessary to take into consideration the nature of the goods or services affected, as well as the actual conditions of the functioning and structure of the market or markets in question".[299]

The strict approach towards what constitutes a restriction of competition by object raises the question of whether the current treatment of certain vertical agreements remains appropriate under the CJEU's own standard. This will be discussed in the following sections for selective distribution (Metro) and internet sales restrictions. The focus will be on the agreement's effects on consumers' decision-making, applying the abovementioned theory of harm. The main economic considerations have already been examined in Chapter 1: neither the treatment of selective distribution agreement outside the Metro exception as restrictions of competition by object nor the treatment of (certain) internet restrictions as restrictions by object are considered justified by economists.[300]

---

[293] Court of Justice, 02/04/2020, Case C-228/18 Budapest Bank, ECLI:EU:C:2020:265, para. 82.

[294] Court of Justice, 02/04/2020, Case C-228/18 Budapest Bank, ECLI:EU:C:2020:265, para. 76.

[295] Court of Justice, 30/01/2020, C-307/18 Generics, ECLI:EU:C:2020:52, para. 103.

[296] Court of Justice, 30/01/2020, C-307/18 Generics, ECLI:EU:C:2020:52, para. 106.

[297] *Ibáñez Colomo*, SSRN 2020.

[298] Court of Justice, 18/11/2021, Case C-306/20 Visma, ECLI:EU:C:2021:935, para. 61.

[299] Court of Justice, 29/06/2023, Case C-211/22 Super Bock Bebidas, ECLI:EU:C:2023:529, para. 35.

[300] See above from p. 68.

II. What to do with Metro?

This section will explore whether the Metro case law can be sustained in two respects: first, its implications as to when a selective distribution agreement is not considered a restriction of competition (cases that fall under the Metro exception). Second, its implications for selective distribution systems that do not fulfil the criteria for the Metro exception.

1. Cases that fall under the Metro exception

Where the Metro criteria are fulfilled, an agreement does not fall within the ambit of Art. 101(1) TFEU.[301] The Metro criteria are partly stricter than the exemption under the VBER.[302] In particular, the exemption applies only to qualitative and not to quantitative criteria. Moreover, it requires that the products in question necessitate the use of the selective distribution system and thus applies only to technically complex or luxury products. In contrast, under the VBER, qualitative and quantitative selective distribution agreements can be exempted, irrespective of the nature of the products. In one important aspect, however, the Metro exception is broader than the VBER as it applies irrespective of the companies' market shares. Thus, even firms with market shares that exceed 30 % can benefit from it.[303]

As explained in Chapter 1, the Metro exception's evaluation from an economic perspective is ambiguous.[304] On the one hand, it allows more flexibility to engage in vertical agreements, which is welcomed from an economic perspective. On the other hand, the Metro exception is uneconomic in that it applies without an analysis of the concrete effects of the agreement. Indeed, the most striking feature of the Metro exception is that it applies without regard to the participating undertakings' market positions. This can make the Metro exception potentially too broad, applying to scenarios with an actual foreclosure risk. This is, to some extent, counterbalanced by the fourth Metro criterion, which requires that other forms of distribution remain available in the market.[305] This criterion, however, is applied rather restrictively.[306] In the case Yves Saint Laurent, for example, the General Court did not consider the criterion fulfilled despite the fact that almost all manufacturers of luxury cosmetics engaged in similar selective distribution systems.[307] In this sense, the Metro exception seems to ignore one of the most important elements of every economic analysis, which is the companies'

---

301 See above from p. 25.

302 Compare *Monti*, World Competition 2013, 489 (493).

303 *Monti*, World Competition 2013, 489 (493).

304 See above from p. 69.

305 See above p. 33.

306 *Kirchhoff*, in: Handbuch Kartellrecht, § 11, para. 378.

307 Court of First Instance, 12/12/1996, Case T-19/92 LeClerc/Yves Saint Laurent, ECLI: EU:T:1996:190, para. 180.

market position. In this regard, the Metro case law risks being too broad and exempting agreements from the ambit of Art. 101(1) TFEU that restrict competition.

Let's examine whether considering consumer autonomy can justify the broad scope of the Metro exception. The theory of harm based on consumer autonomy developed in this thesis would typically not be applicable to agreements which fulfil the Metro requirements. The Metro exception hence appears narrow enough to ensure that no exclusion takes place through harming consumers' decision-making: qualitative selective distribution is unlikely to negatively influence the consumer, and the last Metro criterion (no widespread use of similar systems) ensures that no race to the bottom competition to the detriment of noble competitors occurs. If one were to look at consumer autonomy exclusively, hence, the Metro exception does not appear too broad. However, one must bear in mind that recognizing restrictions of competition based on consumer autonomy would not replace the traditional concepts of restrictions of competition based on merely economic or other consideration. They would instead serve as an additional pathway and do not exclude that restrictions can be found based on purely economic considerations. If Metro is too broad and risks exempting agreements that may restrict competition from a purely economic perspective, it remains flawed even when, purely from the perspective of consumer autonomy, it would not lead to an overly broad exemption.

2. Selective distribution where the Metro criteria are not fulfilled

While Metro does indeed lead to the exclusion of many agreements from the ambit of Art. 101(1) TFEU that will typically not be harmful (except for the abovementioned default that it disregards market power), it does not establish under which circumstances a selective distribution system which does *not* fulfil the criteria *restricts* competition. The Court of Justice considers selective distribution systems outside the Metro exception as restrictions of competition by object.[308] This is somewhat mitigated by the VBER, which exempts selective distribution agreements, in principle, irrespective of the fulfilment of the Metro criteria.[309]

From an economic perspective, selective distribution is considered efficiency-enhancing in most cases.[310] Horizontal concerns, the main concern from an economic perspective, are a relatively unlikely result of selective distribution systems. Thus, the categorization of selective distribution agreements, irrespective of the concrete facts of the case, as restrictions by object is unfounded from an economic perspective. The Vertical Guidelines also state that "where selective distribution is applied by only one supplier in the market, quantitative selective

[308] See above p. 28.
[309] See above from p. 25.
[310] See above from p. 69.

distribution generally does not lead to anti-competitive effects."[311] This appears to conflict somewhat with the Court of Justice's case law on selective distribution but is in line with the Court's most recent case law demanding a restrictive interpretation of restriction by object. In light of various procompetitive justifications for selective distribution and few theories of harm, one can hardly say that there is "sufficiently reliable and robust experience"[312] from an economic perspective as to the expected harms.

This finding leads to the question of whether the perspective of consumer autonomy, which played a significant role in shaping the case law,[313] may provide a justification for the treatment of selective distribution agreements as restriction of competition by object if they do not fulfil the Metro requirements. This question can be answered by applying the theory of harm developed above to selective distribution agreements which do not fulfil the Metro requirements. Agreements fall out of the Metro exception, for example, where they include quantitative selection criteria or where the product in question does not justify the use of a selective distribution system.

First, selective distribution systems that do not fulfil the Metro requirements can diminish consumers' ability to make informed and independent decisions. Especially quantitative selective distribution systems can give retailers the incentive not to give consumers neutral advice but to promote the products of a particular manufacturer.[314] Qualitative criteria can include informational restrictions, such as price comparison or (total) online bans. Other qualitative criteria, on the other hand, do not necessarily restrict consumer autonomy. This is the case, for example, for requirements regarding the presentation of a product (e.g., in a pleasant environment) as long as they do not interfere with the retailer's selection requirements relative to competitors' products (e.g., better placement than competitors).

Second, the exclusion of (noble) rivals is possible but not inherent to selective distribution. A single manufacturer using a selective distribution system, for example, will not necessarily lead to the exclusion of those competitors who don't do the same if they do not have a very strong position in the market. Where agreements do not fulfil the Metro criteria because they include either quantitative requirements or because the nature of the product does not 'require' selective distribution, this does not, as such, indicate any market-wide effect. This appears reasonably probable only where the agreement falls outside of the Metro exception because it does not fulfil the fourth Metro requirement (widespread use that forecloses other distribution systems).

---

[311] Vertical Guidelines, para. 153.

[312] Court of Justice, 02/04/2020, Case C-228/18 Budapest Bank, ECLI:EU:C:2020:265, para. 76.

[313] See above from p. 100.

[314] See above from p. 184.

Third, in many cases, there will be no significant contribution to the exclusionary effect (if there is one at all). This criterion again depends largely on the involved companies' market position. Because Metro disregards the market position, a selective distribution agreement that falls out of the Metro exception could be concluded between companies with high or with very low market shares or anything in between. For companies with low market shares, it appears unlikely that they significantly contribute to any exclusionary effect.

From the mere fact that an agreement does not fulfil the Metro requirements, it can thus not be concluded that it constitutes a restriction of competition based on the theory of harm developed above.

Therefore, both from an economic perspective[315] and from the perspective of consumer autonomy, the characterization of selective distribution agreements as restrictions by object is misguided and should be replaced by a more specific analysis for all selective distribution agreements to identify their competitive harm.

3. Conclusion: abandon Metro altogether

The Metro case law is both too broad and too narrow. It is too broad in that it applies irrespective of the participating undertakings' market positions and too narrow in that it stipulates that all selective distribution agreements that do not fulfil the Metro requirements are restrictions by object. It is neither founded in solid economic theory nor can it be justified by concerns for consumer autonomy. This speaks in favour of abandoning it altogether. The Court's approach in Metro can likely be explained by the fact that before Regulation 1/2003 came into force, the Commission had exclusive power to grant individual exceptions; it would have been impractical if all selective distribution agreements had to be notified to the Commission (as national courts and authorities were not competent).[316] This does not hold true anymore, so this original practical consideration does not justify the Metro exception. Hence, selective distribution systems that are not exempted under the VBER, like other vertical agreements, should be analysed on a more case-by-case basis.

III. Applying the theory of harm to online sales bans

"The information highway will extend the electronic marketplace and make it the ultimate go-between, the universal middleman. Often the only humans involved in a transaction will be the actual buyer and seller. All the goods for sale in the world will be available for you to examine, compare, and, often, customize. [...] Information about vendors and their products and services will be available to any computer connected to the highway. [...] This

[315] See *Szot/Amza*, YARS 2018, 241 (251).
[316] *De Faveri*, Global Antitrust Review 2014, 163 (176).

will carry us into a new world of low-friction, low-overhead capitalism, in which market information will be plentiful and transaction costs low. It will be a shopper's heaven."[317]

As Bill Gates's statement illustrates, at the turn of the 21st century there was tremendous enthusiasm for the internet, with the expectation that lower search costs would boost competition and benefit consumers. In continuation of this rhetoric, competition authorities have emphasized the benefits of e-commerce for the consumer in decisions regarding vertical agreements that limit online sales.[318] The argument behind is that online, consumers do not only find lower prices but are able to make a more informed decision through easier opportunities to compare offers, product characteristics etc., with the help of well-designed online stores and intermediaries such as third-party platforms and price comparison websites.[319] Considering consumer autonomy as a goal of competition law, looking at how bans on the internet raise consumer search costs and influence their decision-making is a legitimate consideration. However, the question arises whether it is justified that EU competition law currently (except if exempted in individual cases under Art. 101(3) TFEU) prohibits all total bans: no product whatsoever may, in principle, be reserved for pure offline sales.[320] As discussed above, vertical agreements that harm consumer autonomy may, in some instances, constitute a restriction of competition. However, competition authorities, in their stance on online sales restrictions, have not developed a convincing theory of why total bans restrict competition in the first place. The reasoning that the internet lowers search costs, therefore prohibiting online sales raises search costs and thus restricts competition, is insufficient. This argumentation neglects competition law's limited scope when it comes to protecting consumer autonomy, which may be concerned only with consumers' functional relationship with the market rather than protecting individual transactions.

This section will discuss whether the strict stance against online sales restrictions can be justified based on the theory of harm developed above. It will test whether and in which circumstances it appears likely that online sales restrictions fulfil the theory of harm (1.–4.). This will be followed by a conclusion (5.).

1. Total online bans

To recall: in the European Union, total online bans are considered restrictions by object[321] (no analysis of the effects required to find a restriction of competition) and hardcore restrictions[322] (no exemption under the VBER). From an economic

[317] *Gates*, The Road Ahead, p. 145.

[318] See above from p. 117.

[319] *Bundeskartellamt*, Vertical Restraints in the Internet Economy, p. 15; *Bundeskartellamt*, Wettbewerbsbeschränkungen im Internetvertrieb, p. 3.

[320] See above p. 35.

[321] Autorité de la Concurrence, 01/07/2019, Décision n° 19-D-14 Bikeurope, para. 82.

[322] Vertical Guidelines, para. 206.

viewpoint this is criticised. A relative laissez-faire approach to online sales bans is desirable because of their potentially efficiency-enhancing effects and the low risk of horizontal effects.[323] The following paragraphs will assess whether the treatment of online sales bans may be justified based on the theory of harm based on consumer autonomy developed above. The question addressed is not whether online bans can have efficiencies that could justify a restriction of competition but under what circumstances they may constitute a restriction of competition in the first place and whether, against this background, the treatment as by object restriction is appropriate.

a) Diminish consumers' ability to make independent and informed decisions

As a first step, it would have to be established that the agreement diminishes consumers' ability to make independent and informed decisions either by distorting retailers' incentives or by directly complicating consumer decisions.

The first question to be asked is whether a total ban incentivizes the retailer to exploit consumer information gaps and not offer neutral advice. As discussed above, retailers usually have the incentive to offer neutral advice.[324] This may change in the case of a total online ban because it reduces intra-brand competition. A total online ban makes it more difficult for consumers to buy the product somewhere else as they would have to go to another physical store rather than being able to simply order the product online. Shopping around and comparing prices becomes hence more costly. The retailer can hence earn an increased margin on the products covered by the total online ban compared to other products which are still available for sale online. However, the exact effect will depend on the specific characteristics of the markets and the products concerned.

To illustrate, consider the following example: producer P of lightbulbs agrees with their retailers on a total ban of online sales, so each retailer can only sell the lightbulbs in physical stores. Retailer R sells lightbulbs from different producers, some of which are also available online. If a consumer now shops for a lightbulb in R's physical store, they could check with their smartphone if a certain lightbulb is available online at a better price than in R's store. However, this won't be possible for lightbulbs produced by P since they are not available online. To compare prices of P-manufactured lightbulbs, the consumer would have to go to another physical store which sells them. Therefore, retailer R faces less (intra-brand) competition when it comes to lightbulbs of producer P compared to lightbulbs of other manufacturers (which are also available from other retailers online). Hence, R is likely to earn a higher margin for lightbulbs from producer P and has thus an interest in selling more of these compared to other producers' lightbulbs. R thus, at least from the outset, has an incentive in steering consumers towards lightbulbs from producer P, e.g., by giving them the best placement in

[323] See above from p. 75.
[324] See above from p. 180.

the store or by advising consumers that they have a better quality. However, the risk in this regard is rather low and depends on the specific circumstances of the market and the product. Since lightbulbs are relatively cheap products that make up only a small fraction of consumers' spending, it is improbable that many consumers compare lightbulb prices in-store with those of online competitors. Moreover, many people buy them spontaneously because a lightbulb in their house just broke. Hence, they do not want to wait for delivery. Therefore, the brick and mortar retailer of lightbulbs already faces only limited competition from online sales. Moreover, where offline retail competition is strong, the retailer will already have low margins. So, if many retailers sell P's lightbulbs offline (e.g., many supermarkets, smaller shops etc.), consumers can already easily switch between retailers. In this case, a ban of online sales for retailers would, in principle, not alter the retailer's incentives.

For other products, the picture might be different. Regarding more expensive products, which are thus more prone to comparison shopping[325], limited intra-brand competition due to an online sales ban could indeed alter retailers' incentives. One could imagine this, for example, for cars or computers or other more extensive purchase decisions[326]. Here, the purchase carries more economic weight for the consumer, so they are likelier to compare different offers, leading to greater price pressure on the retailer.

While bans on online sales, therefore can, in some circumstances, change retailers' incentives and reduce their neutrality, this is not always or even typically the case. Instead, it will depend on the specific circumstances of the case, such as the product's characteristics, the importance of online shopping and comparison for consumers of these products and the situation of the market. Intense competition among existing brick and mortar stores can already provide a sufficient check on retailers' margins to avoid altering their incentives. Therefore, the risk of changing incentives for retailers is low. Nevertheless, it remains a possibility for more expensive and search-intensive products.

The second question to be asked is whether a total ban reduces consumers' ability to make independent and informed decisions by removing information opportunities. For consumers, it is easier to compare competing offers and find information about products that are available online because search costs are typically considerably lower online.[327] The internet offers various tools to consumers that, in principle, allow for more informed decisions.[328]

A total online ban will hence typically reduce information opportunities for consumers. While some information on the product may still be available online

[325] *European Commission*, Study on Consumer Purchasing Behaviour in Europe, p. 5.

[326] See above p. 13.

[327] Bundeskartellamt, 26/08/2015, B2–98/11 ASICS, paras. 79–80; *Buccirossi*, Vertical Restraints for Online Sales, p. 17; *Lieber/Syverson*, in: Handbook of the Digital Economy, 191 (200).

[328] *Buccirossi*, Journal of Competition Law & Economics 2015, 747 (755).

(e.g. test reports), it will typically be more difficult to find information online about products that can be bought only offline. Customer reviews or alike will be available only to a much more limited extent, if at all. While consumers do not necessarily make better choices online, it is not disputed that search costs are lower and that the internet offers important advantages and tools such as comparison websites to make informed decisions.[329] Even less sophisticated consumers who do not make use of specialized websites have some tools for price comparison available in most online stores.[330] Many online stores offer price comparison tools, e.g., the option to sort the products by their price. By making use of this tool, the consumer herself can choose between a high (for example Prada.com in the category: gifts for women, a satin bag for 2.800 €)[331] or low (Prada gifts for women: 75 € for Prada candy eau de parfum)[332] anchor[333] price for their purchase decision. Many websites even allow one to explicitly select a price range. An online consumer could use the tools to avoid anchor heuristics, such as in the pool table example explained in the introduction,[334] by selecting the price range they are willing to pay in the first place (e.g., only to see pool tables that fall in a range between 500 and 700 $). Comparison tools are not limited to prices but can also include comparison matrixes of different products on a website. When shopping online, e.g., for a laptop, many websites offer the consumer to select different models and then list their specific attributes – such as processing power, operating system, working memory (RAM), hard disk space, energy consumption etc. – in direct comparison. Similar comparison tools exist for almost all products that can possibly be compared regarding their specific attributes and are widespread across most major online platforms but also specialized retailers. They facilitate comparison among different options while requiring relatively little cognitive effort, potentially allowing for more informed decisions.[335] Besides reducing anchoring effects, comparison tools may also lead to consumers being more active in their decision-making process. Consumers who are encouraged to compare the attributes of different options tend to make a more involved choice.[336] From a consumer autonomy perspective, having the ability to compare

[329] *Simonson/Rosen*, Absolute Value, p. 8; regarding the increased availability of information for consumers see also *Rezabakhsh et al.*, Journal of Consumer Policy 2006, 3; *Rajagopal et al.*, Consumers and Markets, pp. 185–186; and *Thierer et al.*, University of Miami Law Review 2015, 830 (855).

[330] *Simonson/Rosen*, Absolute Value, pp. 22, 40.

[331] https://www.prada.com/de/de/women/gifts/little_treasures.html#filters=sortBy_4 (accessed: 11 March 2025).

[332] https://www.prada.com/de/de/women/gifts/little_treasures.html#filters=sortBy_3 (accessed: 11 March 2025).

[333] For the anchor heuristic, see above p. 16.

[334] See above p. 16.

[335] *Haubl/Trifts*, Marketing Science 2000, 4.

[336] Compare *Dhar/Gorlin*, Journal of Consumer Psychology 2013, 528 (537).

offers both online *and* offline gives consumers the fullest set of information, empowering them to make independent, well-informed decisions.

The possible counterargument is that a total online ban may have a positive influence on consumers' decision-making where it leads retailers to offer better advice. After all, if the agreement had positive effects (better advice offline) and negative effects (higher search costs if the product is not available online), balancing between these would be necessary to find a net harm to consumer autonomy. This, indeed, would be a challenging exercise. However, the consumer themselves may carry out this balancing, deciding to shop online or offline, depending on their needs. If, absent any online ban, the consumer prefers shopping online, there is little reason to question this choice. This picture may change where there is a risk of free-riding on advisory services provided by brick and mortar stores. In the scenario where without a total ban, online stores would free-ride on brick and mortar advisory services, and this would lead to those stores *not* providing these services anymore, a total ban may improve consumers' decision-making capabilities. However, free-riding on advisory services is rather unlikely and can moreover be addressed under Art. 101(3) TFEU in cases where competition is restricted in the first place.[337] Further, even if total bans can induce additional advice, this will often do little on the inter-brand dimension and thus not help consumers decide among different brands but rather only aim at better advice within a given brand. In Pierre Fabre, for example, a requirement for the distributors was that they can

> "regularly and consistently give the consumer all information concerning the correct use of the products [...], give on-the-spot advice concerning sale of the [...] product that is best suited to the specific health or care matters raised with him or her, in particular those concerning the skin, hair and nails."[338]

While this appears to reveal that the manufacturer cared about informed consumers, this is not necessarily the case. It does not include advice concerning the relative benefits (and disadvantages) of Pierre Fabre products compared to other products or their price. In this case, moreover, the products could only be sold in the presence of a qualified pharmacist. This may have increased consumers' willingness to pay for such products because they associate cosmetic products with health products. In effect, the company may have been free-riding on state regulation designed for pharmaceuticals to impart an aura of medical sophistication

[337] The theory of harm developed in this thesis would, in principle, lead to a more effects-based analysis of vertical agreements and make away with the previous approach that a restriction of competition is often found due to the absence of an objective justification. Therefore, assessing the free-riding defence only under Art. 101(3) TFEU also means that in most cases, such an assessment would be obsolete due to the lack of restriction in the first place. This would likely have benefits from the perspective of procedural economy.

[338] Court of Justice, 13/10/2011, Case C-439/09 Pierre Fabre, ECLI:EU:C:2011:649, para. 11.

to its cosmetics. Had these products been freely available online, that aura – and the resulting price premium – would likely have been diminished.

Against this background, total online bans typically reduce information opportunities for consumers and increase their search costs. Therefore, the first condition of the consumer autonomy-based theory of harm will usually be satisfied for total online bans.

b) Exclusionary effect

As a second condition, it is necessary to establish an exclusionary effect either in the form of classic exclusion, e.g., through raising entry barriers, or in the form of the exclusion of (hypothetical) rivals not willing to copy the practice. The key element is to find an effect on the market as such.

First, a classical exclusionary effect through total internet bans is unlikely. While competing manufacturers might lose some sales offline if retailers push for those brands whose internet sales are restricted, they will typically be able to offset this through increased online sales. If one manufacturer's products are not for sale online, competitors can seize this opportunity and fulfil consumers' online demand by offering similar products online. This could even apply where the manufacturer who bans the sale of their products online has some degree of market power. In fact, restricting a brand's online availability can even create entry opportunities for rivals to capture unmet demand for online sales. That said, in some cases a total ban could raise inter-brand entry barriers. For example, if an incumbent's products account for the bulk of sales across many retailers, hose retailers may be unwilling to invest in an online presence unless they can also sell the incumbent's products – leaving new entrants struggling to find a suitable retailer to carry their products online. Entry without the ability to sell online is often more expensive, so entry barriers would be raised in such a scenario. Yet, a new competitor may also be able to enter the market by distributing the product through their own online store or a marketplace (e.g., Amazon). Where this is an option, exclusion appears rather unlikely. There could, however, be a risk of exclusion for products that consumers are unwilling to buy on platforms or from unknown online retailers, for example, because they require a high level of trust between retailers and consumers (credence goods).[339] Overall, the likelihood of classic, market-wide exclusion stemming from an online sales ban remains low.

Second, it must be assessed whether a total ban has the effect that competitors, to stay in the market, can only react by copying the practice, i.e., also banning their sales online. Such a dynamic may emerge when online bans are used to hide objectively comparable attributes and prices, making imitation of such bans a cheaper alternative to investing in genuine product or quality improvements.

[339] This could be the case for medicinal products, for example. However, for such products distribution is typically regulated so it is a rather hypothetical example.

However, it appears relatively unlikely that this will happen. To copy such a strategy, other manufacturers would have to forego internet sales which have become an important sales channel for many manufacturers. In effect, competitors would face a trade-off between sacrificing online sales and capturing higher margins offline. As a look at some of the cases on total bans decided in Europe reveals, it is indeed typically not the case that rivals react to online bans by adopting similar bans. In STIHL, concerning the distribution of garden equipment, other manufacturers continued to allow their products to be sold online.[340] The same is true for the CMA's Ping case[341]. Here, the golf equipment manufacturer Ping prohibited selling their golf cubs online. However, other manufacturers allowed online sales, including on their own websites or eBay, and there were even online-only specialist e-retailers for golf equipment.[342] The exclusion of noble or, for that matter, any competitor was not discussed by the CMA and, from the facts of the case, seemed not likely.

A case that looks more nuanced is Pierre Fabre.[343] In that case, certain luxury cosmetics could only be sold in the presence of a qualified pharmacist, thereby de facto prohibiting all online sales. This increased consumer search costs for Pierre Fabre products and made it more difficult for consumers to compare their quality and price attributes to those of competitors. Moreover, there was the risk of 'free-riding' on state regulation concerning the distribution of (regulated) pharmaceutical products, inducing a 'health is priceless heuristic'.[344] The exclusion of internet sales was material in this regard, as medicinal products were typically unavailable for sale online. The French competition authority, somewhat unfortunately for this research, defined the market as including only cosmetic products sold under the advice of a pharmacist.[345] In this narrowly defined market, unsurprisingly, few competitors allowed internet sales. Indeed, at the time the French competition authority implemented its decision, none of them had yet authorized internet sales. Therefore, it seems possible that noble competitors were potentially excluded in this case. Considering the facts of the case that pharmacies formerly held a monopoly for the sale of cosmetic products in France,[346] a possibility seems that the distribution system was based on an effort of pharmacies to maintain a de facto monopoly after their de jure monopoly had long expired. However, there was no investigation and discussion in this regard in the decision.

Ultimately, an exclusionary effect of internet bans appears rather unlikely both from a classical economic perspective and from the perspective of consumer autonomy (regarding noble competitors).

---

[340] Autorité de la Concurrence, 24/10/2018, Décision n° 18-D-23 STIHL, paras. 201–212.

[341] Competition and Markets Authority, 24/08/2017, Case 50230 Ping.

[342] Competition and Markets Authority, 24/08/2017, Case 50230 Ping, para. 3.20.

[343] Autorité de la Concurrence, 29/10/2008, Décision n° 08-D-25 Pierre Fabre.

[344] See in this regard also the case Vichy discussed above p. 106.

[345] Autorité de la Concurrence, 29/10/2008, Décision n° 08-D-25 Pierre Fabre, p. 34.

[346] Autorité de la Concurrence, 29/10/2008, Décision n° 08-D-25 Pierre Fabre, p. 8.

c) Significant contribution to the exclusionary effect

Moreover, to find an undertaking liable for a restriction of competition, it must significantly contribute to the exclusionary effect. For undertakings with only marginal market positions, such a contribution is highly improbable.

d) Conclusion: total bans should not constitute a restriction by object

From an economic standpoint, total online bans are often seen as efficiency-enhancing. Therefore, economists criticise the treatment of such restraints as by object restrictions without further analysis of their effects or considering the participating firms' market shares.[347] While this strict treatment may, in part, be motivated by concerns over consumer autonomy[348], such concerns, although they may be normatively relevant,[349] do not in themselves justify the per se categorization of total online bans as by object restrictions. It is true that such bans tend to raise consumers' search costs and make them more reliant on manufacturer-controlled information. However, they do not generally, or in most cases, produce exclusionary effects. This remains the case even under a broader concept of exclusion that includes the exclusion of competitors who refuse to engage in similar practices (i.e., 'noble' rivals). In practice, total online bans are often adopted by only a few manufacturers, while others continue to embrace online channels. This allows consumers who value online information and comparison tools to still benefit from them. Accordingly, a more nuanced assessment of total online bans compared to the current blanket treatment as by object restriction appears warranted.

2. Dual pricing

Under the updated Vertical Guidelines, dual pricing is not considered a hardcore restriction.[350] Consequently, dual pricing agreements will usually not be considered to constitute restrictions of competition by object. This section will analyse whether under the theory of harmed developed above, this treatment is appropriate.

a) Diminish consumers' ability to make informed and independent decisions

Again, the first step is to assess whether dual pricing leads either to adverse retailer incentives or to a diminished ability of consumers to make informed and independent decisions in any other way. Dual pricing affects retailer margins for offline versus online sales. Without dual pricing, retailer margins can potentially

---

[347] See above from p. 75.
[348] See above from p. 108.
[349] See Chapter 2, § 2 (from p. 121).
[350] See above p. 38.

be higher for online sales due to lower costs. Regarding retailer incentives, a distinction must be made between offline and online sales. For offline sales, dual pricing can have similar effects to total online sales bans, although the impact is generally smaller. Like a total internet ban, dual pricing reduces intra-brand price competition from online sellers, albeit without eliminating it entirely. A retailer who sells both products subject to dual pricing and products with unrestricted online sales may achieve a higher margin on the former. However, the effects will be less pronounced than those of total bans. Even total bans do not necessarily lead to adverse retailer incentives.[351] This applies a fortiori to dual pricing. Price competition between retailers as such is not eliminated. More efficient retailers online and offline can bring retailer margins down. When it comes to online sales, retailers' incentives are unlikely to change at all. Even when the retailer also sells products not subject to dual pricing at the same time, they will not typically have a higher margin on the products which are subject to dual pricing. If anything, dual pricing is likely to reduce retailer margins for online sales due to higher wholesale prices.

Dual pricing is also unlikely to impair consumer decision-making: it neither restricts retailers' ability to advertise or provide information, nor does it hinder third parties – such as platforms, price-comparison websites, or search engines – from doing so. A manufacturer, however, can use dual pricing to exclude online sales altogether by setting the wholesale price for products designated for online sales so high that online selling is de facto not possible.[352] In this scenario, dual pricing is nothing else than a total online ban and the reasoning outlined above applies.[353]

b) Exclusionary effect

Classical exclusionary effects appear rather unlikely for dual pricing. Even if dual pricing leads retailers to favor restricted items in their physical stores, competing manufacturers can typically recoup lost offline sales through increased online sales. Unlike total online bans, dual pricing does not diminish other manufacturers' ability to find online retailers willing to carry their products. While in the case of total bans, some retailers might not be willing to open an online store in the first place if they cannot sell the incumbent's products online, dual pricing still allows retailers to sell all products online. Therefore, it is less likely that retailers will refrain from opening online stores in the first place.

Similarly, the exclusion of noble competitors appears unlikely. Dual pricing typically has only a modest impact on retailer margins, so rival manufacturers can continue to reach consumers without adopting the same practice.

---

[351] See above p. 231.

[352] Vertical Guidelines, para. 209.

[353] See above from p. 230.

c) Significant contribution

Even when the first two conditions are met, it remains necessary to show that the agreement significantly contributes to the exclusionary effect. As with total online bans, this is only plausible for firms that hold an important market position.

d) Conclusion

Dual pricing appears unlikely to raise concerns under the consumer autonomy-based theory of harm. Accordingly, it is appropriate not to classify dual pricing agreements as restrictions of competition by object or hardcore restriction. The updated Vertical Guidelines[354] in this regard appear to have struck the right balance, both from an economic perspective as well as when considering consumer autonomy.

3. Price comparison bans

Price comparison websites are recognized in the Vertical Guidelines as a distinct online advertising channel,[355] and an outright ban on their use is treated as a "hardcore" restriction.[356] Only qualitative requirements "which do not directly or indirectly prevent the use of all price comparison services" can be exempted under the VBER.[357] Such qualitative requirements can include the prohibition of the use of "particular price comparison services".[358] According to the Bundeskartellamt, a total price comparison ban is a restriction by object, so no further analysis of the effects would be needed to condemn it as a restriction of competition.[359] As noted above, this approach is difficult to justify on economic grounds.[360] The following paragraphs will discuss under what circumstances price comparison bans can restrict competition based on the theory of harm suggested above and whether, on that basis, they should be treated as restrictions of competition by object.

a) Diminish consumers' ability to make independent and informed decisions

As a first step, it must be established that the agreement diminishes consumers' ability to make independent and informed decisions.

[354] See above p. 38.

[355] *European Commission*, Explanatory Note on the new VBER and Vertical Guidelines, para. 344.

[356] Vertical Guidelines, paras. 203, 347.

[357] Vertical Guidelines, para. 349.

[358] Vertical Guidelines, para. 206.

[359] Bundeskartellamt, 26/08/2015, B2–98/11 ASICS, paras. 244–272; upheld by Bundesgerichtshof, 12/12/2017, KVZ 41/17 ASICS, NZKART 2018, 96.

[360] See above from p. 78.

The first avenue here is limited intra-brand competition and, therefore, an incentive for retailers not to offer neutral advice. Typically, price comparison websites can lead to increased transparency in the market and therefore intensify price competition at the retail level.[361] Conversely, restrictions on their use have the opposite effect: they increase search costs and thus reduce price competition on the retail level.[362] In this regard, they can have effects similar to MAPs. A retailer that can offer lower prices, e.g., because they are more efficient, will be impaired in their ability to draw away consumers from other, potentially less efficient and more expensive retailers. Accordingly, a possible effect of bans on price comparison websites is reduced intra-brand competition and, therefore, higher relative retailer margins. A retailer that sells both, products subject to a price comparison ban and other products which are not subject to such ban, will typically earn a higher margin on the former. They have thus an incentive to sell more of the restricted items rather than other products. Hence, theoretically, the retailer could promote the product for which there is a price comparison ban. Unlike for total bans, the concern here is not so much related to the relative promotion in the retailer's brick and mortar store but rather to promotion within the retailer's online shop. They could, for example, give restricted products a better ranking in search queries on their website. However, the risk will depend on the concrete circumstances of the market, e.g., the availability of the product on large and known websites, the nature of the products (relatively high-priced items here still bear higher risks) and the combination with other restrictions. Platforms, for example, can to some extent substitute price comparison websites. In the US, 74 % of consumers that purchase online start with a product search on Amazon, irrespective of where they ultimately buy the product.[363] If a product is available on Amazon, consumers are quite likely to at least know about the Amazon price even when ultimately shopping somewhere else. Platforms can thus provide a certain check on the retailer's margin even where price comparison websites are banned for the product.

Undisputedly, however, price comparison bans increase consumer search costs. The CMA, in a market study on digital comparison tools, concluded that digital comparison tools "are mostly a force for good: they make it easier for people to shop around, and improve competition – which is a spur to lower prices, higher quality and efficiency."[364] When access to such services is prohibited for specific products, consumers can no longer easily locate alternative dis-

[361] Vertical Guidelines, para. 343.

[362] Vertical Guidelines, para. 347.

[363] *Berthiaume*, Chain Store Age, 26/05/2021, Study: Most Product Searches Begin on Amazon, available at https://chainstoreage.com/study-most-product-searches-begin-amazon; for slightly older figures, see *Competition and Markets Authority*, Online Search: Consumer and Firm Behaviour, p. 14.

[364] *Competition and Markets Authority*, Digital comparison tools market study, p. 5.

tributors of the same item or compare different products across brands.[365] Price comparison platforms serve both to identify multiple retailers for a given product and to facilitate category-wide searches. This additional information opportunity is taken away from consumers if price comparison websites are restricted. Hence, in most, if not all, cases, a total ban on price comparison websites will diminish consumers' information opportunities.

b) Exclusionary effect

As a second condition, there must be an exclusionary effect. This may be simply the potential exclusion of rivals (e.g., who are as efficient) or the exclusion of 'noble rivals'.

When it comes to bans on price comparison websites, traditional exclusion could occur foremost at the retail level. In particular for new or lesser-known retailers, visibility on comparison platforms is often essential to compete with established players.

Yet a single manufacturer's price comparison ban does not necessarily prevent the market entry of newcomers on the retailer level. Where inter-brand competition is high, such a retailer can potentially enter the market with another manufacturer's products. So, the assessment should take into account the level of both inter- and intra-brand competition. In general, exclusionary effects appear, therefore, possible but not a necessary or typical result of price comparison bans. Regarding inter-brand competition, (classic) exclusionary effects appear again relatively unlikely. This is because often competing manufacturers can engage in the same conduct. So where one manufacturer prevents the use of price comparison websites, other manufacturers can do the same. This reaction can chill overall competition without reducing the number of competitors on the inter-brand level. It may risk, however, the exclusion of noble rivals. Competitors not willing to engage in the same conduct may be excluded. Unlike a total online sales ban, a ban on price comparison websites does not hinder the ability to sell online as such. This means that a manufacturer does not forego as many sales as through a total online ban. Well-established brands might not depend on visibility on price comparison websites, particularly if manufacturers operate their own online stores. Overall, the risk of excluding noble rivals appears, therefore, relatively high for price comparison bans.

The German ASICS case may illustrate this point. The running shoe manufacturer ASICS prohibited, inter alia, the use of price comparison websites for their products. The market for running shoes is relatively concentrated, with the three biggest companies, ASICS, Adidas, and Nike, having a cumulated market share of 75 %. ASICS was the market leader with a 25–30 % market share.[366] The Bun-

[365] This was also emphasized by the Bundeskartellamt, see Bundeskartellamt, 26/08/2015, B2–98/11 ASICS, para. 15.

[366] Bundeskartellamt, 26/08/2015, B2–98/11 ASICS (Fallbericht), p. 4.

deskartellamt found a restriction of competition in the agreement, emphasizing that price comparison websites are of paramount importance for consumer search.[367] There was a reduction of consumers' information opportunities for ASICS products due to the vertical agreements: prices of different competitors could be compared less easily. This, according to the Bundeskartellamt, led to a reduction in intra- and inter-brand competition in particular because the other two big competitors (Nike and Adidas) had similar agreements in place.[368] Competitors without similar agreements would potentially have had difficulties surviving in the market as retailers would only earn low margins with the sale of their products. ASICS' conduct was even more harmful because it was part of a long-term strategy: initially, ASICS sold through all distribution channels without restrictions.[369] Only once its brand and name were established did the company restrict its distribution and made price comparison harder for consumers.[370]

c) Significant contribution to the exclusionary effect

Lastly, to find a particular vertical agreement to restrict competition in line with the Delimitis case law[371], this agreement must significantly contribute to the exclusionary effect. This contribution will depend on the structure of the market and the companies' market shares. In ASICS, for example, this requirement appears to have been fulfilled as ASICS had a relatively large market share and strong market position.

d) Conclusion: price comparison bans should not constitute a restriction by object

Price comparison website bans do pose some competitive risks regarding the comparability of products as well as adverse retailer incentives. However, their effects depend on the circumstances of the market. For example, a manufacturer restricting price comparison websites in the market entry phase is unlikely to exclude rivals. Against this background, a more nuanced treatment compared to the current treatment as by object restriction appears warranted also regarding price comparison bans.

4. Platform bans

Unlike price comparison website bans or total online bans, platform bans are not treated as hardcore restrictions in the Vertical Guidelines.[372] The Guidelines also consider restrictions on platforms as, in principle, compatible with the Metro

[367] Bundeskartellamt, 26/08/2015, B2–98/11 ASICS (Fallbericht), pp. 8–10.
[368] Bundeskartellamt, 26/08/2015, B2–98/11 ASICS (Fallbericht), p. 10.
[369] Bundeskartellamt, 26/08/2015, B2–98/11 ASICS, para. 51.
[370] Bundeskartellamt, 26/08/2015, B2–98/11 ASICS (Fallbericht), para. 26.
[371] See above p. 222.
[372] Vertical Guidelines, paras. 332–342.

criteria for selective distribution (thus not restricting competition in the first place) as long as they are proportionate and non-discriminatory.[373] In particular, a manufacturer may not appoint a platform as an authorised retailer but prohibit other retailers from selling their products on the same platform.[374] Outside of the Metro exception, the Guidelines see risks of anti-competitive effects of platform bans mainly where inter-brand competition is limited.[375] The Bundeskartellamt in ASICS, while not explicitly deciding on the matter, expressed a more suspicious view on platform bans.[376] It emphasized, inter alia, that consumers put particular trust in those online platforms and that platforms have a great reach that smaller or medium-sized retailers can barely compensate for.[377] The following paragraphs will assess platform bans under the theory of harm developed above.

a) Diminish consumers' ability to make independent and informed decisions

Platform bans can have effects similar to price comparison bans and total online bans on consumers' ability to make independent and informed decisions. First, they restrict intra-brand competition. Unlike in the case of price comparison bans or total online bans, this is not done so much by making comparison harder (although this effect can also occur because platforms offer valuable comparison tools and make it easy to find the cheapest vendor, at least on that specific platform)[378]. Instead, the effect is linked to limiting intra-brand competition by raising entry barriers for retailers. Selling online on platforms is an easy, fast and cheap way to enter the retail market in the first place.[379] Platforms are especially important for smaller retailers, which consumers often cannot easily find through search engines.[380] Moreover, many consumers have more trust in conducting a purchase through a platform rather than an unknown dealer.[381] Furthermore, platforms often provide rating systems for their vendors, so consumers can inform themselves about the vendor's previous performance, making purchasing from an unknown seller less risky.[382] Where platform bans are in place, existing large (non-platform) online retailers,[383] therefore, face limited competition for the sale of the covered products. This limited competition can lead to increased retail

[373] Vertical Guidelines, para. 338.

[374] Vertical Guidelines, para. 338.

[375] Vertical Guidelines, para. 341.

[376] Bundeskartellamt, 26/08/2015, B2–98/11 ASICS, paras. 40–47.

[377] Bundeskartellamt, 26/08/2015, B2–98/11 ASICS, paras. 41–42.

[378] Bundeskartellamt, 26/08/2015, B2–98/11 ASICS, para. 77.

[379] *Ezrachi*, World Competition 2017, 47 (50).

[380] Bundeskartellamt, 26/08/2015, B2–98/11 ASICS, para. 41.

[381] Bundeskartellamt, 26/08/2015, B2–98/11 ASICS, para. 92; *Ezrachi*, World Competition 2017, 47 (50).

[382] Bundeskartellamt, 26/08/2015, B2–98/11 ASICS, para. 92.

[383] There are, however, relatively few areas where this appears a realistic scenario as most large retailers are also platforms, Amazon being the most prominent example.

margins and give retailers adverse incentives to push for certain products irrespective of their merits. However, as for total online bans, this effect can be offset if intra-brand competition is strong for other reasons. It will thus depend on the product and the circumstances of the market. Besides the potential for adverse effects on retailers' incentives, platform bans also diminish consumers' information opportunities about a particular product. Platforms offer a unique opportunity for consumers to compare different retailers on the one hand and different products on the other hand.[384] Retailers can be easily compared by the price they offer but also regarding previous performances through customer ratings. This can increase intra-brand competition on the merits: retailers that can easily be compared on these dimensions have greater incentives to compete with low prices and good performance regarding delivery, after-sales services and return policies.[385] Products of different manufacturers can also easily be compared. Often platforms automatically offer a direct comparison of different products and their attributes.[386] Of course, this gives considerate influence to the platform as to which products are shown in these comparisons.[387] It is, therefore, an important task of competition authorities to ensure competition among platforms and combat adverse platform incentives.[388] Nevertheless, taking away the opportunity to use platforms from consumers will make obtaining information about the product and the retailer more difficult. Hence, consumers are more dependent on retailers' and manufacturers' potentially one-sided information policy, which can increase information asymmetries.[389]

Against this background, platform bans will typically diminish consumers' information opportunities. There is also an, albeit limited, risk of adverse retailer incentives due to limiting competition from platforms, especially for established online retailers.

b) Exclusionary effect

The next question that must be assessed is whether platform bans are likely to have an exclusionary effect. First, platform bans, as mentioned above, can raise barriers to entry on the intra-brand level. Where inter-brand competition is

---

[384] *Ezrachi*, World Competition 2017, 47 (46).

[385] Bundeskartellamt, 26/08/2015, B2–98/11 ASICS, para. 93; *Ezrachi*, World Competition 2017, 47 (46).

[386] This is the case, for example, on Amazon.com. On many technical products once one is selected and the consumer scrolls down the page, they see a number of comparable products and can directly compare their price and quality attributes.

[387] See *European Commission*, Behavioural study on the transparency of online platforms.

[388] Indeed, this is a concern that has been taken up recently in the Digital Markets Act which requires gatekeepers to not just not engage in self-preferencing but also to apply conditions that are transparent, fair and non-discriminatory (Art. 6 Nr. 5); see also above from p. 132.

[389] *Ezrachi*, World Competition 2017, 47 (51).

strong, this can be offset. If one manufacturer prevents the use of platforms, retailers can turn to other manufacturers' products. The main risk here seems to be widespread platform bans in a specific market by all or almost all manufacturers. If that occurs, the entry on the retail level will be difficult. Widespread platform bans can also influence entry on the inter-brand level. Retailers who earn high margins by selling restricted items might not be willing to take on new brands in their assortment where the new manufacturer cannot guarantee an equally high retailer margin. While a new manufacturer could theoretically distribute their products through online platforms, consumers might not be looking for this product category on platforms in the first place or will be reluctant to try a new brand without the ability to compare it with existing products. Conversely, when only a few manufacturers impose platform bans, the associated risks appear relatively low.

Second, platform bans can, in principle, also exclude noble rivals. A manufacturer who does not restrict platform sales has to face the problem that retailers within their own online shop (where they can also sell platform-restricted items) will prefer to sell restricted items. This can be an issue where retailer-operated online stores are an important online shopping channel for consumers and where it is difficult not to be represented on such a channel. Where platforms continue to play an important role, the manufacturer who does not restrict platform sales can compensate for this through a quantitative advantage on platform sales. Hence, where there are strong platforms which are used widely by consumers for certain products, it seems relatively unlikely that platform bans by individual manufacturers lead to the exclusion of (noble) rivals.

In the Coty case, for example, retailers of Coty luxury cosmetic products could not sell on third-party platforms such as Amazon but could sell online via their own online shop (provided that it fulfilled certain criteria). The OLG Frankfurt a.M., which had referred the preliminary questions to the Court of Justice, in its subsequent judgment[390], criticized the Court of Justice for not considering the importance of online marketplaces, particularly in Germany, where many retailers use online marketplaces.[391] This argument, however, rather seems to go in the opposite direction: because so many retailers sell through marketplaces, manufacturers who do not impose similar restrictions will be particularly attractive to retailers who value the ability to sell on marketplaces. The retailers are, therefore, more likely to provide a check on the manufacturers to impose such restrictions where marketplaces are widely used.

[390] OLG Frankfurt, 12/07/2018, 11 U 96/14 (KART) Coty, GRUR 2018, 1171, para. 71.

[391] See above p. 38.

c) Significant contribution to the exclusionary effect

As an additional criterion, it must be established that the agreement significantly contributes to the exclusionary effect. This will primarily depend on the involved companies' market position.

d) Conclusion: platform bans should not constitute a restriction by object

As with the other restraints on online sales discussed here, platform bans do not appear sufficiently harmful in general to be considered by object restrictions. As long as comparable competing products are available on platforms with a large reach, negative effects are unlikely. A simple test that would at least serve to assess the risk at a first quick look is to check whether comparable products are available on large platforms such as Amazon. Where that is the case, it appears rather unlikely that a platform ban will be harmful. Where platform sales are rare or, because of the introduction of platform bans throughout the market, have significantly declined, a closer look might be appropriate.

5. Online search advertising restrictions

Restrictions on online search advertising can, in principle, be exempted under the VBER.[392] The limit, however, is reached when the restriction prohibits the use of an entire online advertising channel. If a retailer can, for example, not advertise at all on Google, this is likely to constitute a hardcore restriction and restriction by object. This section will examine whether online search advertising restrictions are likely to restrict competition under the theory of harm developed above.

a) Diminish consumers' ability to make independent and informed decisions

First, online search restrictions can lead to adverse incentives for retailers. If retailers cannot advertise on search engines (or be found there at all), this will work in favour of well-known and established (online or offline) retailers who won't have to fear competition from less established retailers which consumers might not find.[393] Established retailers can thus earn higher margins on the covered products than on products of other manufacturers without such restrictions (and for which they hence face more intra-brand competition). Therefore, they have an incentive to steer consumers visiting their (online) store towards the products for which online search advertising is restricted. However, this effect may be limited if intra-brand competition is still vivid. In particular where only search advertising is restricted but price comparison through specialized price comparison websites remains possible, search advertising restrictions may have only limited influence on intra-brand competition. For products for which con-

[392] See above from p. 78.
[393] Vertical Guidelines, para. 29.

sumers often compare prices (e.g., large consumer electronics), price competition can remain strong even where search advertising is restricted. This can hence provide a check on established retailers' prices (and consequently their margins) for the relevant products. It also reduces the effects on the incentives to promote specific products over others because of higher retailer margins. The effects of online search restrictions on retailers' incentives will therefore depend on the specific characteristics of the product in question (e.g., high price v. low price items).

Second, online search restrictions can, in principle, remove information opportunities from consumers. However, this effect may be minimal. While it is true that consumers can use search engines as a starting point to inform themselves, online search advertising restrictions do not principally prevent consumers from informing themselves. Even where search advertising restrictions are in place, consumers can still find retailers through generic (i.e., non-paid) search results. Through such search engines, consumers will be able to find many retailers even where advertising is restricted. Moreover, where search advertising restrictions are not combined with other restrictions, consumers can inform themselves through platforms and price comparison websites. From this perspective, there is, therefore, only a low risk that consumer decisions are made significantly more difficult through online search restrictions.

b) Exclusionary effect

As a second condition it would ne to be assessed whether there can be exclusionary effects. This, too, seems quite unlikely in most scenarios. Suppose a manufacturer deprives their retailers of the ability to advertise through online search engines. In that case, retailers will earn a higher margin on this manufacturer's products, but this will come with the risk of a significant reduction in quantity (due to the difficulty of reaching consumers). Therefore, retailers will have an interest in nevertheless selling other manufacturers' products that are not restricted and for which they can reach consumers more easily. Exclusionary effects on the inter-brand level are thus unlikely. On the intra-brand level, retailers remain free to advertise on search engines for other products. Only where the restricted products are must-have items, or where a combination of several restrictive agreements makes it difficult for new retailers to be found, do the risks of exclusion or foreclosure become more pronounced.

Similarly, the exclusion of noble rivals in most cases does not appear to be a significant concern. Manufacturers who allow their retailers to advertise on search engines are likely to have a greater reach and, consequently, more sales than those who do not. Therefore, it seems unlikely that competitors who do not adopt online search restrictions would be unable to survive in the market.

c) Significant contribution to the exclusionary effect

Lastly, to find a restriction of competition, it must be established that the agreement in question significantly contributes to the exclusionary effect. Again, this will not be the case for every vertical agreement prohibiting online search advertising.

d) Conclusion: online search advertising restrictions should not constitute a restriction by object

Search engine restrictions that do not exclude the appearance in generic search results are unlikely to restrict competition. Risks can occur primarily when they are combined with other restrictions. Therefore, it appears appropriate that online search advertising restrictions are currently not treated as restrictions of competition by object. However, an even more lenient approach might be suitable for advertising restrictions even where they exclude an entire online advertising channel (e.g., a Google ban).

6. Conclusion

How a vertical agreement influences consumers' decision-making is an aspect that may be considered when evaluating whether or not it restricts competition. This is also true when it comes to restrictions on online sales, such as total bans, price comparison bans, platform bans or online search restrictions. Considering their potential impact on consumer autonomy, such agreements can in certain cases, have an anti-competitive effect by either potentially excluding rivals (in the traditional sense) or leading to a race to the bottom competition (exclusion of noble rivals). However, whether this effect occurs depends on the circumstances of the market. Hence, it does not appear appropriate to treat those agreements as restrictions of competition by object. The companies' market position should play an important role in evaluating those agreements. Currently, the treatment depends primarily on the agreement's content (e.g., does the agreement contain a total online ban or not?) rather than on the market conditions. None of the types of agreements analysed here appears sufficiently harmful under the theory of harm based on consumer autonomy that it warrants treatment as restrictions of competition by object. This section has just provided some initial indications as to the intuitive effects of online restrictions. This is not to exclude that more research and practical experience will give a different answer. However, at least currently, there is not enough evidence for treating these bans as restrictions of competition by object. In this regard the evaluation of the discussed agreements when considering consumer autonomy does not lead to a different result than their economic evaluation.

V. Outlook: market share-dependent by object restrictions?

At least the treatment of total online bans as restrictions of competition by object under EU competition law appears not fully aligned with economic theory, nor can it be justified when taking into account consumer autonomy. Hence, further reflections on how such agreements should be evaluated is warranted.

A first avenue may be to recur to an individual assessment irrespective of the type of agreement. This would also correspond to the demands of many economists.[394] However, it would face some of the same challenges of administrability and enforceability of the law that have been raised against such an approach.[395] Therefore, further formalisation appears desirable. One solution in this regard could be to formulate a new approach that combines the type of agreement with a market share requirement to define restrictions by object. A restriction by object would then be defined based on the type of agreement (e.g., internet ban) plus a market share requirement. There is no reason why the current approach to look at either the type of agreement (for hardcore restrictions) or (among other things) the market shares (for other agreements) cannot be combined.[396] Therefore, an approach could be to define a new category of restrictions with reference to a certain market share. (Total) internet bans could, for example, be considered prima facie restrictions where the parties' aggregate market share exceeds 15 %.[397] Depending on their likely effects, other types of agreements could be included with different market share thresholds. This approach could also provide more guidance and legal certainty regarding agreements currently not considered hardcore restrictions. There, too, a (higher) market share threshold could be introduced above which a certain type of agreement constitutes a prima facie restriction. This would respect that there are differences between different types of agreements, on the one hand, when looking at their effects on the consumers' decision-making, but also that most agreements are harmful only depending on the market position of the companies involved. Other market circumstances, such as the type of product in question, the number of competitors etc., would then not necessarily have to be assessed in each case. This new category – it could be called 'object plus restraints' – would fall between what is currently considered a restriction of competition by object and one by effect, although being closer to the first. The Court of Justice has, in some instances, interpreted the notions of competition by object and competition by effect fluidly and blurred their exact boundaries.[398] One may argue that these are not to be understood as allowing a

---

[394] See above p. 82.

[395] See above p. 83.

[396] For a similar suggestion regarding RPM, see *Overstreet*, RPM: Economic Theories and Empirical Evidence, p. 175.

[397] This would also lead to consistency with the De Minimis Notice, see De Minimis Notice, para. 8.

[398] See Court of Justice, 13/03/2013, C-32/11 Allianz Hungaria, ECLI:EU:C:2013:160,

binary distinction but instead stand for two poles of a spectrum; depending on the likelihood and extent of harm of an agreement, more or less analysis of other factors is required.[399] It is not inconceivable that on this spectrum, for certain types of agreements, the only additional necessary factor besides the type of agreement for the analysis is the companies' market shares.[400] This approach may strike the right balance between case-by-case justice on the one hand and practical enforceability and legal certainty on the other hand.[401] While the measurement of market shares is not trivial, it is a well-established exercise regularly conducted by competition authorities and courts, as well as firms, in their self-assessment.[402] It should, however, be noted that there is a debate about the usefulness of market shares as an indicator of market power in the first place.[403] Nevertheless, market shares continue to play an important role under EU competition law.[404] They can, to some extent, provide legal certainty to companies.[405] Already under the current framework, companies will hardly get around assessing their market shares when structuring their vertical relationships with other companies. It hence appears useful to continue relying on market shares to some extent.

Developing this new approach would entail two steps. First, it initially only refers to the question of whether there is a restriction of competition and thus the

---

paras. 34–51; Court of Justice, 11/09/2014, Case C-67/13 P Cartes Bancaires, ECLI:EU:C:2014:2204, paras. 48–87; Court of Justice, 18/11/2021, Case C-306/20 Visma, ECLI:EU:C:2021:935, paras. 50–82; *Hertfelder*, in: FS Möschel, 129 (137); *Ioannidou/Nowag*, European Competition Journal 2015, 340 (348–361); *Wolf*, NZKart 2015, 78 (81).

[399] See Court of Justice, 20/01/2016, Case C-373/14 P Toshiba, ECLI:EU:C:2016:26, para. 29 holding that 'in respect of such [market sharing] agreements, the analysis of the economic and legal context of which the practice forms part may thus be limited to what is strictly necessary in order to establish the existence of a restriction of competition by object.'; similar in Court of Justice, 27/04/2017, Case C-469/15 P FSL Holding, ECLI:EU:C:2017:308, para. 107 regarding price-fixing agreements; *Whish/Bailey*, Competition Law, pp. 130–131; *Wagner-von Papp*, in: Münchener Kommentar Wettbewerbsrecht, § 1GWB, para. 242.

[400] See also *Ioannidou/Nowag*, European Competition Journal 2015, 340 (363–366) suggesting a 'quick effects analysis' for minimum RPM that requires to show 'problematic nature or structure of the market'.

[401] This is one of the reasons for the existence of the 'per object' category, see General Advocate Kokott, 19/02/2009, Case C-8/08 T-Mobile Netherlands, ECLI:EU:C:2009:110, paras. 44–49; *Bailey*, CMLR 2012, 559 (566–570); *Whish/Bailey*, Competition Law, p. 126.

[402] Guidance can be found in the *European Commission*, Market Definition Notice.

[403] Critical towards the use of market shares *Kaplow*, Harvard Law Review 2017, 1303; *Kaplow*, International Journal of Industrial Organization 2015, 148; *Kaplow*, Harvard Law Review 2010, 437; *Landes/Posner*, Harvard Law Review 1981, 937; see also *Kerber/Schwalbe*, in: Münchener Kommentar Wettbewerbsrecht, 1. Teil Grundlagen, B. VII. pointing out the difficulties relating to a direct measurement of market power.

[404] See, for a list of areas where market shares are relevant *Whish/Bailey*, Competition Law, pp. 45–47; the Commission considers market shares to constitute, in principle, a useful indicator of market power, see Vertical Guidelines, para. 280.

[405] *Wurmnest*, Marktmacht und Verdrängungsmissbrauch, pp. 267–268.

interpretation of Art. 101(1) TFEU. The development would thus have to take place through case law and soft law instruments such as the Vertical Guidelines. Second, it would then have to be decided to what extent these agreements can be justified under Art. 101(3) TFEU and the VBER. The current classification as hardcore restrictions would not legally pose an obstacle to pursuing another approach towards what constitutes a restriction of competition by object.[406]

§ 4 Conclusion

[1] Vertical agreements can influence consumers' decision-making in various ways.

[2] First, they can lead to horizontal product differentiation (e.g., altering and creating the product's image) and reduce consumers' subconscious reflection. However, this should a priori not be a concern for competition law. The effects in this regard are ambiguous. It should thus matter neither to find a restriction of competition (Art. 101(1) TFEU) nor to justify a restriction found for other reasons (Art. 101(3) TFEU and VBER).

[3] Second, in some instances, vertical agreements can improve consumers' decisions when they lead to retailers providing better advice. In other instances, they can have negative effects on consumers' decision-making.

[4] Where there are negative effects, this can be one element to find a restriction of competition when considering consumer autonomy as a normative concern of EU competition law.

[5] However, competition law can be concerned with autonomy not for the sake of protecting individual consumer transactions but only to safeguard consumers' functional role as arbiters in the competitive process.

[6] Therefore, to find a restriction of competition, it cannot be sufficient that a vertical agreement can reduce consumer autonomy. It must further be established that it is likely to influence the market structure, either through classical exclusionary effects or through the exclusion of 'noble competitors'. 'Noble competitor' refers to a (hypothetical) competitor who is not willing to engage in the same practice.

[7] On this basis, a theory of harm is suggested to establish a restriction of competition based on concerns for consumer autonomy. This theory of harm would serve to make consumer autonomy a workable concept under EU competition law. Its conditions are the following:

(1) The agreement must diminish consumers' ability to make independent and informed choices,

---

[406] *Goyder*, JECLAP 2011, 327 (338) rightly points out that the Commission does not have the power to define 'by object' restrictions through Block Exemption Regulations in a legally binding way; see also *Bailey*, CMLR 2012, 559 (573); *Whish/Bailey*, Competition Law, p. 132.

(2) there must be an exclusionary effect understood in a broad sense that also encompasses the exclusion of 'noble rivals' who do not engage in similar practices, and

(3) the agreement must significantly contribute to the exclusionary effect.

[8] The emergence of the internet and online shopping has changed the way in which consumers make purchase decisions. It has, however, not necessarily made them more rational or less biased. Nevertheless, there is typically more information available, and search costs are lower for products which are available on the internet.

[9] Considering consumer autonomy as a goal of EU competition law does not in itself justify the strict approach towards online sales restrictions, particularly the treatment of total online bans as restriction of competition by object.

[10] Under the theory of harm suggested, online sales bans or other vertical agreements that regulate the retailer's ability to sell products online will not typically restrict competition. Instead, their impact on competition depends on the concrete market circumstances, particularly the widespread use of similar agreements and the participating undertakings' market position.

[11] In the long run, it may be fruitful to explore whether certain categories of agreement can be treated as 'by object plus' restraints, i.e., agreements that are considered restrictions by object only when certain market share thresholds are met.

Summary

I. Research question

This thesis has carried out to analyse the following research question: Can the treatment of vertical agreements, particularly concerning online sales restrictions, be justified based on a) economic considerations, and/or b) considerations of consumer autonomy?

This can be broken down into the following sub-questions:

(1) Are the current rules on vertical agreements concerning online sales restrictions aligned with economic theory?
(2) If not, can they be explained instead by a desire by courts and competition authorities to protect consumers' autonomous decision-making?
(3) Is consumer autonomy a valid normative concern that can be considered in the application of EU competition law?
(4) How can consumer autonomy, as a goal of competition law, be operationalized in the context of vertical agreements
(5) Can the rules on internet sales restrictions be justified when taking into account consumer autonomy in the analysis?

II. Current treatment of vertical agreements under EU competition law and its economic evaluation

1. The current legal treatment of vertical agreements remains, to some extent, form-based and does not in all cases clearly identify what constitutes a restriction of competition

EU competition law applied to vertical agreements is rather complex.[1] Vertical agreements can, in principle, constitute a restriction of competition under Art. 101(1) TFEU. There are, however, certain types of agreements for which the Court of Justice has developed an exemption from the ambit of Art. 101(1) TFEU. One example in this regard is selective distribution agreements under the

[1] See for an overview on the law above from p. 21.

Metro exception. Selective distribution agreements are held not to restrict competition in the first place where certain criteria are fulfilled.[2] In particular, resellers must be chosen based on objective and qualitative criteria which do not go beyond what is necessary. On the other hand, where these requirements are not fulfilled, the Court of Justice considers selective distribution agreements as restrictions of competition by object.

Where agreements restrict competition, they can be justified under Art. 101(3) TFEU and the Vertical Block Exemption Regulation ('VBER'). Art. 101(3) TFEU allows restrictions of competition which contribute to improving the production or distribution of goods or to promoting technical or economic progress while allowing consumers a fair share of the resulting benefits. The restriction must further be indispensable to the attainment of these objectives and must not eliminate competition in respect of a substantial part of the products in question. The VBER applies to agreements between undertakings whose respective market share does not exceed 30 %. It is then presumed that they generally lead to an improvement in production or distribution and allow consumers a fair share of the resulting benefits. However, the VBER does not apply to agreements containing so-called hardcore restrictions. For these, it is assumed that possible efficiencies do not outweigh the anticompetitive harms resulting from the agreement. Examples of hardcore restrictions include minimum RPM or territorial restrictions in exclusive distribution systems. Hardcore restrictions are also typically considered to constitute restrictions of competition by object. If a certain type of agreement is categorized as a restriction of competition by object, this has important consequences. First, no effects need to be established to find a restriction of competition. Second, the De Minimis Notice does not apply. Even agreements between undertakings with market shares below 15 % are therefore considered to appreciably restrict competition. Third, agreements that restrict competition by object typically do not fulfil the conditions of Art. 101(3) TFEU. Therefore, undertakings face high risks if they want to include those types of agreements in their vertical distribution arrangements.[3]

Recently, there has been a heated debate about the permissibility of restrictions on the sale of products over the internet. In this regard, EU competition law takes a rather strict stance. The current rules on internet sales restrictions[4] can be summarized as follows:

[1] Complete bans of online sales (total bans) cannot be exempted under the VBER and will typically be considered a restriction of competition by object, irrespective of the distribution system. Where they are part of selective distribution agreements, they are not exempted under the Metro case law either.

[2] See above from p. 25.

[3] See above from p. 23.

[4] See above from p. 34.

[2] Qualitative criteria on internet sales can benefit from the VBER. They must, however, not amount to a ban on an entire online advertising channel.
[3] Platform bans can, therefore, in principle, fall under the VBER and the Metro exception.
[4] Price comparison bans constitute a hardcore restriction and restriction of competition by object because they prevent the use of an entire online advertising channel. Qualitative criteria on online price comparison websites, however, can be permissible. The same is true for online search advertising restrictions.

Vertical agreements under EU competition law are still assessed to some extent based on the type of agreement (e.g., selective distribution, RPM, internet bans) rather than on its effects on the market.[5] From the current rules, it is relatively straightforward to identify agreements that either clearly do not restrict competition (e.g., selective distribution agreements where the Metro criteria are fulfilled) or are exempted under the VBER. There is, however, less guidance on when and why other agreements restrict competition. For certain types of agreements, including selective distribution agreements and internet sales restrictions, courts and competition authorities often merely assess whether there is an objective justification for the agreement and assume that where there is no such justification, the agreement restricts competition. The evaluation is thus based on either the existence or the lack of an objective justification, and it remains sometimes unclear why certain types of agreements are considered restrictions of competition (by object) in the first place. The argumentation that every vertical agreement restricts competition absent an objective justification pursued in a proportionate manner, however, is not satisfactory for the application of Art. 101 TFEU. This is also the case for agreements considered hardcore and by object restrictions. It is difficult to draw conclusions from the categorization as hardcore restriction (which is based mainly on efficiency considerations and does not always take into account how severely competition is restricted) regarding whether or not an agreement restricts competition in the first place.

2. Economic evaluation, based on consumer surplus, argues for a more case-by-case approach towards vertical agreements than currently applied under EU law

The EU's treatment of vertical agreements does not fully align with economic theory,[6] which predicts that they will often increase consumer surplus[7]. Vertical

---

[5] See above from p. 25.

[6] See above from p. 68.

[7] Consumer surplus is the difference between the benefits consumers derive from a good, as they themselves perceive it, expressed through their willingness (and ability) to pay and the price. See above from p. 44.

agreements, from an economic perspective, are expected to produce the efficient and appropriate level of services due to inter-brand competition: if consumers do not sufficiently value the services, which they are forced to pay for when buying a product whose retailer is bound by vertical agreements, they will simply move to another manufacturer's product. Furthermore, different types of agreements are seen as largely interchangeable. Therefore, the main argument to be distilled from economic literature is that vertical agreements should be evaluated based on their effects on the market, requiring a case-by-case approach. In particular, in the context of online sales restrictions, economists criticize the EU's approach as overly form-based, arguing that EU competition law protects online sales as a distribution channel without any economic justification. Besides theoretical economics, empirical evidence provides support for a case-by-case analysis of vertical agreements because it has not been able to conclusively show either that vertical agreements are enhancing consumer surplus in most cases or the opposite. The same is true for behavioural economic literature. While behavioural economics can help to better understand vertical agreements' effects on the market, no general conclusions can be drawn from it as to the consumer surplus-reducing or -increasing nature of certain types of restraints. The EU's approach also stands in contrast to the US regime, under which – based on a clear pursuit of solely economic goals – all vertical agreements are assessed on a case-by-case basis. Online sales restrictions are not treated as a distinct category under US antitrust law and are typically considered benign.

III. Consumer autonomy as another pathway to explain EU law on vertical agreements

1. Consumer autonomy may be an argumentative force behind the EU's approach to vertical agreements

Given the conflict with economic theory, this thesis has assessed whether EU competition law in the context of vertical agreements can be explained by the goal of protecting consumer autonomy. Consumer autonomy for the purpose of this thesis is understood as entailing:

(1) The (mental) capacities to form intentions and plan their execution, including some level of rationality; this includes factors such as sufficient information and time to make an informed choice; and
(2) independence of decision-making, in particular, freedom from coercion and manipulation.

If these conditions are fulfilled, the range of options provided by the marketplace can be considered 'adequate'.[8] This puts the consumers' decision-making and

[8] See above from p. 210.

how a vertical agreement affects it at the centre of the antitrust analysis. The Court of Justice has always been concerned with how vertical agreements affect consumers' decision-making.[9] On the one hand, the Court has accepted positive effects as an objective justification for vertical agreements. Preserving specialized retailers for the sake of better consumer advice, for example, was the reason for the development of the Metro exception for selective distribution. On the other hand, negative effects on the consumers' decision-making have played a role in determining whether a vertical agreement restricts competition. The Metro exception's limitation to qualitative rather than quantitative criteria, for example, can be explained by concerns for the consumer's decision-making. The limitation is motivated by the idea that retailers should be neutral marketers and not steer the consumer to the purchase of a particular product for reasons other than that it best fits their needs.[10] Most recently, consumer autonomy has become a centre of attention in the context of the debate on online sales restrictions.[11] Competition authorities have considered their effects on consumers' decision-making in their assessment. The Bundeskartellamt but also the Commission, and the French Competition Authority have emphasized that the internet lowers search costs for consumers as it allows easier price and product comparison and that, therefore, online sales bans restrict competition.

However, neither the Court nor competition authorities have developed a coherent theory of harm that allows distinguishing agreements that restrict competition from those that don't based on their effects on consumers' decision-making. The argument made in the context of online sales restrictions that search costs are lower for consumers on the internet so that no product, no matter how small the manufacturer's market shares are, can ever be prevented from being sold online is a good example thereof. It is indeed too simplistic because it neither considers any effects on the market nor does it sufficiently establish what the concrete harm is. While search costs are lower online, from an economic perspective, it is unclear whether state efforts to reduce search costs are welfare-enhancing.[12]

2. *Consumer autonomy can be a concern of EU competition law*

This thesis has argued that consumer autonomy may plausibly be considered a valid normative concern under EU competition law.[13] The relationship between consumer autonomy, competition and competition law can be described as dialectic: consumers, through their choices, play an important part in the competitive process, and their decisions are a substantial element of competition as a

[9] See above from p. 100.
[10] See above from p. 102.
[11] See above from p. 117.
[12] See above from p. 54.
[13] See above from p. 121.

coordinating process. Competition, on the one hand, serves consumers by providing them with a variety of choices. Competition law, on the other hand, protects competition. Because of the importance of consumer decisions for competition, it must also protect consumers' ability to independently make decisions. This dialectical relationship is reflected in EU competition law procedurally and substantively. Procedurally, the consumer, through their right to claim damages for breaches of competition law that affect her, acts as an agent for enforcing competition law.[14] Substantively, competition law protects consumers' autonomous decision-making to ensure the functioning of competition which in turn benefits consumers. Protecting consumer autonomy also aligns with the EU Treaties' broader goals and values, such as consumer protection and fundamental rights.[15] It also corresponds with the law's ordoliberal tradition and the material understanding of freedom of contract which prevails in the EU.[16]

When it comes to consumer welfare and consumer autonomy, these are not conflicting goals. However, there is a conflict of methods concerning consumer autonomy and the consumer welfare standard.[17] Protecting consumer autonomy would not conflict with *consumer welfare as a goal* as it is applied in EU competition law. EU competition law follows the ordoliberal non-dilemma thesis. Under this view, consumer welfare and protecting competition as a process are compatible with each other: if the competitive process and economic freedoms are protected, this will, at least in the long term, benefit consumers. Consumer welfare, understood in a relatively broad sense,[18] can then serve as a proxy for working competition. There is, however, no primacy of consumers' direct interests over competition as such. Even an effects-based approach, which requires looking at the effects of a practice or an agreement on competition, is compatible with this view. The key point is that the relevant effect that must be evaluated is the effect on the market (e.g., exclusionary effect, raising barriers to entry) rather than only on consumer surplus (e.g., higher prices or lower output). Following this approach, there is no conflict between pursuing consumer welfare goals and protecting consumer autonomy. On the one hand, consumer autonomy can be included in the consumer welfare goals. The ability to make autonomous decisions is an important aspect of consumer well-being and is closely linked to consumer choice. On the other hand, consumer autonomy can be understood as a precondition for making markets work and yield the desired results.

Conflicts can arise only when understanding *consumer welfare as a method* rather than simply as a goal. This understanding is the core of the so-called

[14] See above from p. 139.

[15] See above from p. 121.

[16] See above from p. 141.

[17] See above from p. 158.

[18] Consumer welfare in the EU is typically defined broadly, encompassing low prices, high output, innovation, and consumer choice, and is not limited to those elements of consumer well-being that can be quantified in monetary terms; see above p. 161.

consumer welfare standard.[19] Under the consumer welfare standard, a conduct or an agreement is ultimately evaluated based not on its effects on competition but directly on its impact on consumer welfare. Restriction of competition is then defined as a measurable reduction of consumer welfare, typically through higher prices or lower output due to assumed lower consumer surplus. The consumer welfare standard relies on the revealed preferences approach: any measurement of consumer welfare (defined as consumer surplus) rests on the assumption that consumers, through their consumption behaviour, i.e., the purchase of goods and services, reveal their true preferences. Therefore, the consumer welfare standard "links actions to choices, choices to preferences and preferences to welfare."[20] This prevents us from questioning consumer decisions under the consumer welfare standard. Why a consumer chooses to buy product B over product C does not matter. In contrast, protecting consumer autonomy would, in principle, ask exactly this question: do we believe that the consumer chose B over C based on an autonomous decision? Typically, the assumption that consumer decisions lead to an efficient allocation of resources is true. However, EU competition law, in principle, allows to take into account whether consumer decisions are not taken autonomously, for example, because firms exploit their behavioural biases.

IV. Making autonomy workable in the context of vertical agreements

1. How can vertical agreements influence consumer decisions?

Vertical agreements can influence consumers' decision-making in various ways.[21] Sometimes, they can improve consumers' decisions when they lead retailers to provide better advice. This will, however, typically be only the case for complex products for which outside information is difficult to obtain. In other instances, vertical agreements can have adverse effects on the consumer's decision-making. This is particularly the case where agreements incentivise the retailer to promote a manufacturer's products irrespective of their merits. Vertical agreements can also increase consumers' search costs through obfuscation agreements or informational restrictions that make information on products and prices more difficult for consumers to access and to compare. Examples here include bans on price comparison websites or search engine advertising. In principle, vertical agreements that give retailers an incentive to steer consumers towards the purchase of a particular manufacturer's products or that limit retailers' or third parties' ability to provide objective and relevant information about product attributes and

[19] See above p. 162.

[20] *Lianos*, in: Handbook European Competition Law, 1 (8).

[21] See above from p. 180.

prices to consumers can be a concern for competition law. One aspect of vertical agreements that has recently received a lot of attention is whether they can be justified if they serve to improve the product's image. A better product image under a consumer welfare standard is typically perceived as positive: if it leads to a higher willingness to pay, consumers *must* value it more and derive a greater surplus from purchasing it. From the perspective of consumer autonomy, the effects of image-enhancing vertical agreements are ambiguous. They can make products more distinct, which can sometimes help consumers to decide between different offerings as (perceived) differences are greater. At the same time, they can lock in consumers into a specific brand and make comparisons with other products more difficult due to artificial differences. Given these ambiguous effects, this thesis contends that a vertical agreement should not be condemned as anti-competitive *because* it has the goal or effect of horizontally differentiating brands or products. Where an agreement, however, restricts competition for other reasons, it should not be justified on this basis either. The manufacturer's desire to create a better image for their products and raise consumers' willingness to pay is, as such, not a valid justification for restrictions of competition, nor is it sufficient for finding such a restriction.

2. *When can influencing consumers constitute a restriction of competition?*

Where an agreement negatively impacts consumers' decision-making, this can be relevant to find that an agreement restricts competition. Yet, it is not sufficient that an agreement generates negative effects on consumers' decision-making. Additionally, the agreement must affect the market structure. Competition law is concerned only with aggregate consumer decisions rather than with individual transactions. It does not, in principle, try to prevent consumer mistakes or biases in general but can do so only where they risk influencing the market structure. This limited scope also distinguishes competition law from consumer protection law which purports to protect individual consumer transactions. Competition law would protect consumers' decision-making not for the sake of individual consumer transactions but for consumers' functional role as arbiters of the competitive process. Where a distortion of consumers' decision-making risks influencing the market structure, this can be a concern of competition law.[22] Such a market structure effect can be the erection of barriers to entry or the exclusion of competitors. Moreover, agreements or conduct that harm consumers' decision-making can have a market-wide effect where they force essentially all competitors to copy the same practice. It is true that at first sight, in this scenario, there is no exclusionary effect if competitors can survive in the market by adopting the same strategy, which adversely affects consumer decisions. However, competition law does not protect any type of competition but only competition on the merits[23],

---

[22] See above from p. 212.
[23] See above from p. 208.

i.e., competition in which consumer preferences are the "ultimate controlling force in the process of production."[24] Accepting practices that harm consumer autonomy but which are replicable by competitors (and thus do not exclude them) would mean accepting a form of competition that is nothing more than a race to the bottom. While competitors would not necessarily have to leave the market, competition would, in this case, nevertheless be distorted if firms did not have to invest in the merits of their products. Therefore, excluding rivals that do not engage in similar practices or agreements can be a concern for competition law. If the only possible reaction to a vertical agreement that leads to obfuscation or other harms to consumers' decision-making and thus deviates from competition on the merits is to copy the same agreement, this could then amount to the exclusion of those rivals that are 'noble' enough to not follow ('noble rivals'[25]).[26] What exactly constitutes competition on the merits in this regard is subject to interpretation by courts and competition authorities. The term is an indeterminate legal term which allows a constant update to new scientific evidence and, often relatedly, changing societal moral views.[27]

On this basis, this thesis has developed a theory of harm to assess whether a vertical agreement restricts competition based on its effect on consumer autonomy.[28] It has the following elements:

(1) The agreement must diminish consumers' ability to make independent and informed decisions either by incentivizing the retailer to not give neutral advice but push for the sales of a particular manufacturer's product (e.g., by guaranteeing the retailer a higher margin by shielding it from competition from other retailers) or by directly interfering with the retailer's choice context or the information provided by retailers or third parties (e.g., intermediaries);[29]
(2) there must be an exclusionary effect understood in a broad sense that also encompasses the exclusion of 'noble rivals' who do not engage in similar practices;[30] and
(3) the agreement must significantly contribute to the exclusionary effect[31].

[24] *Vanberg*, in: Competition Policy and the Economic Approach, 44 (56).
[25] The term 'noble' here is inspired by the concept of noble competition developed by *Stucke/Ezrachi*, Competition Overdose, pp. 255–292.
[26] See above from p. 212.
[27] See above from p. 218.
[28] See above from p. 218.
[29] See above from p. 218.
[30] See above from p. 220.
[31] See above from p. 222.

3. Implications for EU competition law

This thesis has investigated whether the EU's approach towards vertical agreements that restrict online sales can potentially be explained and justified based on the normative goal of consumer autonomy.[32] In particular, it questioned whether certain types of vertical agreements (total online bans, dual pricing, price comparison website bans, platform bans and online search advertising restrictions) constitute restrictions of competition by object. It did so against the background of how the internet and online shopping have changed how consumers make purchase decisions. There is typically more information available, and search costs are lower for products available on the internet. Yet, this is in itself insufficient to justify the EU's strict approach towards online sales restrictions, particularly the treatment of total bans as restrictions of competition by object.[33] Under the consumer-autonomy based theory of harm suggested in this thesis, online sales bans or other vertical agreements that regulate the retailer's ability to sell products online (e.g., price comparison or search advertising restrictions) will not typically restrict competition.

Considering autonomy, while it may constitute a valid normative concern, does not in itself justify the rules on internet sales restrictions under EU competition law. Instead, it provides support for a more case-by-case approach that focuses on the agreement's effect on the market. The strict and relatively formal approach towards vertical agreements, which are treated as hardcore restrictions, particularly online sales restrictions, should therefore be reconsidered.

Similarly, the Metro exception for selective distribution agreements should be reconsidered.[34] It is both too broad and too narrow. It is too broad in that it applies irrespective of the participating undertakings' market position and too narrow in that it stipulates that all selective distribution agreements which do not fulfil the Metro requirements are restrictions of competition by object. It is neither founded in solid economic theory nor can it be justified by concerns for consumer autonomy. While selective distribution agreements can influence consumer decisions, this does not have a market-wide effect in most cases.

While, in principle, a more case-by-case approach than currently applied appears thus appropriate, this can lead to problems of enforceability and predictability.[35] Therefore, some formalisation is nevertheless desirable. This formalisation, however, may be more granular than currently the case. A potential way forward could be to formulate a new approach that combines the type of agreement with a market share requirement to define restrictions of competition by object.[36] Total online bans, for example, could be considered restrictions of com-

---

[32] See above from p. 229.

[33] See above p. 237.

[34] See above from p. 226.

[35] See above from p. 83.

[36] See above from p. 249.

petition by object only where the involved companies' combined market shares exceed 15 %.

Bibliography

Achilles, Nastasia, Vom Homo Oeconomicus zum Differenzierten Verbraucher, Baden-Baden 2020

Ackermann, Thomas, Kartellrecht und Verbraucherschutz: Zur Notwendigkeit eines gemeinsamen Verbraucherleitbildes, in: Forschungsinstitut für Wirtschaftsverfassung und Wettbewerb (ed.), Herausforderungen für die Wettbewerbsordnung – Kartellrecht zwischen Industriepolitik und Verbraucherschutz, Köln 2013, 73–90

–, Kartellrecht und Verbraucherschutz, NZKart 2016, 397–398

Ackert, George R., Argument for Exempting Prestige Goods from the Per Se Ban on Resale Price Maintenance, Texas Law Review 1994, 1185–1222

Aghion, Philippe/Bolton, Patrick, Contracts as a Barrier to Entry, American Economic Review 1987, 388–401

Ahlert, Dieter/Kenning, Peter/Olbrich, Rainer/Grewe, Gundula/Schröder, Hendrik, Vielfalt durch Gestaltungsfreiheit im Wettbewerb: ein ökonomisches Manifest zur Deregulierung der Konsumgüterdistribution, Munich 2012

Akerlof, George A., The Market for 'Lemons': Quality Uncertainty and the Market Mechanism, Quarterly Journal of Economics 1970, 488–500

Akhtar, Zia, Resale Price Maintenance, Competition Law and the Identifiable Need for Flexibility in Vertical Restraints Index, EuCML 2018, 5–14

Akman, Pinar, Searching for the Long-Lost Soul of Article 82 EC, Oxford Journal of Legal Studies 2009, 267–303

Akman, Pinar/Kassim, Hussein, Myths and Myth-Making in the European Union: The Institutionalization and Interpretation of EU Competition Policy, JCMS 2010, 111–132

Albert, Max, The Behavioral Challenge to Normative Economics, in: Müller, Christian/Otter, Nils (eds.), Behavioral Economics und Wirtschaftspolitik, Stuttgart 2015, 3–28

Albors-Llorens, Albertina, Competition and Consumer Law in the European Union: Evolution and Convergence, Yearbook of European Law 2014, 163–193

Aldred, Jonathan, The Economic Rationale of Trade Marks: an Economist's Critique, in: Ginsburg, Jane C./Davis, Jennifer/Bently, Lionel (eds.), Trade Marks and Brands: An Interdisciplinary Critique, Cambridge 2008, 267–282

Alexander, Christian, Neue Transparenzanforderungen im Internet – Ergänzungen der UGP-RL durch den "New Deal for Consumers", WRP 2019, 1235–1241

American Bar Association, Vertical Restrictions Limiting Intrabrand Competition, Chicago 1977

Anderson, Simon P./Renault, Régis, Firm Pricing with Consumer Search, in: Corchón, Luis C/Marini, Marco A (eds.), Handbook of Game Theory and Industrial Organization, Volume II, Cheltenham 2018, 177–224

Andriychuk, Oles, The Dialectics of Competition Law: Sketching the Ordo-Austrian Approach to Antitrust, World Competition 2012, 355–384

Apelbaum, Eidan/Gerstner, Eitan/Naik, Prasad A., The Effects of Expert Quality Evaluation versus Brand Name on Price Premiums, Journal of Product & Brand Management 2003, 154–165

Areeda, Phillip/Hovenkamp, Herbert, Antitrust Law, Volume 8, 4th edition, Austin 2015

Asker, John/Bar-Isaac, Heski, Vertical Information Restraints: Pro- and Anticompetitive Impacts of Minimum-Advertised-Price Restrictions, Journal of Law & Economics 2020, 111–148

Atiyah, Patrick S., The Rise and Fall of Freedom of Contract, Oxford 1985

Autorité de la Concurrence, Opinion No 10-A-25 on 'Category Management' Agreements between Retail Grocery Operators and Some of the Suppliers thereof, Paris 2010, available at: https://www.autoritedelaconcurrence.fr/sites/default/files/attachments/2020-07/10a25_en.pdf (accessed: 11 March 2025)

–, Press release of 14/05/2013, The Autorité de la Concurrence fines Sanofi-Aventis, available at: https://www.autoritedelaconcurrence.fr/en/communiques-de-presse/autorite-de-la-concurrence-fines-sanofi-aventis-total-eu406-million (accessed: 11 March 2025)

Averitt, Neil W./Lande, Robert H., Consumer Sovereignty: A Unified Theory of Antitrust and Consumer Protection Law, Antitrust Law Journal 1997, 713–756

–, Using the 'Consumer Choice' Approach to Antitrust Law, Antitrust Law Journal 2007, 175–264

Backhaus, Klaus, Multivariate Analysemethoden: eine anwendungsorientierte Einführung, 16th edition, Wiesbaden 2021

Bailey, David, Restrictions of Competition by Object under Article 101 TFEU, CMLR 2012, 559–600

Baker, Jonathan B./Sallet, Jonathan/Scott Morton, Fiona, Unlocking Antitrust Enforcement, Yale Law Journal 2018, 1916–1920

Bar-Gill, Oren, Competition and Consumer Protection: A Behavioral Economics Account, NYU Law and Economics Research Paper 2011

–, Seduction by Contract: Law, Economics, and Psychology in Consumer Markets, Oxford 2012

Baumeister, Roy F., Yielding to Temptation: Self-Control Failure, Impulsive Purchasing, and Consumer Behavior, Journal of Consumer Research 2002, 670–676

Baye, Michael R./Morgan, John/Scholten, Patrick, Information, Search and Price Dispersion, in: Hendershott, Terrence (ed.), Handbook in Economics and Information Systems, Amsterdam 2006, 323–371

Beater, Axel, Unlauterer Wettbewerb, Tübingen 2011

Becker, Carsten, Bundeskartellamt und Verbraucherschutz, ZWeR 2018, 229–245

Behrens, Peter, The Ordoliberal Concept of 'Abuse' of a Dominant Position and its Impact on Article 102 TFEU, in: Podszun, Rupprecht/Di Porto, Fabiana (eds.), Abusive Practices in Competition Law, Cheltenham 2015, 5–25

–, The Consumer Choice Paradigm in German Ordoliberalism and its Impact on EU Competition Law, in: Nihoul, Paul/Charbit, Nicolas (eds.), Consumer Choice – A New Standard for Competition Law Analysis, New York 2016, 123–152

Benöhr, Iris, European Union Law and Consumer Rights, Oxford 2013

Ben-Shahar, Omri/Schneider, Carl, More Than You Wanted to Know: The Failure of Mandated Disclosure, Princeton 2014

van den Bergh, Roger, Vertical Restraints: The European Part of the Policy Failure, Antitrust Bulletin 2016, 167–185

van den Bergh, Roger/Camesasca, Peter D., Comparative Competition Law and Economics, Cheltenham 2017

Bernhard, Jochen, Die Geoblocking-Verordnung in der Praxis, NJW 2019, 472–476

Bernitz, Ulf, Brand Differentiation between Identical Products: An Analysis from a Consumer Law Viewpoint, Journal of Consumer Policy 1981, 21–38

Berthiaume, Dan, Chain Store Age, 26/05/2021, Study: Most Product Searches Begin on Amazon, available at: https://chainstoreage.com/study-most-product-searches-begin-amazon (accessed: 11 March 2025)

Biedenkopf, Kurt H., Vertragliche Wettbewerbsbeschränkung und Wirtschaftsverfassung: die Ausschliesslichkeitsbindung als Beispiel, Heidelberg 1958

Bishop, Simon, The Economics of EC Competition Law: Concepts, Application and Measurement, 3rd edition, London 2010

von Bogdandy, Armin, Grundprinzipien, in: Bogdandy, Armin/Bast, Jürgen (eds.), Europäisches Verfassungsrecht: Theoretische und dogmatische Grundzüge, Berlin, Heidelberg 2009, 13–71

Böhm, Franz, Wettbewerb und Monopolkampf: eine Untersuchung zur Frage des wirtschaftlichen Kampfrechts und zur Frage der rechtlichen Struktur der geltenden Wirtschaftsordnung, Berlin 1933

–, Die Ordnung der Wirtschaft als geschichtliche Aufgabe und rechtsschöpferische Leistung, Stuttgart 1937

–, Wirtschaftsordnung und Staatsverfassung, Tübingen 1950

–, Das Problem der privaten Macht (1928), in: Mestmäcker, Ernst-Joachim (ed.), Reden und Schriften über die Ordnung einer freien Gesellschaft, einer freien Wirtschaft und über die Wiedergutmachung, Karlsruhe 1960, 25–45

–, Democracy and Economic Power, in: Institut für ausländisches und internationales Wirtschaftsrecht Frankfurt am Main (ed.), Cartel and Monopoly in Modern Law, Karlsruhe 1961, 25–45

–, Freiheit und Ordnung in der Marktwirtschaft, ORDO 1971, 11–27

Bonanno, Giacomo/Vickers, John, Vertical Separation, Journal of Industrial Economics 1988, 257–265

Bordalo, Pedro/Gennaioli, Nicola/Shleifer, Andrei, Salience and Consumer Choice, Journal of Political Economy 2013, 803–843

–, Competition for Attention, Review of Economic Studies 2016, 481–513

Bork, Robert H., The Antitrust Paradox: A Policy at War with itself, New York 1978

Bork, Robert H./Sidak, J. Gregory, What does the Chicago School teach about Internet Search and the Antitrust Treatment of Google?, Journal of Competition Law & Economics 2012, 663–700

Botta, Marco/Wiedemann, Klaus, The Interaction of EU Competition, Consumer, and Data Protection Law in the Digital Economy: The Regulatory Dilemma in the Facebook Odyssey, Antitrust Bulletin 2019, 428–446

Botteman, Yves/Barrio, Daniel, From Pierre Fabre to Coty and Beyond: How far can Suppliers ban Online Sales?, JECLAP 2019, 519–531

Bowman, Ward S. Jr., Prerequisites and Effects of Resale Price Maintenance, University of Chicago Law Review 1954, 825–873

Boyle, Peter J./Kim, Hyoshin/Lathrop, E. Scott, The Relationship between Price and Quality in Durable Product Categories with Private Label Brands, Journal of Product & Brand Management 2018, 647–660

Bradford, Anu/Chilton, Adam/Lancieri, Filippo, The Chicago School's Limited Influence on International Antitrust, University of Chicago Law Review 2020, 297–329

Brauneck, Jens, Brauneck: Google: Missbrauch marktbeherrschender Stellung durch Suchmaschinenbetrieb?, GRUR Int. 2018, 103–110

Brodley, Joseph F., The Economic Goals of Antitrust: Efficiency, Consumer Welfare, and Technological Progress, NYU Law Review 1987, 1020–1053

Brömmelmeyer, Christoph, Selektive Vertriebssysteme und Marktplatzverbote für Luxusartikel, NZKart 2018, 62–69

Bronnenberg, Bart J./Dubé, Jean-Pierre/Gentzkow, Matthew/Shapiro, Jesse M., Do Pharmacists Buy Bayer? Informed Shoppers and the Brand Premium, Quarterly Journal of Economics 2015, 1669–1726

Brunell, Richard M., Overruling Dr. Miles: The Supreme Trade Commission in Action, Antitrust Bulletin 2007, 475–529

Bruns, Hendrik/Kantorowicz-Reznichenko, Elena/Klement, Katharina/Luistro Jonsson, Marijane/Rahali, Bilel, Can Nudges be Transparent and Yet Effective?, Journal of Economic Psychology 2018, 41–59

Buccirossi, Paolo, Vertical Restraints for Online Sales (Background Paper for the OECD Roundtable on Vertical Restraints for Online Sales), Paris 2013, available at: https://www.oecd.org/daf/competition/VerticalRestraintsForOnlineSales2013.pdf (accessed: 11 March 2025)

–, Vertical Restraints on E-commerce and Selective Distribution, Journal of Competition Law & Economics 2015, 747–773

Buch-Hansen, Hubert/Wigger, Angela, Revisiting 50 Yearsof Market-Making: The Neoliberal Transformation of European Competition Policy, Review of International Political Economy 2010, 20–44

Buettner, Thomas/Coscelli, Andrea/Vergé, Thibaud/Winter, Ralph A, An Economic Analysis of the Use of Selective Distribution by Luxury Goods Suppliers, European Competition Journal 2009, 201–226

–, Selective Distribution by Luxury Goods Suppliers: A Response to Kinsella Et Al, European Competition Journal 2009, 613–621

Buiten, Miriam Caroline, Exploitative Abuses in Digital Markets: between Competition Law and Data Protection Law, Journal of Antitrust Enforcement 2021, 270–288

Bundeskartellamt, A Bundeskartellamt/Competition Law Forum Debate on Reform of Article 82: A "Dialectic" on Competing Approaches, European Competition Journal 2006, 211–227

–, Vertical Restraints in the Internet Economy, Bonn 2013, available at: https://www.bundeskartellamt.de/SharedDocs/Publikation/EN/Diskussions_Hintergrundpapiere/Vertical%20Restraints%20in%20the%20Internet%20Economy.pdf?__blob=publicationFile&v=2 (accessed: 11 March 2025)

–, Wettbewerb und Verbraucherverhalten – Konflikt oder Gleichlauf zwischen Verbraucherschutz und Kartellrecht?, Bonn 2016, available at: https://www.bundeskartellamt.de/SharedDocs/Publikation/DE/Diskussions_Hintergrundpapier/AK_Kartellrecht_2016_Wettbewerb_und_Verbraucherverhalten.pdf;jsessionid=CCCF3CD75580AAA8A763EB4053DDD9D3.2_cid371?__blob=publicationFile&v=4 (accessed: 11 March 2025)

–, Wettbewerbsbeschränkungen im Internetvertrieb nach Coty und Asics – wie geht es weiter?, Bonn 2018, available at: https://www.bundeskartellamt.de/SharedDocs/Publikation/DE/Schriftenreihe_Digitales/Schriftenreihe_Digitales_4.pdf;jsessionid=2F9659DD12125374CFE5E0ACF63894D7.2_cid371?__blob=publicationFile&v=2 (accessed: 11 March 2025)

–, Sektoruntersuchung Vergleichsportale, Bonn 2019, available at: https://www.bundeskartellamt.de/SharedDocs/Publikation/DE/Sektoruntersuchungen/Sektoruntersuchung_Vergleichsportale_Bericht.pdf;jsessionid=9BB284C365F28A7D0E87E5745A4C3D52.2_cid362?__blob=publicationFile&v=7 (accessed: 11 March 2025)

–, Press release of 12/01/2022, Google News Showcase, available at: https://www.bundeskartellamt.de/SharedDocs/Meldung/EN/Pressemitteilungen/2022/12_01_2022_Google_News_Showcase.html (accessed: 11 March 2025)

–, Press release of 21/12/2022, Improvements for Publishers using Google News Showcase, available at: https://www.bundeskartellamt.de/SharedDocs/Meldung/EN/Pressemitteilungen/2022/21_12_2022_Google_News_Showcase.html?nn=3591568 (accessed: 11 March 2025)

Busch, Christoph, Mehr Fairness und Transparenz in der Plattformökonomie?, GRUR 2019, 788–796

Caffarra, Christina, Selective Distribution of Luxury Goods, in: Gheur, Charles/Petit, Nicolas (eds.), Vertical Restraints and Distribution Agreements under EU Competition Law, Brussels 2011, 55–78

Calliess, Christian/Ruffert, Matthias (eds.), EUV/AEUV, 6th edition, Munich 2022 (cited: *Author*, in: Calliess/Ruffert)

Canaris, Claus-Wilhelm, Wandlungen des Schuldvertragsrechts – Tendenzen zu seiner "Materialisierung", AcP 2000, 273–364

Carlin, Bruce I., Strategic Price Complexity in Retail Financial Markets, Journal of Financial Economics 2009, 278–287

Carlton, Dennis W./Chevalier, Judith A., Free Riding and Sales Strategies for the Internet, Journal of Industrial Economics 2001, 441–461

Carpenter, Gregory S./Glazer, Rashi/Nakamoto, Kent, Meaningful Brands from Meaningless Differentiation: The Dependence on Irrelevant Attributes, Journal of Marketing Research 1994, 339–350

Carstensen, Peter C., The Competitive Dynamics of Distribution Restraints: the Efficiency Versus the Rent-Seeking, Strategic Alternatives, Antitrust Law Journal 2001, 569–609

Caves, Richard E./Greene, David P., Brands' Quality Levels, Prices, and Advertising Outlays: Empirical Evidence on Signals and Information Costs, International Journal of Industrial Organization 1996, 29–52

Chamberlin, Edward H., Theory of Monopolistic Competition: A Re-Orientation of the Theory of Value, 8th edition, Cambridge 1962

Cheng, Thomas K., A Consumer Behavioral Approach to Resale Price Maintenance, Virginia Law & Business Review 2017, 1–82

Christiansen, Arndt/Kerber, Wolfgang, Competition Policy with Optimally Differentiated Rules Instead of 'Per Se Rules vs. Rule of Reason', Journal of Competition Law & Economics 2006, 215–244

Christodoulou, Kassiani/Holzwarth, Johannes, Die neue Vertikal-GVO: Das moderne Vertriebskartellrecht 3.0, NZKart 2022, 540–547

Colangelo, Giuseppe/Torti, Valerio, Selective Distribution and Online Marketplace Restrictions under EU Competition Rules after Coty Prestige, European Competition Journal 2018, 81–109

Colino, Sandra Marco, Vertical Agreements and Competition Law: A Comparative Study of the EU and US Regimes, Oxford 2010

–, The Antitrust F Word: Fairness Considerations in Competition Law, Journal of Business Law 2019, 329–345

Comanor, William S., Vertical Territorial and Customer Restrictions: White Motor and Its Aftermath, Harvard Law Review 1968, 1419–1438

–, Vertical Price-Fixing, Vertical Market Restrictions, and the New Antitrust Policy, Harvard Law Review 1985, 983–1002

–, The Two Economics of Vertical Restraints, Review of Industrial Organization 1990, 99–126

–, Leegin and its Progeny: Implications for Internet Commerce, Antitrust Bulletin 2013, 107–127

Comanor, William S./Rey, Patrick, Vertical Restraints and the Market Power of Large Distributors, Review of Industrial Organization 2000, 135–153

Compeau, Larry D./Lindsey-Mullikin, Joan/Grewal, Dhruv/Petty, Ross D., Consumers' Interpretations of the Semantic Phrases Found in Reference Price Advertisements, Journal of Consumer Affairs 2004, 178–187

Competition and Markets Authority, Online Search: Consumer and Firm Behaviour, London 2017, available at: https://assets.publishing.service.gov.uk/government/uploads/system/uploads/attachment_data/file/607077/online-search-literature-review-7-april-2017.pdf

–, Digital Comparison Tools Market Study: Final Report, London 2017, available at: https://www.gov.uk/cma-cases/digital-comparison-tools-market-study (accessed: 11 March 2025)

–, Online Choice Architecture – How Digital Design can Harm Competition and Consumers, London 2022, available at: https://www.gov.uk/government/publications/online-choice-architecture-how-digital-design-can-harm-competition-and-consumers (accessed: 11 March 2025)

Congiu, Luca/Moscati, Ivan, A Review of Nudges: Definitions, Justifications, Effectiveness, Journal of Economic Surveys 2022, 188–213

Cooper, James C./Froeb, Luke M./O'Brien, Dan/Vita, Michael G., Vertical Antitrust Policy as a Problem of Inference, International Journal of Industrial Organization 2005, 639–664

Crane, Daniel, Ordoliberalism and the Freiburg School, in: Crane, Daniel A./Hovenkamp, Herbert (eds.), The Making of Competition Policy: Legal and Economic Sources, Oxford 2013, 252–281

Crane, Daniel A., Brands and Market Power: a Bird's-eye View, in: Desai, Deven R./Lianos, Ioannis/Waller, Spencer Weber (eds.), Brands, Competition Law and IP, Cambridge 2015, 128–137

–, How Much Brandeis Do the Neo-Brandeisians Want?, Antitrust Bulletin 2019, 531–539

Cseres, Katalin J., Competition Law and Consumer Protection, The Hague 2005

Dahremöller, Carsten/Fels, Markus, Product Lines, Product Design, and Limited Attention, Journal of Economic Behavior & Organization 2015, 437–456

Daskalova, Victoria, Consumer Welfare in EU Competition Law: What is it (not) about?, Competition Law Review 2015, 133–162

Davis, Peter/Edwards-Warren, Kirsten, An Introduction to the Competitive Effects of Branding, in: Desai, Deven R./Lianos, Ioannis/Waller, Spencer Weber (eds.), Brands, Competition Law and IP, Cambridge, United Kingdom 2015, 13–24

Day, Gregory, Monopolizing Free Speech, Fordham Law Review 2020, 1315–1364

De Faveri, Christina, The Assessment of Selective Distribution Systems Post-Pierre Fabre, Global Antitrust Review 2014, 163–197

Deppe, Michael/Schwindt, Wolfram/Kugel, Harald/Plaßmann, Hilke/Kenning, Peter, Nonlinear Responses Within the Medial Prefrontal Cortex Reveal When Specific Implicit Information Influences Economic Decision Making, Journal of Neuroimaging 2005, 171–182

Dertwinkel-Kalt, Markus/Köster, Mats, Attention to Online Sales: The Role of Brand Image Concerns, Journal of Economics & Management Strategy 2022, 64–89

Desai, Deven R./Lianos, Ioannis/Waller, Spencer Weber (eds.), Brands, Competition Law and IP, Cambridge 2015

Desai, Deven R./Waller, Spencer Weber, Brands, Competition, and Antitrust Law, in: Desai, Deven R./Lianos, Ioannis/Waller, Spencer Weber (eds.), Brands, Competition Law and IP, Cambridge 2015, 75–112

Desai, Preyas S./Purohit, Devavrat/Zhou, Bo, The Effect of Slotting Allowances, in: Augier, Mie/Teece, David J. (eds.), The Palgrave Encyclopedia of Strategic Management, London 2018, 1572–1575

Deutscher, Elias/Makris, Stavros, Exploring the Ordoliberal Paradigm: The Competition-Democracy Nexus, Competition Law Review 2016, 181–214

Dhar, Ravi/Gorlin, Margarita, A Dual-system Framework to Understand Preference Construction Process in Choice, Journal of Consumer Psychology 2013, 528–542

Diamond, Peter A, A Model of Price Adjustment, Journal of Economic Theory 1971, 156–168

Dilbary, Shahar J., Famous Trademarks and the Rational Basis for Protecting Irrational Beliefs, George Mason Law Review 2006, 605–666

Dixit, Avinash/Norman, Victor, Advertising and Welfare, Bell Journal of Economics 1978, 1–17

Dolmans, Maurits, Sustainable Competition Policy, SSRN 2020, available at https://papers.ssrn.com/abstract=3608023

Döpper, Hendrik/MacKay, Alexander/Miller, Nathan/Stiebale, Joel, Rising Markups and the Role of Consumer Preferences, SSRN 2022, available at https://papers.ssrn.com/abstract=3939126

Dreher, Meinrad/Adam, Michael, The More Economic Approach to Art. 82 EC and the Legal Process, ZWeR 2006, 259–277

Dreher, Meinrad/Kulka, Michael, Wettbewerbs- und Kartellrecht: eine systematische Darstellung des deutschen und europäischen Rechts, 11th edition, Heidelberg 2021

Drexl, Josef, Die wirtschaftliche Selbstbestimmung des Verbrauchers: eine Studie zum Privat- und Wirtschaftsrecht unter Berücksichtigung gemeinschaftsrechtlicher Bezüge, Tübingen 1998

–, Wettbewerbsverfassung, in: Bogdandy, Armin/Bast, Jürgen (eds.), Europäisches Verfassungsrecht: Theoretische und dogmatische Grundzüge, Berlin, Heidelberg 2009, 905–958

–, On the (A)political Character of the Economic Approach to Competition Law, in: Drexl, Josef/Kerber, Wolfgang/Podszun, Rupprecht (eds.), Competition Policy and the Economic Approach: Foundations and Limitations, Cheltenham 2011, 311–336

Dreyer, Jan Joachim/Ahlenstiel, Enno, Plattformverbote außerhalb selektiver Vertriebssysteme, NZKart 2019, 130–135

Duivenvoorde, Bram, The Upcoming Changes in the Unfair Commercial Practices Directive: A Better Deal for Consumers?, EuCML 2019, 219–228

Dworkin, Ronald M., Is Wealth a Value?, Journal of Legal Studies 1980, 191–226

Eidenmüller, Horst, Die Rechtfertigung von Widerrufsrechten, AcP 2010, 67–104

Eilmansberger, Thomas, How to Distinguish Good from Bad Competition under Art. 82 EC, CMLR 2005, 129–177

Elhauge, Einer/Geradin, Damien, Global Competition Law and Economics, 2nd edition, Oxford 2011

Ellison, Glenn/Ellison, Sara Fisher, Search, Obfuscation, and Price Elasticities on the Internet, Econometrica 2009, 427–452

–, Search and Obfuscation in a Technologically Changing Retail Environment: Some Thoughts on Implications and Policy, Innovation Policy and the Economy 2018, 1–25

Ellison, Sara Fisher, Price Search and Obfuscation: an Overview of the Theory and Empirics, in: Basker, Emek (ed.), Handbook on the Economics of Retailing and Distribution, Cheltenham 2016, 287–305

Emde, Raimond, Qualitativ-selektive Vertriebssysteme und Internetvertrieb – mehr als ein Jahr nach 'Coty', ZVertriebsR 2019, 69–87

Enchelmaier, Stefan, Selective Distribution and the Internet: Lessons from Case C-439/09 Pierre Fabre Dermo-Cosmétique (13 October 2011), in: Surblytė, Gintarė (ed.), Competition on the Internet, Berlin, Heidelberg 2015, 5–23

Endler, Robert, Verbraucher im Kartellrecht, Tübingen 2021

Englerth, Markus/Towfigh, Emanuel V., § 8 – Verhaltensökonomik, in: Petersen, Niels/Towfigh, Emanuel V. (eds.), Ökonomische Methoden im Recht, Tübingen 2023, 217–248

Eucken, Walter, Wettbewerb, Monopol und Unternehmer, Bad Nauheim 1953

–, Grundsätze der Wirtschaftspolitik, 7th edition, Tübingen 2004

European Commission, Green Paper on Vertical Restraints, Brussels 1997, available at: https://europa.eu/documents/comm/green_papers/pdf/com96_721_en.pdf

–, Green Paper on European Union Consumer Protection, Brussels 2001, available at: https://eur-lex.europa.eu/legal-content/EN/TXT/PDF/?uri=CELEX:52001DC0531&from=DE

–, Online Services, including E-commerce, in the Single Market (Commission Staff Working Document), Brussels 2012, available at: https://eur-lex.europa.eu/legal-content/EN/TXT/?uri=CELEX%3A52011SC1641

–, Final Report on the E-commerce Sector Inquiry, Brussels 2017, available at: https://competition-policy.ec.europa.eu/system/files/2021-10/2017_ecommerce_SI_final_report_en.pdf

–, E-Commerce Sector Inquiry (Commission Staff Working Document), Brussels 2017, available at: https://eur-lex.europa.eu/legal-content/EN/TXT/?uri=CELEX%3A52017SC0154

–, Behavioural Study on the Transparency of Online Platforms: Final Report, Brussels 2018, available at: https://data.europa.eu/doi/10.2818/637090

–, Communication from the Commission to the European Parliament, the Council and the European Economic and Social Committee – A New Deal for Consumers, Brussels 2018, available at: https://eur-lex.europa.eu/legal-content/EN/TXT/?uri=CELEX%3A52018DC0183

–, Study on Consumer Purchasing Behaviour in Europe, Final Report (Support Study for the Evaluation of the VBER), Brussels 2020, available at: https://op.europa.eu/en/publication-detail/-/publication/93f52e95-a92e-11ea-bb7a-01aa75ed71a1/language-en

–, Support Studies for the Evaluation of the VBER: Final Report, Brussels 2020, available at: https://op.europa.eu/en/publication-detail/-/publication/93f52e95-a92e-11ea-bb7a-01aa75ed71a1/language-en

–, Evaluation of the Vertical Block Exemption Regulation (Commission Staff Working Document), 2020, available at: https://ec.europa.eu/competition/consultations/2018_vber/staff_working_document.pdf

–, New Consumer Agenda – Strengthening Consumer Resilience for sustainable Recovery, Brussels 2020, available at: https://eur-lex.europa.eu/legal-content/EN/TXT/?uri=CELEX%3A52020DC0696

–, Impact Assessment Report on the VBER and Vertical Guidelines (Commission Staff Working Document), Brussels 2022, available at: https://competition-policy.ec.europa.e

u/system/files/2022-07/20220510_revised_VBER_and_vertical_guidelines_impact_assessment_report.pdf
–, Explanatory Note on the new VBER and Vertical Guidelines, Brussels 2022, available at: https://competition-policy.ec.europa.eu/system/files/2022-05/explanatory_note_VBER_and_Guidelines_2022.pdf
–, Press Release of 10/10/2022, Commission sends Statement of Objections to Teva, available at: https://ec.europa.eu/commission/presscorner/detail/en/IP_22_6062
Eurostat, 12/2021, Digital Economy and Society Statistics – Households and Individuals, available at: https://ec.europa.eu/eurostat/statistics-explained/index.php?title=Digital_economy_and_society_statistics_-_households_and_individuals
–, 01/2022, E-Commerce Statistics for Individuals, available at: https://ec.europa.eu/eurostat/statistics-explained/index.php?title=E-commerce_statistics_for_individuals
–, 11/04/2022, Online Sales Efforts on the Rise due to the Pandemic, available at: https://ec.europa.eu/eurostat/web/products-eurostat-news/-/ddn-20220411-1
Ezrachi, Ariel, The Ripple Effects of Online Marketplace Bans, World Competition 2017, 47–65
Fabra, Natalia/Montero, Juan Pablo, Product Choice and Price Discrimination in Markets with Search Costs, C.E.P.R. Discussion Paper 2017, available at https://nfabra.uc3m.es/wp-content/uploads/2019/05/05_2019_Product-Lines_NEW.pdf
Fehr, Ernst/Wu, Keyu, Obfuscation in Competitive Markets, University of Zurich Working Paper Series 2021, available at https://papers.ssrn.com/abstract=3864205
Felser, Georg, Werbe- und Konsumentenpsychologie, 4th edition, Berlin, Heidelberg 2015
Festinger, Leon, A Theory of Cognitive Dissonance, Evanston 1957
Fikentscher, Wolfgang, Die Freiheit und ihr Paradox, Gräfeling 1997
Foer, Albert Allen/Durst, Arthur, The Multiple Goals of Antitrust, Antitrust Bulletin 2018, 494–508
Fornasier, Matteo, Freier Markt und zwingendes Vertragsrecht, Berlin 2013
Fox, Craig R./Poldruck, Russal A., Prospect Theory and the Brain, in: Glimcher, Paul W./Fehr, Ernst (eds.), Neuroeconomics: Decision Making and the Brain, 2nd edition, Amsterdam 2014, 533–567
Franck, Jens-Uwe, Zum Schutz des Produktimages im selektiven Vertrieb, WuW 2010, 772–786
–, Europäisches Absatzrecht, Berlin 2011
–, Eine Frage des Zusammenhangs: Marktbeherrschungsmissbrauch durch rechtswidrige Konditionen, ZWeR 2016, 137–164
Fried, Charles, Contract as Promise: A Theory of Contractual Obligation, 2nd edition, New York 2015
Fuchs, Andreas/Weitbrecht, Andreas (eds.), Handbuch Private Kartellrechtsdurchsetzung, Munich 2019 (cited: *Author*, in: Handbuch Private Kartellrechtsdurchsetzung)
Gabaix, Xavier/Laibson, David, Shrouded Attributes, Consumer Myopia, and Information Suppression in Competitive Markets, Quarterly Journal of Economics 2006, 505–540
Galbraith, John Kenneth, The Affluent Society, 3rd edition, London 1976
Gates, Bill, The Road Ahead, London 1995
Gavazza, Alessandro/Lizzeri, Alessandro, Chapter 6 – Frictions in Product Markets, in: Ho, Kate/Hortaçsu, Ali/Lizzeri, Alessandro (eds.), Handbook of Industrial Organization, Volume 4, Amsterdam 2021, 433–484
Gehrig, Thomas/Stenbacka, Rune, Price Discrimination, Competition and Antitrust, Swedish Competition Authority Pros and Cons Series 2005, available at https://www.resear

chgate.net/publication/252685898_Price_Discrimination_Competition_and_Antitrust (accessed: 11 March 2025)

Geiger, Niels, The Rise of Behavioral Economics: A Quantitative Assessment, Social Science History 2017, 555–583

Geiger, Rudolf/Khan, Daniel-Erasmus/Kotzur, Markus (eds.), EUV/AEUV, 7th edition, Munich 2023 (cited: *Author*, in: Geiger/Khan/Kotzur/Kirchmair, EUV/AEUV)

Geradin, Damien, The Uncertainties Created by Relying on the Vague 'Competition on the Merits' Standard in the Pharmaceutical Sector: The Italian Pfizer/Pharmacia Case, JECLAP 2014, 344–352

Geradin, Damien./Layne-Farrar, Anne/Petit, Nicolas, EU Competition Law and Economics, Oxford 2012

Geradin, Damien/Petit, Nicolas, Price Discrimination under EC Competition Law: another Antitrust Doctrine in Search of Limiting Principles?, Journal of Competition Law & Economics 2006, 479–531

Gerber, David J., Constitutionalizing the Economy: German Neo-Liberalism, Competition Law and the 'New' Europe, American Journal of Comparative Law 1994, 25–84

–, Law and Competition in Twentieth-Century Europe: Protecting Prometheus, Oxford 2001

–, Competition Law and Antitrust, Oxford 2020

Gerbrandy, Anna, Solving a Sustainability-Deficit in European Competition Law, World Competition 2017, 539–562

Gilbert, Richard, Looking for Mr. Schumpeter: Where Are We in the Competition-Innovation Debate?, Innovation Policy and the Economy 2006, 159–215

Giocoli, Nicola, Competition Versus Property Rights: American Antitrust Law, the Freiburg School, and the early years of European Competition Policy, Journal of Competition Law & Economics 2009, 747–786

Glick, Mark, The Unsound Theory Behind the Consumer (and Total) Welfare Goal in Antitrust, Antitrust Bulletin 2018, 455–493

Glöckner, Jochen, Europäisches Lauterkeitsrecht, Munich 2006

Gormsen, Liza Lovdahl, The Conflict Between Economic Freedom and Consumer Welfare in the Modernisation of Article 82 EC, European Competition Journal 2007, 329–344

Goyder, Joanna, Cet Obscur Objet: Object Restrictions in Vertical Agreements, JECLAP 2011, 327–339

Graef, Inge, Consumer Sovereignty and Competition Law: From Personalization to Diversity, CMLR 2021, 471–504

Graham, Ben, Retail Markets: Assessing Whether Incentivized Category Management is Compatible with Competition Laws (The Netherlands), JECLAP 2014, 85–87

Grewe, Max, Missbrauchsverbot als Durchsetzungsinstrument: eine Untersuchung der Schnittstellen des Kartellrechts mit dem Datenschutz-, Lauterkeits- und AGB-Recht, Baden-Baden 2020

Griffiths, Andrew, A Law-and-Economics Perspective on Trade Marks, in: Ginsburg, Jane C./Davis, Jennifer/Bently, Lionel (eds.), Trade Marks and Brands: An Interdisciplinary Critique, Cambridge 2008, 241–266

Grimes, Warren S., The Seven Myths of Vertical Price Fixing: The Politics and Economics of a Century-Long Debate Antitrust Symposium: Vertical Restraints in the 1990's, Southwestern University Law Review 1992, 1285–1316

–, Spiff, Polish, and Consumer Demand Quality: Vertical Price Restraints Revisited, California Law Review 1992, 815–855

–, Antitrust Tie-In Analysis After 'Kodak': Understanding the Role of Market Imperfections, Antitrust Law Journal 1994, 263–325

–, Brand Marketing, Intrabrand Competition, and the Multibrand Retailer: The Antitrust Law of Vertical Restraints, Antitrust Law Journal 1995, 83–136

–, A Dynamic Analysis of Resale Price Maintenance: Inefficient Brand Promotion, Higher Margins, Distorted Choices, and Retarded Retailer Innovation, Antitrust Bulletin 2010, 101–149

–, The Two Sides of Brand Marketing: Reconsidering Competition Law Governing Distribution Restraints, in: Desai, Deven R./Lianos, Ioannis/Waller, Spencer Weber (eds.), Brands, Competition Law and IP, Cambridge 2015, 138–145

–, Adam Smith, the Competitive Process, and the Flawed Consumer Welfare Standard, GRUR International 2020, 3–13

von der Groeben, Hans/Schwarze, Jürgen/Hatje, Armin (eds.), Europäisches Unionsrecht, 7th edition, Baden-Baden 2015 (cited: *Author*, in: von der Groeben/Schwarze, Europäisches Unionsrecht)

Gröner, Helmut, Walter Eucken – Wegbereiter der Ordnungspolitik, in: Ordnung in Freiheit: Symposium aus Anlaß des 100. Jahrestages des Geburtstages von Walter Eucken, Tübingen 1992, 79–88

Grubb, Michael D., Behavioral Consumers in Industrial Organization: An Overview, Review of Industrial Organization 2015, 247–258

Grunewald, Barbara/Peifer, Karl-Nikolaus, Verbraucherschutz im Zivilrecht, Berlin, Heidelberg 2010

Gyselen, Luc, Vertical Restraints in the Distribution Process: Strength and Weakness of the Free Rider Rationale under EEC Competition Law, CMLR 1984, 647–668

Habersack, Mathias, Richtigkeitsgewähr notariell beurkundeter Verträge, AcP 1989, 403–424

Hacker, Philipp, Verhaltensökonomik und Normativität, Tübingen 2017

Hamilton, Stephen F./Liaukonyte, Jura/Richards, Timothy J., Pricing Strategies of Food Retailers, Annual Review of Resource Economics 2020, 87–110

Hanson, Jon D./Kysar, Douglas A., Taking Behavioralism Seriously: Some Evidence of Market Manipulation, Harvard Law Review 1999, 1420–1572

Hanson, Jon D/Kysar, Douglas A, Taking Behavioralism Seriously: The Problem of Market Manipulation, NYU Law Review 2000, 630–749

Haubl, Gerald/Trifts, Valerie, Consumer Decision Making in Online Shopping Environments: The effects of Interactive Decision Aids, Marketing Science 2000, 4–21

Hawk, Barry E., System Failure; Vertical Restraints and EC Competition Law, CMLR 1995, 973–939

Hayek, Friedrich A., The Use of Knowledge in Society, American Economic Review 1945, 519–530

–, The Pretence of Knowledge (Nobel Prize Lecture), Stockholm 1974, available at: https://EconPapers.repec.org/RePEc:ris:nobelp:1974_002

–, 'Freie Wirtschaft' und Wettbewerbsordnung, in: Hayek, Friedrich A. (ed.), Individualismus und wirtschaftliche Ordnung, 2nd edition, Salzburg 1976, 141–155

–, Die Verfassung der Freiheit, 2nd edition, Tübingen 1983

–, Der Wettbewerb als Entdeckungsverfahren (1968), in: Streit (ed.), Rechtsordnung und Handelnsordnung – Aufsätze zur Ordnungsökonomik, Tübingen 2003, 132–152

–, Rechtsordnung und Handelnsordnung (1967), in: Streit, Manfred E. (ed.), Rechtsordnung und Handelnsordnung, Aufsätze zur Ordnungsökonomik, Tübingen 2003, 35–73

–, Der Sinn des Wettbewerbs (1946), in: Streit, Manfred E. (ed.), Rechtsordnung und Handelnsordnung, Aufsätze zur Ordnungsökonomik, Tübingen 2003, 107–120

–, Law, Legislation, and Liberty: A New Statement of the Liberal Principles of Justice and Political Economy, London 2022

Heermann, Peter W./Schlingloff, Jochen (eds.), Münchener Kommentar zum Lauterkeitsrecht, Volume 1, 3rd edition, Munich 2020 (cited: *Author*, in: Münchener Kommentar Lauterkeitsrecht)

–/(eds.), Münchener Kommentar zum Lauterkeitsrecht, Volume 2, 3rd edition, Munich 2022 (cited: *Author*, in: Münchener Kommentar Lauterkeitsrecht)

Hefti, Andreas, Limited Attention, Competition and Welfare, Journal of Economic Theory 2018, 318–359

Heinemann, Andreas, Behavioural Antitrust, in: Mathis, Klaus (ed.), European Perspectives on Behavioural Law and Economics, Cham 2015, 211–242

Helfrich, Magdalena/Herweg, Fabian, Context-dependent Preferences and Retailing: Vertical Restraints on Internet Sales, Journal of Behavioral and Experimental Economics 2020, 101556

Hellwig, Martin, Effizienz oder Wettbewerbsfreiheit?: zur normativen Grundlegung der Wettbewerbspolitik, Preprints MPI for Research on Collective Goods 2006, available at https://homepage.coll.mpg.de/pdf_dat/2006_20online.pdf

Hertfelder, Johannes, Die Consumer Welfare im europäischen Wettbewerbsrecht: eine Analyse der Rechtspraxis der Kommission und der europäischen Gerichte, Baden-Baden 2010

–, Die bezweckte Wettbewerbsbeschränkung in Art. 101 Abs. 1 AEUV, in: Bien, Florian/Jickeli, Joachim/Müller-Graff, Peter-Christian (eds.), Maß- und Gradfragen im Wirtschaftsrecht (FS Möschel), Baden-Baden 2021, 129–141

Hetmank, Sven, "Wettbewerbsfunktionales Verständnis" im Lauterkeitsrecht, GRUR 2014, 437–443

Holmes, Simon, Climate Change, Sustainability, and Competition Law, Journal of Antitrust Enforcement 2020, 354–405

Hoppmann, Erich, Workable Competition – Die Entwicklung einer Idee über die Norm der Wettbewerbspolitik, ZBJV 1966, 249–273

–, Wettbewerb als Norm der Wettbewerbspolitik, Ordo 1967, 77–94

Hornkohl, Lena, Kluwer Competition Law Blog, 06/11/2020, Brand Gating: German Competition Authority Once Again Launches An Investigation Into Amazon (and Apple), available at: http://competitionlawblog.kluwercompetitionlaw.com/2020/11/06/brand-gating-german-competition-authority-once-again-launches-an-investigation-into-amazon-and-apple/

Hovenkamp, Herbert, Antitrust Policy After Chicago, Michigan Law Review 1985, 213–285

–, Implementing Antitrust's Welfare Goals, Fordham Law Review 2013, 2471–2496

–, Federal Antitrust Policy – the Law of Competition and its Practice, 5th edition, St. Paul 2016

–, Platforms and the Rule of Reason: The American Express Case, Columbia Business Law Review 2019, 35–92

Huck, Steffen/Zhou, Jidong/Duke, Charlotte, Consumer Behavioral Biases in Competition – a Survey (report prepared for the OFT), 2011, available at: https://mpra.ub.uni-muenchen.de/31794/1/MPRA_paper_31794.pdf

Huffman, Max, Bridging the Divide? Theories For Integrating Competition Law and Consumer Protection, European Competition Journal 2010, 7–45

–, Marrying Neo-Chicago with Behavioral Antitrust, Antitrust Law Journal 2012, 105–145

Huffman, Max/Heidtke, Daniel B., Behavioral Exploitation Antitrust in Consumer Subprime Mortgage Lending, William & Mary Policy Review 2012, 77–109

Hunold, Matthias/Kesler, Reinhold/Laitenberger, Ulrich, Rankings of Online Travel Agents, Channel Pricing, and Consumer Protection, Marketing Science 2020, 92–116

Hunold, Matthias/Muthers, Johannes, Resale Price Maintenance and Manufacturer Competition for Retail Services, RAND Journal of Economics 2017, 3–23

Iacobucci, Edward/Winter, Ralph A., European Law on Selective Distribution and Internet Sales: An Economic Perspective Symposium: European Competition Law, Antitrust Law Journal 2016, 47–64

Ibáñez Colomo, Pablo, Vertical Restraints after Generics and Budapest Bank, SSRN 2020, available at https://papers.ssrn.com/abstract=3683938

Inderst, Roman, An Economic Analysis of 'Price Ownership' by Branded Goods Manufacturers, Report prepared for the Association of Branded Goods Manufacturers ('Markenverband'), 2013, available at: http://www.markenverband.de/publikationen/studien/Branded%20Goods%20and%20Price%20Ownership%20Report%20–%20Roman%20Inderst.pdf (accessed: 11 March 2025)

Inderst, Roman/Maier-Rigaud, Frank, Vertical Restraints and the Forgotten Function of Prices in Brand Management, CPI 2015, available at https://www.competitionpolicyinternational.com/vertical-restraints-and-the-forgotten-function-of-prices-in-brand-management/ (accessed: 11 March 2025)

Inderst, Roman/Pfeil, Sebastian, Branding, Quality, and 'Price Ownership' through RPM, SSRN 2013, available at https://papers.ssrn.com/abstract=2395258

Ioannidou, Maria, Enhancing the Consumers' Role in EU Private Competition Law Enforcement: A Normative and Practical Approach, Competition Law Review 2011, 59–85

Ioannidou, Maria/Nowag, Julian, Can two wrongs make a right? Reconsidering minimum resale price maintenance in the light of Allianz Hungária, European Competition Journal 2015, 340–366

Ippolito, Pauline M., Resale Price Maintenance: Empirical Evidence from Litigation, Journal of Law & Economics 1991, 263–294

Issacharoff, Samuel, Disclosure, Agents, and Consumer Protection, JITE 2011, 56–71

Italianer, Alexander, 07/03/2014, Speech at the Competition Policy in the Digital Age 47th Innsbruck Symposium – 'Real sector economy and the internet – digital interconnection as an issue for competition policy', available at: http://ec. europa.eu/competition/speeches/text/sp2014_01_en.pdf.

Janal, Ruth, Die Plattform-Ökonomie vor dem EuGH, EuZW 2017, 844–849

Jansson-Boyd, Cathrine V., Perception and Consumption, in: Zawisza, Madgalena J./Jansson-Boyd, Cathrine V. (eds.), Routledge International Handbook of Consumer Psychology, London 2016, 85–101

–, Perception and Consumption, in: Jansson-Boyd, Cathrine V./Zawisza, Madgalena J. (eds.), Routledge International Handbook of Consumer Psychology, London 2016, 85–101

Jarass, Hans D., Zum Verhältnis von Grundrechtecharta und sonstigem Recht, EuR 2013, 29–45

–/(ed.), Jarass, EU-Grundrechte-Charta, 4th edition, Munich 2021 (cited: *Author*, in: EU-Grundrechtecharta)

Jolls, Christine/Sunstein, Cass R./Thaler, Richard H., A Behavioral Approach to Law and Economics, Stanford Law Review 1998, 1471–1550

Jolls, Christine/Sunstein, Cass R., Debiasing through Law, Journal of Legal Studies 2006, 199–242

Jones, Alison, Left Behind by Modernisation? Restrictions by Object Under Article 101(1), European Competition Journal 2010, 649–676

Jones, Clifford, Private Enforcement of Antitrust Law in the EU, UK and USA, Oxford, New York 1999

Jullien, Bruno/Rey, Patrick, Resale Price Maintenance and Collusion, RAND Journal of Economics 2007, 983–1001

Junqian, Xu, China Daily, 28/03/2013, Vera Wang cancels fitting fees following criticism, available at: http://www.chinadaily.com.cn/china/2013-03/28/content_16353645.htm (accessed: 11 March 2025)

Kahneman, Daniel, Maps of Bounded Rationality: Psychology for Behavioral Economics, American Economic Review 2003, 1449–1475

Kahneman, Daniel/Krueger, Alan B., Developments in the Measurement of Subjective Well-Being, Journal of Economic Perspectives 2006, 3–24

Kahneman, Daniel/Tversky, Amos, Prospect Theory: An Analysis of Decision under Risk, Econometrica 1979, 263–291

–, Choices, Values, and Frames, American Psychologist 1984, 341–350

Kaplow, Louis, Why (ever) Define Markets?, Harvard Law Review 2010, 437–517

–, Market Definition, Market Power, International Journal of Industrial Organization 2015, 148–161

–, On the Relevance of Market Power, Harvard Law Review 2017, 1303–1407

Katz, Michael L., The Welfare Effects of Third-Degree Price Discrimination in Intermediate Good Markets, American Economic Review 1987, 154–167

Kellerbauer, Manuel, Die Bedeutung des 'as efficient competitor' bei der Feststellung von Verstößen gegen Art. 102 AEUV, EuZW 2015, 261–265

Kerber, Wolfang, Should Competition Law Promote Efficiency? Some Reflections of an Economist on the normative Foundations of Competition Law, in: Drexl, Josef/Idot, Laurence/Monéger, Joel (eds.), Economic Theory and Competition Law, Cheltenham 2009, 93–120

Kerber, Wolfgang/Vezzoso, Simonetta, EU Competition Policy, Vertical Restraints, and Innovation: An Analysis from an Evolutionary Perspective, World Competition 2005, 507–532

Khan, Lina, The New Brandeis Movement: America's Antimonopoly Debate, JECLAP 2018, 131–132

Kimel, Dori, Neutrality, Autonomy, and Freedom of Contract, Oxford Journal of Legal Studies 2001, 473–494

–, Personal Autonomy and Change of Mind in Promise and in Contract, in: Klass, Gregory/Letsas, George/Saprai, Prince (eds.), Philosophical Foundations of Contract Law, Oxford 2014, 96–115

Kingston, Suzanne, Integrating Environmental Protection and EU Competition Law: Why Competition isn't Special, European Law Journal 2010, 780–805

–, Greening EU Competition Law and Policy, Cambridge 2012

Kinsella Obe, Stephen/Melin, Hanne/Schropp, Simon, Comments on the CRA Paper Entitled "An Economic Analysis of the Use of Selective Distribution by Luxury Goods Suppliers", European Competition Journal 2009, 227–260

Kirchgässner, Gebhard, Homo Oeconomicus: The Economic Model of Behaviour and Its Applications in Economics and Other Social Sciences, New York 2008

Klagge, Julian, Normative Kohärenz des deutschen Lauterkeitsrechts, Berlin 2016

Klaus, Wertenbroch/Schrift, Rom Y./Alba, Joseph W./Alixandra, Barasch/Amit, Bhattacharjee/Giesler, Markus/Joshua, Knobe/Lehmann, Donald R./Matz, Sandra/Gideon, Nave/Parker, Jeffrey R./Stefano, Puntoni/Yanmei, Zheng/Yonat, Zwebner, Autonomy in Consmer Choice, Marketing Letters 2020, 429–439

Klein, Benjamin, Assessing Resale Price Maintenance after Leegin, in: Elhauge, Einer (ed.), Research Handbook on the Economics of the Law, Cheltenham 2012, 174–201

–, Resale Price Maintenance of Online Retailing, in: Blair, Roger D./Sokol, D. Daniel (eds.), The Oxford Handbook of International Antitrust Economics, Volume 2, 2014, 277–303

Klein, Benjamin/Murphy, Kevin M., Vertical Restraints as Contract Enforcement Mechanisms, Journal of Law & Economics 1988, 265–297

Klement, Jan Hendrik, Wettbewerbsfreiheit, Tübingen 2015

Kohler, Christian, Zum Verbot des Geoblocking im europäischen Binnenmarkt: Angriff auf die Vertragsfreiheit und Schwächung des Verbraucherschutzes?, ZEuP 2020, 253–263

Köhler, Helmut, Zur Konkurrenz lauterkeitsrechtlicher und kartellrechtlicher Normen, WRP 2005, 645–654

Köhler, Helmut/Bornkamm, Joachim/Feddersen, Jörn (eds.), UWG, 41th edition, Munich 2023 (cited: *Author*, in: Köhler/Bornkamm/Feddersen, UWG)

Kokkoris, Ioannis, The Google Case in the EU: Is There a Case Symposium: Some Critical Differences in U.S. and EU Competition Policy, Antitrust Bulletin 2017, 313–333

Körber, Torsten/Schweitzer, Heike/Zimmer, Daniel (eds.), Wettbewerbsrecht, 6th edition, Munich 2019 (cited: *Author*, in: Immenga/Mestmäcker)

Korn, Laura, A Rule of Reason in the EU? A Critical Comparison of the US and EU Antitrust Approaches to Resale Price Maintenance, ZEuP 2020, 618–644

Kőszegi, Botond/Heidhues, Paul, Chapter 6, Behavioral Industrial Economics, in: Douglas, Bernheim/DellaVigna, Stefano/Laibson, David (eds.), Handbook of Behavioral Economics – Foundations and Applications, Volume 1, Amsterdam Oxford 2018, 517–612

Kroeber-Riel, Werner/Gröppel-Klein, Andrea, Konsumentenverhalten, 11th edition, Munich 2019

Kroese, Floor M./Marchiori, David R./de Ridder, Denise T. D., Nudging Healthy Food Choices: a Field Experiment at the Train Station, Journal of Public Health 2016, e133–e137

Krüger, Tobias/Vogel, Tobias/Wänke, Michaela, Framing Effects in Consumer Judgement and Decision Making, in: Jansson-Boyd, Cathrine V./Zawisza, Madgalena J. (eds.), Routledge International Handbook of Consumer Psychology, London 2016, 349–369

Kumkar, Lea Katharina, Online-Märkte und Wettbewerbsrecht: Implikationen der Platform Revolution für das EU-Vertriebskartellrecht, Baden-Baden 2017

Künzler, Adrian, Effizienz oder Wettbewerbsfreiheit?: zur Frage nach den Aufgaben des Rechts gegen private Wettbewerbsbeschränkungen, Tübingen 2008

–, Economic Content of Competition law: the Point of regulating Preferences, in: Zimmer, Daniel (ed.), The Goals of Competition Law, Cheltenham 2015, 182–213

–, Dilution Law, Vertical Agreements, and the Construction of Consumption, Oxford Journal of Legal Studies 2017, 75–104

–, Restoring Consumer Sovereignty: How Markets Manipulate Us and What the Law Can Do About It, Oxford 2017

–, Competition Law Enforcement on Digital Markets – Lessons from Recent EU Case Law, Journal of Antitrust Enforcement 2019, 249–278

Künzler, Adrian/Warlouzet, Laurent, National Traditions of Competition Law: A Belated Europeanization through Convergence?, in: Patel, Kiran Klaus/Schweitzer, Heike (eds.), The Historical Foundations of EU Competition Law, Oxford 2013, 89–124

Lafontaine, Francine/Slade, Margaret, Exclusive Contracts and Vertical Restraints: Empirical Evidence and Public Policy, in: Buccirossi, Paolo (ed.), Handbook of Antitrust Economics, Cambridge 2007, 391–414

Lancieri, Hilippo/Posner, Eric A./Zingales, Luigi, The Political Economy of the Decline of Antitrust Enforcement in the United States, SSRN 2022, available at https://papers.ssrn.com/sol3/papers.cfm?abstract_id=4011335

Landeo, Claudia, Exclusionary Vertical Restraints and Antitrust: Experimental Law and Economics Contributions, in: Teitelbaum, Joshua C./Zeiler, Kathryn (eds.), Research Handbook on Behavioral Law and Economics, Cheltenham 2018, 75–100

Landes, William M./Posner, Richard A., Market Power in Antitrust Cases, Harvard Law Review 1981, 937–996

Lang, John Temple, Selective Distribution Remarks, Fordham International Law Journal 1984, 323–361

Latzel, Clemens, Verhaltenssteuerung, Recht und Privatautonomie, Berlin, Heidelberg 2020

Leavitt, Harold J., A Note on Some Experimental Findings About the Meanings of Price, Journal of Business 1954, 205–210

Lee, Freddy, Wine and the Consumer Price-perceived Quality Heuristics, International Journal of Marketing Studies 2012, 31–35

Lee, Timothy B., Vox, 05/03/2015, Mattress stores want to rip you off. Here's how to fight back., available at: https://www.vox.com/2015/3/5/8151607/mattress-buying-tips-savings (accessed: 11 March 2025)

Leibenstein, Harvey, Bandwagon, Snob, and Veblen Effects in the Theory of Consumers' Demand, Quarterly Journal of Economics 1950, 183–207

Lenaerts, Koen, Die Werte der Europäischen Union in der Rechtsprechung des Gerichtshofs der Europäischen Union: eine Annäherung, EuGRZ 2017, 639–641

Lenaerts, Koen/Gutierrez-Fons, Jose A., To Say What the Law of the EU Is: Methods of Interpretation and the European Court of Justice, Columbia Journal of European Law 2013, 3–61

Lettl, Tobias, Missbräuchliche Ausnutzung einer marktbeherrschenden Stellung nach Art. 102 AEUV, § 19 GWB und Rechtsbruch, WuW 2016, 214–221

Lianos, Ioannis, Some Reflections on the Question of the Goals of EU Competition Law, in: Lianos, Ioannis/Geradin, Damien (eds.), Handbook on European Competition Law, Substantive Aspects, Cheltenham 2013, 1–84

Lichtenstein, Donald R./Burton, Scot, The Relationship Between Perceived and Objective Price-Quality, Journal of Marketing Research 1989, 429–443

Lieber, Ethan/Syverson, Chad, Online versus Offline Competition, in: Peitz, Martin/Waldfogel, Joe (eds.), The Oxford Handbook of the Digital Economy, Oxford 2012, 191–218

Lindsay, Michael A., The Antitrust Source, 04/2017, Overview of State RPM, available at: https://www.dorsey.com/–/media/files/newsresources/publications/2017/apr17_lindsay_chart.pdf?la=en (accessed: 11 March 2025)

Lindsey-Mullikin, Joan/Petty, Ross D., Marketing Tactics Discouraging Price Search: Deception and Competition, Journal of Business Research 2011, 67–73

Litman, Jessica, Breakfast with Batman: The Public Interest in the Advertising Age, Yale Law Journal 1999, 1717–1735

Loewenstein, George/Bryce, Cindy/Hagmann, David/Rajpal, Sachin, Warning: You are about to be nudged, Behavioral Science & Policy 2015, 35–42

Lohse, Andrea, Drittplattformverbote: Kernbeschränkungen des Internetvertriebs?, WuW 2014, 120–130

Lowe, Philip, "Consumer Welfare and Efficiency—New Guiding Principles of Competition Policy?", Speech at the 13th International Conference for Competition, 2007, available at: https://ec.europa.eu/competition/speeches/text/sp2007_02_en.pdf

Lubberger, Andreas, Plattformverbote verboten?, WRP 2015, 14–24

Lugard, Paul, Some Reflections on the Treatment of Resale Price Maintenance under EU Competition Law in Light of Leegin, in: Gheur, Charles/Petit, Nicolas (eds.), Vertical Restraints and Distribution Agreements under EU Competition Law, Brussels 2011, 193–212

Lukes, Rudolf, Der Kartellvertrag: das Kartell als Vertrag mit Außenwirkungen, Munich, Berlin 1959

Lüttringhaus, Jan D., Vertragsfreiheit und ihre Materialisierung im Europäischen Binnenmarkt: Die Verbürgung und Materialisierung unionaler Vertragsfreiheit im Zusammenspiel von EU-Privatrecht, BGB und ZPO., Tübingen 2018

Lux, Jochen, Der Tatbestand der allgemeinen Marktbehinderung: ein Beitrag zu den Grenzen des Lauterkeitsrechts, Tübingen 2006

Lynch, John G./Ariely, Dan, Wine Online: Search Costs Affect Competition on Price, Quality, and Distribution, Marketing Science 2000, 83–103

MacKay, Alexander/Smith, David Aron, The Empirical Effects of Minimum Resale Price Maintenance, SSRN 2014, available at https://ssrn.com/abstract=2513533

Mäger, Thorsten/Schreitter, Florian von, Vertikale Wettbewerbsbeschränkungen und das Internet: Schutz des Verbrauchers oder Behinderung effizienter Vertriebsstrukturen?, NZKart 2015, 62–73

de la Mano, Miguel/Duquesne, Guillaume/Bowman, Thomas, Reform of the Vertical Block Exemption Regulation and the Accompanying Vertical Guidelines: a Last Call for an Economic Perspective, Competition Law & Policy Debate 2022, 12–20

de la Mano, Miguel/Jones, Alison, Vertical Agreements Under EU Competition Law: Proposals for Pushing Article 101 Analysis, and the Modernization Process, to a Logical Conclusion, in: Healey, Deborah/Michael, Jacobs/Smith, Rhonda L. (eds.), Research Handbook on Methods and Models of Competition Law, Cheltenham 2020, 167–203

Marchiori, David R./Adriaanse, Marieke A./De Ridder, Denise T.D., Unresolved Questions in Nudging Research: Putting the Psychology Back in Nudging, Social and Personality Psychology Compass 2017, e12297

Marshall, Alfred, Principles of Economics, Basingstoke 2013

Marvel, Howard P./McCafferty, Stephen, Resale Price Maintenance and Quality Certification, RAND Journal of Economics 1984, 346–359

Melamed, A. Douglas/Petit, Nicolas, The Misguided Assault on the Consumer Welfare Standard in the Age of Platform Markets, Review of Industrial Organization 2019, 741–774

Mestmäcker, Ernst-Joachim, Über das Verhältnis des Rechts der Wettbewerbsbeschränkungen zum Privatrecht, AcP 1968, 235–262

–, Wettbewerbsfreiheit und unternehmerische Effizienz. Eine Erwiderung auf Schmidtchen, ORDO 2008, 185–208

–, *Böhm, Franz*, in: Grundmann, Stefan/Riesenhuber, Karl (eds.), Deutschsprachige Zivilrechtslehrer des 20. Jahrhunderts in Berichten ihrer Schüler, Band 1, 2011, 31–54

–, Wettbewerbsfreiheit und Wohlfahrt. Ein ideengeschichtlicher Beitrag zum Verhältnis von Ökonomie und Recht, ORDO 2012, 429–448

–, Europäische Prüfsteine der Herrschaft und des Rechts: Beiträge zu Recht, Wirtschaft und Gesellschaft in der EU, Baden-Baden 2016

Mestmäcker, Ernst-Joachim/Schweitzer, Heike, Europäisches Wettbewerbsrecht, 3rd edition, Munich 2014

Metzlaff, Karsten, Category Management und Kartellrecht, ZVertriebsR 2012, 138–151

Meyer, Jürgen/Hölscheidt, Sven (eds.), Charta der Grundrechte der Europäischen Union, 5th edition, Baden-Baden 2019 (cited: *Author*, in: Meyer/Hölscheidt, EU-Grundrechtecharta)

Mises, Ludwig Von, Human Action: A Treatise on Economics, Auburn 2012

Mitsukuni, Nishida/Remer, Marc, Lowering Consumer Search Costs can lead to higher Prices, Economics Letters 2018, 1–4

Mohr, Jochen, Sicherung der Vertragsfreiheit durch Wettbewerbs- und Regulierungsrecht Domestizierung wirtschaftlicher Macht durch Inhaltskontrolle der Folgeverträge, Tübingen 2015

Möller, Silke, Verbraucherbegriff und Verbraucherwohlfahrt im europäischen und amerikanischen Kartellrecht, Baden-Baden 2008

Monti, Giorgio, Article 81 EC and Public Policy, CMLR 2002, 1057–1099

–, Restraints on Selective Distribution Agreements, World Competition 2013, 489–511

Moraga-González, José Luis/Sándor, Zsolt/Wildenbeest, Matthijs R., Prices and heterogeneous search costs, RAND Journal of Economics 2017, 125–146

Morell, Alexander, Behavioral Antitrust and Merger Control: Comment, JITE 2011, 143–148

–, (Behavioral) Law and Economics im Europäischen Wettbewerbsrecht: Missbrauchsaufsicht über Schwellenrabatte, Baden-Baden 2011

–, Nachfrage, Angebot und Märkte, in: Towfigh, Emanuel V./Petersen, Niels (eds.), Ökonomische Methoden im Recht: Eine Einführung für Juristen, Tübingen 2023, 41–76

Möschel, Wernhard, Wettbewerbspolitik aus ordoliberaler Sicht, in: von Gamm, Otto Friedrich (ed.), Strafrecht, Unternehmensrecht, Anwaltsrecht: Festschrift für Gerd Pfeiffer, Köln 1988, 707–727

–, The Proper Scope of Government Viewed from an Ordoliberal Perspective: The Example of Competition Policy, JITE 2001, 3–13

Motta, Massimo, Competition Policy: Theory and Practice, Cambridge 2004

Mullan, Hugh/Timan, Natalie, Does Economic Theory Justify a Difference in Treatment of Restrictions of Competition on PCTs versus Marketplaces Symposium: The E-Commerce Sectory Inquiry, Competition Law & Policy Debate 2017, 11–23

Müller, Friedrich/Christensen, Ralph, Juristische Methodik, Band II: Europarecht, 3rd edition, Berlin 2012

Mundt, Andreas, Die neue Vertikal-GVO – Bereit für die Zukunft?, ZVertriebsR 2022, 205–207

Nagy, Csongor István, The Distinction between Anti-competitive Object and Effect after Allianz: The End of Coherence in Competition Analysis?, World Competition 2013, 541–564

Nermuth, Manfred/Pasini, Giacomo/Pin, Paolo/Weidenholzer, Simon, The informational divide, Games and Economic Behavior 2013, 21–30 *von Neumann, John/Morgenstern, Oskar*, Theory of Games and Economic Behavior: 60th Anniversary Commemorative Edition, Princeton 2004

Newman, John M., The Output-Welfare Fallacy: A Modern Antitrust Paradox, Iowa Law Review 2022, 563–619

Nihoul, Paul, 'Freedom of Choice': the Emergence of a Powerful Concept in European Competition Law, in: Nihoul, Paul/Charbit, Nicolas (eds.), Consumer Choice: A New Standard for Competition Law Analysis, New York 2016, 9–40

Nipperdey, Hans Carl, Wettbewerb und Existenzvernichtung, Kartell-Rundschau 1930, 127–152

North, Adrian C./Hargreaves, David J./McKendrick, Jennifer, In-store Music affects Product Choice, Nature 1997, 132–132

Nowag, Julian, Environmental Integration in Competition and Free-Movement Laws, Oxford 2016

OECD, Roundtable on Vertical Restraints for Online Sales, Paris 2013, available at: https://www.oecd.org/daf/competition/VerticalRestraintsForOnlineSales2013.pdf (accessed: 11 March 2025)

Ohly, Ansgar/Sosnitza, Olaf (eds.), Gesetz gegen den unlauteren Wettbewerb, 7th edition, 2016

Oppermann, Bernd/Chmeis, Ahmad, The Uniform Application of Articles 101 and 102 TFEU in German Competition Law, in: Almăşan, Adriana/Whelan, Peter (eds.), The Consistent Application of EU Competition Law: Substantive and Procedural Challenges, Cham 2017, 195–220

Orbach, Barak, The Image Theory: RPM and the Allure of High Prices, Antitrust Bulletin 2010, 277–307

–, How Antitrust Lost its Goal, Fordham Law Review 2012, 2253–2278

Ornstein, Robert E., Multimind: A wew Way of looking at Human Behavior, Los Altos 2003

Overstreet, Thomas R., Resale Price Maintenance: Economic Theories and Empirical Evidence (Report prepared for the FTC), Washington D.C. 1983, available at: https://www.ftc.gov/sites/default/files/documents/reports/resale-price-maintenance-economic-theories-and-empirical-evidence/233105.pdf (accessed: 11 March 2025)

Parret, Laura, Shouldn't We Know What We Are Protecting? Yes We Should! A Plea for a Solid and Comprehensive Debate About the Objectives of EU Competition Law and Policy, European Competition Journal 2010, 339–376

Patel, Kiran Klaus/Schweitzer, Heike, Introduction, in: Patel, Kiran Klaus/Schweitzer, Heike (eds.), The Historical Foundations of EU Competition Law, Oxford 2013

Patterson, Mark R., Antitrust Law in the New Economy: Google, Yelp, LIBOR, and the Control of Information, Cambridge 2017

Pechstein, Matthias/Drechsler, Carola, § 7. Die Auslegung und Fortbildung des Primärrechts, in: Riesenhuber, Karl (ed.), Europäische Methodenlehre, 4th edition, Berlin 2021, 181–208

Pechstein, Matthias/Nowak, Carsten/Häde, Ulrich (eds.), Frankfurter Kommentar EUV/GRC/AEUV, Tübingen 2017 (cited: *Author*, in: Frankfurter Kommentar EUV/GRC/AEUV)

Pera, Alberto, Changing Views of Competition, Economic Analysis and Ec Antitrust Law, European Competition Journal 2008, 127–168

Pereira, Joseph, Wall Street Journal, 28/08/2016, Price-Fixing Makes Comeback After Supreme Court Ruling, available at: https://www.wsj.com/articles/SB121901920116148325 (accessed: 11 March 2025)

Pereira, Pedro, Do lower Search Costs reduce Prices and Price Dispersion?, Information Economics and Policy 2005, 61–72

Pérez, Sigfrido M. Ramírez/Scheur, Sebastian van de, The Evolution of the Law on Articles 85 and 86 EEC [Articles 101 and 102 TFEU]: Ordoliberalism and its Keynesian Challenge, in: Patel, Kiran Klaus/Schweitzer, Heike (eds.), The Historical Foundations of EU Competition Law, Oxford 2013, 19–53

Persch, Johannes, The Role of Fundamental Rights in Antitrust Law – a special Responsibility for Undertakings with Regulatory Power under Art. 102 TFEU?, European Competition Journal 2021, 542–566

–, Is Taking Away User Traffic Anti-Competitive? Munich Court Stops Cooperation between Google and the German Federal Ministry of Health, JECLAP 2021, 694–697

Petersen, Jens, Rechtsordnung und Wirtschaftsordnung nach Eucken, Berlin 2019

Petty, Ross D., Product Strategy and Antitrust: A Consumer Choice Perspective, Journal of Consumer Affairs 2018, 252–285

Piccolo, Salvatore/Tedeschi, Piero/Ursino, Giovanni, How limiting deceptive Practices harms Consumers, RAND Journal of Economics 2015, 611–624

Pichler, Philipp, Das Verhältnis von Kartell- und Lauterkeitsrecht: eine Standortbestimmung nach den Novellen von GWB und UWG, Baden-Baden 2009

Picht, Peter Georg, The EU Geo-Blocking Regulation from a Competition Law Perspective, JECLAP 2020, 244–256

Plassmann, Hilke/O'Doherty, John/Shiv, Baba/Rangel, Antonio, Marketing actions can modulate neural representations of experienced pleasantness, Proceedings of the National Academy of Sciences 2008, 1050–1054

Podszun, Rupprecht, The Role of Economics in Competition Law, EuCML 2018, 57–65

–, Digital Ecosystems, Decision-Making, Competition and Consumers – On the Value of Autonomy for Competition, SSRN 2019, available at https://ssrn.com/abstract=342069 2

–, Der Verbraucher als Marktakteur: Kartellrecht und Datenschutz in der Facebook-Entscheidung des BGH, GRUR 2020, 1268–1276

Podszun, Rupprecht/Busch, Christoph/Henning-Bodewig, Frauke, Behördliche Durchsetzung des Verbraucherrechts?, Berlin 2018, available at: https://www.bmwk.de/Redaktion/DE/Publikationen/Studien/behoerdliche-durchsetzung-des-verbraucherrechts.pdf?__blob=publicationFile&v=13 (accessed: 11 March 2025)

Posner, Richard A., Working Paper III: Advertising and Product Differentiation, Antitrust Law & Economics Review 1968, 47–50

–, Antitrust Law: An Economic Perspective, Chicago 1976

–, The Rule of Reason and the Economic Approach: Reflections on the Sylvania Decision, University of Chicago Law Review 1977, 1–20

–, The Next Step in the Antitrust Treatment of Restricted Distribution: Per Se Legality, University of Chicago Law Review 1981, 6–26

Potacs, Michael, Wertkonforme Auslegung des Unionsrechts?, EuR 2016, 164–176

Pratkanis, Anthony/Aronson, Elliot, Age of Propaganda – The everyday Use and Abuse of Persuasion, New York 1992

Rajagopal/Castano, Raquel/Flores Villalba, David R., Consumers and Markets: Analyzing Behavioral Shifts and Emerging Challenges, New York 2016

Ramello, Giovanni B./Silva, Francesco, Appropriating Signs and Meaning: the elusive Economics of Trademark, Industrial and Corporate Change 2006, 937–963

Rao, Anita, Information or Obfuscation? The Case of the 'No High Fructose Corn Syrup' Label, SSRN 2022, available at https://papers.ssrn.com/abstract=4020395

Raz, Joseph, The Morality of Freedom, Oxford 1986

Reich, Norbert, Protection of Consumers' Economic Interests by the EC, Sidney Law Review 1992, 23–61

Reich, Norbert/Micklitz, Hans-W., Europäisches Verbraucherrecht, Baden-Baden 2003

Renckens, An, Welfare Standards, Substantive Tests, and Efficiency Considerations in Merger Policy: Defining the Efficiency Defense, Journal of Competition Law & Economics 2007, 149–179

Rey, Patrick/Caballero-Sanz, Francisco, The Policy Implications of the Economic Analysis of Vertical Restraints (European Commission Economic Papers), Brussels 1996, available at: http://aei.pitt.edu/41521/1/A5627.pdf

Rey, Patrick/Stiglitz, Joseph, Vertical Restraints and Producers' Competition, European Economic Review 1988, 561–568

Rey, Patrick/Vergé, Thibaud, Economics of Vertical Restraints, in: Buccirossi, Paolo (ed.), Handbook of Antitrust Economics, Boston 2008, 354

Rezabakhsh, Behrang/Bornemann, Daniel/Hansen, Ursula/Schrader, Ulf, Consumer Power: A Comparison of the Old Economy and the Internet Economy, Journal of Consumer Policy 2006, 3–36

Rhodes, Andrew/Wilson, Chris M., False Advertising, RAND Journal of Economics 2018, 348–369

Rhodes, Andrew/Zhou, Jidong, Consumer Search and Retail Market Structure, Management Science 2019, 2607–2623

Richards, Timothy J./Klein, Gordon/Bonnet, Céline/Bouamra-Mechemache, Zohra, Strategic Obfuscation and Retail Pricing, Review of Industrial Organization 2020, 859–889

Rinner, William/Tor, Avishalom, Behavioral Antitrust: A New Approach to the Rule of Reason After Leegin, University of Illinois Law Review 2011, 805–864

Riziotis, Dimitris, Efficiency Defence in Article 82 EC, in: Mackenrodt, Mark-Oliver/Gallego, Beatriz Conde/Enchelmaier, Stefan (eds.), Abuse of Dominant Position: New Interpretation, New Enforcement Mechanisms?, Berlin, Heidelberg 2008, 89–115

Robbins, Lionel, Interpersonal Comparisons of Utility: A Comment, Economic Journal 1938, 635–641

Robertson, Viktoria, Online Sales under the European Commission's Block Exemption Regulation on Vertical Agreements: Part 2, ECLR 2012, 179–184

Rooney, William H./Fleming, Timothy G./Swaminathan, Sruti, Amex in Context: Tracing the Application of the Rule of Reason to Vertical Restraints The NYSBA 2018 William Howard Taft Lecture: After Amex, Columbia Business Law Review 2019, 1–34

Roth, Wulf-Henning, Kartell- und Wettbewerbsrecht, in: Riesenhuber, Karl (ed.), Privatrechtsgesellschaft, Tübingen 2007, 179–206

Säcker, Franz Jürgen/Meier-Beck, Peter (eds.), Münchener Kommentar zum Wettbewerbsrecht, Band 2, 4th edition, Munich 2022 (cited: *Author*, in: Münchener Kommentar Wettbewerbsrecht)

Säcker, Franz Jürgen/Meier-Beck, Peter/Bien, Florian/Montag, Frank (eds.), Münchener Kommentar zum Wettbewerbsrecht, Band 1, 3rd edition, Munich 2020 (cited: *Author*, in: Münchener Kommentar Wettbewerbsrecht)

Sagers, Chris, Coty, Amazon, and the Future of Vertical Restraints: Evolving Distribution Norms on Both Atlantic Shores International Developments: Essay, Antitrust 2019, 103–108

Salop, Steven C., Question: What Is the Real and Proper Antitrust Welfare Standard – Answer: The True Consumer Welfare Standard, Loy. Consumer L. Rev. 2009, 336–353

Scheele, Rachel, Facebook: From Data Privacy to a Concept of Abuse by Restriction of Choice, JECLAP 2021, 34–37

Scherer, Frederic M., The Economics of Vertical Restraints, Antitrust Law Journal 1983, 687–718

–, Industrial Market Structure and Economic Performance, 3rd edition, Boston 1990

–, Vertical Relations in Antitrust: Some Intellectual History, Antitrust Bulletin 2004, 841–858

Scherer, Frederic M./Steiner, Robert L./Comanor, William S., Vertical Antitrust Policy as a Problem of Inference: The Response of the American Antitrust Institute, SSRN 2005, available at https://papers.ssrn.com/abstract=1103589

Schirmbacher, Martin/Schmidt, Stephanie, Verbraucherrecht 2014 – Handlungsbedarf für den E-Commerce, Computer und Recht 2014, 107–119

Schmidtchen, Dieter, Wettbewerbsfreiheit oder Effizienz? Zur Zweisamkeit von Recht und Ökonomie im Bereich der Wettbewerbspolitik, ORDO 2008, 143–184

Schmidt-Rimpler, Walter, Grundfragen einer Erneuerung des Vertragsrechts, AcP 1941, 130–197

–, Zum Problem der Geschäftsgrundlage, in: Dietz, Rolf/Hueck, Alfred/Reinhardt, Rudolf (eds.), Festschrift für Hans Carl Nipperdey zum 60. Geburtstag, 1955, 1–30

–, Zum Vertragsproblem, in: Baur, Fritz (ed.), Funktionswandel der Privatrechtsinstitutionen: Festschrift für Ludwig Raiser, Tübingen 1974, 3–26

Schmitt, Lennart, Das unionsrechtliche Verbraucherleitbild: Rechtsgebietsspezifische Rezeption und Binnendifferenzierung des Leitbilds vom informierten, aufmerksamen und verständigen Durchschnittsverbraucher, Baden-Baden 2018

Schmitz, Stefan, The European Commission's Decision in GE/Honeywell and the Question of the Goals of Antitrust Law, University of Pennsylvania Journal of International Law 2002, 539–595

Schwaderer, Melanie Ariane, Resale Price Maintenance in Consumer Good Markets: an Economic Justification for the Prohibition of RPM, Thesis, Florence (European University Institute) 2019

Schweda, Marc/Rudowicz, Jan-Christoph, Verkaufsverbote über Online-Handelsplattformen und Kartellrecht, WRP 2013, 590–600

Schweitzer, Heike, The History, Interpretation and Underlying Principles of Sec. 2 Sherman Act and Art. 82 EC, in: Ehlermann, Dieter/Marquis, Mal (eds.), European Competition Law Annual 2007: A reformed approach to Article 82 EC, Oxford 2008, 119–164

–, The Art to Make Gatekeeper Positions Contestable and the Challenge to Know What Is Fair: A Discussion of the Digital Markets Act Proposal, ZEuP 2021, 503–544

Schweitzer, Heike/Haucap, Justus/Kerber, Wolfgang/Welker, Robert, Modernisierung der Missbrauchsaufsicht für marktmächtige Unternehmen, Baden-Baden 2018

Schweitzer, Heike/Patel, Kiran Klaus, EU Competition Law in Historical Context: Continuity and Change, in: Schweitzer, Heike/Patel, Kiran Klaus (eds.), The Historical Foundations of EU Competition Law, Oxford 2013, 207–230

Scitovsky, Tibor, The State of Welfare Economics, American Economic Review 1951, 303–315

Secrieru, Oana, The Economic Theory of Vertical Restraints, Journal of Economic Surveys 2006, 797–822

Shapiro, Carl, Antitrust in a Time of Populism, International Journal of Industrial Organization 2018, 714–748

Sheff, Jeremy N., Biasing Brands, Cardozo Law Review 2010, 1245–1314
–, Veblen Brands, Minnesota Law Review 2012, 769–832
Shepard, Lawrence, The Economic Effects of Repealing Fair Trade Laws, Journal of Consumer Affairs 1978, 220–236
Siciliani, Paolo, Consumer Theories of Harm: an Economic Approach to Consumer Law enforcement and Policy Making, Oxford 2019
Simon, Herbert A., Bounded Rationality, in: Eatwell, John/Milgate, Murray/Newman, Peter (eds.), Utility and Probability, London 1990, 15–18
–, Invariants of Human Behavior, Annual Review of Psychology 1990, 1–20
Simonson, Itamar, Get closer to your Customers by Understanding how they make Choices, California Management Review 1993, 68–84
Simonson, Itamar/Rosen, Emanuel, Absolute Value – What Really Influences Customers in the Age of (Nearly) Perfect Information, New York 2014
Simonson, Itamar/Tversky, Amos, Choice in Context: Tradeoff Contrast and Extremeness Aversion, Journal of Marketing Research 1992, 281–295
Smith, Ethan, Wallstreet Journal, 31/08/2015, StubHub Gets Out of 'All-In' Pricing, available at: http://www.wsj.com/articles/stubhub-gets-out-of-all-in-pricing-1441065436 (accessed: 11 March 2025)
Sokol, Daniel D., The Transformation of Vertical Restraints: Per Se Illegality, the Rule of Reason, and Per Se Legality Symposium: Robert Bork and Antitrust Policy, Antitrust Law Journal 2014, 1003–1016
Solomon, Michael R., Consumer Behavior: Buying, Having, and Being, 13th edition, Boston, Munich 2019
Sosnitza, Olaf, Wettbewerbsbeschränkungen durch die Rechtsprechung: Erscheinungsformen und Ursachen auf dem Gebiet des Lauterkeitsrechts, Baden-Baden 1995
Spiegler, Ran, Competition Over Agents with Boundedly Rational Expectations, Theoretical Economics 2006, 207–231
Statista, Statista, 14/11/2022, U.S.: Digital Buyer Penetration 2017–2025, available at: https://www.statista.com/statistics/273958/digital-buyer-penetration-in-the-united-states/ (accessed: 11 March 2025)
Steinbaum, Marshall/Stucke, Maurice E., The Effective Competition Standard, University of Chicago Law Review 2020, 595–623
Steiner, Robert L., The Nature of Vertical Restraints, Reprints for Antitrust Law and Economics 1990, 143–197
–, The Inverse Association Between the Margins of Manufacturers and Retailers, Review of Industrial Organization 1993, 717–740
Stiglitz, Joseph E., Chapter 13 Imperfect Information in the Product Market, in: Schmalensee, Richard/Willig, Robert (eds.), Handbook of Industrial Organization, Volume 1, Amsterdam 1989, 769–847
Stole, Lars A., Chapter 34 Price Discrimination and Competition, in: Armstrong, M./Porter, R. (eds.), Handbook of Industrial Organization, Volume 3, Amsterdam 2007, 2221–2299
Stucke, Maurice E., Does the Rule of Reason Violate the Rule of Law, U.C. Davis Law Review 2008, 1375–1490
–, Reconsidering Antitrust's Goals, Boston College Law Review 2012, 551–630
Stucke, Maurice E./Ezrachi, Ariel, Competition Overdose: How Free Market Mythology Transformed Us from Citizen Kings to Market Servants, New York 2020
Stuyck, Jules, European Consumer Law After the Treaty of Amsterdam: Consumer Policy In or Beyond the Internal Market?, CMLR 2000, 367–400

–, EC Competition Law After Modernisation: More than Ever in the Interest of Consumers, Journal of Consumer Policy 2005, 1–30

Stylianou, Konstantinos/Iacovides, Marios, The Goals of EU Competition Law – A Comprehensive Empirical Investigation, Legal Studies 2022, 620–648

Sullivan, Lawrence A./Grimes, Warren S., The Law of Antitrust: An integrated Hanbook, 3rd edition, St. Paul 2016

Sullivan, Mary W., Economic Analysis of Hotel Resort Fees (Report for the FTC), Washington D.C. 2017, available at: https://www.ftc.gov/system/files/documents/reports/economic-analysis-hotel-resort-fees/p115503_hotel_resort_fees_economic_issues_paper.pdf (accessed: 11 March 2025)

Szot, Patrycja/Amza, Ana, Marketplace Restrictions and Selective Distribution after Coty Germany Legislation and Case Law Reviews, YARS 2018, 241–284

Taylor, Greg, Raising Search Costs to Deter Window Shopping can Increase Profits and Welfare, RAND Journal of Economics 2017, 387–408

Telser, Lester G., Why Should Manufacturers Want Fair Trade?, Journal of Law & Economics 1960, 86–105

Thaler, Richard H., Toward a positive Theory of Consumer Choice, Journal of Economic Behavior & Organization 1980, 39–60

–, Mental Accounting and Consumer Choice, Marketing Science 1985, 199–214

–, Nudge: Improving Decisions about Health, Wealth, and Happiness, New Haven 2008

–, Behavioral Economics: Past, Present, and Future, American Economic Review 2016, 1577–1600

Thierer, Adam/Koopman, Christopher/Hobson, Anne/Kuiper, Chris, How the Internet, the Sharing Economy, and Reputational Feedback Mechanisms Solve the Lemons Problem, University of Miami Law Review 2015, 830–878

Thomas, Stefan, Wettbewerb in der Digital Economy: Verbraucherschutz durch AGB-Kontrolle im Kartellrecht?, NZKart 2017, 92–98

–, Die digitale Ökonomie zwischen vertikaler und horizontaler Wettbewerbsbeschränkung, ZHR 2020, 223–248

Tirole, Jean, Theory of Industrial Organization, 14th print, Cambridge 2003

Towfigh, Emanuel V., Das ökonomische Paradigma, in: Towfigh, Emanuel V./Petersen, Niels (eds.), Ökonomische Methoden im Recht: Eine Einführung für Juristen, Tübingen 2023, 23–40

Trevena, Helen/Neal, Bruce/Dunford, Elizabeth/Haskelberg, Hila/Wu, Jason H. Y., A Comparison of the Sodium Content of Supermarket Private-Label and Branded Foods in Australia, Nutrients 2015, 7027–7041

Trstenjak, Verica/Beysen, Erwin, The Growing Overlap of Fundamental Freedoms and Fundamental Rights in the Caselaw of the CJEU, ELR 2013, 293–316

Tull, D. S./Boring, R. A./Gonsior, M. H., A Note on the Relationship of Price and Imputed Quality, Journal of Business 1964, 186–191

Turner, Vanessa/Reyna, Augustin/Fafchamps, Nicolas, Vertical Restraints in an Online World – the Consumer Perspective, Competition Law & Policy Debate 2022, 30–37

Tversky, Amos/Kahneman, Daniel, Judgment under Uncertainty: Heuristics and Biases, Science 1974, 1124–1131

–, The Framing of Decisions and the Psychology of Choice, Science 1981, 453–458

–, Extensional Versus Intuitive Reasoning: The Conjunction Fallacy in Probability Judgment, in: Adler, Jonathan E./Rips, Lance J. (eds.), Reasoning: Studies of Human Inference and its Foundations, Cambridge 2008, 114–135

Ulmer, Peter, Der Begriff 'Leistungswettbewerb' und seine Bedeutung für die Anwendung von GWB und UWG-Tatbeständen, GRUR 1977, 565–580

US Congress Antitrust Subcommittee, Investigation of Competition in Digital Markets – Majority Staff Report and Recommendations, 2020, available at: https://www.govinfo.gov/content/pkg/CPRT-117HPRT47832/pdf/CPRT-117HPRT47832.pdf (accessed: 11 March 2025)

US DoJ, 04/10/2010, Press Release of 04/10/2010, Justice Department Sues American Express, Mastercard and Visa to Eliminate Rules Restricting Price Competition, available at: https://www.justice.gov/opa/pr/justice-department-sues-american-express-mastercard-and-visa-eliminate-rules-restricting (accessed: 11 March 2025)

Valdivia, Eduardo Aguilera, The Scope of the Special Responsibility upon Vertically Integrated Dominant Firms after the Google Shopping Case: Is There a Duty to Treat Rivals Equally and Refrain from Favouring Own Related Business?, World Competition 2018, 43–68

Vanberg, Viktor J., Consumer Welfare, Total Welfare and Economic Freedom: on the normative Foundations of Competition Policy, in: Drexl, Josef/Kerber, Wolfang/Podszun, Rupprecht (eds.), Competition Policy and the Economic Approach: Foundations and Limitations, Cheltenham 2011, 44–71

Varian, Hal, Chapter 10 – Price Discrimination, in: Schmalensee, Richard/Armstrong, Mark (eds.), Handbook of Industrial Organization, Volume 1, Amsterdam 1989, 598–647

Varian, Hal R., Intermediate Microeconomics: a modern Approach, 9th edition, New York, London 2014

Veblen, Thorstein, The Theory of the Leisure Class, Reprint, Auckland 2009

Vergé, Thibaud, An Economic Appraisal of the Draft Guidelines on Vertical Restraints, in: Gheur, Charles/Petit, Nicolas (eds.), Vertical Restraints and Distribution Agreements under EU Competition Law, Brussels 2011, 31–53

Verouden, Vincent, Vertical Agreements and Art. 81 (1) EC: The evolving Role of Economic Analysis, Antitrust Law Journal 2003, 525–575

–, Vertical Agreements: Motivation and Impact, in: Collins, Wayne D (ed.), Issues in Competition Law and Policy, Volume III, Chicago 2008, 1813–1840

Vesterdorf, Bo, Theories of Self-Preferencing and Duty to Deal – Two Sides of the Same Coin Hot Topic: Google, CLPD 2015, 4–9

Vezzoso, Simonetta, Zur Beurteilung vertikaler Beschränkungen in der europäischen Wettbewerbspolitik aus evolutionsökonomischer Sicht, Bern 2007

Vogel, Louis, Efficiency versus Regulation: The Application of EU Competition Law to Distribution Agreements, JECLAP 2013, 277–284

Völckner, Franziska, The Dual Role of Price: Decomposing Consumers' Reactions to Price, Journal of the Academy of Marketing Science 2008, 359–377

Völckner, Franziska/Hofmann, Julian, The Price-Perceived Quality Relationship: A Meta_Analytic Review and Assessment of its Determinants, Marketing Letters 2007, 181–196

Waelbroeck, Denis/Davies, Zachariah, Coty, Clarifying Competition Law in the Wake of Pierre Fabre, JECLAP 2018, 431–442

Wagner, Gerhard, The Economics of Harmonization: the Case of Contract Law, CMLR 2002, 995–1023

Wardhaugh, Bruce, Intel, Consequentialist Goals and the Certainty of Rules: The Same Old Song and Dance, My Friend, Competition Law Review 2016, 215–238

–, Competition, Effects and Predictability: Rule of Law and the Economic Approach to Competition, London 2020

Warlouzet, Laurent, The EEC/EU as an Evolving Compromise between French Dirigism and German Ordoliberalism (1957–1995), JCMS 2019, 77–93

Wartinger, Stefan/Solek, Lukas, Restrictions of Third-Party Platforms within Selective Distribution Systems, World Competition 2016, 291–305

Weise, Karen, The New York Times, 19/12/2019, Prime Power: How Amazon squeezes the Businesses behind its Store, available at: https://www.nytimes.com/2019/12/19/technology/amazon-sellers.html (accessed: 11 March 2025)

Werden, Gregory J./Froeb, Luke M./Shor, Mikhael, Behavioral Antitrust and Merger Control, JITE 2011, 126–142

Whish, Richard/Bailey, David, Competition Law, 10th edition, Oxford, New York 2021

Wiedemann, Gerhard (ed.), Handbuch des Kartellrechts, 4th edition, 2020 (cited: *Author*, in: Handbuch Kartellrecht)

Wigger, Angela/Nölke, Andreas, Enhanced Roles of Private Actors in EU Business Regulation and the Erosion of Rhenish Capitalism: the Case of Antitrust Enforcement, JCMS 2007, 487–513

Wilson, Chris M., Ordered Search and Equilibrium Obfuscation, International Journal of Industrial Organization 2010, 496–506

Wilson, Chris M./Price, Catherine Waddams, Do Consumers Switch to the Best Supplier?, Oxford Economic Papers 2010, 647–668

Winter, Ralph, Vertical Restraints and Antitrust Policy: A Reaction to Cooper, Froeb, O'Brien, and Vita, CPI 2006, 75–88

Winter, Ralph/Iacobucci, Ed, Vertical Restraints Across Jurisdictions, in: Blair, Roger D./Sokol, D. Daniel (eds.), The Oxford Handbook of International Antitrust Economics, Volume 2, Oxford 2014, 351–386

Wissing, Christian, Konsumentenwohlfahrt als Ziel der Wettbewerbspolitik, WuW 2020, 593–594

Witt, Anne C., Restrictions on the Use of Third-party Platforms in Selective Distribution Agreements for Luxury Goods, European Competition Journal 2016, 435–461

Wolf, Christoph, Bezweckte Wettbewerbsbeschränkungen nach dem Urteil "Groupement des cartes bancaires", NZKart 2015, 78–85

Wolf, Maik, Behördliche Durchsetzung des Lauterkeitsrechts zur Optimierung des Wettbewerbsschutzes, WRP 2019, 283–293

Wolinsky, Asher, True Monopolistic Competition as a Result of Imperfect Information, Quarterly Journal of Economics 1986, 493–511

Wörsdörfer, Manuel, Von Hayek and Ordoliberalism on Justice, Journal of the History of Economic Thought 2013, 291–317

Wright, Joshua D., The Antitrust/Consumer Protection Paradox: Two Policies at War with Each Other, Yale Law Journal 2012, 2216–2268

Wright, Joshua D./Ginsburg, Douglas, The Goals of Antitrust: Welfare Trumps Choice, Fordham Law Review 2013, 2405–2423

Wright, Joshua D./Stone, Judd E., Misbehavioral Economics: The Case Against Behavioral Antitrust, Cordoza Law Review 2012, 1517–1533

Wu, Tim, After Consumer Welfare, Now What? The 'Protection of Competition' Standard in Practice, CPI 2018, available at https://scholarship.law.columbia.edu/faculty_scholarship/2291

–, OneZero, 19/11/2019, The Utah Statement: Reviving Antimonopoly Traditions for the Era of Big Tech, available at: https://onezero.medium.com/the-utah-statement-reviving-antimonopoly-traditions-for-the-era-of-big-tech-e6be198012d7

Wurmnest, Wolfgang, Marktmacht und Verdrängungsmissbrauch, 2nd edition, Tübingen 2012

Yang, Huanxing, Targeted Search and the Long Tail Effect, RAND Journal of Economics 2013, 733–756

Zäch, Roger/Künzler, Adrian, Efficiency or Freedom to Compete? Towards an axiomatic Theory of Competition Law, ZWeR 2009, 269–288

Zelger, Bernadette, "By object" Restrictions Pursuant to Article 101(1) TFEU: a Clear Matter or a Mess, and a Critical Analysis of the Court's Judgement in Expedia?, European Competition Journal 2017, 356–389

–, Restrictions of Online Sales and Vertical Agreements: Bundeskartellamt vs. Commission? Why Coty and Asics are compatible, European Competition Journal 2018, 445–461

Zhou, Jidong, Reference Dependence and Market Competition, Journal of Economics & Management Strategy 2011, 1073–1097

Zimmer, Daniel, Consumer Welfare, Economic Freedom and the Moral Quality of Competition Law – Comments on Gregory Werden and Victor Vanberg, in: Drexl, Josef/ Kerber, Wolfgang/Podszun, Rupprecht (eds.), Competition Policy and the Economic Approach: Foundations and Limitations, Cheltenham 2011, 72–78

Zimmerman, Ann, Wallstreet Journal, 23/05/2012, Sony, Samsung rein in Retailers' Discounts on TVs, available at: http://online.wsj.com/article/SB10001424052702304791704577420383631021786.html

Index